To Simon

On the occasio[n]

36 Something o[r] [o]the[r]s!

Love Dad & Tricia
xxx

8 Oct'

THE COMPLETE
ENCYCLOPEDIA OF
RIFLES &
CARBINES

THE COMPLETE ENCYCLOPEDIA OF

RIFLES & CARBINES

A comprehensive guide to rifles
& carbines from around the world

A. E. HARTINK

REBO
PUBLISHERS

© 1997 Rebo International b.v., The Netherlands

This 2nd edition reprinted 2004

Text: A. E. Hartink
Cover design: Minkowsky Graphics, Enkhuizen, The Netherlands
Production: TextCase, Groningen, The Netherlands
Translation: First Edition Translations Ltd, Cambridge, Great Britain
Typesetting: Hof&Land Typografie, The Netherlands

ISBN 90 366 15127

Contents

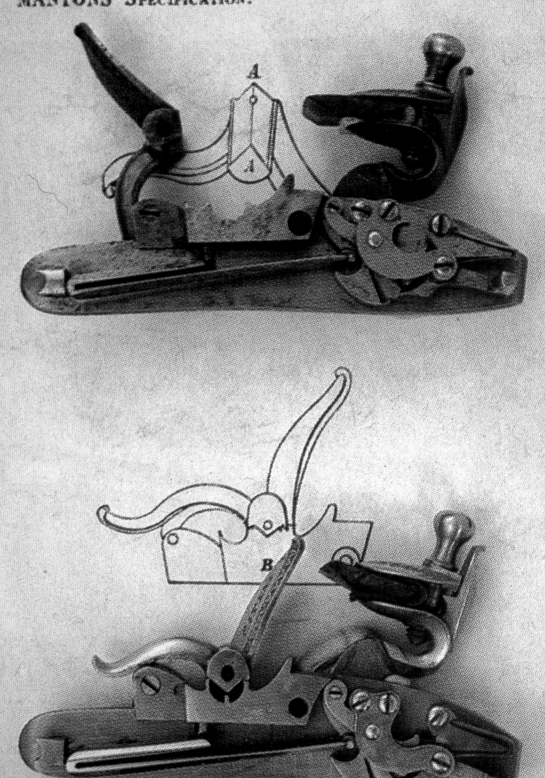

1. The development of firearms

People have always been fascinated by weapons. In earlier times, these weapons were daggers and close-quarter spears, then bows, slings, and throwing javelins. The primary function of these weapons was for hunting and occasionally for self-defence against rival tribes. The evolution of weapons across the centuries has more or less mirrored the development of man. Until about half-way through the Middle Ages, most weapons were hand to hand, and early drawings document the first recorded use of projectiles in ancient China. In a Chinese document that can be dated to 1040 and that only became known in the west in the fifteenth century, mention is made of a form of gunpowder that was used in fireworks. Some believe that this "alchemist's secret" was brought out of China by the famous Venetian merchant venturer, Marco Polo, on his trading expeditions across Europe to China and Beijing. He presumably witnessed the use of Chinese fireworks. Others believe, however, that gunpowder was discovered in Europe, and the names of a Franciscan monk, Roger Bacon, and another monk, Berthold Schwarz from Freiburg in Germany, are associated with these claims. Blackpowder (Schwarzpulver in German) does not owe its name to its grey-black colour but to Berthold Schwarz. Blackpowder is generally composed of 75% saltpetre, 15% sulphur, and 10% charcoal. When it was discovered some time in the fourteenth century that, in addition to making fine fireworks, heavy projectiles could also be shot into the air using blackpowder, the foundation had been laid for the development of firearms. The first hand cannon appeared at this time. These were little more than a short metal tube closed at one end which were attached to long wooden poles that acted as a butt. Soon after, cannons on gun carriages made their appearance. The cannon dating from 1449 from Mons in Belgium is a good example of this.

Firing a blackpowder cannon

Igniting the gunpowder

Although firearms technology has advanced enormously over the centuries, the basic principles remain the same: a metal tube closed at one end with a small opening made or left in it. The gunpowder and the projectile were fed into the open end of the tube and rammed to the far end. The gunpowder was then ignited through the small hole, and the projectile - usually a stone, lead or other metal ball - was shot from the tube. At first, the powder was ignited by glowing wood chips but these were later replaced by matches or fuses.

The gases generated from the combustion

Matchlock gun, manufactured by Zeughaus HEGE-öberlingen

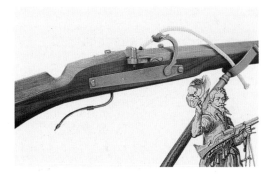

Manton's specification flintlock by HEGE

of the gunpowder expanded so quickly and at such high pressures that the projectile or bullet was ejected from the tube. This firing happened at such a high velocity that, once the bullet exited the tube (or barrel), it continued on its way for some distance.

Matchlock

Using a match or fuse for ignition involved a naked flame and was therefore very difficult to achieve in poor weather conditions. There was therefore no shooting in wet weather, and a glowing match or fuse would also give away the shooter's position at night. Consequently a better means of ignition was sought: the wheel-lock.

The unusual combination of a matchlock and a wheel-lock

Wheel-lock

The wheel-lock is a metal disc combined with a coil spring, that is wound up with a key and then secured - an action known as locking. When the wheel-lock is released by pressing the trigger, the tension of the spring causes the metal disc to spin backwards, scraping against a flint as it does. This causes a shower of sparks that ignites the fine gunpowder in the pan. This technique is still widely used for modern cigarette lighters.

Flintlock

Because the wheel-lock system was complicated and expensive to make, a simpler, cheaper alternative was developed: the flintlock.

The flint was secured in the jaws of a kind of hammer. This hammer or cock, as it is called, was fixed to the side of the weapon and could be drawn backwards (cocked) against the tension of the spring and locked into position.

When the trigger was pressed, the flint struck a metal plate close to the flash hole. The resulting sparks ignited the gun-

A flintlock by HEGE

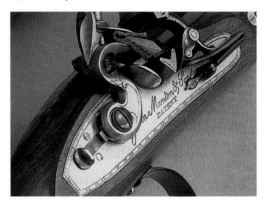

powder in the flash hole. The flintlock system underwent several centuries of development. During the course of its development, one of its variations was the snaphaunce lock. This system consisted of two hammers. The first had a kind of screw claw into which a flint could be fixed. This hammer could be drawn back against the pressure of the hammer spring. The second hammer was a sort of anvil or steel situated just above the flash hole. When the trigger was pulled, the hammer with the flint struck against the steel. This produced sparks that fell into the flash hole. The fine gunpowder in the flash hole was ignited which, in turn, set off the main charge in the barrel.

A further development was the true flintlock. Because the snaphaunce lock was rather sensitive to weather conditions, a cover was devised to protect the flash hole. This cover's vertical metal plate also acted as the steel for the flint.

Percussion ignition

A major breakthrough in ignition mechanisms was achieved when a Scottish priest, Alexander Forsyth - from Belhelvie in Aberdeenshire - invented the percussion primer (or at least the main principles of the system).

In 1799 he published a scientific paper about a chemical com-pound, known as fulminate, that exploded when struck. The next step, to enclose the fulminate in a soft metal percussion primer or cap, was a small one.

Around 1820, a highly explosive chemical compound was developed that could be

Percussion lock by HEGE

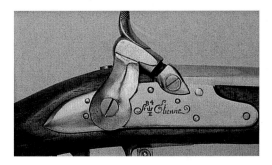

accommodated in a small cap. The problem of using a naked flame for ignition became a thing of the past.

Firearms at this time were still largely based on the old principles - a metal tube closed at one end. The chamber (the place in the barrel where the charge was placed) still had to be loaded with both the powder and the ball through the muzzle. For ignition, however, the percussion cap was fixed by a small attachment to the flash hole. This attachment is known as the nipple or piston. To hit the percussion cap really hard, a hammer mechanism was developed similar to the flintlock. This hammer was located immediately behind

the barrel chamber. The hammer (or cock) was drawn backwards against the pressure of a spring and locked in position. By pulling the trigger, the hammer was released to hit the percussion cap so forcibly that it exploded. The resulting flash passed through the nipple to ignite the gunpowder charge in the chamber. This percussion system was used for a long time for rifles, pistols, and later in more modern five- and six-shot black-powder revolvers. The bullet evolved at the end of the eight-eenth and beginning of the nineteenth century. Guns with rifling in their barrels to make the bullet's flight more stable also appeared at this time, so that a target could be hit with greater accuracy.

Development of the cartridge

The next important step in the evolution of firearms was the creation of the cartridge. At first this was simply a casing of paper or cardboard, and later of brass. The components of the cartridge - gunpowder, percussion cap and case - were assembled in one unit.

Cartridges like this could no longer be loaded via the muzzle but had to be placed in the chamber of the barrel through the back of the firearm. This meant that the rear of the barrel had to be open to load the weapon. After loading, the barrel then had to be strong enough and securely closed to prevent it from splitting or springing open when the charge exploded. The solution to this problem was the bolt-action chamber.

Cut-away drawing of a rifle cartridge. Percussion cap: 1. steel or anvil; 2. firing point; 3. brass cap.
Bullet: 1. casing; 2. lead core; 3. flute

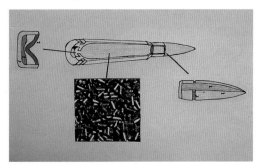

A pair of HEGE percussion duelling pistols

Rimfire and pinfire cartridges

Rimfire cartridges and the pinfire system are variations in the evolution of cartridges. In the rimfire cartridge, the means of ignition is not housed in a brass cap but is moulded into the rim of the cartridge case itself. Rimfire ammunition is still used widely in small calibre weapons.

The pinfire cartridge also has its ignition charge inside its case. This is ignited by a blow from the hammer against a protruding pin at the rear of the cartridge case. This cartridge system was used for only a relatively short period of time.

Lefaucheux-type pinfire revolver

The invention of nitro-powder

The third important step in the development of weapons was the invention of the chemically compounded nitro-powder. Gas expansion using this powder was much greater and at a far higher pressure than gunpowder. As a result, part of the pressure could be used to open the bolt

Cross-section of a 5.7mm calibre caseless cartridge by Voere

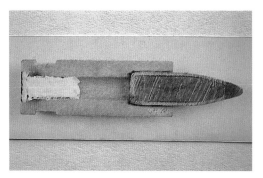

automatically. This led to the development of semi-automatic weapons such as pistols, sub-machine guns, rifles and carbines.

Although the basic principles of chamber, charge, bullet, firing the charge and the barrel remain unchanged, there have been tremendous breakthroughs in firearms and ammunition technology. These continue to this day with electronic ignition and caseless cartridges, for example.

Recent developments

Early firearms took a great deal of time to prepare for firing. Dry and preferably calm conditions were also needed to ensure the powder would ignite. Even under ideal circumstances it was more a matter of luck than judgement whether the target was hit. Nowadays there are firearms that can fire 600 rounds per minute and that can be used reliably under all weather conditions and with great accuracy. Magazine changes can be accomplished in a matter of seconds.

Modern light firearms can be subdivided into hand guns and shoulder firearms. This is a generalization since many sub-machine guns and (semi-)automatic guns and carbines can be used as either hand guns or shoulder weapons by means of fold-out stocks and barrel extensions.

Hand guns

Hand guns can be subdivided into:
- Revolvers: blackpowder, small calibre rimfire, large calibre centre-fire.
- Pistols: blackpowder pistols, small calibre rimfire, large calibre centre-fire.

Large calibre revolver: Smith & Wesson Model 686 with 6in (152mm) barrel

Several blackpowder revolvers by HEGE:
1. Roger & Spencer; 2. same in stainless steel; 3.
Remington Army

Several 'Parker of London' percussion pistols
by HEGE

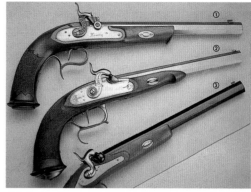

Large calibre pistol: Sig-Sauer P226-Sport

Small .22 calibre revolver: Ruger new Model Single-Six

Shoulder firearms

Shoulder firearms can be subdivided into:
- Rifles and carbines: blackpowder, breech opening, bolt action, lever action, pump action, semi- and fully automatic.

- Shotguns: breech opening, bolt action, pump action, semi- and fully automatic.

Small .22 calibre pistol: Browning Buckmark Target
51/2in (140mm)

Single-shot rifle with breech opening by Heym

HEGE-Bristlen-Pedersoli blackpowder match rifle

Browning European bolt-action rifle

Winchester lever-action repeating rifle

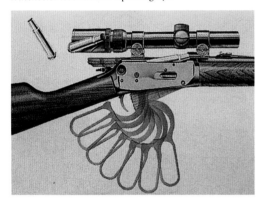

Semi-automatic Browning BAR Safari rifle

Browning pump-action repeater "slug" gun

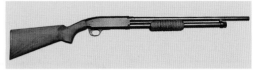

Sig SG551-Swat Automatic rifle

Browning B-25 breech-opening shotgun

Browning A-bolt Stalker bolt-action rifle

Semi-automatic Browning Auto-5 shotgun

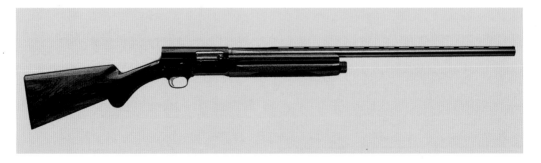

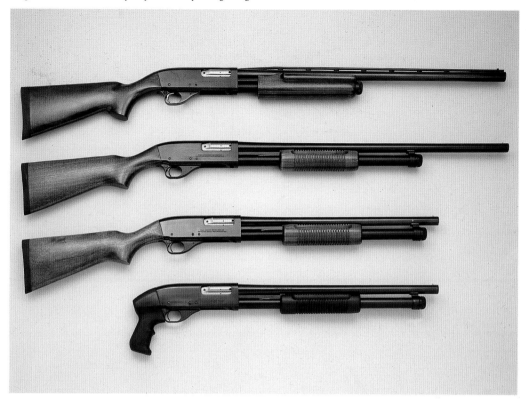

Developments in ammunition

The most popular calibre cartridge at the beginning of the twentieth century was the British .303in, used in the various Enfield and Lee-Enfield rifles that were made in Britain. The US army had its own calibre of .30-06 for Springfield, and later Garand rifles.

After the establishment of NATO, these calibres were dropped in favour of a standardized 7.62mm NATO calibre (also known as 7.62 x 51mm or .308in Winchester). This in turn made way for the smaller and lighter .223in Remington calibre. At the outset of the Vietnam war, Colt had developed an army rifle that was to become legendary: the Colt M16, which also served as a light machine gun. The Americans were the first to utilize this new rifle and new calibre, followed later by the other NATO partners. This ammunition is not suitable for use with sniper's rifles because its lightweight bullet is susceptible to side winds. Sniper's rifles are principally made in the .308in Winchester calibre or other Magnum ca-

libres of a similar diameter. Further developments since the 1980s, such as caseless cartridges, have many advantages over conventional ammunition.

The amount of ammunition an infantryman has to carry is much lighter now than before, and the construction of the weapon is simpler because it does not have to eject a cartridge case. A good example of this is the experimental G-11 carbine by Heckler & Koch which has a 4.7mm diameter and cartridge length of 21mm. This prototype is not likely to progress beyond the development stage. Another example is the caseless cartridge with electronic firing manufactured by Voere that is principally intended for sporting and hunting use.

2. Technology

Before going into the technical details of rifles and carbines, this chapter provides a general introduction to weapon technology for those who have little knowledge about this aspect of firearms and for those who may wish to refresh their knowledge. In order to appreciate a firearm as a piece of technology, it is essential to understand how it works and to be able to recognize the names of the various parts to avoid misunderstandings. One person might refer to the butt of a rifle and another to its stock, which could lead to confusion. An example is the way the terms "cartridge holder" and "magazine" are mixed up. A cartridge holder is a removable holder in which cartridges are lodged. A magazine is a fixed internal store for cartridges.

What is a rifle and what is a carbine?

The term "rifle" is often used incorrectly for any shoulder weapon, whether its barrel is rifled or not. A few non-rifled guns are also included in this book.
The terms "rifle" and "carbine" are often interchanged. For the sake of clarity they are defined as follows.

Rifle

A rifle is a shoulder firearm with a rifled barrel - the inside of the barrel has spiral

SIG SSG 3000 sniper's or sharpshooter's rifle

Left: receiver with the mechanism housing and stock of a Bushmaster XM15-E2S

grooves machined in it. These grooves make the bullet spin when it is shot out of the barrel so that its flight is as stable as possible. This rifling extends from the chamber to the muzzle. The extent to which the barrel is rifled is known as its "twist". This twist is directly related to the length of the barrel together with the bullet's weight and velocity.
Rifles can be subdivided into two types:

Weatherby Custom Varmint Master

Anschåtz match rifle model 1907

- By use: military, hunting, and target shooting.
- By action: bolt (single shot or not), breech loading (hinged), pump-action repeater, lever-action repeater, or semi-automatic (worked by recoil or gas pressure).

Carbine

A carbine is a short, lightweight rifle with a barrel length of up to 22in (56cm). Carbines were originally developed as military weapons. The same subdivision applies as for rifles above. Since the technical details are the same for both rifles and carbines (apart from barrel length and therefore overall length), the different parts of these firearms are not discussed separately here.

The main groups

A rifle or carbine consists of a number of main groups of parts. The number and types of main groups depend upon the type of weapon and its system. These groups can consist of

a. the receiver, mechanism housing, or breech opening
b. the bolt, bolt head, or locking mechanism
c. the barrel, cartridge chamber, and sights
d. the stock
e. the trigger mechanism
f. the magazine or cartridge holder.

The receiver, mechanism housing, or breech opening

Manufacturing stages of a receiver for a Zoli AZ-1900

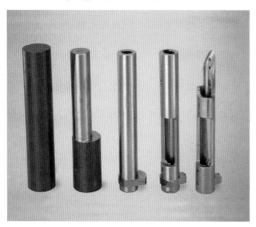

Mechanism housing or receiver of a Bushmaster XM15-E2S rifle

The receiver is the housing for the rifle's bolt or breech. The barrel is attached to the receiver. The bolt can be moved backwards and forwards in the receiver to close the barrel chamber. Usually, the trigger group is also attached to the

The breech opening of a hinged barrel gun by New England Firearms

receiver. Other than in single-shot weapons, there is an opening beneath the receiver for an internal magazine or removable cartridge holder.

With semi-automatic or lever-action repeating rifles, the term "mechanism cover" is sometimes used instead of receiver. The repeating mechanism is located within the mechanism housing, together with the trigger group and cartridge holder.

The mechanism cover with the trigger group and trigger group/cartridge holder of the Bushmaster XM15-E2S

Opening breeches are usually only found in shotguns, but some hinged barrel rifles have their barrels attached by a hinge to the breech block, together with the trigger group and stock.

The bolt, bolt head, or locking mechanism

The bolt is a solid piece of metal that closes the weapon. The bolt also loads the weapon by pushing a cartridge into

Breech-opening drilling rifle by Merkel, with three barrels

Manufacturing stages of the bolt for a Zoli AZ-1900

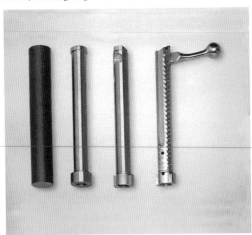

Cut-away model of a Bushmaster receiver with barrel. The locking lugs can be seen clearly together with the cartridge in the chamber. Part of the firing pin can also be seen in the cut-away section of the bolt head

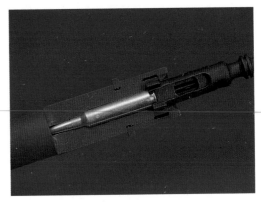

the chamber of the barrel. The bolt is then turned until lugs locate with recesses in the receiver.

The cartridge is now in the chamber and the breech is locked. The firing pin, which is also located in the bolt, is cocked by the bolt action. When the trigger is pulled, the firing pin is released. The firing-pin spring makes the pin strike the per-

cussion cap at the rear of the cartridge case. The shot then goes off. When the bullet has exited the barrel, the bolt is reopened and pulled to the rear. The cartridge extractor at the front of the bolt removes the empty cartridge from the chamber and ejects it.

Breech of the Springfield 'Trapdoor' rifle. To load this weapon, the breech has to be opened by unlocking the lever next to the hammer. The breech then hinges upwards to give access to the chamber

Cross-section of a Zoli AZ-1900 bolt

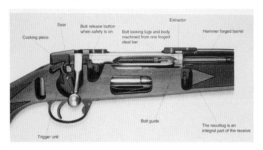

Front view of a Zoli AZ-1900 bolt

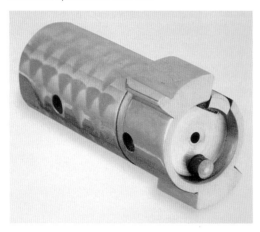

type, calibre, and manufacturer. Small to medium calibres generally use a two-lug system, frequently based on the principles of the Mauser bolt. In larger Magnum calibres, more lugs are generally used on both the front and rear of the bolt. The handle of the bolt also locates in a recess in the receiver to act as a further lock for the breech. In small calibre bolt-action rifles this is often the only form of locking but it is sufficient.

Front view of a Weatherby Magnum bolt with nine locking lugs

Bolt heads are mainly found in semi-automatic weapons. In small calibre rifles, the bolt head is driven backwards by the recoil from the shot. This happens after the round has been discharged from the barrel.

In larger calibre weapons, the bolt head is usually driven back by gas pressure. After the cartridge in the chamber has been fired, the bullet is forced down the barrel. While the bullet is still in the barrel, a small proportion of the gas pressure is

Gas-pressure repeating mechanism: 1. barrel; 2. gas vent; 3. gas pressure chamber; 4. pisto;, 5. return spring rod

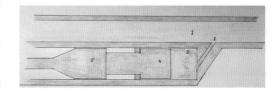

Locking lugs are located on the front of the bolt or bolt head together with the firing pin. The extractor, which may operate by spring action, is usually situated here so that the spent cartridge can be ejected by opening and returning the bolt. The number of lugs varies according to

diverted down a small vent positioned about half-way along the barrel to a gas cylinder mounted under or above the barrel. The piston inside this cylinder drives the return spring rod, which in turn drives the bolt head back. The bolt head has much the same function as the bolt, and similarly it incorporates the locking lugs, firing pin, and cartridge extractor. By means of this extractor, the spent cartridge is removed from the chamber and then ejected by an ejector mechanism.

Cartridge extractor of the Winchester Model 70 rifle

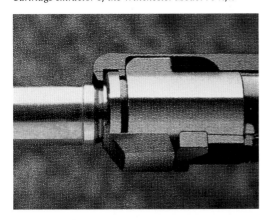

The backwards movement of the bolt head creates tension in the return spring. This ensures that, when the bolt head has reached the limit of its backwards travel, it is pushed forward again. When the bolt head is pushed forward, it rams a new round into the chamber and cocks the firing-pin mechanism. Once the trigger is pressed, the new round will be fired and the whole cycle is repeated. The bolt head also has lugs. Semi-automatic weapons

Return spring of a Bushmaster XM15-E2S rifle. The return spring can be seen at the end of the bolt head. The cocking lever can also be seen above it

mainly use a rotating system by which the lugs on the bolt head locate in and are guided by grooves. This ensures that when the bolt head rotates, the lugs engage in the recesses in the receiver or breech block. This completes the locking action. Some makes of weapon incorporate ingenious bolt lug systems, such as the FN-Browning BAR rifle.

The FN-Browning BAR rifle has a rotating bolt head with seven different lugs that lock into the receiver.

Some military weapons, such as the Colt M16, are provided with additional means of returning the bolt head. In this rifle, a knob attached to the breech housing increases the force necessary to push the bolt head home should dirt otherwise prevent it from locating fully.

Rotation lugs of the Browning BAR II bolt head

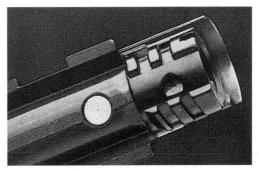

This system was invaluable in the jungles of Vietnam.

Locking mechanisms that operate by other systems than the bolt or bolt head usually have a vertical sliding lock with a reciprocating bolt that moves up and down. This mechanism is operated by a lever such as that seen on Sharps rifles and carbines. This lever is an extension of the trigger mechanism and when it is pushed forward, the locking piece drops down to open the chamber. This weapon can be loaded with one round by hand. When the lever is pulled back, the locking piece moves upwards to close the breech. The firing pin in such weapons is usually located in the locking piece in much the same way as when sited in the bolt or bolt head.

Button (next to the finger) for increasing pressure to the bolt head on a Bushmaster XM15-E2S

The barrel of an Anschütz rifle, complete with receiver, bolt, and trigger group

The breech block of a Sharps rifle with a lever-action locking mechanism

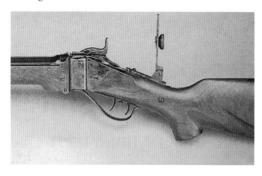

The barrel is usually a round tube although some older weapons had polygon-section barrels. On the inside of the barrel are the spiral grooves known as

The barrel and cartridge chamber

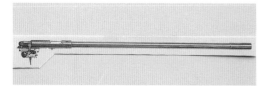

rifling. The purpose of rifling is to make the bullet spin around its longitudinal axis.

The bullet is made to spin when it is driven down the barrel. The extent of this spinning is known as the twist. A barrel's twist is dependent on both the length of

An example of rifling in a barrel (photograph from HEGE)

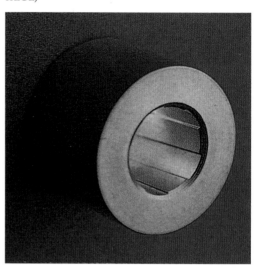

the barrel and the number of complete 360 degree rotations through which the rifling turns. For example, a twist of 305mm (12in) indicates that rifling turns through one complete rotation in 305mm (12in). To make sure the bullet spins, the bullet's outer diameter is slightly larger than the diameter of the raised fields inside the barrel. The bullet is consequently forced past these ridges, which cut into the bullet's outer jacket, thus causing it to spin. Spin gives the bullet greater stability in flight. Without spin, the bullet would tumble so that the accuracy and predictability of its aim would be impaired.

The first part of the barrel into which the cartridge is loaded is the chamber. The chamber is thicker than the rest of the barrel so that it can withstand the force of the charge's explosion and the very high temperatures this creates. If the chamber were too thin it could split open. The gas pressure generated by a rifle cartridge can be as high as 4,000 bar. The chamber is tapered so that the cartridge sits firmly in place. This is necessary to prevent the cartridge from being pushed too far into the barrel, which would prevent the firing pin from striking the percussion cap.

Some makes of weapon have attachments on their muzzles which have various

Cut-away section showing the barrel chamber with a cartridge in the chamber (Bushmaster)

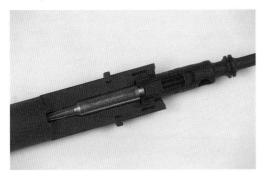

functions, such as flash suppression. A flash suppressor is used mainly on military weapons. As its name implies, a flash suppressor reduces the flash or flame at the muzzle so that the infantryman's position is not given away. Another type of attachment is the muzzle compensator. The recoil when using larger calibres can give the person firing the weapon severe problems.

A muzzle compensator utilizes some of the gas pressure that is pushed out with the bullet to dampen the recoil. A system similar to this is used in match pistols. Compensators come in a variety of types

Flash suppressor of a Galil SAR rifle

and sizes and they are sometimes built into the barrel. In such weapons, small slots are machined into the barrel close to the muzzle.

The gas pressure escapes through these just before the bullet leaves the barrel.

Muzzle compensator of an LAR-Grizzly .50 MBG sniper's rifle

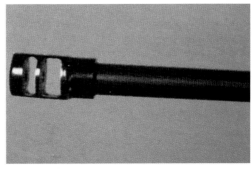

This method of compensation is often known as the Magna-Port system.

Another type of muzzle attachment is the Winchester Boss system, which was devised to increase the weapon's accuracy. It works as follows.
As the bullet travels down the barrel it sets up high levels of vibration because of the speed and force at which it is pushed through the rifled fields.

Rifle compensators by the GOL company

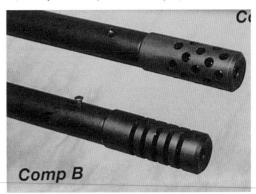

This vibration does not stop until the bullet has left the muzzle. The vibration is at its maximum the moment the bullet

The Boss system of Browning and Winchester

reaches the muzzle, which can cause a deviation in the bullet's trajectory. This deviation in trajectory will not be exactly the same with every shot and so long-range rifles are often equipped with thicker-than-usual barrels to reduce this vibration effect.

With the Winchester Boss system, the nature of the vibration can be controlled - that is, the amount of vibration cannot be regulated but its frequency can.

This means that, with each shot, the frequencies of the vibration are more or less identical when the bullet leaves the barrel.

The Boss system: left-hand arrow points to the micrometer adjuster for the barrel vibration; centre arrow indicates the compensator which reduces recoil by 30-50%; right-hand arrow indicates the adjustable barrel weight which tunes the barrel vibration frequencies

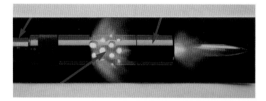

This system also acts as a muzzle compensator, reducing recoil by between 30 and 50%.

Winchester introduced a new version, the Boss-CR, in 1996, which works in a similar way but does not incorporate a muzzle compensator.

The Boss-CR system that does not include a compensator

The sights

Sights are mounted on the barrel and, frequently, also on the receiver. Simple sights usually just consist of a notched sight at the rear of the rifle. These may or may not be adjustable and have a V or U-shaped notch in the plate. At the muzzle

The fixed-notch sight used for Browning rifles

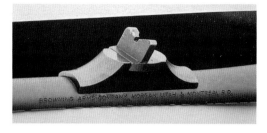

end of the barrel is a bead or post. Aiming is achieved by lining up the top of the bead in the V or U-shaped notch.

The adjustable micrometer sight used for Browning rifles

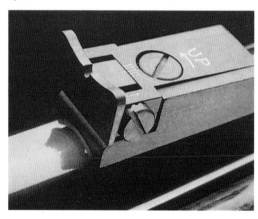

There are many variations of this, from fold-away sights to notched sights that can be adjusted finely by a micrometer. Another type of sight is the ramped tangent sight that can be adjusted to set distance ranges.

The illustration shows how the CZ tangent sight can be adjusted in incre-

The notched tangent sights with a ramp as used by CZ

ments of 25m (27yd) - up to 200m (218yd).

Some rifles have a series of pop-up notched sights, one behind the other, for different ranges. These are battle sights that are used principally on larger calibre weapons. The battle sights shown on the CZ rifle are adjustable in 100m (109yd) increments.

If the target is at 200m (218yd), then the sight for this range is lifted, similarly for 300m (328yd). Some battle sights extend to 500m (546yd).

Optical sights usually consist of a base with a tube that has a small aperture at its

The battle sights on a CZ rifle

centre. In simple versions such as military sights, these usually fold away and have a ramp on which adjustments for range can be made.

Other systems have turnable cylinders that have different apertures for different range distances. A dioptric match sight works on a similar principle but it is equipped with a micrometer for precise

The pop-up battle sight of a Galil SAR rifle

adjustments. Special match rifles often have a circular bead plus cross hairs that, when matched with the bead on the front sight, ensure a perfect hit.

Some rifles have a protective shroud around their beads. This not only protects the bead from damage but also reduces any distracting glare during aiming.

The stock

Stocks come in a very wide variety of

An Anschütz optical sight with full dioptric adjustment (dioptre no. 6805)

Optical tube and bead from an AnschÅtz sight

shapes, sizes and materials. Certain types are recognized as standard international types. The basic styles are as follows:

- The straight or English stock
The bottom of this stock runs in a straight

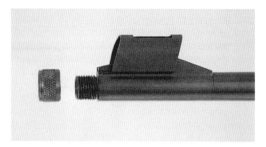

line to the butt. This stock is used particularly with lever-action repeating rifles as it allows the room needed for the enlarged trigger guard, which also acts as the cocking lever.

A swallow-tail rail for attaching telescopic sights to a CZ-550 rifle

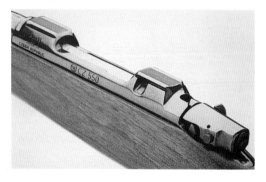

- The standard stock with pistol grip
The upper side of this stock runs straight to the butt but the underside has a clear pistol grip. This is a very popular type of stock that is used widely for rifles.

Predrilled and tapped mounting points for bolting on telescopic sights (CZ)

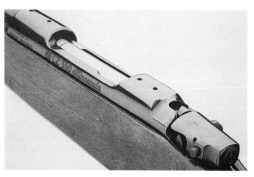

- The stock with pistol grip and raised cheek
A de-luxe version of the standard stock. This stock has both a pistol grip and a

Telescopic sights for Weatherby rifles

raised cheek which makes it easier to aim the rifle.

- Stock with pistol grip and hog's back
This type of stock has a straight upper line until half-way down the back of the stock. The line then slants down to the butt.

A pistol grip is also incorporated into this stock. When the weapon is put to the shoulder it sits higher than other types of stock. This type is also known as the German stock.

- Monte Carlo stock
This type of stock has a very definite pistol grip and, towards the rear of the stock,

A straight or English stock without pistol grip of a Winchester rifle

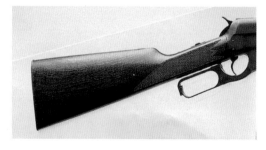

a very pronounced sloping line to the butt.
The cheek of the butt is also very pronounced. This type of stock is mainly used with the larger calibres and for match rifles.

A CZ rifle with a standard stock with pistol grip but no raised cheek

- Match stock

Match rifles frequently have special stocks with a very definite pistol grip that may also have a thumb hole in it. The butts of

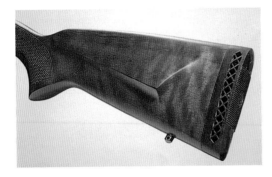
A de-luxe stock with raised cheek on a CZ rifle

A German stock on an AnschÅtz rifle

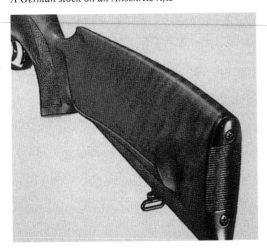

match stocks are often equipped with separate adjustable shoulder grips that can be positioned under the armpit. These stocks often incorporate all manner of adjustment possibilities.

Nowadays, stocks are made from all manner of materials but in the past they were mainly made of wood, usually walnut. Cheaper rifles had beech stocks that were sometimes made to look like walnut. Modern stocks are often made from laminated wood.

Monte Carlo stock on a CZ rifle

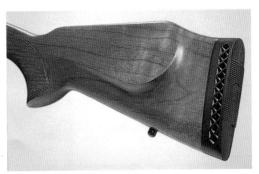

A block of timber laminate is machined into a stock which creates interesting patterns in the wood. Sometimes different types and colours of wood are laminated together to achieve a veryattractive decorative finish.

Another modern material is carbon fibre, which is made up in a similar fashion to

A fully adjustable match stock on an AnschÅtz rifle

glass reinforced polyester but which is stronger and lighter. Kevlar and Zytel are the trade names of some of these materials.

Stocks of carbon fibre and other artificial materials come in a range of colours, such as black, grey, or white, or in different camouflage colours.

In larger calibre rifles, the rear of the butt of the stock is usually finished with a thick rubber buffer to absorb the recoil.

A multicoloured laminated wooden stock by AnschÅtz

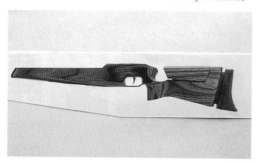

The trigger mechanism

Rifles have different trigger mechanisms according to their intended purpose:

Artificial material stock by Weatherby

- Immediate trigger. This trigger mechanism is similar to that used in shotguns. There is no separate pressure point or any free play with the trigger. When the trigger is pressed, the shot is fired immediately.

- Pressure-point trigger. With this type of trigger, there is a small amount of free play before the trigger meets a definite resistance. Having checked the aim, the shot is fired by continuing to press the trigger beyond the pressure point.

A butt buffer pad of rubber with a honeycomb structure to absorb the recoil

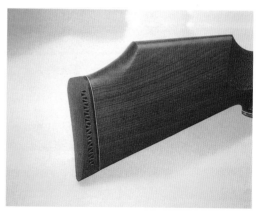

With more expensive models, both the amount of free play before the pressure point and the amount of pressure required to fire the shot can be adjusted.

- Pre-set trigger. With this type of trigger

Immediate trigger (AnschÅtz 1432ED)

mechanism it is possible to reduce the trigger pressure significantly. By pushing forward either the trigger or a small catch next to the trigger, the trigger is set to react more rapidly.
When the trigger is subsequently pressed, only a light squeeze is needed to fire the shot. The Germans call this trigger RÅckstecher. A similar trigger mechanism has two combined triggers. By pressing the trigger lever that sticks out, the main trigger is activated so that it only requires a little pressure to fire the shot.

Pressure-point trigger mechanism (AnschÅtz 1432E trigger)

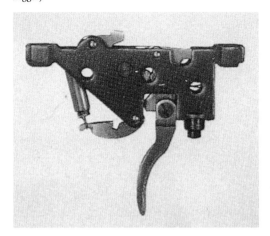

A trigger mechanism with means of switching the trigger pressure. The front "trigger" activates a lower trigger pressure for the rear trigger (AnschÅtz 1432EKSt)

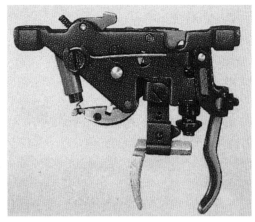

- Double-action trigger. This mechanism has twin triggers. The rear trigger acts as the switch to activate the front trigger to work at a lower trigger pressure. The front trigger can be used on its own but would then need a much higher trigger pressure. This should not be confused with the twin triggers of a double-barrelled shotgun or rifle.

- Match trigger. These triggers are characterized by the extensive range of adjustments they permit. Match rifles often have the capability for fine adjustments of the free movement of the trigger, the trigger pressure, trigger position, pressure point, and follow-through after firing the shot. Simpler match triggers are limited to step less adjustments of trigger pressure from, for example, 281/4 to 53oz (800 to 1,500g).

Double- or twin-action trigger (Anschütz 1432ESt)

The match trigger in the illustration has the following adjustment capabilities:

1. A screw to adjust free movement before the pressure point.
2. A screw to adjust the tumbler.

A pre-set trigger by Browning

Match trigger mechanism by AnschÅtz (type 5018)

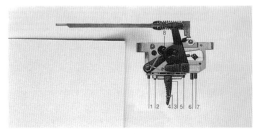

3. A screw to adjust the trigger's horizontal movement.
4. An adjustment ring for a very light trigger pressure.
5. An adjustment screw for the follow-through - the amount of movement after the shot has been fired to keep the rifle steady.
6. A screw for adjusting the trigger pressure before the pressure point.
7. A screw to adjust the pressure at the pressure point.
8. An adjustment for changing the angle at which the bottom of the trigger lever engages with the firing lever.

The magazine or cartridge holder

The term "magazine" often leads to confusion. A repeating rifle, whether semi-automatic or bolt action, has an opening for a magazine or a magazine shaft to which a separate and removable cartridge holder can be attached.
Some repeating rifles have a different form of internal magazine, with a removable or hinged cover which may or may not be located on the underside of the rifle. With internal magazines, the cartridges are housed safely in the body of the rifle. A disadvantage of this system is that capacity is limited. Additionally, in most cases the magazine has to be loaded from above via the breech.

The advantage of removable cartridge holders is that they can usually be loaded outside the weapon. The holder is then inserted into the magazine opening and

fastened in position with the cartridge holder or magazine catch. Moreover, the weapon can be reloaded rapidly with a replacement cartridge holder.

A great many military weapons make use of separate cartridge holders. One dis-

An example of a removable cartridge holder by CZ. The magazine catch is located at the front of the trigger guard

Separate cartridge holder from a CZ rifle

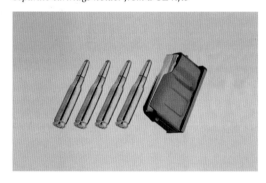

Example of a cartridge holder catch on a CZ-511 rifle

The hinged cover plate of an internal magazine (CZ)

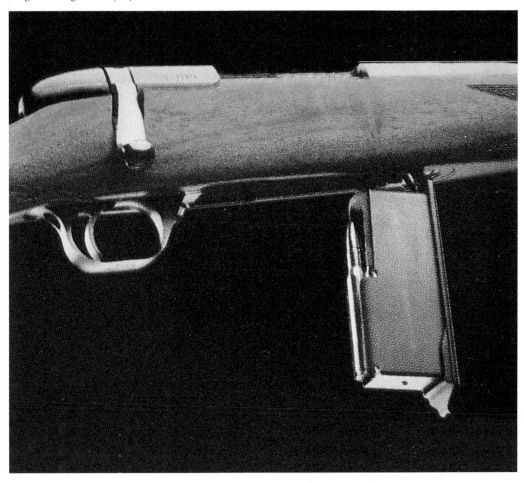

advantage of using these - particularly when the cartridge holder is large - is that they can stick out, which causes problems when shooting in a prone position. This system is also easily damaged. A compromise between the fixed magazine and the removable cartridge holder is the CZ hinged cartridge holder. The catch for removing the cartridge holder is usually situated close to the magazine or trigger mechanism is often found in lever-action repeating rifles and also in semi-automatics. Cartridges can be loaded one at a time into a tube located under the barrel. Loading is sometimes from the muzzle end, sometimes via the butt or stock, but in certain cases through a side loading port or even from beneath the breech block.

The tubular magazine beneath the barrel of a Winchester lever-action repeating rifle

3. Safety in the use of firearms

This chapter considers safe handling and use of firearms. To make sure firearms are used safely, there are twelve "golden rules":

1. *Treat every firearm as if it is loaded.* This is the most important rule. If someone hands you a gun to look at and says that the weapon is not loaded, do not take their word for it. Check for yourself. This may save you a great deal of misery in the end.

2. *Always point the barrel in a safe direction* and never point it in a direction you do not want to shoot at! Never wave a weapon around.

Open the bolt or breech to convince yourself that there is no round in the chamber. With repeating rifles, first always remove the cartridge holder or empty the magazine

3. *Keep your finger away from the trigger* and use the safety catch, even if you are sure the weapon is not loaded. Only move your finger to the trigger on the firing range and only then when the weapon is aiming at the intended target from the firing position.
After the shot has been fired, remove your finger immediately from the trigger. Keep your finger straight alongside the trigger guard.

Only place your finger on the trigger when the weapon is aiming at the intended target

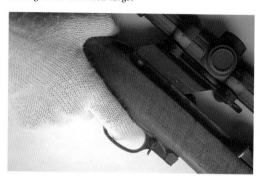

4. *Never play with a gun.* A firearm may be a technically and aesthetically pleasing object but it can also be extremely dan-

Is your weapon aiming at the target? If not, then keep your finger straight alongside the trigger guard

gerous. A firearm deserves respect and to be handled very carefully. It is certainly not a toy.

5. *Practise loading and unloading* a new weapon in a safe place until you have perfected the drill.

6. *Never leave a loaded or unloaded gun unattended.* This is vitally important, especially where there are children. Children love to imitate adults and they could be waving your gun around before you know it.

7. *Keep your weapons and ammunition separate* from each other and out of reach of your own or anyone else's children. Lock your weapons and ammunition securely away. This will also prevent a burglar from having instant access to a loaded firearm.

8. *Service your weapons regularly.* Check before you service your gun that it really is not loaded. If you intend using your gun after it has not been used for some time, make sure that the barrel is not blocked by a wad of cleaning cloth, for example. If this should prove to be the case, you will need a new weapon after taking the first shot.

9. *Establish a distinct routine* when handling your guns and ammunition. Take care to keep different kinds of ammunition separate. Be very careful when filling new cartridges yourself. Remember that an additional boost for a cartridge is a precise matter of tenths of a grain, and that one grain weighs 0.0025oz (0.0648g)! Beginners in this field would be wise to seek advice of experienced hand-loaders. They must also have good reference books to hand, and be familiar with all the theoretical "ins and outs" of hand-loading.

10. *Always wear ear protection* and shooting or safety glasses. A significant proportion of all shooting accidents are caused by technical defects in the guns or ammunition of the person injured or in the guns and ammunition of people shooting nearby. Make sure your eyes are protected from powder debris, escaping gas pressure, or ejected cartridge cases.

11. *NEVER combine shooting with alcohol* or, even worse, with drugs in whatever form or strong medicines (check the instructions for the medicine's use first). Alcohol or drugs will disturb your perception, judgement, and behaviour. Drink

Shooting glasses by Wischo

your beer or dram after shooting and after you have unloaded and stored your guns safely. And of course, at the end of a shooting session if you have to drive yourself home, don't drink and drive!

12. *Point out any unsafe behaviour to fellow shooters.* Beginners never learn unless someone tells them what to do or what not to do. Try to explain the proper use of guns in a polite way. Even experienced shooters make mistakes. Avoid the company of "know-it-alls" who think they know better than anyone else. They are a source of potential danger.

Various Wischo ear protectors

4. Safety systems

After previous chapters on technical aspects, this chapter gives more detailed information about the various safety systems that are used with rifles and carbines.

Safety systems in practice

For the sake of clarity, it is important to define the concept of a safety system. This is a manually operated system which, when put in operation, prevents a weapon from being fired unintentionally. Most safety systems prevent any movement of the trigger lever but the firing-pin can also be locked by certain systems and, in addition, some weapons lock the trigger mechanism itself. With bolt-action rifles, the bolt is generally locked by the safety system. Some safety systems combine some or all of these methods. However, there are also different automatically-operated safety systems that can be lifted mechanically by pulling the trigger, such as firing-pin safety mechanisms.

Safety catch immediately behind the bolt (CZ)

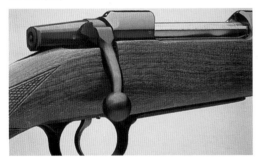

The safety catch

A safety catch is operated manually. Depending on the make, type, and model of weapon, it blocks the hammer or internal firing-pin, and/or the trigger mechanism, and/or the trigger lever, and sometimes also prevents the breech or the bolt from being opened. Various combinations can be used.

With the majority of bolt-action rifles, the safety catch is mounted on the receiver

A simple but effective safety catch on a Marlin bolt-action rifle

group, right next to the bolt lever. The safety catch usually shows a red dot when it is in the firing position, and a white dot

Safety catch in the front of the trigger guard (Marlin)

in the safe position. A variation on this is for the safety catch to be mounted at the front of the trigger guard. The safety catch is operated using the trigger finger. Good examples of this can be found in older military weapons, such as the Garand rifle, or similar systems on model 45 and 9 Marlin carbines. This type of safety catch usually just blocks the trigger lever.

Pinion or rotating safety catch

Pinion-operated safety catches are usually found on bolt-action rifles. The catch is operated by a rotating pinion at the rear of the bolt that blocks both the bolt and the firing-pin. A good example can be found on the type 98 Mauser rifle. This type of safety catch has been employed by many manufacturers, including Winches-

Pinio- operated safety catch at the rear of the bolt (Mauser)

Rotating safety catch of Browning

ter, with their rotating safety catch on the .30 M1 carbine. The catch on this weapon is mounted on the trigger guard and it

Rotating safety catch of a Winchester .30 M1 carbine

Rotating safety catch of a Bushmaster XM15-E2S rifle (Colt system)

blocks the trigger lever. A further example of a rotating safety catch can be found on the mechanism housing of the Colt M16/AR-15 and similar rifles.

Sliding-lever safety catch

Sliding-lever safety catches are used on both bolt-action and semi-automatic weapons. The slider is sometimes mounted on top of the pistol grip of the stock,

Sliding-lever safety catch on the receiver (round knob beneath the hammer) of a Marlin lever-action repeating rifle

in an extension of the mechanism housing. The slider usually blocks the trigger lever and/or the trigger mechanism. The slider can also be mounted on the side of the mechanism housing or the breech.

Press-button safety catch

This system is usually located in the trigger guard. The mechanism is frequently of the push-through type, whereby the catch is pushed through from one side of the trigger guard to the other. When set to safe, a red ring is usually visible.

A different type of press-button catch is that used by Winchester, where a button is sited in the side of the mechanism housing. This push button passes through the receiver and it blocks the hammer.

Press-button safety catch located to rear of the trigger lever, in the trigger guard

Press-button safety catch on the mechanism housing of a Winchester lever-action repeating rifle

The disc-operated catch of Thompson

Single-shot pistols and rifles made by Thompson/Centre have a unique safety system. When the weapon is broken to open the breech in order to load a round into the chamber, the safety mechanism is automatically engaged.

The safe, or locked position, is only released when the trigger lever is pulled. In addition, there is a selector switch above the hammer that sets the firing-pin to one of three positions: position 1 for rim-fire,

Disc-operated safety catch of the Thompson Contender rifle

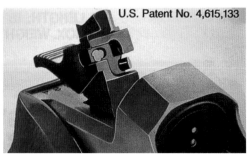

U.S. Patent No. 4,615,133

2 for safe, and 3 for centre-fire. This system does not lock either the hammer or the trigger lever. Should the hammer accidentally be released, any cartridge in the chamber will not be fired, because the firing-pin on the hammer is withdrawn.

Magazine safety

Few rifles and carbines utilize a safety system linked to the magazine but for those that do, the system starts from the principle that to clean a weapon, the magazine has to be removed. With this safety system, once the magazine has been removed, either the trigger mechanism is locked, or the trigger action is disengaged from the mechanism to prevent a shot from being fired accidentally.

The half-cock

This system is sometimes utilized with

The half-cock, combined with a hammer-head that can be withdrawn, of Browning

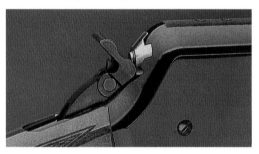

rifles and carbines with locking for the cocking lever that generally have an external hammer. If the hammer is pulled partially backwards by means of the cocking lever, the trigger mechanism locates a recess in the base of the hammer. This blocks the trigger mechanism until the cocking lever is fully pushed to the rear, cocking the weapon, ready to fire. This action also loads a new round into the chamber. The illustration above shows this system combined with an additional safety fea-ture with which the hammer of this lever-action rifle can also be pulled backwards in the half-cocked position.

The slide safety

Almost all rifles and carbines have a slide

safety. This system prevents a cartridge from being fired if the slide is not fully home, for instance because of dirt or because of a cartridge that does not fit properly into the chamber, or whatever the reason may be. In most semi-automatic weapons this system functions as follows. A lug on the trigger bar has to match with a recess at the bottom of the inner side of the slider. If this is not done, so that the slide is not fully engaged, the trigger bar is blocked so that the trigger mechanism or hammer cannot fire a shot. Manually operated systems block the hammer or otherwise prevent it striking the firing-pin. Other systems without internal or external hammers have a trigger mechanism that is directly connected to a lug on the firing-pin. Provided the locking action is not fully engaged, the connection between the trigger mechanism and firing-pin is not made.

The load indicator

This system is sometimes used for match rifles but is mainly used for hunting rifles. The load indicator shows whether there is

The load, or readiness indicator of CZ. The prominent stub at the rear of the bolt indicates that the rifle is cocked

In this illustration of a CZ rifle, the weapon is not loaded or cocked The load indicator, at the rear of the bolt, does not stick out.

a round in the chamber and it can also provide an indication with some firearms of whether the firing-pin is cocked. This can be seen by, for example, a stub or boss that protrudes through the rear of the bolt or bolt-head, or one that protrudes from the top of a hinged breech.

The automatic firing-pin safety

The automatic firing-pin safety is mainly used with double-action pistols. Several makes and types of rifle do, however, use a similar system, normally in combination with slide safety. In this case the firing-pin is usually comprised of two parts. When the breech or bolt is opened, the rear of the firing-pin is moved out of range of the hammer. Provided the breech or bolt are not fully closed, the firing-pin remains out of range of the hammer.
The illustration above shows the cut-away mechanism of a Marlin lever-action repeating rifle.
1. A firing-pin, comprising two parts,

Cut-away illustration of the mechanism housing of a Marlin lever-action repeating rifle, showing the safety systems: firing-pin safety, trigger safety, half cock/-hammer safety, and a safety catch for locking the trigger

whereby the rear is kept out of range of the hammer until the breech is fully closed (a type of firing-pin safety). 2. Trigger mechanism locked if the cocking lever is not fully engaged. 3. Half-cock/hammer safety, with which the hammer can be manually pulled back and locked in the halfway position. The hammer cannot be released forward by pressing the trigger, the hammer has first to be pulled fully to the rear. It can then be fired by pressing the trigger. 4. The hammer can be locked by means of the sliding-lever safety catch.

5. Locking systems

Earlier chapters have discussed the enormous forces that are unleashed in the chamber of a rifle when a cartridge is fired. Those forces have to be harnessed and properly directed to prevent a weapon becoming a lump of twisted steel scrap. The tremendous gas-pressure in the fired cartridge must only exit in the one safe direction - the open barrel. The forces which drive the bullet out of the cartridge case and down the barrel also recoil in the opposite direction. The breech in the barrel that is necessary to be able continually to load new cartridges must be safely closed until the gas-pressure has subsided to a safe level. This closing of the chamber is known as locking. Different weapons have their own locking mechanisms. The terms bolt-head or slide and bolt are repeatedly used in this context.

Slide or bolt

Before dealing with the locking systems of rifles and carbines, I will deal with the terms slide and bolt.
With semi-automatic weapons, the term slide is normally used. This is a massive block of steel which is driven back by the recoil to re-cock the weapon. A bolt is an equally massive block of steel that is manually operated.
The slide or bolt have to be connected to the receiver when they are closed in order to withstand the considerable gas-pressure. This is usually achieved by means of lugs or cams on the slide or bolt that engage in corresponding recesses in the receiver or breech block that form an extension of the barrel. The term receiver is also used where the slide or bolt are located in a partially open track.
A receiver or mechanism housing is a mainly enclosed housing in which the bolt-slide can move backwards and forwards. The mechanism housing usually incorporates the trigger group and magazine.

Locking systems in use

The different locking systems used in rifles and carbines are described below.

Locking lugs

Depending on the system used, the manually-operated bolt is equipped with a number of locking lugs to the front and/or rear of the bolt. In closing or locking-up, these lugs fit into notches which ensure that the bolt and receiver are firmly connected to each other.
This is a robust and reliable system that can withstand very high gas-pressures and is therefore suitable for use with heavy calibre ammunition. The number of lugs can be as many as nine, depending on the make and system.
Single lug bolts are used with smaller calibre rifles and nine can be found, for example on the powerful Weatherby rifles. With some makes both the front and rear of the bolt has a number of lugs, so that the bolt is firmly locked to the receiver. The Sauer bolt has a slightly different system. This has locking lugs that fold inwards but extend outwards to engage in notches in the receiver by the rotating action of the bolt.

Bolt lugs of an M70 Winchester bolt-action rifle

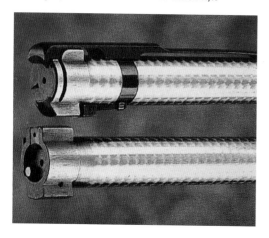

Weatherby bolt locking system with nine lugs

Sauer bolt with extendible lugs

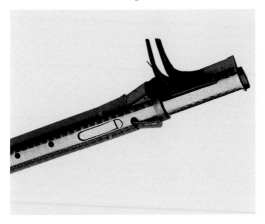

Yet another system is that used with the Blaser R93 rifle. The locking lugs are arranged around the bolt behind its face. There are 18 small segments that are pushed outwards by the locking action of the bolt to form a collar that grasps the barrel.

Blaser R93 rifle with eighteen extendible lugs for 360˚ locking

Inertia action

Detail from an exploded drawing of the Krico small calibre rifle. The bolt head (no. 201 101) acts as a decelerating mass. Part no. 210 300 is the recoil spring

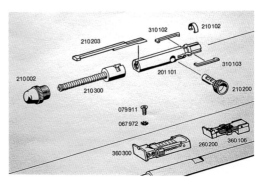

This system is usually used in smaller calibre rifles and carbines. The locking of these weapons is achieved by the weight or mass of the bolt head or slide combined with the pressure of the return spring that together ensure the slide remains in the forward, closed position. The slide is pressed against the rear of the cartridge chamber by the tension in the recoil spring. The system works as follows: when a shot is fired, gas-pressure develops impelling the bullet from the cartridge case through the rifling in the barrel. The explosion/gas-pressure and acceleration of the bullet through the barrel cause a force in the opposite direction against the inside of the back of the cartridge case that ensures the chamber is gas tight. This also tries to propel the cartridge case backwards out of the chamber but this is prevented by the bolt or slide. The tension of the recoil spring together with the mass of the steel bolt or slide are calculated to delay this action until the bullet has exited the barrel. At this point, the system can safely be disengaged. The mass of the slide is sufficient that when the recoil commences, the backward movement continues until it is halted at the end of its travel. The sequence is as follows:

- the shot is fired
- the slide is forced back by gas-pressure
- this in turn more or less simultaneous-

ly tensions the springs of the firing-pin, the hammer, and the return spring, and cocks the weapon. The spent cartridge is removed from the chamber by the cartridge extractor as the slide moves backwards, and is ejected
- because the return spring is compressed to its maximum, this is tensioned so that it pushes the slide forwards
- the slide removes a new cartridge from the cartridge holder as it is forced forwards, and rams this into the chamber.

The return spring is usually located behind the slide.

Rotation locking

Slide with rotation locking (Bushmaster)

Certain semi-automatic rifles and carbines use a rotation locking system.
The weapon's slide, which is mounted in the receiver or mechanism housing, is equipped with a number of locking lugs at its front. When the slider (or bolt head) is closed, these lugs engage with notches in the rear of the barrel.

Bolt-action roller system of Heckler & Koch

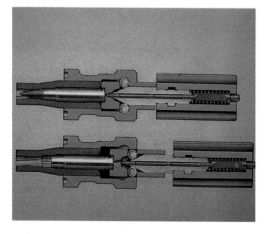

Depending upon the type of weapon, this is the receiver or breech.
The recoil or gas-pressure causes the slide to turn a certain number of degrees so that the lugs disengage from the notches in the receiver or breech.

Bolt-action roller system

This system is mainly used in rifles, carbines, and even pistols made by the German company of Heckler & Koch. The system operates in the following way. Two hemispherical recesses are situated in longitudinal extensions to the barrel. Within these are located two steel rollers that are also connected to the slide. When the weapon is locked, the two steel rollers drop into recesses at the side of the barrel. After firing, the slide is forced backwards by gas-pressure. The two rollers swing inwards and when disengagement is completed, the slide continues backwards. After that, the cycle of extracting, ejecting, and reloading begins again.

There are two advantages to this system. First, the locked action after firing the cartridge is very stable and, secondly, the recoil is delayed because the two rollers first have to swing inwards. This reduces discomfort for shooters when using powerful ammunition. One disadvantage is the high production cost of this system, because it requires very fine tolerances in manufacture. A further disadvantage is the system's sensitivity to variations in ammunition.

Gas-pressure locking system

Semi-automatic weapons that are operated by gas-pressure are nothing new. Experiments into such systems were carried out in the nineteenth century with the Cei-Rigotti rifle, for example, that was demonstrated to the Italian army in 1895. Various prototype weapons were built in Germany from 1901 and the commander of the British army at that time dismissed the Farquhar-Hill automatic as too complicated.
The working of a semi-automatic gas-pressure system general operates in the following way. Gas-pressure develops when a cartridge is fired.

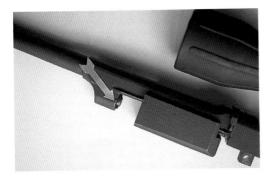

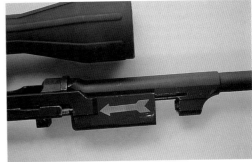

This drives the bullet from the cartridge case and impels it towards the muzzle. Half way along the barrel there is a small hole or gas vent. Because the bullet is still in the barrel, the pressure in the barrel is very high and some of that pressure escapes via the vent to a small cylinder. The cylinder has a piston which is driven back by the sudden increase in pressure. The piston is usually connected to a return lever that is in turn connected to the slide. The blow back of the piston forces the slide backwards.

Now the bullet has left the barrel, and the gas-pressure returns to normal but the slide has been set in motion and continues backwards. In most cases, the slide rotates as it is pushed through grooves, disengaging it from the end of the barrel. The cartridge is simultaneously pulled from the chamber and ejected. The firing-pin and/or the hammer (or internal striking mechanism) is cocked and the slide is stopped in its rearwards travel. During this process, the recoil or return spring has also been tensioned. The pressure of that spring now pushes the slide forwards once more, inserting a new cartridge from the magazine in the chamber. When that cartridge is fired, the entire cycle is repeated.

The gas vent is either located under (as the .30-M1 carbine) or on the top of the barrel (as the Kalashnikov AK-47), depending upon the maker and model.

The gas-pressure system is not really a locking system, rather a propulsion or repeater mechanism, since the true locking is performed by lugs and grooves on the rotating slide and the end of the barrel.

This gas-pressure system is used in various forms in rifles, carbines, machine-guns, machine-pistols, and even shotguns.

Pump-action repeating system

Rotation locking of the Browning pump-action repeating system

The pump-action repeating system works much like the gas-pressure system. The main difference is the form of propulsion. With the pump-action system, the repeating mechanism is manually driven by the handle under the barrel which is pulled to the rear and then pushed forwards again. The slide, which usually has locking lugs, is disengaged, the empty shell is ejected, and the firing-pin is re-cocked. The forward motion inserts a new round in the chamber. The conclusion of the sequence is when the slide is rotated so that the locking lugs engage with matching recesses in the breech or receiver. This method is also used for shotguns.

Hinged breech-action lock

Hinged breech-action lock of CZ

Hinged breech-action locks are mainly used in shotguns, where the barrel is attached by a hinge to the locking mechanism, the trigger group, and the stock. The system is found with some single-shot rifles, such as the Thompson Contender carbine, the Handi-Rifle of New England Firearms, and the special large calibre rifles by Heym.

The barrel is attached to the rest of the weapon by a hinge at the breech and it is locked by a sliding or swivel-action catch. When this is opened, the barrel can be "broken."

Cartridges can then be removed from, and inserted directly into the end of the barrel. This system can withstand extremely high gas-pressures, making it suitable for use with powerful ammunition.

Lever-action locking

The lever-action locking system is principally found on old-fashioned "cowboy" rifles and carbines of the "wild west." An enlarged trigger guard is coupled with the slide or bolt. When the lever is pushed forwards, the bolt (which may or may not rotate) is disengaged from locking lugs in the breech and/or end of the barrel, and moves backwards and the cartridge extractor in the breech ejects the spent cartridge. The rearwards travel of the slide forces the hammer back and cocks it. Simultaneously, the cartridge loader drops to the level of the tubular magazine and the magazine spring pushes a round into the loader. Once the lever is pulled back, the cartridge loader rises up level with the chamber.

With larger calibres, the slide (or bolt) is equipped with locking lugs. Browning uses a special toothed rack as a locking system

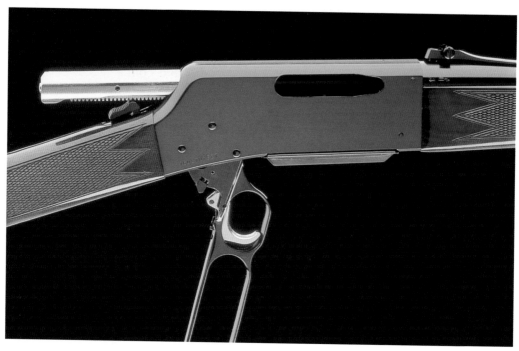

Lever-action by Uberti: for smaller calibres, the lever-action alone is the locking system

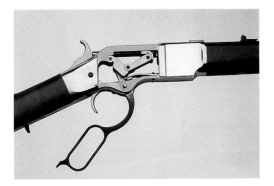

The slide then pushes forwards over the cartridge loader and inserts the round into the chamber. The lever-action then comes to a neutral position and the slide clicks into the locked position. Certain variations of this system rotate the slide so that it can engage with locking lugs at the rear of the barrel. The weapon is then ready to fire.

Roller or drop-block locking

The roller-block system, such as that used by Remington, is operated by a special locking lever at the rear of the receiver that at first glance appears to be a second hammer. The actual hammer is positioned behind the locking lever, as can be seen from the illustration. Pulling the locking lever backwards and downwards opens the chamber so that the weapon can be unloaded and reloaded. After loading, the lever is first pushed forwards to close the chamber, then the weapon can be fired. The drop-block action is operated, rather like the lever-action, with

Remington rolling block-vergrendeling

an enlarged trigger guard that acts as a lever. When this is pushed forwards, the entire breech block drops down on runners.

This gives access to the chamber to remove and/or load a cartridge. Once the lever is pulled back, the breech block returns into alignment with the barrel, closing the chamber. This system can be combined with a cartridge loader that provides a new round from a tubular magazine.

The Sharps drop-block action (Navy Arms)

Trapdoor action

This very old system was used mainly on the ancient Springfield model 1868 Trapdoor rifle. The chamber at the end of the barrel is closed by a receiver and the barrel end which are hinged from above the barrel and connected to each other by a catch or handle.

The hinged barrel end also incorporates the firing-pin.

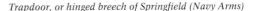

Trapdoor, or hinged breech of Springfield (Navy Arms)

6. Maintenance

The shooter is usually very enthusiastic about match shooting or hunting but finds the cleaning of weapons less enjoyable. Yet the good functioning of the rifle or carbine and its precision depend to a great extent upon the manner in which the gun is maintained. A barrel in which the rifling is clogged up with powder residues or with copper and lead swarf will not perform properly. Quite apart from the potential for the gas-pressure to increase to dangerous levels, the bullet has insufficient spin imparted upon it and it is likely to tumble in its flight.

The easiest way is to clean the weapon each time it is used. The marksman who participates in long-range competitions or bench-rest shooter who pulls through his barrel after each group of shots does so for a purpose.

Check before every cleaning session that the weapon is not loaded. A large proportion of shooting accidents occur during cleaning of weapons.

Cleaning the barrel

To clean the barrel properly, the cleaning rod needs to be pushed through it with a piece of wadding smeared with gun oil. This is followed by cleaning with a brass wire brush of the right diameter for the calibre. Never use a steel wire brush. If the barrel is very dirty, special barrel cleaning agents will be needed such as Hoppe's No. 9, Robla Solo, Kleenbore, and the products of Frankonia and Kettner.

The barrel, as said, has to be cleaned with a good cleaning rod that is not made of iron or steel. This has to be done always from the chamber towards the muzzle and never in the opposite direction.

The cleaning rod is worked in and out a number of times, until all the powder residues and carbon deposits from combustion are fully removed.

Different types of cleaning rods:
1. aluminium rod for shotguns; 2. steel rod for hand guns; 3. universal plastic-covered steel rod; 4. plastic-coated rifle cleaning rod

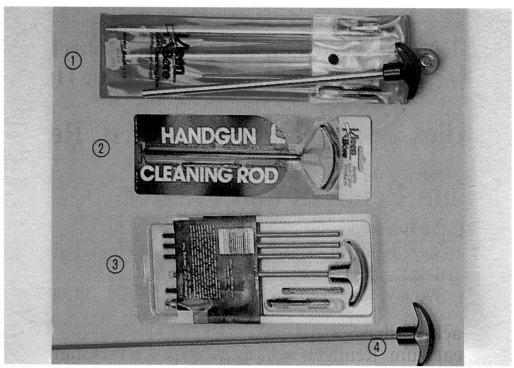

The next step is to clean the chamber thoroughly with a larger brush since the diameter of the chamber is greater than that of the barrel. An old toothbrush and clean wadding is ideal for this purpose.

A number of mistakes are often made during cleaning the barrel. One major one, is to hold the weapon upright and to pour oil into the muzzle with the intention of giving the dirt a good soaking to loosen it. The mess in the barrel does indeed become loose and it streams with the oil down the barrel to the chamber where it ends up on the front of the bolt or slide, continuing on to coat the firing-pin. With automatic weapons, there is also the danger that the oil will enter the gas vent, affecting the repeating mechanism with all the problems that can entail. Far better is to remove the bolt or slide and to use the cleaning rod.

Lubricating a firearm

After the cleaning, the barrel has to be pulled through with pieces of wadding until these come out clean. The barrel is then lightly smeared with oil.

Most cleaning kits include a felt brush for this purpose. The bolt or slide does not have to be removed every time the weapon is fired. The bolt head does have to be cleaned though; accumulation of dirt does not improve the functioning of the cartridge extractor. After wiping the bolt or slide clean, it needs to be lightly smeared with oil, preferably with a silicone oil that ensures even lubrication. The stock is best coated with special oil for the stock, since the normal gun oil can bleach it.

If the stock has a hard varnish coating, it can be wiped clean with a damp cloth. The front and rear sights can be cleaned easily with a stiff paintbrush.

Finally, the external steel parts of the weapon can be wiped over with a silicon cloth. This prevents etching of the metal by acids from your skin.

Major servicing

Once a year it is necessary to carry out a major service, preferably at the end of the hunting or shooting season. It is sensible to strip the gun down as much as possible in order to clean every part thoroughly. For this purpose, I use a metal container with diesel oil to which I add a little gun oil to make it a little less harsh. All the parts, with the exception of the stock, are allowed to soak in the liquid, after which they are thoroughly brushed clean. Of course, I handle each weapon separately to avoid mixing up the parts.

After cleaning, every part is lightly smeared with oil (with the emphasis on "lightly") and the weapon is reassembled. Before firing the weapon after such a cleaning session, it is necessary to remove the film of oil from the barrel. This is done thoroughly, using dry wadding with a cleaning rod.

Those shooters who are not confident about stripping and reassembling their weapons provide work for the gunsmith who will carry out such a major service for a price.

7. Ammunition

Rifle and carbine cartridges are available in a wide range of types and sizes. Certain calibres can be used for both hand guns and for rifles and carbines. This is true, for example, of the .22 LR cartridge (Long Rifle) and also of the .357 and .44 Magnum revolver cartridges and even the .30-M1 carbine ammunition. The last of these is used with the AMT Automag III pistol and for other hand guns. This chapter deals solely with the normal rifle and carbine ammunition, with some mention of certain special types. The number of calibres available is so great that this on its own could fill a book.

How the cartridge works

Almost all cartridges are made up of four different components:
- The case
- The priming cap
- The powder
- The bullet

Sectional drawing through a Winchester rifle cartridge:
1. the primer; 2. the powder charge; 3. the case;
4. the bullet

The sequence of firing a cartridge is as follows.
The firing-pin of the weapon strikes the priming cap of the cartridge. The cap is filled with a small quantity of highly explosive compound that can be set off by a light blow. Within milliseconds, the little charge explodes, and the sharp flash of flame ignites the powder. The bottom of the cartridge is equipped with one (Boxer system) or more small gaps (Berdan system) which direct the flame to the main charge. In a fraction of a second, the gunpowder burns fiercely, creating a high gas-pressure. This pressure is entirely contained because the cartridge case is enclosed on virtually all sides - from behind by the bolt or slide, and at the sides by the wall of the chamber. The cartridge case is made of brass which is a

soft and pliable material. Because the case expands during ignition and is pressed against the chamber wall, a gas-tight seal is formed. This is essential so that all the available gas-pressure can be used to impel the bullet. The only outlet for the gas to escape is forwards, but the bullet is in the way. The high pressure forces the bullet from its casing and in a very short space of time, the bullet accelerates to a very high velocity which increases as the gas expands behind it as it passes along the barrel.

The gas-pressures that are created during ignition are dependant upon the powder charge, but they can become extremely high. An 8 x 57mm Mauser cartridge has a reasonable pressure of "only" 35,000 psi (pounds per square inch) or 2,465kg/cm^2. Compare that with the air pressure in your tyres. A more modern cartridge such as a .223 Remington develops a higher gas-pressure, that can increase to 55,000 psi (3,873kg/cm2). A larger calibre does not automatically mean that the gas-pressure is of the levels of "Magnum" cartridges. A powerful Magnum cartridge like the .458 Winchester Magnum does not exceed 3,477kg/cm^2. Depending upon the calibre and type of weapon, the bullet flies several hundred to several thousand metres/yards. The gas-pressure ensures that the bullet travels at an exceptional velocity towards its target. A general rule of thumb with rifle and carbine cartridges is that the lighter the bullet, the higher its velocity but this is not always the case. A light bullet from a .223 calibre Remington reaches a muzzle velocity of about 1,000m per second (3,280ft per second). A .308 Winchester cartridge also has similar muzzle velocity. The speed of a bullet is grossly underestimated - especially by popular television series which show heroes dodging asbullets whistle past. When they hear the shot, they manage to duck their heads back around the cover of a wall without coming to harm.
The reality is quite different.

Speed and precision

From the moment that the shooter wishes to fire, it takes about 0.2 seconds for the message from the brain to reach the fingers and for them to react. The firing-pin strikes the primer cap about 0.005 seconds later. The ignition in the cartridge then takes about 0.0004 seconds, making a total of 0.2054 seconds. The ignition flame sets of the powder charge and gas-pressure begins to develop. This chemical reaction continues even after the bullet has left the barrel. After about 0.004 seconds, the bullet escapes from the cartridge case and begins its trajectory towards the target. The bullet has a "modest" muzzle velocity of 1,000m per second (3,280ft per second) as it leaves the barrel having been pressed through the rifled fields in the weapon about 0.0012 seconds later. Depending on the rate of twist and certain other factors, the bullet leaves the barrel turning at 3,000 revolutions per second. If the target is at a range of 100m (328ft), the bullet will reach it in 0.15 seconds. So the total time from firing before the bullet hits its target is 0.3606 seconds. Even more interesting is that the shooter does not feel the recoil until 0.2 seconds after the bullet has exited the barrel.

Ballistics

The study of the behaviour of ammunition is known as ballistics. In general there are two kinds of ballistic properties: the internal ballistics examines the behaviour of the cartridge in the chamber and of the bullet in the barrel. The external ballistics cover the performance after the bullet has exited the muzzle. There is a third type of ballistic property, that examines the behaviour of the bullet when it hits its target. Internal and external ballistics partially overlap. The speed with which a bullet leaves the barrel is known as the muzzle velocity. This is dependant upon the cross-section and to a lesser extent, the shape of the bullet but also of the type of cartridge. A cartridge with a heavy charge will in general achieve higher velocity because greater gas-pressures will be developed. The velocity of the bullet is often important because of the kinetic energy of the bullet. The velocity is not of great interest for a cartridge for a match hand gun because accuracy is only required to about 25 or 50 metres/yards. Velocity is important, how-ever, for competitors at the longer ranges of, for instance, 300 meters/yards because this has a bearing on the deviation of the bullet. A high velocity will usually pro-duce a flat trajectory. The kinetic energy, expressed in Joules, is calculated by a simple formula: bullet velocity 2 x weight of bullet in grams: 2,000 = number of Joules. The result in Joules is not of much interest to match shooters but it is to hunters.

Hunting ammunition

Hunters have to determine what game can be shot with which ammunition. Many countries have specific regulations governing this. Everyone can understand that there is little point in trying to shoot a deer at 100 metyres/yards with a small calibre weapon, regardless of whether they approve. With larger calibres, the choice is more difficult. Most European countries have the following legal requirements:
- Roe deer: cartridge must have a minimum kinetic energy of 980 Joules at 100m (109yds).

Calibre examples:

Calibre	Bullet velocity		Kinetic energy of bullet	
	V0	V100	E0	E100
.222 Remington (3.6)	910	750	1,491	1,013
.223 Remington (3.6)	1,000	860	1,800	1,331
.243 Winchester (6.5)	918	807	2,739	2,117

- Red deer, fallow deer, and wild boar: cartridge must have a minimum kinetic energy of 2,200 Joules at 100m (109yds).

Calibre Bullet	velocity		Kinetic energy of bullet	
	V0	V100	E0	E100
.270 Remington (8.4)	853	792	3,056	2,635
7 x 57mm (10.5)	800	720	3,360	2,722
8 x 57mm (12.1)	800	730	3,872	3,224
.30-06 Springfield (11.6)	823	762	3,929	3,368
.308 Winchester (11.6)	796	729	3,675	3,082

Larger game than this really means Magnum cartridges with a kinetic muzzle energy greater than 4,500 Joules at 100m (109yds), such as .375 Magnum or larger.
V0   = Velocity (bullet's velocity at 0m: muzzle velocity)
V100 = The same at 100m (109yds)
E0   = Kinetic energy of bullet at the muzzle
E100   The same at 100m (109yds)
The figures in brackets e.g. (8.4) are the bullet's weight in grams.

Effective range

Generally speaking, standard ammunition in use in standard rifles is used at ranges of between 100 and 300m (328yds).
Special sniper's rifles have an effective range that can easily achieve 300m (328yds) and even farther. The modern large calibre sniper's rifles such as the .50 calibre BMG (Browning Machine Gun, based upon machine-gun ammunition) are precise to a range of 2,500m (2,734yds). Marksmen fire at targets of 3-5cm (11/4-2in) diameter at ranges of 300m (328yds). This requires considerable practice and specially adapted ammunition. Both factors push a sports shooter towards self-loading of cartridges.
In addition to the experience of the shooter, target-shooting also depends upon the powder charge, the type of bullet, type of primer, and the type of weapon used.
The barrel of a rifle and carbine has spiral grooves on its inside that impart a spin on the bullet as it travels through the barrel. This rotation stabilizes the bullet in its flight, to keep it on target. Without this, the bullet would tumble.

The subtle differences in stability, trigger system, cartridge loading, sights, power, ease of handling, and ergonomic comfort of a weapon are often not recognized or given sufficient importance by newcomers to the sport of shooting. For experienced shooters, these factors can be quickly distinguished and play a major role in their choice of new weapon.
Below you will find a general description of the most current calibres of rifle and carbine cartridges, together with illustrations of these cartridges.

Rimfire ammunition

The .22 Short, Long, Long Rifle, and .22 WMR (Winchester Magnum Rimfire) cartridges belong to the family of rimfire cartridges. This means that the fulminate compound has been pressed inside the thin-walled case rim, where it is ignited by the strike of the firing-pin. There is not, of course, much of this priming compound. In the case of RWS cartridges, it is only 0.035g of the non-corrosive material "Sinoxid." Cartridges such as .22 WMR are widely used with small-bore hunting rifles for shooting birds.

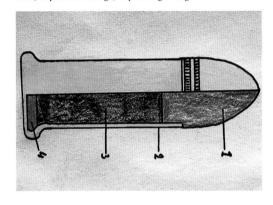
Cross-section through a rimfire cartridge: 1. bullet; 2. case; 3. powder charge; 4. priming charge

The rimfire cartridge .22 Short is used in rapid-fire pistols. As well as the normal cartridges, special indoor cartridges are available with a significantly reduced powder charge for shooting at short range in enclosed spaces.
The Hi-Speed or high velocity cartridges have a considerably higher muzzle velocity and in combination with a hollow point bullet, have a totally different effect on targets than standard bullets. Such cartridges have no advantage for the sports shooter in terms of precision. Quite the contrary has been proved from numerous tests. This rimfire ammunition is often called the "Flobert cartridge", which is not correct.

The range of rimfire cartridges (from left to right): .22 Short; .22 LR; .22 LR-Yellow Jacket; .22 LR-Stinger; .22 WMRSerie randvuurpatronen, van links naar rechts: .22 Short; .22 LR; .22 LR-Yellow Jacket; .22 LR-Stinger; .22 WMR

The .22 Short

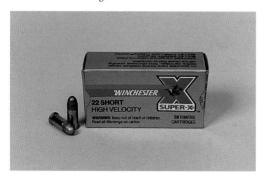

The history of the .22 Short cartridge goes back some way. The rimfire cartridge was developed in the USA from the European 6mm Flobert cartridge. The first gun with this calibre was the Smith & Wesson First Model revolver that was introduced in 1857. The cartridge was initially provided with a 29 grain (1.9g) bullet and a 4 grain (0.26g) charge of black powder. The cartridge quickly became popular for the sport of disc shooting with heavy single-shot match rifles. Following the invention of smokeless, or nitro powder in 1887, this cartridge became widely used in competitive shooting circles, and in 1930, a high-speed version was introduced. Many small bore-rifles and carbines equipped for .22 LR can also fire this cartridge. It is not suitable for ranges above 50m (164ft).

The .22 Long

This cartridge was first introduced in 1871. It is often regarded as an intermediate stage between the .22 Short and the .22 LR cartridges. This is not the case. This cartridge was introduced in 1871 as a revolver cartridge, about sixteen years before the .22 LR. The .22 Long originally had a 29 grain (1.9g) bullet and was loaded with black powder. The potential usage of this cartridge was significantly reduced by the introduction of the .22 LR cartridge.

The .22 LR

It is accepted that this cartridge was developed by the American firm J. Stevens Arms and Tool Company. This ammunition was introduced in 1887. The cartridge initially had a 40 grain (2.6g) bullet and a black powder charge of 5 grain (0.32g). The first High-Speed versions of this cartridge were introduced by Remington in about 1930. There were two versions: a 40 grain (2.6g) solid bullet or a 37 grain (2.4g) hollow bullet. This last type was specifically intended for the hunting of small game to a range of 80m (262ft). The .22 LR cartridge has been produced in higher quantities than any other ammunition. Almost every manufacturer of ammunition makes the .22 LR in a wide range of different versions. The maximum range of the bullet is about 1,000m (1,093yds), fired at a trajectory of about 30 degrees. Do not underestimate this cartridge.

The .22 WMR (Winchester Magnum Rimfire)

Winchester developed this rimfire cartridge in 1959. The American firms of Ruger and Smith & Wesson both introduced a revolver for this calibre, followed in 1960 by the Winchester model 61 pump-action rifle.

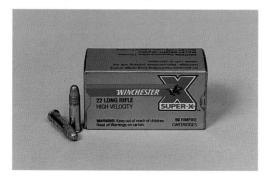

There is an enormous variety of handguns, rifles, and carbines that use this cartridge, particularly for hunting. The cartridge has never been of any significance to the sport of target shooting. The effective range of this cartridge is about 125m (136yds).

The table below gives the bullet's velocity and kinetic energy for the different cartridges.

Cartridge	Type	Bulletweight	Gas-pressure	VO velocity	EO
		g	bar	m/s	Joule
6mm	Flobert	1.0	800	200	20
.22 Long	Z(immer	1.8	1,000	220	44
.22 Short	Standard	1.8	1,800	260	61
.22 LR	Subsonic	2.6	1,800	305	121
.22 LR	Standard	2.6	1,800	330	141
.22 LR	High velocit	2.6	1,800	400	208
.22 LR	Stinger	2.1	1,900	510	273
.22 Magnum	WMR	2.6	1,900	615	491

VO = muzzle velocity in metres per second
EO = kinetic energy of the bullet at the muzzle
WMR = Winchester Magnum Rimfire, the original name of the .22 Magnum rimfire cartridge. This is a longer rimfire cartridge, that cannot be fired in weapons designed for .22 Short/ .22 Long /.22 LR cartridges.

Centre-fire cartridges

Calibre .22 Hornet

Calibre .22 Hornet rifle cartridge

At the beginning of the 1930s, this cartridge was developed by a group of re-loaders from a .22 Winchester Centre-Fire cartridge as a "wild-cat" cartridge.

Since the start of modern cartridges, a number of privately developed "wild-cat" cartridges have been added to their range by munitions manufacturers.
The .22 Hornet was originally fired from adapted Springfield model 1903 rifles. Today there are many rifles for this calibre. The cartridge is primarily used for hunting wild game to a range of 200m (219yds).

Calibre	Bullet weight		VO	EO
	grains	g	m/s	Joules
.22 Hornet	46	3.0	820	1,009

Calibre .222 Remington

This cartridge was introduced by Remington in 1950. The .222 calibre cartridge

The .222 Remington cartridge

was not based on an existing calibre or developed as a "wild cat" but developed as a new cartridge by Remington themselves. It was introduced at the same time as the Remington model 722 bolt-action rifle of this calibre. The .222 Remington cartridge is used for bench rest target shooting but also for hunting small game up to 250m (273yds). There has been tremendous development in the field of bench rest target shooting and the cartridges for this purpose since 1950 which has reduced the importance of the .222 Remington cartridge.

Calibre	Bullet weight		VO	EO
	grains	g	m/s	Joules
.222 Remington	50	3.2	957	1,465
.222 Remington	55	3.6	920	1,524

The .223 Remington cartridge

Calibre .223 Remington

The development of the .223 Remington cartridge was linked to the development of the US Army rifle of this calibre - the AR-15, later to become M-16. This Armalite rifle was developed by Eugene Stoner and this military calibre was introduced in 1957. A year later,
Remington introduced it as a commercial cartridge. The .223 Rem. is an extremely popular calibre, particularly because it is the most widely used military cartridge. Munitions components are widely available for purchase at a reasonable price. This cartridge is currently the official standard calibre of NATO.

Calibre	Bullet weight		VO	EO
	grains	g	m/s	Joules
.223 Remington	55	3.6	988	1,757
.223 Remington	55	3.6	1,006	1,822

Calibre .243 Winchester

The .243 Winchester cartridge is renowned for its exceptionally flat trajectory

This cartridge was introduced by Winchester in 1955. At that time there was considerable interest in "wild-cat" 6mm cartridges. The .223 Remington is in fact a .308 Winchester cartridge case in which the case opening has been reduced to 6mm diameter. The calibre is ideal for hunting because of the exceptionally flat trajectory of the bullet. This cartridge is extensively used in the United States as a long-range cartridge for shooting small game such as prairie dogs and ground squirrels at a range of 300m (328yds).

Calibre	Bullet weight		VO	EO
	grains	g	m/s	Joules
.243 Winchester	80	5.2	1,042	2,823
.243 Winchester	100	6.5	902	2,644

Calibre .270 Winchester

Calibre .270 Winchester

This cartridge was introduced by Winchester in 1925 at the same time as their model 54 bolt-action rifle. The .270 Winchester is really a .30-06 Springfield cartridge in which the case opening has been reduced to 7mm (.277in).
The cartridge is mainly popular in the United States.
This cartridge is principally used to shoot medium-sized game. The cartridge has an extremely flat trajectory with outstanding accuracy. The effective range is about 300m (328yds)

Calibre	Bullet weight		VO	EO
	grains	g	m/s	Joules
.270 Winchester	100	6.5	1,061	3,659
.270 Winchester	130	8.4	884	3,790
.270 Winchester	150	9.7	884	3,790

.30-M1 Carbine calibre

The .30-M1 Carbine calibre for the
Winchester .30-M1 carbine

The .30-M1 cartridge was developed by
Winchester in 1941 because of the requirement of the US Army for the .30-M1
carbine. The carbine was due to replace
the .45 ACP army pistol and was intended
to be a compromise between a hand-gun
and a normal-sized army rifle. After World
War II, a lot of carbines were disposed of
by the army and these became available
for sports shooters. This calibre has little
potential for hunters because it is not sufficiently accurate at longer range. For target shooting to 100m (109yds) though, it
is ideally suited and very popular. There
are many clubs and/or competitions in
many countries specializing in the M1 carbine. The M1 carbine was largely developed by David Marshall "Carbine" Williams of the Winchester Repeating Arms
Company. During World War II, the carbine was made by many companies, including Inland, Underwood, Quality Hardware and Machine Corporation (HMC.),
Rock-Ola, Irwin-Pedersen, Saginaw,
National Postal Meter, Standard Products, and IBM.

Calibre	Bullet weight		VO	EO
	grains	g	m/s	Joules
.30-M1 Carbine	110	7.1	607	1,308

Calibre .30-30 Winchester

The .30-30 Winchester cartridge dates from
the nineteenth century. It was introduced
in 1895 for the Winchester model 1894

and 1895 rifles with lever-action repeating
mechanisms. The designation of this cartridge appears linked to a time of black
powder but this is not the case. The
designation indicates a cartridge with a
bullet calibre of .30in diameter that contains about 30 grains of smokeless powder.
This latter specification is very generalized because the powder charge is very
dependent upon the type of powder used,
as hand-loaders know very well. This cartridge is widely used in the United States
to hunt medium-sized game such as roe
and fallow deer. The effective range is
150m (164yds).

Calibre	Bullet weight		VO	EO
	grains	g	m/s	Joules
.30-30 Winchester	150	9.7	728	2,560
.30-30 Winchester	170	11.0	671	2,476

.30-30 Winchester cartridge

Calibre 7.62 x 39mm (Russian)

This cartridge is the Russian equivalent of
the .308 Winchester calibre, that is also
known as 7.62 x 51mm within NATO.
This calibre was developed back in 1943,
during World War II. The Americans
became acquainted with this cartridge
during the Vietnam War, because this is
the calibre used in the famous Kalashnikov AK-47 rifle. After the Iron Curtain
fell and the Cold War ended, this cartridge became available throughout the
West. An indication of the change in times
is that Colt now makes a civilian version
of its M-16 army rifle in this calibre. That
is also true of Ruger with their Mini-Thirty carbine.

The 7.62 x 39mm cartridge for the Kalashnikov AK-47 army rifle

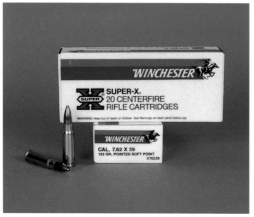

Calibre	Bullet weight		VO	EO
	grains	g	m/s	Joules
7.62 x 39	123	8.0	715	2,045

Calibre .303 British

The British .303 cartridge for the Lee-Enfield army rifle and other weapons

This cartridge originates from the former British Empire of the nineteenth century. It was introduced into service with the British Army in 1888 and saw service in all the former colonies in Africa, India, and elsewhere. It was originally intended to use black powder but the calibre was adapted in 1892 for use with smokeless powder. After World War II, with the formation of the North Atlantic Treaty Organization, this calibre was replaced by the now standard NATO cartridge of 7.62 x 51mm, or .308 Winchester calibre. This cartridge continues to be widely used in target shooting but virtually never for hunting purposes.

Calibre	Bullet weight		VO	EO
	grains	g	m/s	Joules
.303 British	180	11.7	770	3,469

Calibre .30-06 Springfield

The .30-06 Springfield cartridge used in (among other weapons) the famous Garand rifle

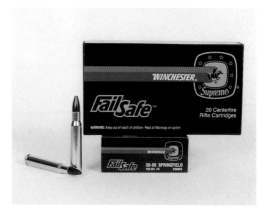

This cartridge was introduced into service with the American armed forces in 1906 for use with the Springfield model 1903-A3 rifle and later in 1936 for use with the famous Garand rifle. The designation .30-06 is derived from .30 calibre (.308in to be precise) from 1906. The addition of Springfield results from the company being a state enterprise until the 1950s, known as US Springfield Arsenal. The calibre saw service during World War II and also during the Korean War. This calibre is exceptionally popular in North and South America as a sporting calibre in use for hunting every type of game.

Calibre	Bullet weight		VO	EO
	grains	g	m/s	Joules
.30-06 Springfield	110	7.1	1.030	3,766
.30-06 Springfield	150	9.7	890	3,842
.30-06 Springfield	180	11.7	825	3,982
.30-06 Springfield	220	14.3	735	3,863

Calibre .308 Winchester

This calibre was developed for the US Army after World War II by the

De .308 Winchester-patroon voor o.a. de FN-Fal en de Springfield M14

The 8 x 57mm Mauser cartridge

Ordnance Department. The military designation of this cartridge is 7.62 x 51mm NATO, because it was adopted in 1953 as the official NATO calibre. Winchester was permitted in 1952 to make this cartridge available for the civilian market under the name .308 Winchester. The US Army used this cartridge for its M1A rifle, or Springfield M14 as it was also known. This cartridge was used in Europe for the FN-FAL army rifle. Initially, this cartridge was less popular in the civilian market than the .30-06 Springfield but gradually it gained popularity. Now, the .308 Winchester is widely used with sporting rifles, including long-range target shooting at 300m (328yds). The calibre is less used for hunting weapons in Europe.

Calibre	Bullet weight		V0	E0
	grains	g	m/s	Joules
.308 Winchester	110	7.1	1,000	3,550
.308 Winchester	150	9.7	860	3,587
.308 Winchester	180	11.7	800	3,744

Calibre 8 x 57mm Mauser

The 8 x 57mm Mauser or 8mm Mauser cartridge was developed in 1888 as military ordnance. Another designation for this round was 8 x 57mm-J. The original diameter of the bullet was 8.08mm (.318in). In 1903, the cartridge was modified but the original designation was retained with the addition of "S" - hence 8 x 57mm-S or JS. The bullet of this cartridge has a diameter of 8.20mm (.323in). This is rather confusing, since the firing of

an "S" cartridge in a "J" rifle can lead to dire consequences. Mauser rifles of the type G98 or K98 are built to this newer calibre and only the Mauser rifles commissioned in 1888 have the older "J" calibre. This calibre is extremely popular outside Europe for hunting game at a range of about 300m (328yds).

Calibre	Bullet weight		V0	E0
	grains	g	m/s	Joules
8 x 57mm Mauser	170	11.0	785	3,219
8 x 57mm Mauser	195	12.7	770	3,765

Calibre .338 Winchester Magnum

The .338 Winchester Magnum cartridge, a true hunter's calibrebut one that is also widely used for marksmen and snipers

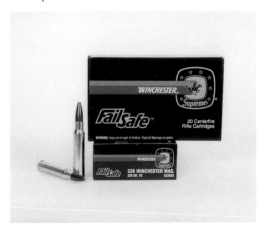

The .338 Winchester Magnum cartridge was introduced in 1959 for the Winchester model 70 Alaskan rifle.

The cartridge is derived from the .458 Winchester Magnum calibre with the cartridge case opening reduced to .338in (8.585mm). The case has a strengthened collar at its base. The cartridge is intended for hunting and is rarely used for target shooting.

Calibre	Bullet weight		VO	EO
	grains	g	m/s	Joules
.338 Winchester Magnum	200	13.0	900	5,265

Larger calibres

A brief overview is given below of the larger calibres.

Some of the larger calibre cartridges, such as the .358 Win., .357 Win., .357 H & H Magnum,. 45-70 Government, and the .458 Win. Mag.

Calibre .358 Winchester Magnum

The .358 Winchester cartridge was introduced in 1955 for use with the model 70 bolt-action rifle. The case of this cartridge is based on the .308 Winchester cartridge, with the cartridge opening and neck expanded.

Calibre	Bullet weight		VO	EO
	grains	g	m/s	Joules
.358 Winchester Magnum	250	16.2	680	3,745

Calibre .375 Winchester

This cartridge was specially developed in 1978 for the Winchester Big Bore model lever-action repeating rifle.

Calibre	Bullet weight		VO	EO
	grains	g	m/s	Joules
.375 Winchester	200	13.0	671	2,927

Calibre .375 Holland & Holland Magnum

The .375 Holland & Holland Magnum is of British origin and was introduced in 1912 for big game hunting in Africa.

Calibre	Bullet weight		VO	EO
	grains	g	m/s	Joules
.375 H & H Magnum	270	17.5	820	5,884

Calibre .45-70 Government

This cartridge was originally developed for the Springfield model 1873 "Trapdoor" rifle. It seems a powerful cartridge but when compared with more recent large calibre cartridges, its performance is below par.

Calibre	Bullet weight		VO	EO
	grains	g	m/s	Joules
.45-70 Government	300	26.2	405	2,149

Calibre .458 Winchester Magnum

Winchester introduced a special version of their model 70 bolt-action rifle in 1956 which they called "Africa." The cartridge is developed for the largest and most dangerous wild life in Africa and is also known as the "elephant calibre." Since then various manufacturers have brought out rifles for this Magnum calibre, such as the Remington model 700 bolt-action rifle. This cartridge delivers phenomenal kinetic energy levels at its target. The recoil for the shooter is also quite enormous. This is not a calibre for shooting a series of 50 targets in competition with. What is more, the cartridges are also very costly.

Calibre	Bullet weight		VO	EO
	grains	g	m/s	Joules
.458 Winchester Magnum	510	33.0	643	6,822

Dakota cartridges

A range of Dakota calibres

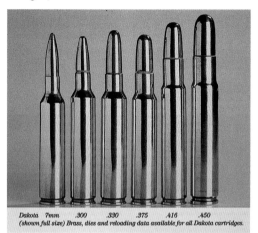

Dakota 7mm .300 .330 .375 .416 .450
(shown full size) Brass, dies and reloading data available for all Dakota cartridges.

Dakota originated as a company producing custom-made rifles. The Dakota cartridges are shot with Dakota model 76 bolt-action rifles. Most Dakota cartridges are based on the .404 Jeffery case, named after a famous American munitions designer.

Calibre	Bullet weight		VO	EO
	grains	g	m/s	Joules
.450 Dakota	500	32.4	747	9,040

Weatherby cartridges

Weatherby cartridges are specially devel-

Example of Weatherby cartridges

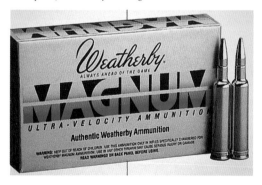

oped for Weatherby Magnum bolt-action rifles. These rifles are built to withstand the highest levels of gas-pressure.

Weatherby solely make hunting rifles. The author is not aware of any attempts by the company to enter military markets for snipers' rifles or such like. The calibres for this make vary from .224 Weatherby Magnum to .460 Weatherby Magnum.

Calibre	Bullet weight		VO	EO
	grains	g	m/s	Joules
.224 Weatherby Mag.	55	3.6	1,1113	2,230
.300 Weatherby Mag.	180	11.7	1,006	5,920
.378 Weatherby Mag.	300	19.4	892	7,718
.460 Weatherby Mag.	500	32.4	793	10,187

Calibre .50 BMG (Browning Machine Gun)

The .50 BMG (Browning Machine Gun) cartridge shown here isthe military tracer version

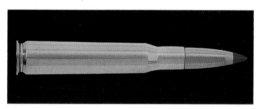

This cartridge was developed in 1921 by the renowned American weapon designer, John Moses Browning. The calibre was intended for his .50 calibre machine-gun. It is moving that this weapon still sees service in NATO after 75 years, where it is used on armoured vehicles, tanks, and as an aircraft machine-gun. The calibre is also currently in use with snipers' bolt-action rifles for ranges in excess of 1,500m (1,640yds). The first companies to make rifles for this calibre are the American concerns Barret, McMillan, and Harris. This calibre is growing in popularity for target shooting. The weapon and cartridge are not much used in Western Europe because of the lack of suitable civilian firing ranges.

Calibre	Bullet weight		VO	EO
	grains	g	m/s	Joules
.50 BMG	720	46.7	857	17,149

8. Explanation of exploded drawings

Exploded drawings have nothing to do with explosions! The term means a dimensional drawing of all the parts that are assembled in a rifle or carbine.

In this encyclopaedia of rifles and carbines, a lot of words are used that might confuse the reader. Most firearms have more or less the same technical basis. These drawings can provide a guide to both the parts and functioning of these weapons.

Below is an exploded drawing of a Krico bolt-action rifle, a Krico small-calibre semi-automatic rifle, and a Ruger Mini 14 semi-automatic large-calibre rifle. The names of the various parts from which these (and similar) weapons are assembled are listed.

Exploded drawing of a bolt-action rifle

Below is a Krico bolt-action rifle with a list of the parts used to construct this and similar rifles.

370002	sling swivel
610001	receiver or breech
610001	back stop
610002	cartridge extractor with plunger (610102) and cartridge extractor spring (001041)
610103	ejector with ejector spring (111043) and retaining pin (014811)
610200	bolt
610400	firing-pin with firing-pin spring
610500	bolt handle
620000	barrel
630000	trigger group
630300	trigger group (immediate trigger)
630302	trigger guard for trigger group 630300
630600	trigger group (match trigger)
631400	pre-set trigger

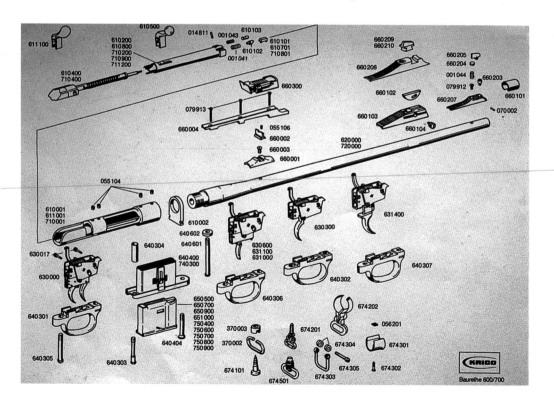

640301	trigger guard for trigger group 630000
640306	trigger guard for trigger group 630600
640307	trigger guard for trigger group 631400
640400	magazine
640404	cartridge holder
660001	mount for simple sights with sight (660002)
660004	mount for hunting sight (Battue version)
660101	bead tunnel
660103	mount for adjustable bead
660207	mount for adjustable bead
660208	bead sights mount
660209	bead sights
660300	rack sight
674201	sling swivel
674202	sling swivel
674303	sling swivel
674501	sling swivel

210210	retaining spring
210203	firing-pin
210300	return or recoil spring with return spring rod
220300	barrel
230000	trigger group
240101	trigger guard
260200	rack sight
310102	cartridge extractor
310103	cartridge extractor
340000	magazine
350000	cartridge holder
360300	rack sight
360502	mount for bead sight
360503	bead sight
370002	sling swivel
660101	bead tunnel

Exploded drawing of a small-calibre semi-automatic rifle

This exploded drawing shows the Krico small-calibre semi-automatic rifle (with inertia locking).

210101	slide
210102	springs for both cartridge extractors

Exploded drawing of a large-calibre semi-automatic rifle

The weapon used for this drawing is a Ruger Mini-14 semi-automatic rifle.

MS00100	receiver
MS00200	trigger guard
MS00300	barrel

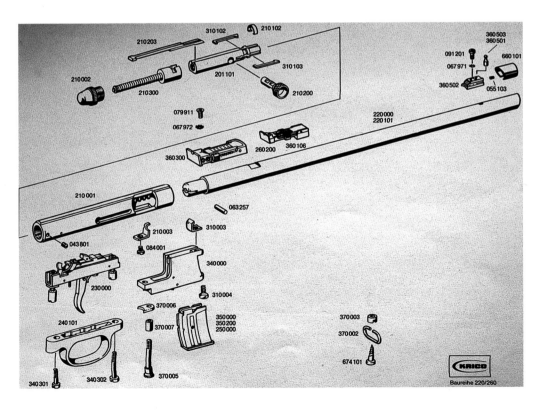

MS0040   stock
MS0070   stock reinforcing frame (sub-frame with magazine aperture)
KMS00800   ejector with ejector spring (MS070000)
KMS01100   firing-pin
MS01300   trigger housing
MS01400   cartridge extractor with plunger (KMS01600) and spring (KMS01500)
MS01700   hammer
MS01800   trigger spring-connecting rod with trigger spring (MS04700)
MS02000   trigger
MS02300   tumbler with tumbler spring (MS02400)
MS02700   cartridge holder
MS03000   loading guide (of cartridge holder) with spring (MS02800) and cartridge holder bottom cover (MS03400) and spring clip (MS02600)
MS03100   cartridge holder or magazine catch with spring (MS05000) and rod (KMS04000)
MS03500   top: connecting ring for hand guard
MS03500   bottom: gas-pressure cylinder
MS03600   gas piston

MS03900   return rod with return spring (MS05100)
KMS04400   bead ring with bead
MS04500   pin for slide catch
MS04800   trigger spring
MS05200   optical sight
MS05500   mount for optical sight
MS05900   adjustment screw for sideways sight adjustment
MS07400   adjustment screw for height adjustment of optical sight
KMS07500   front sling swivel
MS13200   slide catch
MS13800   safety catch (in trigger guard) with spring (MS04900)
MS23700   breech block
B-64   butt plate with butt-plate screw (B-63)
B-120   rear sling swivel
MFH   hand guard

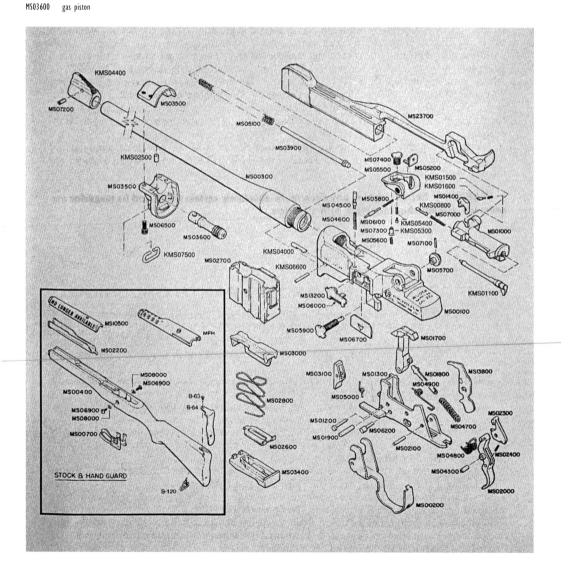

Guide to the symbols for use or purpose

In this encyclopaedia, you will find symbols next to each weapon. This will give you quick reference of the purpose of each individual weapon. There are no hard and fast rules, however. A marksman's rifle, which is intended for police use, might be ideal for long range shooting in certain branches of the sport but it has not be primarily designed for that function. At the other extreme, a smallbore match rifle with an optical sight and fully adjustable stock that weighs less than 5kg (11lbs) is not readily used for hunting small game. The target shooting category for small-bore carbines, which is a very popular discipline, has on the other hand been directly developed from hunting practice. Strangely enough, the .308 Winchester calibre is rarely used for hunting and yet it is a favourite marksman's calibre.

From this, you will appreciate that these symbols merely provide a rough guide. The indications are based upon the construction, type, calibre, repeating mechanism, and sights of the rifle or carbine. Many manufacturers for instance offer excellent hunting rifles with bolt-action that with a different stock and sight can also be a superb match or sniper's rifle. I do not expect any comments from readers who can testify that a person with a typical hunting rifle can constantly return full marks when shooting at 300m (328yds).

This book does not provide a classification either of which weapon is suitable for shooting which type of game. Such matters are closely related to the calibre, and information about this is available from the respective rifle and ammunition makers. In short, the symbols are concerned with general applications for the average shooter (which includes the author of this book).

Symbols of use

: sporting rifle/carbine for competition and leisure

: match rifle - specially adapted for competitive target shooting

: sporting rifle for long range, bench rest, silhouette, and sniper's rifle

: military-style sporting rifle

: hunting rifle/hunting-sporting rifle - hunting rifle for hunting and for the existing and developing sport of "hunting" target shooting such as Running Bore. A number of European countries limit to two the number of cartridges that can be loaded in magazines or cartridge-holders of semi-automatic weapons.

CZ magazine cover

1. Springfield Armory National Match rifle
2. Ruger Mini-14 Stainless with collapsible stock
3. Galil SAR rifle

9. An A-Z of rifles and carbines

AMT rifles

The American manufacturer Arcadia Machine and Tool Inc., abbreviated to AMT, was founded in 1969 by Harry W. Sanford. The company was originally called the AutoMag Corporation (AMC). Several years later, the company became bankrupt and parts of it were bought by the Thomas Oil Company. Under the name Trust Deed Estates Corporation (TDE), the company continued to assemble complete firearms from parts, and later to produce them. The company was based in North Hollywood but moved to El Monte in California shortly after the foundation of TDE. Sanford, the original founder of the company, bought back the company in 1985, when AMT acquired its current name. The company is mainly known for its large-calibre pistols, such as the Automag. The company also produces a number of excellent small-calibre rifles in stainless steel, including the .22 Magnum (Winchester Magnum Rimfire) hunting rifle for small game. This rifle can be obtained with a plastic stock or an attractive laminated wooden stock.

AMT Magnum Hunter Auto Rifle

TECHNICAL DETAILS

Calibre	: .22 WMR (Winchester Magnum Rimfire)
Cartridge capacity	: 5 rounds
Magazine catch	: magazine catch behind magazine aperture
Action	: semi-automatic
Locking	: inertia or spring locking
Weight	: 6lb (2.7kg)
Length	: 40½in (102.9cm)
Barrel length	: 20in (50.8cm)
Sight	: none:mounting for telescopic sight
External safety	: safety catch on right of receiver, slide can be fixed in rear position
Internal safety	: locking

CHARACTERISTICS

• material	: stainless steel
• finish	: none
• stock	: black plastic

AMT Magnum Hunter Auto Rifle

TECHNICAL DETAILS

Calibre	: .22 WMR (Winchester Magnum Rimfire)
Cartridge capacity	: 5 rounds (10 rounds also available)
Magazine catch	: magazine catch behind magazine aperture
Action	: semi-automatic
Locking	: inertia or spring locking
Weight	: 6lb (2.7kg)
Length	: 40½in (102.9cm)
Barrel length	: 20in (50.8cm)
Sight	: none: mounting for telescopic sight
External safety	: safety catch on right of receiver, slide can be fixed in rear position

Internal safety   : locking
CHARACTERISTICS
• material   : stainless steel
• finish   : none
• stock   : laminated wood

Anschütz

The firm of Anschütz was founded in about 1850 by Julius Gottfried Anschütz.

In those days, the company was based at Zella-Mehus in the German province of Thuringia. The company had become a sizeable concern by 1897, when it employed 75 people. Both sons of the founder, Otto and Fritz Anschütz, joined the company at an early age to learn craft skills. It has remained a family business. At the end of World War II, the allied forces closed the factory but in 1950, the company was reborn at Ulm in southern Germany. The name of Anschütz is mainly linked to its wide range of match and hunting rifles. Almost every shooting club in Western Europe must possess at least one small-bore Anschütz rifle. This will usually be one of the older but excellent Match 54 bolt-action rifles. This rifle was the first model to be made by the new company based at Ulm in 1953. The more recent types, such as the Super Match model 2013 with its fully-adjustable stock and shoulder rest are a byword in target-shooting circles. Other manufacturers even ensure that their rifles will accept the wide range of Anschütz accessories, such as optical sights, bead tunnels, and balancing weights for the barrel. Some also make their rifles so that Anschütz stocks will fit them. Several years ago Anschütz developed a special short barrel of 69cm (27¼in) for small-bore match rifles with a 50cm (193/4in) extension piece to attach to the muzzle. This achieves the optimum ballistic properties from the .22 Long Rifle cartridge, while maintaining a maximum length for the accuracy of the sights. The company makes a wide range of rifle parts, including barrels, receivers, and stocks, which shooters can use to custom-build rifles to their own requirements. In addition to small- and full-bore rifles, Anschütz also make air-powered weapons and the famous Anschütz Exemplar hunting and silhouette pistol. In addition, they also make a range of light hunting rifles and carbines for calibres .22 LR, .22 WMT, .22 Hornet, and .222 Remington, that are intended for hunting small game.

Anschütz model 1395

TECHNICAL DETAILS
Calibre   : .22 LR
Cartridge capacity : single round
Magazine catch   : not applicable
Action   : bolt-action
Locking   : locking-lugs
Weight   : 2.3kg (5lb 1oz)
Length   : 108cm (42½in)
Barrel length   : 65cm (25⅝in)
Sight   : optical sight and bead tunnel
External safety   : safety catch on right of receiver
Internal safety   : locking
CHARACTERISTICS
• material   : steel
• finish   : blued
• stock   : walnut

Anschütz model 1416 D/St

TECHNICAL DETAILS
Calibre   : .22 LR
Cartridge capacity : 5 or 10 rounds
Magazine catch   : catch behind magazine aperture
Action   : bolt-action
Locking   : locking-lugs
Weight   : 2.8kg (6lb 2oz)
Length   : 104cm (41in)
Barrel length   : 58cm (22⅞in)

Sight	: adjustable folding sight and bead tunnel
External safety	: safety catch on right of receiver
Internal safety	: locking

CHARACTERISTICS
- material : steel
- finish : blued
- stock : walnut

Model designation:
D = immediate trigger
St = double-action trigger:
(Stecher) see chapter on technology

Anschütz model 1416 D/St Classic

TECHNICAL DETAILS
Calibre	: .22 LR
Cartridge capacity	: 5 or 10 rounds cartridge holder
Magazine catch	: catch behind magazine aperture
Action	: bolt-action
Locking	: locking-lugs
Weight	: 2.8kg (6lb 2oz)
Length	: 104cm (41in)
Barrel length	: 58cm (22⅞in)
Sight	: adjustable folding sigh tand bead tunnel
External safety	: safety catch on right of receiver
Internal safety	: locking

CHARACTERISTICS
- material : steel
- finish : blued
- stock : walnut

Model designation:
D = pressure-point trigger
St = double-action trigger:
(Stecher) see chapter on technology

Anschütz model 1416/1518 St

TECHNICAL DETAILS
Calibre	: .22 LR
Cartridge capacity	: 5 or 10 rounds cartridge holder
Magazine catch	: catch behind magazine aperture
Action	: bolt-action
Locking	: locking-lugs
Weight	: 2.5kg (5lb 8oz)
Length	: 96cm (37¾in)
Barrel length	: 50cm (19¾in)
Sight	: adjustable folding sight and bead tunnel
External safety	: safety catch on left of receiver
Internal safety	: locking

CHARACTERISTICS
- material : steel
- finish : blued
- stock : walnut stock continues under barrel

Model designation:
Model 1418 is .22 LR calibre and Model
1518 is .22 WMR calibre
St = double-action trigger: (Stecher) see
chapter on technology

Anschütz model 1432 E/ED/ESt/EKSt

TECHNICAL DETAILS
Calibre	: .22 Hornet
Cartridge capacity	: single round
Magazine catch	: not applicable
Action	: bolt-action

Locking	: locking-lugs
Weight	: 4kg (8lb 13oz)
Length	: 109cm (42⅞in)
Barrel length	: 60cm (23⅝in)
Sight	: none, mounting for telescopic sight
External safety	: winged safety catch at rear of bolt
Internal safety	: locking, load indicator (protruding pin at rear of bolt)

CHARACTERISTICS

• material	: steel
• finish	: blued
• stock	: walnut with pistol grip

Model designation:
E   = Match pressure-point trigger
ED   = Immediate match trigger (comparable with shotguns)
ESt   = Stecher (double-action trigger: see chapter on technology)
EKSt   = combined match pressure-point trigger with double-action trigger

Anschütz model 1432 Stainless E/ED/ESt/EKSt

TECHNICAL DETAILS

Calibre	: .22 Hornet
Cartridge capacity	: single round
Magazine catch	: not applicable
Action	: bolt-action
Locking	: locking-lugs
Weight	: 4kg (8lb 13oz)
Length	: 109cm (42⅞in)
Barrel length	: 60cm (23⅝in)
Sight	: none, mounting for telescopic sight
External safety	: winged safety catch at rear of bolt
Internal safety	: locking, load indicator (protruding pin at rear of bolt)

CHARACTERISTICS

| • material | : steel receiver, stainless ste-barrel |

| • finish | : blued receiver, no finish for barrel |
| • stock | : walnut with pistol grip |

Model designation:
E   = Match pressure-point trigger
ED   = Immediate match trigger (comparable with shotguns)
ESt   = Stecher (double-action trigger: see chapter on technology)
EKSt   = combined match pressure-point trigger with double-action trigger

Anschütz model 1450 Biathlon

TECHNICAL DETAILS

Calibre	: .22 LR
Cartridge capacity	: 5 rounds
Magazine catch	: catch behind magazine aperture
Action	: bolt-action
Locking	: locking-lugs
Weight	: 4kg (8lb 13oz)
Length	: 93cm (36⅝in)
Barrel length	: 50cm (19⅜in)
Sight	: optical sight and bead tunnel
External safety	: safety catch on right of receiver
Internal safety	: locking

CHARACTERISTICS

• material	: steel
• finish	: blued
• stock	: walnut with shoulder grip

The model has a special Biathlon shoulder sling (rucksack model)

Anschütz model 1451/1451 D Achiever

TECHNICAL DETAILS

| Calibre | : .22 LR |
| Cartridge capacity | : 5 or 10 rounds |

External safety : safety catch on right of
                  receiver
Internal safety : locking
CHARACTERISTICS
• material : steel
• finish : blued
• stock : wood

Anschütz model 1466 D Luxus

TECHNICAL DETAILS
Calibre : .22 LR
Cartridge capacity : 5 rounds
Magazine catch : at front of magazine
                  aperture
Action : bolt-action
Locking : locking-lugs
Weight : 2.9kg (6lb 6oz)
Length : 107cm (42 ⅛in)
Barrel length : 58cm (22⅞in)
Sight : adjustable folding sight
        and bead tunnel;rail and
        mounting for telescopic
        sight
External safety : safety catch at rear ofbolt
Internal safety : locking
CHARACTERISTICS
• material : steel
• finish :blued
• stock :walnut with pistol grip
         and specially-formed cheek

Magazine catch : catch behind magazine
                  aperture
Action : bolt-action
Locking : locking-lugs
Weight : 2.3kg (5lb 1oz)
Length : 104cm (41in)
Barrel length : 58cm (22⅞in)
Sight : adjustable height rack
        (1451-F), or fully adjustable
        rack (1451-Kv)
External safety : safety catch on right of
                  receiver
Internal safety : locking
CHARACTERISTICS
• material : steel
• finish : blued
• stock : wood

D   = pressure-point trigger

Anschütz model 1451 Achiever Super Target

Anschütz model 1710D

TECHNICAL DETAILS
Calibre : .22 LR
Cartridge capacity : 5 or 10 rounds
Magazine catch : catch behind magazine
                  aperture
Action : bolt-action
Locking : locking-lugs
Weight : 2.9kg (6lb 6oz)
Length : 101cm (39¼in)
Barrel length : 56cm (22in)
Sight : optical sight and bead
        tunnel

TECHNICAL DETAILS

Calibre : .22 LR
Cartridge capacity : 5 and 10 rounds
Magazine catch : behind magazine aperture
Action : bolt-action
Locking : locking-lugs
Weight : 3kg (6lb 10oz)
Length : 109cm (42⅞in)
Barrel length : 60cm (23⅝in)
Sight : adjustable folding sight and bead tunnel
External safety : winged safety catch at rear of bolt
Internal safety : locking, load indicator (protruding pin at rear of bolt)

CHARACTERISTICS

• material : steel
• finish : blued
• stock : wood (Monte-Carlo or pistol grip with hog's back)

D = immediate trigger

Anschütz model 1710D-FWT, 1710 St/FWT

TECHNICAL DETAILS

Calibre : .22 LR
Cartridge capacity : 5 and 10 rounds
Magazine catch : behind magazine aperture
Action : bolt-action
Locking : locking-lugs
Weight : 3kg (6lb 10oz)
Length : 109cm (42⅞in)
Barrel length : 60cm (23⅝in)
Sight : none, suitable for mounting telescopic sight
External safety : winged safety catch at rear of bolt
Internal safety : locking, load indicator (protruding pin at rear of bolt)

CHARACTERISTICS

• material : steel

• finish : blued
• stock : black plastic Monte Carlo stock

D = immediate trigger
St = double-action trigger (Stecher)

Anschütz model 1710/1730/1740 D/St

TECHNICAL DETAILS

Calibre : .22 LR (M1710); .22 Hornet (M1730);.222 Rem. (M1740)
Cartridge capacity : 5 rounds
Magazine catch : behind magazine aperture
Action : bolt-action
Locking : locking-lugs
Weight : 3kg (6lb 10oz)
Length : 109cm (42⅞in) (.22LR); 110cm (43¼in)(.22 Hornet)
Barrel length : 60cm (23⅝in)
Sight : adjustable folding sight and bead tunnel
External safety : winged safety catch at rear of bolt
Internal safety : locking, load indicator (protruding pin at rear of bolt)

CHARACTERISTICS

• material : steel
• finish : blued
• stock : wooden Monte-Carlo stock or German-style pistol grip with hog's back

D = immediate trigger
St = double-action trigger (Stecher)

 ## Anschütz model 1712 D-FWT

TECHNICAL DETAILS

Calibre : .22 LR
Cartridge capacity : single round
Magazine catch : not applicable
Action : bolt-action

CHARACTERISTICS
• material : steel
• finish : blued
• stock : wood, continues under
barrel to muzzle

Locking	: locking-lugs
Weight	: 2.85kg (6lb 6oz)
Length	: 102cm (40⅛in)
Barrel length	: 55cm (21⅝in)
Sight	: none, mounting rail and tapped holes for telescopic sight
External safety	: winged safety catch at rear of bolt
Internal safety	: locking, load indicator

CHARACTERISTICS
• material : steel
• finish : blued
• stock : black plastic with pistol grip and raised cheek

Anschütz model 1733 D/St

TECHNICAL DETAILS

Calibre	: .22 Hornet
Cartridge capacity	: 5 rounds
Magazine catch	: behind magazine aperture
Action	: bolt-action
Locking	: locking-lugs
Weight	: 2.9kg (6lb 6oz)
Length	: 99cm (39in)
Barrel length	: 50cm (19¾in)
Sight	: adjustable folding sight and bead tunnel
External safety	: winged safety catch at rear of bolt
Internal safety	: locking, load indicator on rear of bolt (protruding pin)

Anschütz model 1808 MS-R (Metallic Silhouette)

TECHNICAL DETAILS

Calibre	: .22 LR
Cartridge capacity	: 5 rounds
Magazine catch	: in front of magazine aperture
Action	: bolt-action (Match 54)
Locking	: locking-lugs
Weight	: 3.5kg (8lb 6oz)
Length	: 102cm (40⅛in)
Barrel length	: 49cm (19¼in)
Sight	: mounting rail for telescopic sight
External safety	: winged safety catch at rear of bolt
Internal safety	: locking, load indicator on rear of bolt (protruding pin)

CHARACTERISTICS
• material : steel
• finish : blued
• stock : walnut with pistol grip and thumb-hole

Anschütz model 1827 (Biathlon)

TECHNICAL DETAILS

Calibre	: .22 LR
Cartridge capacity	: 5 rounds
Magazine catch	: in front of magazine aperture
Action	: bolt-action (Match 54)
Locking	: locking-lugs

Weight	: 4.1kg (9lb 1oz)
Length	: 104cm (41in)
Barrel length	: 55cm (21⅝in)
Sight	: optical sight and bead tunnel
External safety	: safety catch to left of receiver
Internal safety	: locking, load indicator on rear of bolt (protruding pin)

CHARACTERISTICS

• material	: steel
• finish	: blued
• stock	: walnut with shoulder grip

Anschütz model 1827 Fortner (Biathlon)

TECHNICAL DETAILS

Calibre	: .22 LR
Cartridge capacity	: 5 rounds
Magazine catch	: behind magazine aperture
Action	: horizontal bolt
Locking	: locking knee
Weight	: 4kg (8lb 13oz)
Length	: 104cm (41in)
Barrel length	: 55cm (21⅝in)
Sight	: optical sight and bead tunnel
External safety	: safety catch to left of receiver
Internal safety	: locking, load indicator at rear of bolt

CHARACTERISTICS

• material	: steel
• finish	: blued
• stock	: walnut with shoulder-grip

Anschütz model 1903

TECHNICAL DETAILS

Calibre	: .22 LR
Cartridge capacity	: single round
Magazine catch	: not applicable
Action	: bolt-action (Match 54)
Locking	: locking-lugs
Weight	: 4.5kg (9lb 14oz)
Length	: 110cm (43¼in)
Barrel length	: 65cm (21⅝in)
Sight	: optical sight and bead tunnel
External safety	: safety catch to right and rear of bolt handle
Internal safety	: locking, load indicator at rear of bolt

CHARACTERISTICS

• material	: steel
• finish	: blued
• stock	: specially coloured laminate

Anschütz model 1907

TECHNICAL DETAILS

Calibre	: .22 LR
Cartridge capacity	: single round
Magazine catch	: not applicable
Action	: bolt-action (Match 54)
Locking	: locking-lugs
Weight	: 4.9kg (10lb 13oz)
Length	: 113cm (44½in)
Barrel length	: 66cm (26in)
Sight	: optical sight and bead tunnel
External safety	: safety catch left-handside

Internal safety   : locking, load indicator
                      on rear of bolt

CHARACTERISTICS
- material   : steel
- finish   : blued
- stock   : walnut (lower model), light
                      beech (top)

Anschütz model 1907-Laminate

TECHNICAL DETAILS
Calibre   : .22 LR
Cartridge capacity : single round
Magazine catch   : not applicable
Action   : bolt-action (Match 54)
Locking   : locking-lugs
Weight   : 4.9kg (10lb 13oz)
Length   : 113cm (44½in)
Barrel length   : 66cm (26in)
Sight   : optical sight and bead
                      tunnel
External safety   : winged safety catch left-
                      hand side of receiver
Internal safety   : locking, load indicator
                      on rear of bolt

CHARACTERISTICS
- material   : steel
- finish   : blued
- stock   : specially coloured laminate

Anschütz model 1910

TECHNICAL DETAILS
Calibre   : .22 LR

Cartridge capacity : single round
Magazine catch   : not applicable
Action   : bolt-action (Match 54)
Locking   : locking-lugs
Weight   : 7kg (15lb 6oz)
Length   : 117cm (46in)
Barrel length   : 69cm (27⅛in)
Sight   : optical sight and bead
                      tunnel
External safety   : safety catch left-hand
                      side of receiver
Internal safety   : locking, load indicator
                      on rear of bolt

CHARACTERISTICS
- material   : steel
- finish   : blued
- stock   : walnut, shoulder grip

The models illustrated are 1910 (top) and
1911 (lower)

Anschütz model 1911

TECHNICAL DETAILS
Calibre   : .22 LR
Cartridge capacity : single round
Magazine catch   : not applicable
Action   : bolt-action (Match 54)
Locking   : locking-lugs
Weight   : 5.4kg (11lb 6oz)
Length   : 116cm (45⅝in)
Barrel length   : 69cm (27⅛in)
Sight   : optical sight and bead
                      tunnel
External safety   : safety catch left-hand
                      side of receiver
Internal safety   : locking, load indicator
                      on rear of bolt

CHARACTERISTICS
- material   : steel
- finish   : blued
- stock   : beech

The models illustrated are 1910 (top) and
1911 (lower)

Anschütz model 1913 National

TECHNICAL DETAILS
Calibre	: .22 LR
Cartridge capacity	: single round
Magazine catch	: not applicable
Action	: bolt-action (Match 54)
Locking	: locking-lugs
Weight	: 7kg (15lb 6oz)
Length	: 117cm (46in)
Barrel length	: 69cm (27⅛in)
Sight	: optical sight and bead tunnel
External safety	: safety catch left-hand side of receiver
Internal safety	: locking, load indicator on rear of bolt

CHARACTERISTICS
• material	: steel
• finish	: blued
• stock	: walnut (top) or beech (lower)

Anschütz model 1913 Super Match

TECHNICAL DETAILS
Calibre	: .22 LR
Cartridge capacity	: single round
Magazine catch	: not applicable
Action	: bolt-action (Match 54)
Locking	: locking-lugs
Weight	: 7kg (15lb 6oz)
Length	: 116cm (45⅝in)
Barrel length	: 69cm (27⅛in)
Sight	: optical sight and bead tunnel

External safety	: safety catch left-hand side of receiver
Internal safety	: locking, load indicator on rear of bolt

CHARACTERISTICS
• material	: steel
• finish	: blued
• stock	: walnut (lower) or specially coloured laminate, with thumb-hole and shoulder grip

Anschütz model 2007

TECHNICAL DETAILS
Calibre	: .22 LR
Cartridge capacity	: single round
Magazine catch	: not applicable
Action	: bolt-action (Match 54)
Locking	: locking-lugs
Weight	: 5.4kg (11lb 14oz)
Length	: 116cm (45⅝in)
Barrel length	: 69cm (27⅛in)
Sight	: optical sight and bead tunnel
External safety	: winged safety catch at rear of bolt
Internal safety	: locking, load indicator on rear of bolt

CHARACTERISTICS
• material	: steel
• finish	: blued
• stock	: walnut or beech with thumb-hole

The barrel of the upper rifle is shortened to 50cm (19 3/4in) and has special extension tubes with additional weight.

Anschütz model 1913 Super Match Special

TECHNICAL DETAILS
Calibre	: .22 LR
Cartridge capacity	: single round

Magazine catch	: not applicable
Action	: bolt-action (Match 54)
Locking	: locking-lugs
Weight	: 7kg (15lb 6oz)
Length	: 117cm (46in)
Barrel length	: 69cm (27⅛in)
Sight	: optical sight and bead tunnel
External safety	: safety catch left-hand side of receiver
Internal safety	: locking, load indicator on rear of bolt

CHARACTERISTICS
• material	: steel
• finish	: blued
• stock	: adjustable walnut stock with thumb-hole and shoulder grip

The barrel of the upper rifle is shortened to 50cm (19¾in) and has special extension tubes with additional weight.

Anschütz model 2013/690 Super Match Aluminium

TECHNICAL DETAILS
Calibre	: .22 LR
Cartridge capacity	: single round
Magazine catch	: not applicable
Action	: bolt-action (Match 54)
Locking	: locking-lugs
Weight	: 7kg (15lb 6oz)
Length	: 117cm (46in)
Barrel length	: 69cm (27⅛in)
Sight	: optical sight and bead tunnel
External safety	: winged safety catch on rear of bolt
Internal safety	: locking, load indicator on rear of bolt

CHARACTERISTICS
• material	: steel, aluminium
• finish	: blued
• stock	: adjustable aluminium stock frame with laminated pistol grip, raised cheek and front grip. The butt has a shoulder grip. This exceptional stock also fits the Keppeler full-bore precision rifle

Anschütz model 525

TECHNICAL DETAILS
Calibre	: .22 LR
Cartridge capacity	: 5 and 10 rounds (2 round cartridge holder also available)
Magazine catch	: behind magazine aperture
Action	: semi-automatic
Locking	: inertia
Weight	: 2.9kg (6lb 6oz)
Length	: 110cm (43¼in)
Barrel length	: 61cm (24in)
Sight	: adjustable folding sight and bead tunnel plus mounting for telescopic sight
External safety	: safety catch at right of trigger guard
Internal safety	: locking

CHARACTERISTICS
• material	: steel
• finish	: blued
• stock	: wood

Anschütz model 54.18 MS (Metallic Silhouette)

TECHNICAL DETAILS

Calibre	: .22 LR
Cartridge capacity	: single round
Magazine catch	: not applicable
Action	: bolt-action (Match 54)
Locking	: inertia
Weight	: 4.2kg (9lb)
Length	: 105cm (41⅜in)
Barrel length	: 57cm (22½in)
Sight	: none, mounting for telescopic sight
External safety	: safety catch on left of receiver
Internal safety	: locking, load indicator at rear of bolt

CHARACTERISTICS
- material : steel
- finish : blued
- stock : wood with pistol grip

The model 54.18-MS is shown above with Model 64-MS below.

Anschütz model 64 MS (MetallicSilhouette)

TECHNICAL DETAILS

Calibre	: .22 LR
Cartridge capacity	: single round
Magazine catch	: not applicable

Action	: bolt-action (Match 54)
Locking	: locking-lugs
Weight	: 3.7kg (8lb 3oz))
Length	: 104cm (41in)
Barrel length	: 55cm (21¾in)
Sight	: none, mounting for telescopic sight
External safety	: safety catch on right of receiver
Internal safety	: locking

CHARACTERISTICS
- material : steel
- finish : blued
- stock : wood with pistol grip

The model 54.18-MS is shown above with Model 64-MS below.

Anschütz model 54.18 MS-R (Metallic Silhouette Repeater)

TECHNICAL DETAILS

Calibre	: .22 LR
Cartridge capacity	: 5 rounds
Magazine catch	: at front of magazine aperture
Action	: bolt-action (Match 54)
Locking	: locking-lugs
Weight	: 3.7kg (8lb 3oz))
Length	: 100cm (39⅜in)
Barrel length	: 54.4cm (21½in)
Sight	: none, mounting for telescopic sight
External safety	: safety catch on right behind bolt knob
Internal safety	: locking, load indicator at rear of bolt

CHARACTERISTICS
- material : steel
- finish : blued
- stock : hardwood match stock with pistol grip

The model 54.18-MS-R is shown above
with Model 64-MS-R below.

Anschütz model 64 MS-R
(MetallicSilhouette Repeater)

TECHNICAL DETAILS

Calibre	: .22 LR
Cartridge capacity	: 5 rounds
Magazine catch	: at front of magazine aperture
Action	: bolt-action (Match 64)
Locking	: locking-lugs
Weight	: 3.7kg (8lb 3oz))
Length	: 100cm (39⅜in)
Barrel length	: 54.4cm (21½in)
Sight	: none, mounting for telescopic sight
External safety	: winged safety catch on rear of bolt
Internal safety	: locking, load indicator at rear of bolt

CHARACTERISTICS
- material   : steel
- finish   : blued
- stock   : hardwood match stock with pistol grip

Length	: 105cm (41⅜in)
Barrel length	: 58cm (22⅞in)
Sight	: none, mounting for telescopic sight
External safety	: safety catch on left of receiver
Internal safety	: locking, load indicator at rear of bolt

CHARACTERISTICS
- material   : steel
- finish   : blued
- stock   : beech with specially flattened bench-rest front grip

Armscor-KBI

Armscor rifles, made in The Philippines,
are of the highest quality. They are imported into North and South America by KBI
Inc. of Harrisburg, Pennsylvania. This
company also imports a Hungarian version of the famous AK-47 rifle in the standard Russian calibre 7.62 x 54 R. The
Armscor versions of the Colt M-16 and
the AK-47 in .22 calibre are justifiably
successful.

The model 54.18-MS-R is shown above
with Model 64-MS-R below.

Anschütz model BR-50 (Bench Rest)

TECHNICAL DETAILS

Calibre	: .22 LR
Cartridge capacity	: single round
Magazine catch	: not applicable
Action	: bolt-action (Match 54)
Locking	: locking-lugs
Weight	: 5.2kg (11b 8oz)

Armscor-KBI model M-14P

TECHNICAL DETAILS

Calibre : .22 LR
Cartridge capacity : 10 rounds
Magazine catch : front of magazine
  aperture
Action : semi-automatic
Locking : inertia
Weight : 3.1kg (6lb 13oz))
Length : 104.1cm (41in)
Barrel length : 56.1cm (22$^1/_{10}$in)
Sight : adjustable folding;
  mounting for telescopic
  sight
External safety : safety catch on right of
  receiver
Internal safety : locking

CHARACTERISTICS

• material : steel
• finish : blued
• stock : hardwood with pistol
  grip

From top to bottom: models M-14P, M-20P, and M-12Y.

Armscor-KBI model M-20P

TECHNICAL DETAILS

Calibre : .22 LR
Cartridge capacity : 10 rounds
Magazine catch : front of magazine aperture
Action : bolt-action
Locking : 2 locking-lugs
Weight : 2.9kg (6lb 4oz)
Length : 102.9cm (40½in)
Barrel length : 52.7cm (20¾in)
Sight : adjustable folding sight;
  mounting for telescopic
  sight
External safety : safety catch on right of
  receiver
Internal safety : locking

CHARACTERISTICS

• material : steel
• finish : blued
• stock : hardwood with pistol grip

From top to bottom: models M-14P, M-20P, and M-12Y.

Armscor-KBI model M-12Y (Youth)

TECHNICAL DETAILS

Calibre : .22 LR
Cartridge capacity : single round
Magazine catch : not applicable
Action : bolt-action
Locking : 2 locking-lugs
Weight : 1.9kg (4lb)
Length : 86.7cm (34$^1/_{10}$in)
Barrel length : 44.5cm (17½in)
Sight : adjustable folding sight;
  mounting for telescopic
  sight
External safety : safety catch on right of
  receiver
Internal safety : locking

CHARACTERISTICS

• material : steel
• finish : blued
• stock : hardwood with pistol grip

From top to bottom: models M-14P, M-20P, and M-12Y.

Armscor-KBI model M-1600

TECHNICAL DETAILS

Calibre	: .22 LR
Cartridge capacity	: 10 rounds
Magazine catch	: front of magazine aperture
Action	: semi-automatic
Locking	: inertia
Weight	: 2.8kg (6lb 3oz)
Length	: 97.8cm (38½in)
Barrel length	: 46.4cm (18¼in)
Sight	: adjustable military optical sight
External safety	: safety catch on right of trigger guard
Internal safety	: locking

CHARACTERISTICS

- material : steel
- finish : blued
- stock : black painted hardwood with pistol grip

This rifle is a small-bore version of the military M-16 or AR-15. Illustrated are the M-1600 (top) and model AK-22 (below).

Armscor-KBI model AK-22

TECHNICAL DETAILS

Calibre	: .22 LR
Cartridge capacity	: 10 rounds
Magazine catch	: front of magazine aperture
Action	: semi-automatic
Locking	: inertia
Weight	: 3.4kg (7lb 8oz)
Length	: 96.5cm (38in)
Barrel length	: 46.4cm (18¼in)
Sight	: adjustable folding sight and bead tunnel
External safety	: safety catch on mechanism housing
Internal safety	: locking

CHARACTERISTICS

- material : steel
- finish : blued

- stock : hardwood with pistol grip

This rifle is a small-bore version of the militaryAK-47. Illustrated are the M-1600 (top) and model AK-22 (below).

Armscor-KBI model M-2000S

TECHNICAL DETAILS

Calibre	: .22 LR
Cartridge capacity	: 10 rounds
Magazine catch	: front of magazine aperture
Action	: semi-automatic
Locking	: inertia
Weight	: 2.9kg (6lb 4oz)
Length	: 102.9cm (40½in)
Barrel length	: 52.7cm (20¾in)
Sight	: adjustable folding sight, mounting for telescopic sight
External safety	: safety catch on receiver
Internal safety	: locking

CHARACTERISTICS

- material : steel
- finish : blued
- stock : hardwood with pistol grip

Illustrated are the M-1800S (below) and model M-2000S (top).

Armscor-KBI model M-1800S

TECHNICAL DETAILS

Calibre : .22 Hornet
Cartridge capacity : 5 rounds
Magazine catch : front of magazine aperture
Action : bolt-action
Locking : 2 locking-lugs
Weight : 3kg (6lb 9oz)
Length : 104.8cm (41¼in)
Barrel length : 56.1cm (22⅛in)
Sight : adjustable folding sight,
  mounting for telescopic
  sight
External safety : safety catch on right of
  receiver
Internal safety : locking

CHARACTERISTICS

• material : steel
• finish : blued
• stock : hardwood with pistol grip

This rifle is also available for calibre .22 LR (model M-1400S) and .22 WMR (model M-1500S). Illustrated are (top) models M-2000S and (below) M-1800S.

Armscor-KBI model M-1800SC

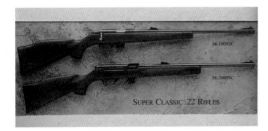

TECHNICAL DETAILS

Calibre : .22 Hornet
Cartridge capacity : 5 rounds
Magazine catch : front of magazine aperture
Action : bolt-action
Locking : 2 locking-lugs
Weight : 3kg (6lb 9oz)
Length : 104.8cm (41¼in)
Barrel Length : 56.1cm (22⅛in)
Sight : adjustable folding sight,
  mounting for telescopic
  sight
External safety : safety catch on right
  behind bolt
Internal safety : locking

CHARACTERISTICS

• material : steel
• finish : blued
• stock : walnut with pistol grip

This rifle is also available for calibre: .22 LR (model M-1400SC) and .22 WMR (model M-1500SC). Illustrated are (top) models M-1800SC and (below) M-2000SC.

Armscor-KBI model M-2000SC

TECHNICAL DETAILS

Calibre : .22 LR
Cartridge capacity : 10 rounds
Magazine catch : front of magazine aperture
Action : semi-automatic
Locking : inertia
Weight : 2.9kg (6lb 4oz)
Length : 102.9cm (40½in)
Barrel Length : 52.7cm (20¾in)
Sight : adjustable folding sight,
  mounting for telescopic
  sight
External safety : safety catch on right of
  receiver
Internal safety : locking

CHARACTERISTICS

• material : steel
• finish : blued
• stock : walnut with pistol grip

Illustrated are the M-1800SC (top) and model M-2000SC (below).

Armscor-KBI model M-20C

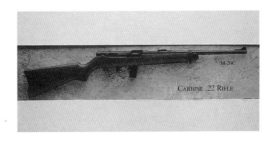

TECHNICAL DETAILS

Calibre : .22 LR
Cartridge capacity : 10 rounds
Magazine catch : front of magazine aperture
Action : semi-automatic
Locking : inertia
Weight : 2.8kg (6lb 3oz)
Length : 96.5cm (38in)
Barrel Length : 46.4cm (18¼in)
Sight : adjustable folding sight, mounting for telescopic sight
External safety : safety catch on right of receiver
Internal safety : locking

CHARACTERISTICS
• material : steel
• finish : blued
• stock : hardwood with pistol grip

Benelli

The Italian firm of Benelli is based in Urbino in the foothills of the Umbrian Apennines. The company was founded by the brothers Filippo and Giovanni Benelli. The name Benelli was associated for a long time with mopeds and the company also made tools and machines. Weapons were made on a small scale from about 1920. Since 1975, the company has concentrated on firearms and the name was changed to Benelli Armi. In 1975, a subsidiary was set up in Vitoria, in Spain, where the majority of the Spanish armaments industry is located. The barrels for Benelli rifles are produced in France at Saint-Etienne and at Brescia in Italy. Benelli also makes a range of excellent pistols, semi-automatic shotguns, and a pair of small-calibre carbines. Among pistols, the MP5, B80S, and MP3S models are very well known. Benelli brought out its first semi-automatic gauge 12 shotgun, the Extralusso, in 1969. The Benelli M1 Super 90 is highly regarded as a police weapon.

Benelli Athena

TECHNICAL DETAILS

Calibre : .22 LR
Cartridge capacity : 10 rounds
Magazine catch : front of magazine aperture
Action : semi-automatic

Locking : inertia
Weight : 2.95kg (6lb 8oz)
Length : 96.5cm (38in)
Barrel Length : 46.4cm (18in)
Sight : adjustable folding sight, suitable for mounting a telescopic sight
External safety : press button safety catch on front of trigger guard
Internal safety : locking

CHARACTERISTICS
• material : steel
• finish : blued
• stock : hardwood

Benelli Athena Elegant

TECHNICAL DETAILS

Calibre : ..22 LR
Cartridge capacity : 10 rounds
Magazine catch : front of magazine aperture
Action : semi-automatic
Locking : inertia
Weight : 3.6kg (8lb)
Length : 103.5cm (40¾in)
Barrel Length : 52.7cm (20¾in) including muzzle compensator
Sight : adjustable folding sight, suitable for mounting a telescopic sight
External safety : press button safety catch on front of trigger guard

Internal safety : locking
CHARACTERISTICS
• material : steel
• finish : blued
• stock : walnut

Beretta

Beretta is one of the oldest weapon manufacturers in Europe. Bartolomeo Beretta
had already established a workshop in the
fifteenth century in Gardone in the Val Trom-
pa region of Italy. He chiefly made barrels
for other gunsmiths. His son, Giovannino,
followed in his father's footsteps and became
a master gunsmith. In those days, the business
was mainly occupied with making muskets
and shotguns. At the end of the eighteenth
century, Pietro Beretta ruled the family firm.
He won huge orders to deliver guns to Na-
poleon's army. After the battle of Waterloo,
the market for weapons collapsed. Beretta
switched to making sporting and hunting
weapons. Pietro's son, Giuseppe, was blessed
with great business foresight and he expanded
the business between 1840 to 1865 into a
major concern. His son, also named Pietro,
instituted modern production techniques at
the beginning of the twentieth century. The
subsequent generation, Giuseppe and Carlo
Beretta, turned the business into a true mul-
tinational, with subsidiaries in the United
States, France, Brazil, and Greece. The present-day management is in the hands of Ugo
Gussalli Beretta and the company is now a
major name for military firearms, shotguns,
sporting rifles, and pistols. A major breakthrough was the choice by the US Army in
1986 of the Beretta M92-F 9mm parabellum
calibre: pistol. To mitigate against American
protests at a foreign pistol being selected, a
separate company was formed, called Beretta USA Corporation, based in Accokeek,
Maryland.

Beretta model 70 Sport

TECHNICAL DETAILS
Calibre : .222 Rem., .223 Rem.
Cartridge capacity : 5, 8, or 30 rounds
Magazine catch : front of trigger guard
Action : semi-automatic
Locking : rotating slide
Weight : 3.8kg (8lb 5oz)
Length : 95.5cm (37⅝in)
Barrel Length : 45cm (17¾in)
Sight : optical military sight
External safety : rotating safety catch on left
  of casing
Internal safety : locking
CHARACTERISTICS
• material : steel
• finish : matt black
• stock : plastic stock with hand
  guard and pistol grip

Beretta model 455-EELL Express

TECHNICAL DETAILS
Calibre : see below
Cartridge capacity : double-barrelled, 1 round
  per chamber
Magazine catch : not applicable
Action : breech action
Locking : breech lock
Weight : 5kg (11lb)
Length : 100.9cm (39¾in)
Barrel Length : 65cm (25⅝in)
Sight : folding sight
External safety : sliding safety catch on neck
  of stock
Internal safety : prevention of double firing
CHARACTERISTICS
• material : steel
• finish : blued barrels, engraved
  bare metal pivot mounting
• stock : walnut

Available Calibres: .375 H & H Mag., .416
Rigby, .458 Win. Mag., 470 NE, .500 NE

Beretta model 500

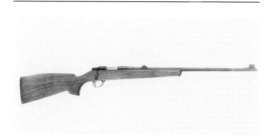

TECHNICAL DETAILS

Calibre	: .222 Rem., .223 Rem.
Cartridge capacity	: 5 rounds
Magazine catch	: not applicable; push-button for hinged magazine cover in front of trigger guard
Action	: bolt-action
Locking	: 2-lug bolt
Weight	: 3.1kg (6lb 13oz)
Length	: 109cm (43in)
Barrel Length	: 61cm (24in)
Sight	: adjustable sight with bead tunnel
External safety	: safety catch at rear of bolt
Internal safety	: locking

CHARACTERISTICS

• material	: steel
• finish	: blued
• stock	: walnut

Beretta model 501

TECHNICAL DETAILS

Calibre	: .243 Win., .308 Win.
Cartridge capacity	: 5 rounds
Magazine catch	: not applicable; push-button for hinged magazine cover in front of trigger guard
Action	: bolt-action
Locking	: 2-lug bolt
Weight	: 3.4kg (7lb 8oz)

Length	: 109cm (43in)
Barrel Length	: 61cm (24in)
Sight	: none, drilled and tapped for telescopic sight
External safety	: safety catch at rear of bolt
Internal safety	: locking

CHARACTERISTICS

• material	: steel
• finish	: blued
• stock	: walnut

Beretta model 501-DL

TECHNICAL DETAILS

Calibre	: .243 Win., .308 Win.
Cartridge capacity	: 5 rounds
Magazine catch	: not applicable; push-button for hingedmagazine cover in front of trigger guard
Action	: bolt-action
Locking	: 2-lug bolt
Weight	: 3.4kg (7lb 8oz)
Length	: 109cm (43in)
Barrel Length	: 61cm (24in)
Sight	: adjustable sight with bead tunnel, drilled and tapped for telescopic sight
External safety	: safety catch at rear of bolt
Internal safety	: locking

CHARACTERISTICS

• material	: steel

* finish : blued
* stock : selected walnut

Beretta model S689 Gold Sable

TECHNICAL DETAILS
Calibre : .30-06 Spr., 9.3 x 74R
Cartridge capacity : double-barrelled, 1 round
per chamber
Magazine catch : not applicable
Action : breech action
Locking : breech lock
Weight : 3.5kg (7lb 11oz)
Length : 104.8cm (41¼in)
Barrel Length : 60cm (23⅝in)
Sight : folding sight
External safety : sliding safety catch on
neck of stock
Internal safety : prevention of double
firing

CHARACTERISTICS
* material : steel
* finish : blued barrels, tempered
and engraved pivot moun-
ting
* stock : walnut with raised cheek

An exchangeable barrel in shotgun gauge
20 is available.

Beretta model SS06

TECHNICAL DETAILS
Calibre : 9.3 x 74R, .375 H & H
Mag., .458 Win. Mag.

Cartridge capacity : double-barrelled, 1 round
per chamber
Magazine catch : not applicable
Action : breech action
Locking : breech lock
Weight : 5kg (11lb)
Length : 104.8cm (41¼in)
Barrel Length : 62cm (24½in)
Sight : folding sight
External safety : sliding safety catch on
neck of stock
Internal safety : prevention of double
firing

CHARACTERISTICS
* material : steel
* finish : blued barrels, tempered and
engraved pivot mounting
* stock : walnut with raised
cheek

An exchangeable barrel in shotgun gauge
20 is available.

Beretta model SS06-EELL

TECHNICAL DETAILS
Calibre : 9.3 x 74R, .375 H & H
Mag., .458 Win. Mag.
Cartridge capacity : double-barrelled, 1 round
per chamber
Magazine catch : not applicable
Action : breech action
Locking : breech lock
Weight : 5kg (11lb)
Length : 104.8cm (41¼in)
Barrel Length : 62cm (24½in)
Sight : folding sight
External safety : sliding safety catch on neck
of stock
Internal safety : prevention of double
firing

CHARACTERISTICS
* material : steel
* finish : blued barrels, temperedand
engraved pivot mounting

- stock   : walnut with raised cheek

An exchangeable barrel in shotgun gauge 12 is available.

Beretta Super Olimpia-X

TECHNICAL DETAILS

Calibre	: .22 LR
Cartridge capacity	: 5 or 10 rounds cartridge holder
Magazine catch	: behind magazine aperture
Action	: semi-automatic
Locking	: inertia
Weight	: 3.7kg (8lb 3oz)
Length	: 109cm (42¾in)
Barrel Length	: 60cm (23⅝in)
Sight	: optical match sight with bead tunnel, mounting for telescopic sight
External safety	: press-button safety catch in rear of trigger guard
Internal safety	: locking

CHARACTERISTICS

• material	: steel
• finish	: blued
• stock	: walnut

This rifle has a switch to select manually-operated repeating.

Beretta Super Sport-X

TECHNICAL DETAILS

Calibre	: .22 LR
Cartridge capacity	: 5 or 10 rounds cartridge holder

Magazine catch	: behind magazine aperture
Action	: semi-automatic
Locking	: inertia
Weight	: 3.3kg (7lb 6oz)
Length	: 106.5cm (42in)
Barrel Length	: 60cm (24in)
Sight	: adjustable sight, mounting for telescopic sight
External safety	: press-button safety catch in rear of trigger guard
Internal safety	: locking

CHARACTERISTICS

• material	: steel
• finish	: blued
• stock	: walnut

Bernardelli

The history of the Italian Bernardelli company from Gardone Val Trompia in the Italian Alps stretches back to 1721 when it was founded. The firm was officially registered by Vincenzo Bernardelli in 1865, and is primarily known for its magnificent shotguns that often bear wonderful model names such as Saturno, Hemingway, and Holland. The company also produce competition pistols, and also police and sporting pistols in various calibres. A number of twin-bore rifles are also made for hunting large game. These are not shotguns, but rifles for large-calibre: cartridges. This type of rifle is designated Express. They often have a special folding sight with three or more leaves for different ranges.

Bernardelli Express 2000

TECHNICAL DETAILS

Calibre	: 9.3 x 74R, 8 x 57mm, 7 x 65R, 30-06 Spr.,.375 H& H Mag.
Cartridge capacity	: double-barrelled rifle
Magazine catch	: not applicable

Action	: breech action
Locking	: breech lock on top of pivot
Weight	: 3.1kg (6lb 13oz)
Length	: 102-107cm
	(40⅛-42⅛in)
Barrel Length	: 55-60cm
	(21¾-23⅝in)
Sight	: Express folding sight
External safety	: safety catch slider on
	back of pistol grip
Internal safety	: locking

CHARACTERISTICS
- material : steel
- finish : blued
- stock : walnut

Bernardelli Express Minerva

TECHNICAL DETAILS
Calibre	: 9.3 x 74R
Cartridge capacity	: double-barrelled rifle
Magazine catch	: not applicable
Action	: breech action
Locking	: breech lock on top of pivot
Weight	: 3.2kg (7lb 3oz)
Length	: 101cm (39¾in)
Barrel Length	: 60cm (23⅝in)
Sight	: Express folding sight
External safety	: safety catch slider on back
	of pistol grip
Internal safety	: locking

CHARACTERISTICS
- material : steel
- finish : blued with bare metal side
  plates and external hammers
- stock : specially selected walnut

Bernardelli Express VB

TECHNICAL DETAILS
Calibre	: 9.3 x 74R, 8 x 57mm,
	7 x 65R, 30-06 Spr.,.375
	H& H Mag.
Cartridge capacity	: double-barrelled rifle

Magazine catch	: not applicable
Action	: breech action
Locking	: breech lock on top of pivot
Weight	: 3.2kg (7lb 3oz)
Length	: 101-106cm (39¾-41¾in)
Barrel Length	: 55-60cm (21¾-23⅝in)
Sight	: Express folding sight
External safety	: safety catch slider on back
	of pistol grip
Internal safety	: locking

CHARACTERISTICS
- material : steel
- finish : blued with bare metal side
  plates and external hammers
- stock : walnut

Bernardelli Express VB De Luxe

TECHNICAL DETAILS
Calibre	: 9.3 x 74R, 8 x 57mm,
	7 x 65R, 30-06 Spr.,.375
	H& H Mag.
Cartridge capacity	: double-barrelled rifle
Magazine catch	: not applicable
Action	: breech action
Locking	: breech lock on top of pivot
Weight	: 3.2kg (7lb 3oz)
Length	: 101-106cm (39¾-41¾in)
Barrel Length	: 55-60cm (21¾-23⅝in)
Sight	: Express folding sight
External safety	: safety catch slider on back
	of pistol grip
Internal safety	: locking

CHARACTERISTICS

- material : steel
- finish : blued with bare metal side plates and external hammers
- stock : specially selected walnut

Bernardelli Express VB-E

TECHNICAL DETAILS

Calibre	: 9.3 x 74R, 8 x 57mm, 7 x 65R, 30-06 Spr.,.375 H& H Mag.
Cartridge capacity	: double-barrelled rifle
Magazine catch	: not applicable
Action	: breech action
Locking	: breech lock on top of pivot
Weight	: 3.2kg (7lb 3oz)
Length	: 101-106cm (39¾-41¾in)
Barrel Length	: 55-60cm (21¾-23⅝in)
Sight	: Express folding sight
External safety	: safety catch slider on back of pistol grip
Internal safety	: locking

CHARACTERISTICS

- material : steel
- finish : blued
- stock : walnut

Bernardelli VB-Target carbine

TECHNICAL DETAILS

Calibre	: .22 LR
Cartridge capacity	: 5 or
Magazine catch	: in front of magazine aperture
Action	: semi-automatic
Locking	: inertia
Weight	: 2.3kg (5lb 1oz)
Length	: 103cm (40½in)
Barrel Length	: 53cm (20⅞in)
Sight	: adjustable folding
External safety	: push-button safety catch slider on left of trigger guard
Internal safety	: locking

CHARACTERISTICS

- material : steel
- finish : blued
- stock : hardwood

Blaser

The German company Blaser Jagdwaffen GmbH is based in Isny im Allgäu in Baden-Württemberg, close to the border between Bavaria and Austria in the Allgäuer Alps. The firm was set up in 1977 by Horst Blaser and was taken over by the company's master gunsmith, Gerhard Blenk, in 1986. The company specialises in making high-quality hunting rifles with exceptionally fine engravings. Most models are equipped with breech actions of the type used with shotguns. These rifles are often equipped with quality telescopic sights by makers such as Zeiss, Swarovski, Schmidt & Bender, and Leupold. The Blaser rifles can be provided on request with Mag-Na-Port recoil suppressors or a Kickstop recoil absorber in the stock.

A new single shot R-93 UIT standard rifle and new 10-rounds bolt-action rifle R-93 CISM were introduced in 1993 at the IWA international weapons exhibition in Nuremberg in Germany. Both these weapons are match rifles for competing at 300m (328yds). The bolt action is specific to this maker, in that the bolt can be pulled directly back without first having to be turned. The bolt head has a 360° ring with 12 locking-lugs that are pushed outwards when the weapon is locked to engage in a circular rim around the chamber. The R-93 rifle also has a system for simple exchange of barrels which makes it easy to change Calibre. Blaser has also developed a special process for preventing rust which it uses to treat its weapons. The parts are treated with the so-called Blaser-Q process in which the parts are subjected to nitrogen that permeates to 0.2mm into the surface of the steel.

Calibres available: (top barrel): .22 Hornet, .222 Rem., 5.6 x 50R Mag.; (lower barrel): 5.6 x 50R Mag., 5.6 x 50R, .243 Win., .25-06, 5.6 x 57R, 5.6 x 65 RWS, .270 Win., 7 x 57R, 7 x 65R, .308 Win., .30-06 Spr., .30R Blaser, 8 x 57 IRS, 8 x 75 RS, 9.3 x 74R

Blaser B750/88 mountain carbine (Bergstutzen) double-bore

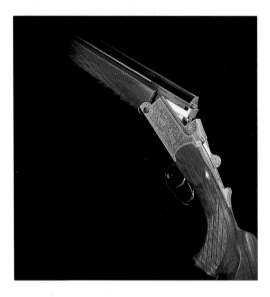

TECHNICAL DETAILS

Calibre	: see below
Cartridge capacity	: double-barrel
Magazine catch	: not applicable
Action	: breech-action
Locking	: breech-lock on rear of pivot
Weight	: 3.1kg (6lb 13oz)
Length	: 102cm (40⅛in)
Barrel Length	: 60cm (23⅝in)
Sight	: fixed leaf; special Blaser mount for telescopic sight
External safety	: safety catch slider on rear of pistol grip
Internal safety	: locking, after loading, the weapon is automatically made safe; it canbe cocked before the shot by means of the safety catch

CHARACTERISTICS

- material : steel
- finish : blued barrel, engravedbare metal breech and pivot
- stock : flame-treated walnut with pistol grip

Blaser R 93 Jagdmatch Luxus Holz (hunting/match wood)

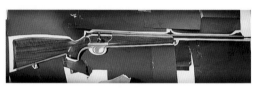

TECHNICAL DETAILS

Calibre	: .222 Rem.
Cartridge capacity	: 3 rounds
Magazine catch	: internal magazine
Action	: bolt-action
Locking	: special 360˚ locking
Weight	: 4.4kg (9lb 11oz)
Length	: 107cm (42⅛in)
Barrel Length	: 62.7cm (24¾in)
Sight	: fixed leaf; special Blaser mount for telescopic sight
External safety	: safety catch slider on rear of pistol grip
Internal safety	: locking, after loading, the weapon is automatically made safe; it can be cocked before the shot by means of the safety catch

CHARACTERISTICS

- material : steel
- finish : blued barrel, engraved bare metal breech and pivot with walnut inlay
- stock : flame-treated walnut with pistol grip

Blaser R 93 Royal

TECHNICAL DETAILS

Calibre	: see below
Cartridge capacity	: 3 rounds

Magazine catch	: internal magazine
Action	: bolt-action
Locking	: special 360° locking
Weight	: 3-3.2kg (6lb 9oz-7lb 3oz)
Length	: 102-107cm (40⅛-42⅛in)
Barrel Length	: 57.7-62.7 (22¾-24¾in)
Sight	: fixed leaf; special Blaser mount for telescopic sight
External safety	: safety catch slider on rear of pistol grip
Internal safety	: locking, after loading, the weapon is automatically made safe; it can be cocked before the shot by means of the safety catch

CHARACTERISTICS
- material : steel
- finish : blued barrel, engraved bare metal breech and pivot
- stock : flame-treated walnut with pistol grip

Calibres available: (small-bore): .222 Rem., .223 Rem., 5.6 x 50R Mag.; (full-bore): .243 Win., 6.5 x 57, 6.5 x 55, 6.5 x 65R RWS, .270 Win., 7 x 57, 7 x 64, .308 Win., .30-06 Spr., 8 x 57 IS, 9.3 x 74R; (medium calibre): 6.5 x 68, 7.5 x 55, 8 x 68S, 9.3 x 64; (Magnum calibre): 7mm Rem. Mag., .300 Win. Mag., .300 Wby. Mag., .338 Win. Mag., .375 H &H Mag.

Blaser K 95 Luxus

TECHNICAL DETAILS

Calibre	: see below
Cartridge capacity	: single round
Magazine catch	: not applicable
Action	: breech-action
Locking	: breech-lock on rear of breech pivot
Weight	: 2.4-2.6kg (5lb 3oz- 5lb 11oz)
Length	: 102-107cm (40⅛-42⅛in)
Barrel Length	: 60-65cm (23⅝-25⅝in)
Sight	: adjustable leaf; special Blaser mount for telescopic sight
External safety	: safety catch slider on rear of pistol grip
Internal safety	: locking, after loading, the weapon is automatically made safe; it can be cocked before the shot by means of the safety catch.

CHARACTERISTICS
- material : steel
- finish : blued barrel, engraved bare metal breech and pivot
- stock : walnut with pistol grip

Available calibres: .22 Hornet, .222 Rem., 5.6 x 50R Mag., 5.6 x 52R, .243 Win., 6.5 x 57R, 6.5 x 65R RWS, 6.5 x 68R, .270 Win., 7 x 57R, 7 x 65R, 7mm Rem. Mag., .308., .30-06 Spr., .30R Blaser, 7.5 x 55, .300 Win. Mag., .300 Wby. Mag., 8 x 57 IRS, 8 x 75 RS, 8 x 68RS, 9.3 x 74R.

Brown

The American firm of Brown Precision Inc., based in Los Molinos, California, USA, is no mass-producer. Chet Brown is a gunsmith who makes special rifles to order. Brown set up as a gunsmith in 1970 and began experimenting with plastic rifle stocks. Their stocks became quickly popular with bench-rest shooters, who need a stock that is not susceptible to weather conditions in the way natural wood is. In addition, a plastic stock is much lighter than a wooden one. Hunters too soon discovered the advantages of plastic stocks, particularly those of reduced weight. Brown also makes use of stainless steel and gives ordinary steel parts a nickel-plated finish or Teflon coating. The Brown rifles are built around Remington 700 or 40X, or Winchester M-70 receivers and bolts. These receivers are attached to stainless steel match barrels by Shilen. The client determines the calibre:, the barrel length, the type of stock, and the finish. Every mechanical part is precisely hand-finished to fine tolerances. The customer can order a rifle in any imaginable calibre:, including one to his own design. Brown has a number of standard configurations to make comparisons easier, but these can be tailored to individual requirements. Brown also makes a special marksman's rifle. The "plastic" stocks are made these days of Kevlar or glass-fibre.

Brown High Country Custom

TECHNICAL DETAILS
Calibre	: to choice
Cartridge capacity	: 3-5 rounds
Magazine catch	: at front of trigger guard
Action	: bolt-action
Locking	: 2 locking-lugs (Remington 40X)
Weight	: from 5lb 1oz (2.3kg)
Length	: from 40½in (103cm)
Barrel Length	: from 22in (55.8cm)
Sight	: none, special mount for telescopic sight
External safety	: safety catch behind bolt knob
Internal safety	: locking

CHARACTERISTICS
• material	: steel
• finish	: matt black
• stock	: matt black or camouflage plastic with pistol grip

Brown High Country Youth

TECHNICAL DETAILS
Calibre	: see below
Cartridge capacity	: 3-5 rounds
Magazine catch	: at front of trigger guard

Action	: bolt-action
Locking	: 2 locking-lugs (Remington 700)
Weight	: 7-8lb 14oz (3.2-3.9kg)
Length	: 40½in (103cm)
Barrel Length	: 22in (55.8cm)
Sight	: none, special mount for telescopic sight
External safety	: safety catch behind bolt knob
Internal safety	: locking

CHARACTERISTICS
• material	: steel
• finish	: blued
• stock	: grey plastic with pistol grip

Available calibres: .223 Rem., .243 Win., 7mm-08 Rem., 6mm Rem., .308 Win.

Brown Pro-Hunter

TECHNICAL DETAILS
Calibre	: to choice
Cartridge capacity	: 3-5 rounds
Magazine catch	: at front of trigger guard
Action	: bolt-action
Locking	: 2 locking-lugs (Remington 700)
Weight	: from about 7lb 11oz-9lb 14oz (3.5-4.5kg)
Length	: from 40½-44½in (103-113cm)
Barrel Length	: from 22-24in (55.8-61cm)

excluding muzzle
compensator

Sight	: leaf, special mount for telescopic sight
External safety	: safety catch behind bolt knob
Internal safety	: locking

CHARACTERISTICS

• material	: steel, stainless-steel barrel
• finish	: bare metal, untreated barrel, nickel-plated receiver
• stock	: black plastic with pistol grip

Brown Pro-Hunter Elite

TECHNICAL DETAILS

Calibre	: to choice
Cartridge capacity	: 3-5 rounds
Magazine catch	: at front of trigger guard
Action	: bolt-action
Locking	: 2 locking-lugs (Remington M70)
Weight	: from about 7lb 11oz-9lb 14oz (3.5-4.5kg)
Length	: from 40½-44½in (103-113cm)
Barrel Length	: from 22-24in (55.8-61cm)
Sight	: leaf, special mount for telescopic sight
External safety	: winged safety catch behind bolt knob
Internal safety	: locking

CHARACTERISTICS

• material	: steel, stainless-steel barrel
• finish	: bare metal, untreated barrel, nickel-plated receiver
• stock	: black plastic with pistol grip

Brown Pro-Varminter

TECHNICAL DETAILS

Calibre	: to choice
Cartridge capacity	: 3-5 rounds

Magazine catch	: at front of trigger guard
Action	: bolt-action
Locking	: 2 locking-lugs (Remington 700 or 40X)
Weight	: from about 7lb 11oz-9lb 14oz (3.5-4.5kg)
Length	: from 40½-44½in (103-113cm)
Barrel Length	: from 22-24in (55.8-61cm)
Sight	: none, special mount for telescopic sight
External safety	: winged safety catch on right of receiver, behind bolt knob
Internal safety	: locking

CHARACTERISTICS

• material	: steel, stainless-steel barrel
• finish	: bare metal, matt-finish barrel, nickel-plated receiver
• stock	: black plastic with pistol grip

Brown Tactical Elite

TECHNICAL DETAILS

Calibre	: see below
Cartridge capacity	: 3-5 rounds or removable cartridge holder
Magazine catch	: at front of trigger guard
Action	: bolt-action
Locking	: 2 locking-lugs (Remington 700)
Weight	: from about 9lb 14oz (4.5kg) excluding telescopic sight
Length	: from 40½in (103cm)
Barrel Length	: from 24in (61cm)
Sight	: none, special mount for telescopic sight
External safety	: safety catch on right of receiver, behind bolt knob
Internal safety	: locking

CHARACTERISTICS

• material	: steel
• finish	: matt black
• stock	: black Kevlar with pistol grip and adjustable butt-plate

Calibres available: .223 Rem., .308 Win., .300 Win. Mag., or any other calibre: required.

Browning/FN-Browning

John Moses Browning lived from 1855 to 1926. From 1883, he designed a considerable number of weapons and worked closely with Winchester. In 1898, he was awarded a patent for his design of a semiautomatic shotgun, the Automatic-5. He wanted to sell this design to Winchester but the head of the company at that time rejected it. Browning's price was too much and the machine shop at Winchester was not suitable for such a gun. Browning contacted Remington but on the day of his appointment with them, the head of the company, Marcellus Hartley, died of a heart attack. Browning decided to take his design to Europe. Various pistols designed by him were already being made there by the Belgian company Fabrique National (FN) in Herstal near Liege.

FN were happy to produce Browning's Automatic-5. In 1925, the American designed his B25 shotgun with the revolutionary idea - at that time - of placing the two barrels on top of each other instead of side-by-side. This gun came into production in 1926 and it is still being made. Browning died that same year of a heart attack he suffered when in Liege. After his death, his son, Val Browning, continued the family tradition by designing weapons. Today's company has establishments in the United States and Canada. It also has links to the munitions giant Winchester. The FN-Browning High Power (HP-35) pistol is very well known. The company also makes a wide range of small-bore and full-bore hand guns. FN is really the world leader though in the manufacture of small-bore rifles and of shotguns for clay pigeon shooting. A number of shotguns are made for Browning by Miroku, in Japan. The customizing department of Browning has a wide range of artistic engravings for every type of Browning firearm.

Browning A-bolt II (Standard)

TECHNICAL DETAILS

Calibre	: see below
Cartridge capacity	: 3 rounds (.22 Hornet/.223 Rem.: 4 rounds)
Magazine catch	: at front of trigger guard
Action	: bolt-action
Locking	: 2 locking-lugs
Weight	: 6lb 2oz (2.8kg)
Length	: 39½in (103.3cm)
Barrel Length	: 20in (50.8cm)
Sight	: none, special mount for telescopic sight
External safety	: safety catch on pistol grip behind receiver
Internal safety	: locking, load indicator

CHARACTERISTICS

• material	: steel
• finish	: blued
• stock	: walnut with pistol grip

Calibres available: .243 Win., .308 Win., 7mm-08 Rem., .22-250 Rem., .223 Rem., .22 Hornet.

Magazine catch	: at front of trigger guard
Action	: bolt-action
Locking	: 2 locking-lugs
Weight	: 6lb 6oz-7lb 5oz (2.9-3.3kg)
Length	: 41¾-46¾in (106.1-118.8cm)
Barrel Length	: 22-26in (55.9-66cm)
Sight	: none, special mount for telescopic sight
External safety	: safety catch on pistol grip behind receiver
Internal safety	: locking, load indicator

CHARACTERISTICS

• material	: steel
• finish	: blued
• stock	: black carbon fibre

Calibres available (group1, long bolt) Magnum: .338 Win. Mag., .300 Win. Mag., 7mm Rem. Mag.; (group 2, long bolt): .25-06 Rem., .270 Win., .280 Rem., .30-06 Spr.; (group 3, short bolt): .243 Win., .308 Win., 7mm-08 Rem., .22-250 Rem., .223 Rem.

This rifle can be equipped with the Boss system

Browning A-bolt II Eclipse Varmint

TECHNICAL DETAILS

Calibre	: .308 Win., .22-250 Rem., .223 Rem.
Cartridge capacity	: 4 rounds (.223 Rem.: 6 rounds)
Magazine catch	: at front of trigger guard
Action	: bolt-action
Locking	: 2 locking-lugs
Weight	: 9lb 1oz (4.1kg)
Length	: 44½in (113cm)
Barrel Length	: 26in (66cm) with Boss system
Sight	: none, special mount for telescopic sight

Browning A-bolt II Composite Stalker

TECHNICAL DETAILS

Calibre	: see below
Cartridge capacity	: 3 rounds (.223 Rem.: 6 rounds)

| External safety | : safety catch on pistol grip behind receiver |
| Internal safety | : locking, load indicator on rear of receiver |

CHARACTERISTICS
- material : steel
- finish : blued
- stock : laminated hardwood with thumb-hole

Browning A-bolt II Hunter

TECHNICAL DETAILS

Calibre	: see below
Cartridge capacity	: 3 rounds (.223 Rem.: 4 rounds)
Magazine catch	: at front of trigger guard
Action	: bolt-action
Locking	: 2 locking-lugs
Weight	: 6lb 11oz-7lb 5oz (3-3.3kg)
Length	: 41¾-46¾in (106.1-118.8cm)
Barrel Length	: 22-26in (55.9-66cm)
Sight	: adjustable folding sight and bead tunnel
External safety	: safety catch on pistol grip behind receiver
Internal safety	: locking, load indicator on rear of receiver

CHARACTERISTICS
- material : steel
- finish : blued
- stock : walnut with pistol grip

Calibres available (group1, long bolt) Magnum: .338 Win. Mag., .300 Win. Mag., 7mm Rem. Mag.; (group 2, long bolt): .25-06 Rem., .270 Win., .280 Rem., .30-06 Spr.; (group 3, short bolt): .243 Win., .308 Win., 7mm-08 Rem., .22-250 Rem., .223 Rem.

Browning A-bolt II Stainless Stalker

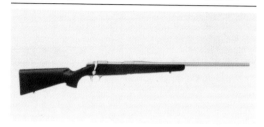

TECHNICAL DETAILS

Calibre	: see below
Cartridge capacity	: 3 rounds (.223 Rem.: 6 rounds)
Magazine catch	: at front of trigger guard
Action	: bolt-action
Locking	: 2 locking-lugs
Weight	: 6lb 6oz-7lb 5oz (2.9-3.3kg)
Length	: 41¾-46¾in (106.1-118.8cm)
Barrel Length	: 22-26in (55.9-66cm)
Sight	: none, special mount for telescopic sight
External safety	: safety catch on pistol grip behind receiver
Internal safety	: locking, load indicator at rear of receiver

CHARACTERISTICS
- material : steel
- finish : blued
- stock : black carbon fibre

Calibres available (group1, long bolt) Magnum: .375 H & H, .338 Win. Mag., .300 Win. Mag., 7mm Rem. Mag.; (group 2, long bolt): .25-06 Rem., .270 Win., .280 Rem., .30-06 Spr.; (group 3, short bolt): .243 Win., .308 Win., 7mm-08 Rem., .22-250 Rem., .223 Rem.

This rifle can be equipped with the Boss system

Browning A-bolt II Varmint

TECHNICAL DETAILS

Calibre	: .308 Win., .22-250 Rem., .223 Rem.
Cartridge capacity	: 4 rounds (.223 Rem.: 6 rounds)
Magazine catch	: at front of trigger guard
Action	: bolt-action
Locking	: 2 locking-lugs

Calibres available: (Magnum) .338 Win. Mag., .300 Win. Mag., 7mm Rem. Mag.; (standard): .30-06 Spr., .270 Win., .308 Win., .243 Win.
This BAR rifle is equipped with the Boss system.

Weight	: 9lb (4.1kg)
Length	: 44½in (113cm)
Barrel Length	: 26in (66cm) with Boss system
Sight	: none, special mount for telescopic sight
External safety	: safety catch on pistol grip behind receiver
Internal safety	: locking, load indicator on rear of receiver

CHARACTERISTICS
- material : steel
- finish : blued
- stock : laminated hardwood

Browning BAR Mark II Safari

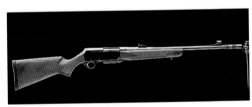

TECHNICAL DETAILS
Calibre	: see below
Cartridge capacity	: 3 rounds (Magnum) or 4 (standard)
Magazine catch	: at front of trigger guard
Action	: semi-automatic, gas-pressure
Locking	: 7-lugs rotating slide
Weight	: 7lb 9oz-8lb 9oz (3.5-3.9kg)
Length	: 43-45in (109-114cm)
Barrel Length	: 22-24in (55.9-61cm)
Sight	: adjustable folding, drilled and tapped for telescopic sight
External safety	: push-button safety catch behind trigger guard
Internal safety	: locking

CHARACTERISTICS
- material : steel
- finish : blued
- stock : walnut with pistol grip

Browning BAR Mark II Safari-Hunter

TECHNICAL DETAILS
Calibre	: see below
Cartridge capacity	: 3 rounds (Magnum) or 4 (standard)
Magazine catch	: at front of trigger guard
Action	: semi-automatic, gas-pressure
Locking	: 7-lugs rotating slide
Weight	: 7lb 9oz-8lb 9oz (3.5-3.9kg)
Length	: 43-45in (109-114cm)
Barrel Length	: 22-24in (55.9-61cm)
Sight	: none, drilled and tapped for telescopic sight
External safety	: push-button safety catch behind trigger guard
Internal safety	: locking

CHARACTERISTICS
- material : steel
- finish : blued
- stock : walnut with pistol grip

Calibres available: (Magnum) .338 Win. Mag., .300 Win. Mag., 7mm Rem. Mag.; (standard): .30-06 Spr., .270 Win., .308 Win., .243 Win.
This BAR rifle can be equipped with the Boss system as an accessory.

Browning BL-22

TECHNICAL DETAILS
Calibre	: .22 LR, .22Long, .22 Short
Cartridge capacity	: 15, 17, or 22 rounds respectively

Magazine catch   : tubular magazine with
                        closing cap at front
Action   : lever-action
Locking   : lever-action
Weight   : 5lb (2.3kg)
Length   : 36¾in (93.4cm)
Barrel Length   : 20in (50.8cm)
Sight   : adjustable folding sight
External safety : when weapon is cocked,
                        trigger is disen gaged from
                        trigger mechanism
Internal safety : locking, half-cock on
                        hammer, inert firing pin

CHARACTERISTICS
• material   : steel
• finish   : blued
• stock   : walnut

Browning BLR model 81 Long Action

TECHNICAL DETAILS
Calibre   : see below
Cartridge capacity : 4 rounds
Magazine catch   : at front of magazine
                        aperture
Action   : lever-action
Locking   : lever-action
Weight   : 7lb 3oz-8lb 9oz (3.2-3.9 kg)
Length   : 39¾-44½ in (101-113cm)
Barrel Length   : 20⅛-22⅛in (51-56cm)
Sight   : adjustable sight, holes
                        provided in receiver for
                        telescopic sight
External safety : none
Internal safety : locking, half-cock on safety

CHARACTERISTICS
• material   : steel

• finish   : blued
• stock   : straight English stock of
                        walnut
Available calibres: .270 Win., .30-06 Spr., 7mm
Rem. Mag.

Browning European Standard Affût (hunting gun)

TECHNICAL DETAILS
Calibre   : see below
Cartridge capacity : 3-4 rounds
Magazine catch   : front of trigger guard
Action   : bolt-action
Locking   : 2 locking-lugs
Weight   : 6lb 13oz-7lb 1oz (3.1-3.2kg)
Length   : 42½-47⅝in (108-121cm)
Barrel Length   : 22-26in (56-66cm)
Sight   : adjustable folding sight and
                        bead tunnel
External safety : safety catch slide on neck of
                        the stock behind receiver
Internal safety : locking, load indicator on
                        rear of receiver

CHARACTERISTICS
• material   : steel
• finish   : blued
• stock   : walnut with pistol grip

Calibres available: (group1 Magnum):
.300 Win. Mag.; (group 2, long bolt): .270
Win., .30-06 Spr., 6.5 x 55m, 7 x 64mm;
(group 3, short bolt): .243 Win., .257
Roberts, .308 Win., 7mm-08 Rem., .22-
250 Rem.

Browning European Standard Affût-Boss (hunting gun)

TECHNICAL DETAILS
Calibre   : see below
Cartridge capacity : 3-4 rounds
Magazine catch   : front of trigger guard
Action   : bolt-action

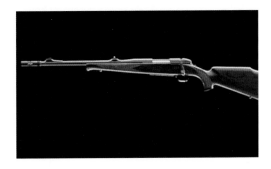

Locking	: 3 locking-lugs
Weight	: 6lb 13oz-7lb 1oz (3.1-3.2kg)
Length	: 42½-47⅝in (108-121cm) excluding Boss
Barrel Length	: 22-26in (56-66cm)
Sight	: adjustable folding sight and bead tunnel
External safety	: safety catch slide on neck of the stock behind receiver
Internal safety	: locking, load indicator on rear of receiver

CHARACTERISTICS
- material : steel
- finish : blued
- stock : walnut with pistol grip

Calibres available: (group1 Magnum): .300 Win. Mag.; (group 2, long bolt): .270 Win., .30-06 Spr., 6.5 x 55m, 7 x 64mm; (group 3, short bolt): .243 Win., .257 Roberts, .308 Win., 7mm-08 Rem., .22-250 Rem.

Browning Lightning BLR model Long Action

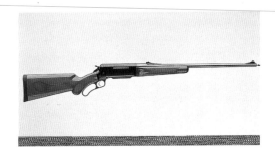

TECHNICAL DETAILS

Calibre	: see below
Cartridge capacity	: 3-4 rounds
Magazine catch	: at front of magazine aperture
Action	: lever-action
Locking	: lever-action
Weight	: 7lb 2oz-7lb 6oz (3.3-3.6 kg)
Length	: 43-44¾in (109-113.8cm)
Barrel Length	: 22-24in (55.9-61cm)
Sight	: adjustable sight, holes provided in receiver for telescopic sight
External safety	: none
Internal safety	: locking, half-cock on safety, fold-away hammer

CHARACTERISTICS
- material : steel, light metal mechanism housing
- finish : blued
- stock : walnut with pistol grip

Available calibres: .270 Win., .30-06 Spr., 7mm Rem. Mag.

Browning Lightning BLR model Short Action

TECHNICAL DETAILS

Calibre	: see below
Cartridge capacity	: 4-5 rounds
Magazine catch	: at front of magazine aperture
Action	: lever-action
Locking	: lever-action
Weight	: 6lb 13oz (3.1kg)
Length	: 39½in (100.3cm)
Barrel Length	: 20in (50.8cm)
Sight	: adjustable sight, holes provided in receiver for telescopic sight
External safety	: none
Internal safety	: locking, half-cock on safety, fold-away hammer

CHARACTERISTICS
- material : steel, light metal mechanism housing
- finish : blued
- stock : walnut with pistol grip

Available calibres: .222 Rem., .223 Rem., .22-250 Rem., .243 Win., .284 Win., .257 Roberts, 7mm-08 Rem., .308 Win., .358 Win.

Browning model 1885 "High Wall"

TECHNICAL DETAILS

Calibre	: see below
Cartridge capacity	: single shot
Magazine catch	: not applicable
Action	: cocking-lever combined with trigger guard
Locking	: drop block action
Weight	: 8lb 1oz (3.7kg)
Length	: 43½in (110.5cm)
Barrel Length	: 28in (71.1cm)
Sight	: none, suitable for telescopic sight
External safety	: none
Internal safety	: locking, half-cock on hammer

CHARACTERISTICS
- material : steel, light metal mechanism housing
- finish : blued
- stock : slim-line walnut

Calibres available: .22-250 Rem., .270 Win., .30-06 Spr., 7mm Rem. Mag., 45-70 Govt.

Browning model 1885 "Low Wall"

TECHNICAL DETAILS

Calibre	: .22 Hornet, .223 Rem., .243 Win.

Cartridge capacity	: single shot
Magazine catch	: not applicable
Action	: cocking-lever combined with trigger guard
Locking	: drop block action
Weight	: 6lb 6oz (2.9kg)
Length	: 39½in (100.3cm)
Barrel Length	: 24in (61cm)
Sight	: none, suitable for telescopic sight
External safety	: none
Internal safety	: locking, half-cock on hammer

CHARACTERISTICS
- material : steel, light metal mechanism housing
- finish : blued
- stock : walnut with pistol grip

Browning model 1895 Lever-action

TECHNICAL DETAILS

Calibre	: .30-06 Spr.
Cartridge capacity	: magazine for 4 rounds
Magazine catch	: at rear of magazine
Action	: lever-action
Locking	: lever-action
Weight	: 8lb (3.6kg)
Length	: 42in (106.7cm)
Barrel Length	: 24in (61cm)
Sight	: adjustable height leaf
External safety	: safety catch on neck of stock
Internal safety	: locking, blocking rod

CHARACTERISTICS
- material : steel,
- finish : blued, engraved action cover
- stock : straight walnut stock

This nostalgic model was made in 1995, in limited quantities.

Browning Semi-Auto 22 (Grade VI)

TECHNICAL DETAILS

Calibre : .22 LR
Cartridge capacity : 11 rounds
Magazine catch : none, tubular magazine
Action : semi-automatic slide
Locking : inertia
Weight : 4lb 6oz (2kg)
Length : 37in (94cm)
Barrel Length : 19¼in (48.9cm)
Sight : folding sight, suitable for telescopic sight
External safety : safety catch on front of trigger guard
Internal safety : locking

CHARACTERISTICS

• material : steel
• finish : blued
• stock : wooden stock with pistol grip and loading access for tubular magazine

Animals figures are engraved on the receiver and inlaid with 24 carat gold. A locking knob in front of the trigger guard enables the weapon to be split into two parts.

BSA

Birmingham Small Arms Ltd, better known as BSA, harks back to a long tradition. The city of Birmingham was involved in the weapons-industry as early as the thirteenth century. No firearms were made of course, but swords, daggers and other metalwork were, for the wars of those days. In 1854, fourteen master gunsmiths founded the Birmingham Small Arms and Metal Company, which mainly manufactured rifles for the British Army. From 1869 until about 1880, BSA made the Le Mat revolver under licence. This was a combination weapon with both a shotgun and rifled barrel. In 1924, the company developed a .50 calibre machine-gun for anti-aircraft use. A water-cooled version was developed for the British Navy. The firm's production was later broadened to include rifles and shotguns for hunting and sport shooting. Today the company is known as BSA Guns Ltd. The company made a range of first-class rifles but unfortunately these are no longer made. Because they were made in large numbers, these weapons have been included in this book. Nowadays, BSA solely makes air rifles and air pistols such as the Meteor, Scorpion, and Airsporters.

BSA CF2 Carbine

TECHNICAL DETAILS

Calibre : see below
Cartridge capacity : 3-5 rounds depending upon Calibre Magazine catch at front of trigger guard
Action : bolt-action
Locking : 2 locking-lugs
Weight : 7lb 8oz-8lb (3.4-3.6kg)
Length : 41⅜in (105.2cm)
Barrel Length : 20⅛in (52.3cm)
Sight : adjustable Williams sight, suitable for telescopic sight
External safety : safety catch behind bolt
Internal safety : locking, load indicator at rear of bolt

CHARACTERISTICS

• material : steel
• finish : blued
• stock : hardwood with pistol grip

Available calibres: .222 Rem., .223 Rem., .22-250 Rem., .243 Win., 6.5 x 55mm, 7 x 57mm, 7 x 64mm, 7mm Rem. Mag., .270 Win., .308 Win., .30-06 Spr., .300 Win. Mag.

The British firm of BSA (Birmingham Small Arms) no longer makes this rifle.

BSA CF2 Heavy Barrel Rifle

TECHNICAL DETAILS

Calibre : see below
Cartridge capacity : 4-5 rounds depending upon Calibre:
Magazine catch : at front of trigger guard
Action : bolt-action
Locking : 2 locking-lugs
Weight : 9-9½lb (4.1-4.3kg)
Length : 44⅜in (112.8cm)
Barrel Length : 60cm (23⅝in)
Sight : adjustable Williams sight, suitable for telescopic sight
External safety : safety catch behind bolt
Internal safety : locking, load indicator at rear of bolt

CHARACTERISTICS

• material : steel
• finish : blued
• stock : hardwood with pistol grip

Available calibres: .222 Rem., .223 Rem., .22-250 Rem., .243 Win.; other calibres were made to special order.

The British firm of BSA (Birmingham Small Arms) no longer makes this rifle.

BSA CF2 Hunting Rifle

TECHNICAL DETAILS

Calibre : see below

Cartridge capacity : 3-5 rounds depending upon Calibre
Magazine catch : at front of trigger guard
Action : bolt-action
Locking : 2 locking-lugs
Weight : 7lb 8oz-8lb (3.4-3.6kg)
Length : 44⅜in (112.8cm)
Barrel Length : 23⅝in (60cm)
Sight : adjustable Williams sight, suitable for telescopic sight
External safety : safety catch behind bolt
Internal safety : locking, load indicator at rear of bolt

CHARACTERISTICS

• material : steel
• finish : blued
• stock : hardwood with pistol grip

Available calibres: .222 Rem., .223 Rem., .22-250 Rem., .243 Win., 6.5 x 55mm, 7 x 57mm, 7 x 64mm, 7mm Rem. Mag., .270 Win., .308 Win., .30-06 Spr., .300 Win. Mag.

Illustrated: BSA Model CF-2 Hunting Rifle (above) and CF-2 Hunting Carbine (below)

The British firm of BSA (Birmingham Small Arms) no longer makes this rifle.

BSA CF2 Hunting Carbine

TECHNICAL DETAILS

Calibre : see below
Cartridge capacity : 4-5 rounds depending upon Calibre
Magazine catch : at front of trigger guard
Action : bolt-action
Locking : 2 locking-lugs
Weight : 7lb 8oz-8lb (3.4-3.6kg)
Length : 41⅜in (105.2cm)
Barrel Length : 20⅝in (52.3cm)
Sight : adjustable Williams sight, suitable for telescopic sight

| External safety | : safety catch behind bolt |
| Internal safety | : locking, load indicator at rear of bolt |

CHARACTERISTICS
- material : steel
- finish : blued
- stock : hardwood with pistol grip

Available calibres: .222 Rem., .223 Rem., .22-250 Rem., .243 Win., 6.5 x 55mm, 7 x 57mm, 7 x 64mm, .270 Win., .308 Win., .30-06 Spr.

Illustrated: BSA Model CF-2 Hunting Rifle (above) and CF-2 Hunting Carbine (below)
The British firm of BSA (Birmingham Small Arms) no longer makes this rifle.

Action	: lever-action
Locking	: drop block locking
Weight	: 11lb (5kg)
Length	: 47⅝in (121cm)
Barrel Length	: 26½in (67.3cm)
Sight	: optical sight and bead tunnel
External safety	: none
Internal safety	: locking, load indicator at rear of bolt

CHARACTERISTICS
- material : steel
- finish : blued
- stock : walnut with pistol grip

BSA no longer make this target rifle for a range of 300m (328yds).

BSA CF2 Target Rifle

TECHNICAL DETAILS
Calibre	: .308 Win.
Cartridge capacity	: single shot
Magazine catch	: not applicable

BSA Martini Target

TECHNICAL DETAILS
Calibre	: .22 LR.
Cartridge capacity	: single shot
Magazine catch	: not applicable
Action	: lever-action
Locking	: drop block locking
Weight	: 12lb (5.4kg)
Length	: 49¼in (125cm)
Barrel Length	: 24in (61cm)
Sight	: optical sight and bead tunnel
External safety	: none
Internal safety	: locking, load indicator at rear of bolt

CHARACTERISTICS
- material : steel
- finish : blued
- stock : beech

Bushmaster

The American firm Quality Parts Company was set up in 1979 and is based in Windham, Maine. Initially, the company made weapon parts for the US Army and the police. Subsequently many products were added for the civilian market, such as spare parts for the AR-15/M-16 rifle. Recently, the company began making accessories for Fal, Heckler & Koch, Ruger, and AK-47 rifles, together with components for Colt .45 ACP pistols and Uzi pistols and carbines. The subsidiary company, Bushmaster Firearms Inc. makes special versions of the Colt M-16/AR-15 rifle under the name XM15. During the Gulf War (Operation Desert Storm), the company received a large contract to make the M16-A2-M4 carbine for the US Army. The company makes the XM15-E2S rifles and carbines for the civilian market. The appendix "S" stands for semi-automatic. These rifles are copies of the AR-15 but they are better made. Bushmaster also makes match versions of these rifles for competing at 800m (874yds). In common with the Colt M16, there is a knob to the right of the receiver mechanism to manually assist the slide to close. The repeating mechanism can become sluggish due to dirt or overheating in the chamber.

Bushmaster X17S Bullpup rifle

TECHNICAL DETAILS

Calibre	: .223 Rem.
Cartridge capacity	: 30 rounds
Magazine catch	: magazine catch on left of magazine housing
Action	: semi-automatic, gas-pressure
Locking	: 7-lugs rotating slide
Weight	: 8lb 6oz (3.8kg)
Length	: 30in (76cm)
Barrel Length	: 21½in (54.6cm)
Sight	: standard sight in carrying handle; mounting for telescopic sight
External safety	: safety catch on right of receiver housing, indication of firing position on left
Internal safety	: locking

CHARACTERISTICS

• material	: steel
• finish	: black phosphate coated
• stock	: plastic

The cartridge holder is located in the butt of the rifle.

Bushmaster XM 15 E2S "Shorty" carbine

TECHNICAL DETAILS

Calibre	: .223 Rem.
Cartridge capacity	: 30 rounds
Magazine catch	: magazine catch on left of magazine housing
Action	: semi-automatic, gas-pressure
Locking	: 7-lugs rotating slide
Weight	: 7lb (3.2kg)
Length	: 34¾in (88.3cm)
Barrel Length	: 16in (40.6cm)
Sight	: adjustable folding optical sight
External safety	: safety catch on right of receiver housing, indication of firing position on left
Internal safety	: locking

CHARACTERISTICS

• material	: steel
• finish	: black phosphate coated
• stock	: plastic

Bushmaster XM 15 E2S Dissipator carbine

TECHNICAL DETAILS

Calibre : .223 Rem.
Cartridge capacity : 30 rounds
Magazine catch : magazine catch on left of magazine housing
Action : semi-automatic, gas-pressure
Locking : 7-lugs rotating slide
Weight : 7lb 6oz (3.4kg)
Length : 34½in (87.6cm)
Barrel Length : 16in (40.6cm)
Sight : adjustable folding optical sight
External safety : safety catch on right of receiver housing, indication of firing position on left
Internal safety : locking

CHARACTERISTICS

• material : steel
• finish : black phosphate coated
• stock : plastic

This rifle has a hand guard that is equipped with a heat dissipator.

Bushmaster XM 15 E2S "Dissipator" V-Match carbine

TECHNICAL DETAILS

Calibre : .223 Rem.
Cartridge capacity : 30 rounds

Magazine catch : magazine catch on left of magazine housing
Action : semi-automatic, gas-pressure
Locking : 7-lugs rotating slide
Weight : 7lb 6oz (3.4kg)
Length : 34½in (87.6cm)
Barrel Length : 16in (40.6cm)
Sight : none, mounting for telescopic sight
External safety : safety catch on right of receiver housing, indication of firing position on left
Internal safety : locking

CHARACTERISTICS

• material : steel
• finish : black phosphate coated, mechanism housing has no carrying handle
• stock : plastic

This rifle has a hand guard that is equipped with a heat dissipator.

Bushmaster XM 15 E2S Target rifle

TECHNICAL DETAILS

Calibre : .223 Rem.
Cartridge capacity : 30 rounds
Magazine catch : magazine catch on left of magazine housing
Action : semi-automatic, gas-pressure
Locking : 7-lugs rotating slide
Weight : 8lb 10oz (3.9kg)
Length : 38¼in (97cm)
Barrel Length : 20in (51cm)
Sight : adjustable folding sight
External safety : safety catch on right of receiver housing, indication of firing position on left
Internal safety : locking

CHARACTERISTICS

• material : steel

• finish	: black phosphate coated, mechanism housing has no carrying handle
• stock	: plastic

This rifle is also available with a
 24in (61cm) or 26in (66cm) length barrel.

Bushmaster XM 15 E2S V-Match Competition rifle

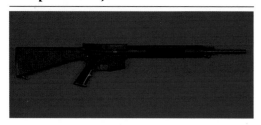

TECHNICAL DETAILS
Calibre	: .223 Rem.
Cartridge capacity	: 30 rounds
Magazine catch	: magazine catch on left of magazine housing
Action	: semi-automatic, gas-pressure
Locking	: 7-lugs rotating slide
Weight	: 8lb 5oz (3.8kg)
Length	: 38¼in (97cm)
Barrel Length	: 20in (51cm)
Sight	: none, mounting for telescopic sight
External safety	: safety catch on right of receiver housing, indication of firing position on left
Internal safety	: locking

CHARACTERISTICS
• material	: steel
• finish	: black phosphate coated, mechanism housing has no carrying handle
• stock	: plastic

This rifle is also available with a 24in (61cm) or 26in (66cm) length barrel.

Calico

The American maker, California Instrument Company, was founded in Bakersville, California in 1982. Originally, they made specialized tools for the oil industry before deciding in 1985 to make a range of weapons. Calico developed light automatic and semi-automatic weapons with an unusual cartridge holder - a cylindrical box with a spiral magazine that is sited on the top of the weapon. The rows of cartridges are pushed forwards by a spring and the rotation of the cylinder around its central axis. The cartridges are delivered one at a time to the chamber from the front underside of the cartridge holder. As each round is fired, the row of cartridges moves forward as room is made for them. The first weapon produced by Calico was a 100-round smallbore pistol in .22 LR Calibre. In June, 1989, the company introduced a 50- and 100-round carbine using 9mm parabellum ammunition with a spiral-acting magazine based on the same principles. The company fell foul though of new tougher firearms laws that were introduced in the United States. Weapons with a capacity in excess of 10 rounds are no longer per-mitted to be sold to the civilian market. Calico is now restricted to selling its weapons to Government departments and export to countries where such restrictions do not apply.

Calico Liberty 50 carbine

TECHNICAL DETAILS
Calibre	: .9 Para.
Cartridge capacity	: external magazine for 50 rounds
Magazine catch	: magazine catch on left of magazine housing
Action	: semi-automatic
Locking	: inertia
Weight	: 7lb (3.2g)
Length	: 34½in (87.6cm)
Barrel Length	: 16in (40.9cm)
Sight	: fixed leaf with adjustable bead
External safety	: doubled-sided push-button
Internal safety	: locking, separate position for inspecting chamber without cocking weapon or loading a round

CHARACTERISTICS

- material : stock, hand grip, and external magazine of robust
  plastic, barrel and receiver
  mechanism of steel
- finish : black coating
- stock : brown plastic stock and
  hand grip

Calico Liberty 100 carbine

TECHNICAL DETAILS

Calibre	: .9 Para.
Cartridge capacity	: external magazine for 100 rounds
Magazine catch	: magazine catch on left of magazine housing
Action	: semi-automatic
Locking	: inertia
Weight	: 7lb (3.2g)
Length	: 34½in (87.6cm)
Barrel Length	: 16in (40.9cm)
Sight	: fixed leaf with adjustable bead
External safety	: doubled-sided push-button
Internal safety	: locking, separate position for inspecting chamber without cocking weapon or loading a round

CHARACTERISTICS

- material : stock, hand grip, and external magazine of robust
  plastic, barrel and receiver
  mechanism of steel
- finish : black coating
- stock : brown plastic stock and
  hand grip

Chapuis

A factory in the village of Saint-Bonnet-le-Château beside the river Loire in France was busy at the end of the nineteenth century making consumer goods.

Along side this diligent industry, the factory also made parts such as barrels and pivot breeches for the nearby major armaments factory at Saint-Étienne. André Chapuis was a home-worker gunsmith who specialised in making breeches and barrels. Because his son Jean wanted to join him in the making of firearms, the pair of them decided to set up on their own in a small way to make complete weapons. They specialized in making hunting guns. Production was forced to stop during World War II but got under way again in 1945. Under the present head of the company, René Chapuis, the company is an important supplier of shotguns and Express hunting rifles of very high quality, with much of the production still being done by hand. The single-barrel breech-opening Oural rifle was introduced in 1990 for hunting medium-sized game.

Chapuis Double Express Prestige

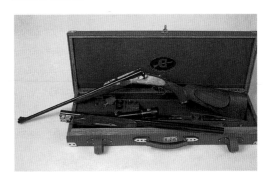

TECHNICAL DETAILS

Calibre	: 9.3 x 74R, 8 x 57mm, 7 x 65R
Cartridge capacity	: double-barrelled rifle
Magazine catch	: not applicable
Action	: breech-action
Locking	: breech-lock on top of pivot-breech
Weight	: 3.3-3.4kg (7lb 5oz-7lb 8oz)
Length	: 109cm (43in)
Barrel Length	: 60cm (23⅝in)
Sight	: folding sight, suitable for telescopic sight
External safety	: sliding catch on back of pistol grip
Internal safety	: locking

CHARACTERISTICS
- material : steel
- finish : blued, bare metal engraved breech pivot with side-locking
- stock : walnut

⊥

Chapuis Double Express Progress

TECHNICAL DETAILS
Calibre	: 9.3 x 74R, 7 x 65R, 8 x 57mm.
Cartridge capacity	: double-barrelled rifle
Magazine catch	: not applicable
Action	: breech-action
Locking	: breech-lock on top of pivot-breech
Weight	: 3.3kg (7lb 5oz)
Length	: 102.5cm (40⅜in)
Barrel Length	: 60cm (23⅝in)
Sight	: folding sight, suitable for telescopic sight
External safety	: sliding catch on back of pistol grip
Internal safety	: locking

CHARACTERISTICS
- material : steel
- finish : blued, bare metal engraved breech pivot with side-locking
- stock : walnut

⊥

Chapuis Double Express Progress 375 Savanna

TECHNICAL DETAILS
Calibre	: .375 H & H Mag.
Cartridge capacity	: double-barrelled rifle
Magazine catch	: not applicable
Action	: breech-action
Locking	: breech-lock on top of pivot-breech
Weight	: 3.85kg (8lb 8oz)
Length	: 109cm (43in)
Barrel Length	: 65cm (25⅛in)

Sight	: Express folding sight, suitable for telescopic sight
External safety	: sliding catch on back of pistol grip
Internal safety	: locking

CHARACTERISTICS
- material : steel
- finish : blued, bare metal engraved breech pivot with side-locking
- stock : walnut

⊥

Chapuis Double Express Progress Imperial

TECHNICAL DETAILS
Calibre	: 9.3 x 74R, 8 x 57mm, 7 x 65R
Cartridge capacity	: double-barrelled rifle
Magazine catch	: not applicable
Action	: breech-action
Locking	: breech-lock on top of pivot-breech
Weight	: 3.3-3.3kg (7lb 1oz-7lb 4oz)
Length	: 109cm (43in)
Barrel Length	: 65cm (25⅛in)
Sight	: folding sight, suitable for telescopic sight

External safety	: sliding catch on back of pistol grip
Internal safety	: locking

CHARACTERISTICS
- material : steel
- finish : blued, bare metal engraved breech pivot with side-locking
- stock : walnut

Chapuis Gevaudan 2000 Affût (hunting rifle)

TECHNICAL DETAILS

Calibre	: 7 x 64, .300 Win. Mag.
Cartridge capacity	: 4 rounds
Magazine catch	: internal magazine
Action	: bolt-action
Locking	: 2 locking-lugs
Weight	: 3.2-3.3kg (7lb 1oz-7lb 4oz)
Length	: 113.5-118.5cm (44¾-4611/16in)
Barrel Length	: 60-65cm (23⅝-25⅝in)
Sight	: special sight for driven-game, suitable for telescopic sight
External safety	: safety catch on right, behind bolt
Internal safety	: locking, load indicator

CHARACTERISTICS
- material : steel
- finish : blued
- stock : walnut with pistol grip

Chapuis Gevaudan 2000 Battue (hunting rifle)

TECHNICAL DETAILS

Calibre	: 7 x 64, 9.3 x 62mm, .300 Win. Mag.

Cartridge capacity	: 4-5 rounds
Magazine catch	: internal magazine
Action	: bolt-action
Locking	: 2 locking-lugs
Weight	: 3.1-3.6kg (6lb14oz-8lb)
Length	: 107-113.5cm (42⅛in-44¾in)
Barrel Length	: 53-60cm (20⅞-23⅝in)
Sight	: special driven-game sight, suitable for telescopic sight
External safety	: sliding catch on back of pistol grip
Internal safety	: locking

CHARACTERISTICS
- material : steel
- finish : blued
- stock : walnut

Chapuis Gevaudan 2000 Battue Stutzen (hunting carbine)

TECHNICAL DETAILS

Calibre	: 7 x 64, 9.3 x 62mm, .300 Win. Mag.
Cartridge capacity	: 4-5 rounds
Magazine catch	: internal magazine
Action	: bolt-action
Locking	: 2 locking-lugs
Weight	: 3.1kg (6lb 14oz)
Length	: 107cm (42⅛in)
Barrel Length	: 53cm (20⅞in)
Sight	: special sight for driven-game, suitable for telescopic sight
External safety	: sliding catch on back of pistol grip
Internal safety	: locking

CHARACTERISTICS
- material : steel
- finish : blued
- stock : walnut, running full length under barrel, with pistol grip

Chapuis Oural Luxe

TECHNICAL DETAILS

Calibre	: see below
Cartridge capacity	: single shot
Magazine catch	: not applicable
Action	: breech-action
Locking	: breech lock catch on top
Weight	: 2.8kg (6lb 3oz)
Length	: 102.5cm (40⅜in)
Barrel Length	: 60cm (23⅝in)
Sight	: folding sight, suitable for mounting telescopic sight
External safety	: sliding catch on back of pistol grip
Internal safety	: locking

CHARACTERISTICS

• material	: steel
• finish	: blued, bare metal engraved breech pivot with side-locking
• stock	: walnut

Calibres available: 6 x 62R Frères, 6.5 x 57R, 7 x 65R, .270 Win., .300 Win. Mag.

This rifle is equipped with a double-action trigger.

Colt

The Colt Manufacturing Company Inc. is based at Hartford, Connecticut, on the east coast of the United States. The company has produced firearms for more than 160 years, beginning with revolvers but adding other semi-automatic pistols at the start of the twentieth century. In 1911, Colt introduced the famous Colt model 1911 .45 ACP pistol that was designed by John Moses Browning. Many years ago, Colt made a range of rifles such as the Colt Colteer and Stagecoach carbine in .22 LR Calibre. They also made a pump-action shotgun, called the Standard Pump. These firearms have long since vanished from the company's range. The company has made a number of civilian versions of its very well-known Colt M-16 automatic army rifle with the designation AR-15. The M-16 was designed by the American weapon designer Eugene Stoner on behalf of the Armalite company. The firm was at that time a subsidiary of Fairchild Engine and Airplane, for whom Stoner was Chief Engineer. Colt took over the production in 1959. During the Vietnam War, the M-16 was also produced by Harrington & Richardson, and by General Motors. About 3,440,000 Colt M-16 rifles have been made in all the versions. The current range of rifles from Colt consists of the Colt Match Target rifle in seven different versions. This is an adapted civilian version of the M-16 army rifle. The Colt Match Target is available in Calibres .223 Rem., 9mm Para., and the Russian calibre:, 7.62 x 39mm. The company introduced a double-barrelled shotgun in 1995, the Colt Armsmear.

Colt Match Target HBAR (Heavy Barrel)

TECHNICAL DETAILS

Calibre	: .223 Rem.
Cartridge capacity	: 5 rounds
Magazine catch	: magazine catch on left of magazine aperture
Action	: semi-automatic, gas-pressure
Locking	: 7-lugs rotating slide
Weight	: 8lb (3.6kg)
Length	: 39in (99.1cm)
Barrel Length	: 20in (51cm)

Sight	: adjustable folding optical sight
External safety	: safety catch on right of mechanism housing
Internal safety	: locking

CHARACTERISTICS
- material : steel
- finish : black phosphate coating
- stock : plastic

This rifle is also available for 9mm Para. or 7.62 x 39mm and in a lightweight version at 6lb 11oz (3kg).

Colt Sporter HBAR (Heavy Barrel)/Armalite

TECHNICAL DETAILS

Calibre	: .223 Rem.
Cartridge capacity	: 5, 20, or 30 rounds
Magazine catch	: magazine catch on left of magazine aperture
Action	: semi-automatic, gas-pressure
Locking	: 7-lugs rotating slide
Weight	: 7lb 8oz (3.4kg)
Length	: 39in (99.1cm)
Barrel Length	: 20in (51cm)
Sight	: adjustable folding optical sight
External safety	: safety catch on right of mechanism housing
Internal safety	: locking

CHARACTERISTICS
- material : steel
- finish : black phosphate coating
- stock : plastic

CZ

CZ is short for Ceska Zbrojovka established in the small town of Uhersky Brod, in the foothills of the Carpathian mountains in Moravia in the Czech Republic. Czechoslovakia built up an extensive armaments industry after World War I because its national army had to be equipped. Plants of Zbrojovka Brno, Ceska Zbrojovka Strakonice, and Zavody Skoda are the best-known firms in the weapons business. The first company, based at Brno was responsible for developing the light machine-gun GB-33. A production licence was sold to the British government Enfield Ordnance Factory which produced the LMG as the world famous Bren gun.

The present company of Ceska Zbrojovka, or CZ, was established in 1936 because of the threat from Nazi-Germany. A factor in choosing Uhersky Brod was that it was out of range of the German bombers. Czechoslovakia was in any event occupied by Germany. The factory was forced to produce machine-guns for the Wehrmacht between 1939 and 1945. After World War II, the country came into the Russian sphere of influence and the firm made large numbers of Kalashnikov rifles. During the sixty years that the company has been in existence in its present form, a range of pistols and rifles were also made. The company is currently the largest manufacturer of light weapons and it exports to more than seventy countries. A number of firearms, such as the CZ-75 pistol, have been used as a model by many other weapons makers who have made their own adaptation of the design. The present range includes a wide assortment of bolt-action rifles, semi-automatic pistols, shotguns, and air weapons. The products were little known during the time of the Cold War and Iron Curtain. Since then, however, CZ weapons have become enormously popular in view of their favourable price to high quality relationship.

CZ ZKM 452 2E Deluxe

TECHNICAL DETAILS

Calibre : .22 LR, .22 WMR
Cartridge capacity : 10 rounds
Magazine catch : magazine catch at front of
magazine aperture
Action : bolt-action
Locking : 2 locking-lugs
Weight : 3kg (7lb 10oz)
Length : 108.3cm (42⅝in)
Barrel Length : 57.1cm (22½in)
Sight : adjustable folding sight and
bead tunnel
External safety : safety catch behind bolt
Internal safety : locking

CHARACTERISTICS

• material : steel
• finish : blued
• stock : wood with pistol grip

CZ ZKM 452 Junior carbine

TECHNICAL DETAILS

Calibre : .22 LR, .22 WMR
Cartridge capacity : 10 rounds
Magazine catch : magazine catch at front of
magazine aperture
Action : bolt-action
Locking : 2 locking-lugs
Weight : 1.8kg (4lb)
Length : 81.7cm (32¼in)
Barrel Length : 41.2cm (16¼in)
Sight : height adjustable sight and
bead tunnel
External safety : safety catch behind bolt
Internal safety : locking

CHARACTERISTICS

• material : steel
• finish : blued
• stock : wood with pistol grip

CZ 452-2E ZKM Special

TECHNICAL DETAILS

Calibre : .22 LR, .22 WMR
Cartridge capacity : 10 rounds
Magazine catch : magazine catch at front of
magazine aperture
Action : bolt-action
Locking : 2 locking-lugs
Weight : 3kg (7lb 10oz)
Length : 108.3cm (42⅝in)
Barrel Length : 63cm (24¾in)
Sight : adjustable folding sight and
bead tunnel, mounting for
telescopic sight
External safety : safety catch behind bolt
Internal safety : locking

CHARACTERISTICS

• material : steel
• finish : blued
• stock : beech with pistol grip

CZ 452-2E ZKM Standard

TECHNICAL DETAILS

Calibre : .22 LR, .22 WMR
Cartridge capacity : 10 rounds
Magazine catch : magazine catch at front of
magazine aperture
Action : bolt-action
Locking : 2 locking-lugs
Weight : 3kg (7lb 10oz)

Length	: 108.3cm (42⅝in)
Barrel Length	: 63cm (24¾in)
Sight	: adjustable folding sight and bead tunnel, mounting for telescopic sight
External safety	: safety catch behind bolt
Internal safety	: locking

CHARACTERISTICS
- material : steel
- finish : blued
- stock : beech with pistol grip

CZ 452-2E ZKM Synthetic

TECHNICAL DETAILS
Calibre	: .22 LR, .22 WMR
Cartridge capacity	: 10 rounds
Magazine catch	: magazine catch at front of magazine aperture
Action	: bolt-action
Locking	: 2 locking-lugs
Weight	: 2.7kg (6lb)
Length	: 108.3cm (42⅝in)
Barrel Length	: 63cm (24¾in)
Sight	: adjustable folding sight and bead tunnel, mounting for telescopic sight
External safety	: safety catch behind bolt
Internal safety	: locking

CHARACTERISTICS
- material : steel
- finish : nickel-plated
- stock : plastic, with pistol grip

CZ model CZ 511

TECHNICAL DETAILS
Calibre	: .22 LR
Cartridge capacity	: 8-rounds
Magazine catch	: magazine catch at front of magazine aperture
Action	: semi-automatic

Locking	: inertia
Weight	: 2.5kg (5lb 8oz)
Length	: 98cm (38⅝in)
Barrel Length	: 56.4cm (22¼in)
Sight	: adjustable folding sight and bead tunnel, mounting for telescopic sight
External safety	: press-button safety catch behind trigger
Internal safety	: locking

CHARACTERISTICS
- material : steel
- finish : blued
- stock : beech with pistol grip

CZ model CZ 511 Lux

TECHNICAL DETAILS
Calibre	: .22 LR
Cartridge capacity	: 8-rounds
Magazine catch	: magazine catch at front of magazine aperture
Action	: semi-automatic
Locking	: inertia
Weight	: 2.5kg (5lb 8oz)
Length	: 98cm (38⅝in)
Barrel Length	: 56.4cm (22¼in)
Sight	: adjustable folding sight and bead tunnel, mounting for telescopic sight
External safety	: press-button safety catch behind trigger
Internal safety	: locking

CHARACTERISTICS
- material   : steel
- finish   : blued
- stock   : walnut with pistol grip

CZ 513 Farmer

TECHNICAL DETAILS
Calibre   : .22 LR
Cartridge capacity : 10 rounds
Magazine catch   : magazine catch at front of magazine aperture
Action   : bolt-action
Locking   : 2 locking-lugs
Weight   : 2.8kg (6lb 3oz)
Length   : 99cm (39in)
Barrel Length   : 53cm (20⅞in)
Sight   : adjustable height sight and bead tunnel
External safety   : safety catch behind bolt
Internal safety   : locking
CHARACTERISTICS
- material   : steel
- finish   : blued
- stock   : beech with pistol grip

CZ 527

TECHNICAL DETAILS
Calibre   : .22 Hornet, .222 Rem., .223 Rem.
Cartridge capacity : 5-rounds cartridge holder

Magazine catch   : on right of cartridge holder
Action   : bolt-action
Locking   : 2 locking-lugs (Mauser type)
Weight   : 2.8kg (6lb 3oz)
Length   : 107.7cm (42⅜in)
Barrel Length   : 46.2cm (18¼in)
Sight   : fixed sight and sight and bead tunnel, mounting for telescopic sight
External safety   : safety catch behind bolt
Internal safety   : locking
CHARACTERISTICS
- material   : steel
- finish   : blued
- stock   : beech with pistol grip

CZ 527 FS

TECHNICAL DETAILS
Calibre   : .22 Hornet, .222 Rem., .223 Rem.
Cartridge capacity : 5-rounds cartridge holder
Magazine catch   : on right of cartridge holder
Action   : bolt-action
Locking   : 2 locking-lugs (Mauser type)
Weight   : 2.7kg (6lb)
Length   : 98cm (38½)
Barrel Length   : 52cm (20½in)
Sight   : fixed sight and bead tunnel, mounting for telescopic sight
External safety   : safety catch to right of bolt
Internal safety   : locking
CHARACTERISTICS
- material   : steel
- finish   : blued
- stock   : beech stock runs right through under barrel, with pistol grip

CZ 527 Lux

TECHNICAL DETAILS
Calibre : .22 Hornet, .222 Rem., .223 Rem.
Cartridge capacity : 5-rounds cartridge holder
Magazine catch : on right of cartridge holder
Action : bolt-action
Locking : 2 locking-lugs (Mauser type)
Weight : 2.7kg (6lb)
Length : 107.7cm (42⅜in)
Barrel Length : 60cm (23⅝in)
Sight : fixed sight plus bead tunnel, mounting for telescopic sight
External safety : safety catch behind bolt
Internal safety : locking

CHARACTERISTICS
• material : steel
• finish : blued
• stock : walnut with pistol grip

CZ 537

TECHNICAL DETAILS
Calibre : .243 Win., .308 Win.
Cartridge capacity : 4 rounds
Magazine catch : not applicable, internal magazine

Action : bolt-action
Locking : 2 locking-lugs (Mauser type)
Weight : 3.3kg (7lb 5oz)
Length : 113.5cm (44¾in)
Barrel Length : 60cm (23⅝in)
Sight : fixed sight plus bead tunnel, mounting for telescopic sight
External safety : safety catch behind bolt
Internal safety : locking

CHARACTERISTICS
• material : steel
• finish : blued
• stock : beech with pistol grip

This rifle is also available with a removable 5-rounds cartridge holder for Calibres 6.5 x 55mm, 7 x 57mm, 7 x 64mm, and .270 Win.

CZ 537 FS

TECHNICAL DETAILS
Calibre : .243 Win., .308 Win.
Cartridge capacity : 4 rounds
Magazine catch : not applicable, internal magazine
Action : bolt-action
Locking : 2 locking-lugs (Mauser type)
Weight : 3.1kg (6lb 13oz)
Length : 105.5cm (41½in)
Barrel Length : 52cm (20½in)
Sight : fixed sight plus bead tunnel, mounting for telescopic sight
External safety : safety catch behind bolt
Internal safety : locking

CHARACTERISTICS
• material : steel
• finish : blued
• stock : beech stock continues fully under barrel, with pistol grip

This rifle is also available with a removable 5-rounds cartridge holder for calibres

6.5 x 55mm, 7 x 57mm, 7 x 64mm, and .270 Win.

CZ 537 Sport

TECHNICAL DETAILS

Calibre	: .308 Win.
Cartridge capacity	: 4 rounds
Magazine catch	: not applicable, internal magazine
Action	: bolt-action
Locking	: 2 locking-lugs (Mauser type)
Weight	: 4.7kg (10lb 6oz)
Length	: 115cm (45¼in)
Barrel Length	: 65cm (25⅝in)
Sight	: Anschütz optical sight, mounting for telescopic sight
External safety	: safety catch behind bolt
Internal safety	: locking

CHARACTERISTICS

• material	: steel
• finish	: blued
• stock	: special match stock with pistol grip

CZ 537 Sniper

TECHNICAL DETAILS

Calibre	: .308 Win.
Cartridge capacity	: 4 rounds
Magazine catch	: not applicable, internal magazine
Action	: bolt-action
Locking	: 2 locking-lugs (Mauser type)
Weight	: 5.25kg (11lb 10oz)
Length	: 115cm (45¼in)
Barrel Length	: 65cm (25⅝in)
Sight	: none, mounting for telescopic sight
External safety	: safety catch behind bolt
Internal safety	: locking

CHARACTERISTICS

• material	: steel
• finish	: blued
• stock	: special stock with pistol grip and bipod

CZ 550

TECHNICAL DETAILS

Calibre	: see below
Cartridge capacity	: 4-6 rounds
Magazine catch	: at front of magazine aperture
Action	: bolt-action
Locking	: 4 locking-lugs
Weight	: 3.3kg (7lb 5oz)
Length	: 113.5cm (44¾in)
Barrel Length	: 60cm (23⅝in)
Sight	: none, mounting for telescopic sight
External safety	: safety catch behind bolt
Internal safety	: locking

CHARACTERISTICS

• material	: steel
• finish	: blued

- stock : walnut with pistol grip

Available Calibres: .243 Win., .270 Win., .308 Win., .30-06 Spr.

CZ 550-Battue (hunting rifle)

Length : 105.5cm (41½in)
Barrel Length : 52cm (20½in)
Sight : adjustable sight and bead tunnel, mounting for telescopic sight
External safety : safety catch behind bolt
Internal safety : locking
CHARACTERISTICS
- material : steel
- finish : blued
- stock : walnut stock continues full-length under barrel, with pistol grip

Available calibres (fixed magazine): 6.5 x 55mm, .270 Win., 7 x 57mm, 7 x 64mm, .30-06 Spr., 9.3 x 62mm; (removable cartridge holder): .243 Win., .308 Win.

TECHNICAL DETAILS
Calibre : see below
Cartridge capacity : 4-6 rounds
Magazine catch : at front of magazine aperture
Action : bolt-action
Locking : 4 locking-lugs
Weight : 3.1kg (6lb 13oz)
Length : 105cm (41½in)
Barrel Length : 52cm (20½in)
Sight : special sight for driven game and bead tunnel, mounting for telescopic sight
External safety : safety catch behind bolt
Internal safety : locking
CHARACTERISTICS
- material : steel
- finish : blued
- stock : walnut with pistol grip

Available Calibres: .243 Win., .270 Win., .308 Win., ,30-06 Spr.

CZ 550-FS Battue (hunting rifle)

TECHNICAL DETAILS
Calibre : see below
Cartridge capacity : 4-6 rounds
Magazine catch : at front of magazine aperture
Action : bolt-action
Locking : 4 locking-lugs
Weight : 3.1kg (6lb 13oz)
Length : 105.5cm (41½in)
Barrel Length : 52cm (20½in)
Sight : special sight for driven game and bead tunnel, mounting for telescopic sight

CZ 550 FS

TECHNICAL DETAILS
Calibre : see below
Cartridge capacity : 4-5 rounds
Magazine catch : at front of magazine aperture
Action : bolt-action
Locking : 4 locking-lugs
Weight : 3.1kg (6lb 13oz)

External safety   : safety catch behind bolt
Internal safety   : locking
CHARACTERISTICS
• material   : steel
• finish   : blued
• stock   : walnut stock continues full-
                     length under barrel, with
                     pistol grip

Available calibre:s: .243 Win., .270 Win.,
.308 Win., .30-06 Spr.

CZ 550 Lux

TECHNICAL DETAILS
Calibre   : see below
Cartridge capacity : 4-5 rounds
Magazine catch   : at front of magazine
                     aperture
Action   : bolt-action
Locking   : 4 locking-lugs
Weight   : 3.3kg (7lb 5oz)
Length   : 113.5cm (44¾in)
Barrel Length   : 60cm (23⅝in)
Sight   : adjustable, mounting for
                     telescopic sight
External safety   : safety catch behind bolt
Internal safety   : locking
CHARACTERISTICS
• material   : steel
• finish   : blued
• stock   : walnut with pistol grip

Available calibres (fixed magazine): 6.5 x
55mm, .270 Win., 7 x 57mm, 7 x 64mm,
.30-06 Spr., 9.3 x 62mm; (removable cartridge holder): .243 Win., .308 Win.

CZ 550 Magnum

TECHNICAL DETAILS
Calibre   : see below
Cartridge capacity : 5 rounds (internal magazine)

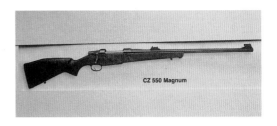

CZ 550 Magnum

Magazine catch   : at front of magazine
                     aperture
Action   : bolt-action
Locking   : 4 locking-lugs
Weight   : 4.2kg (9lb 5oz)
Length   : 118cm (46½in)
Barrel Length   : 63.5cm (25in)
Sight   : adjustable Express folding
                     sight, mounting for
                     telescopic sight
External safety   : safety catch behind bolt
Internal safety   : locking
CHARACTERISTICS
• material   : steel
• finish   : blued
• stock   : walnut with pistol grip

Available calibres (fixed magazine): 7mm
Rem. Mag., .300 Win. Mag., .375 H & H
Mag., .416 Rem. Mag., .458 Win. Mag.

CZ 550 MC

TECHNICAL DETAILS
Calibre   : see below
Cartridge capacity : 5 rounds
Magazine catch   : at front of magazine
                     aperture
Action   : bolt-action
Locking   : 4 locking-lugs
Weight   : 3.3kg (7lb 5oz)

Length	: 113.5cm (44¾in)
Barrel Length	: 60cm (23⅝in)
Sight	: folding sight and bead tunnel, mounting for telescopic sight
External safety	: safety catch behind bolt
Internal safety	: locking

CHARACTERISTICS
- material : steel
- finish : blued
- stock : walnut Monte Carlo pattern stock, with pistol grip

Available calibre:s: .270 Win., 7 x 57mm, 7 x 64mm, 6,5 x 55 SE, .30-06 Spr., 9.3 x 62mm

CZ 550 Minnesota

TECHNICAL DETAILS

Calibre	: see below
Cartridge capacity	: 4-5 rounds
Magazine catch	: at front of magazine aperture
Action	: bolt-action
Locking	: 4 locking-lugs
Weight	: 3.3kg (7lb 5oz)
Length	: 113.5cm (44¾in)
Barrel Length	: 60cm (23⅝in)
Sight	: none, mounting for telescopic sight
External safety	: safety catch behind bolt
Internal safety	: locking

CHARACTERISTICS
- material : steel
- finish : blued
- stock : walnut with pistol grip

Available calibres (fixed magazine): 6.5 x 55mm, .270 Win., 7 x 57mm, 7 x 64mm, .30-06 Spr., 9.3 x 62mm; (removable cartridge holder): .243 Win., .308 Win.

CZ 550 Standard

TECHNICAL DETAILS

Calibre	: see below
Cartridge capacity	: 4-5 rounds
Magazine catch	: at front of magazine aperture
Action	: bolt-action
Locking	: 4 locking-lugs
Weight	: 3.3kg (7lb 5oz)
Length	: 113.5cm (44¾in)
Barrel Length	: 60cm (23⅝in)
Sight	: none, mounting for telescopic sight
External safety	: safety catch behind bolt
Internal safety	: locking

CHARACTERISTICS
- material : steel
- finish : blued
- stock : walnut with pistol grip

Available calibres (fixed magazine): 6.5 x 55mm, .270 Win., 7 x 57mm, 7 x 64mm, .30-06 Spr., 9.3 x 62mm; (removable cartridge holder): .243 Win., .308 Win.

CZ ZKK 600

TECHNICAL DETAILS

Calibre	: see below
Cartridge capacity	: 5 rounds
Magazine catch	: push-button at front of trigger guard
Action	: bolt-action
Locking	: 2 locking-lugs (Mauser type)
Weight	: 3.25kg (7lb 3oz)

Length	: 111cm (43¾in)
Barrel Length	: 60cm (23⅝in)
Sight	: fixed sight plus bead tunnel, mounting for telescopic sight
External safety	: safety catch behind bolt
Internal safety	: locking

CHARACTERISTICS

• material	: steel
• finish	: blued
• stock	: wood with pistol grip

Available calibre:s: 6.5 x 55mm, 7 x 57mm, 7 x 64mm, .270 Win., .30-06 Spr.

CZ ZKK 601

TECHNICAL DETAILS

Calibre	: .243 Win., .308 Win.
Cartridge capacity	: 5 rounds
Magazine catch	: not applicable
Action	: bolt-action
Locking	: 2 locking-lugs (Mauser type)
Weight	: 3.25kg (7lb 3oz)
Length	: 109.5cm (43⅛in)
Barrel Length	: 60cm (23⅝in)
Sight	: fixed sight plus bead tunnel, mounting for telescopic sight
External safety	: safety catch behind bolt
Internal safety	: locking

CHARACTERISTICS

• material	: steel
• finish	: blued
• stock	: walnut with pistol grip

CZ ZKK 602

TECHNICAL DETAILS

Calibre	: .375 H & H, .458 Win. Mag.
Cartridge capacity	: 4 rounds

Magazine catch	: push-button at rear of magazine aperture
Action	: bolt-action
Locking	: 4 locking-lugs
Weight	: 4.2kg (9lb 5oz)
Length	: 115cm (45⅞in)
Barrel Length	: 63.5cm (25in)
Sight	: 3 position adjustable Express sight and bead tunnel, mounting for telescopic sight
External safety	: safety catch behind bolt
Internal safety	: locking

CHARACTERISTICS

• material	: steel
• finish	: blued
• stock	: wood with pistol grip

CZ ZKK 611

TECHNICAL DETAILS

Calibre	: .22 WMR
Cartridge capacity	: 6 rounds
Magazine catch	: in front of trigger guard
Action	: semi-automatic
Locking	: inertia
Weight	: 2.8kg (6lb 3oz)
Length	: 99cm (39in)
Barrel Length	: 51cm (20in)
Sight	: adjustable folding sight and bead tunnel, mounting for telescopic sight
External safety	: push-button safety catch above trigger guard
Internal safety	: locking

CHARACTERISTICS

• material	: steel
• finish	: blued
• stock	: walnut with pistol grip

Daewoo

The Korean armaments factory of Daewoo Precision Industries Ltd in Seoul is part of the massive conglomerate Daewoo. The parent company has a wide industrial base that includes machinery, shipbuilding, aerospace, and a major car industry. Daewoo make both pistols and rifles. The DR200 rifle in .223 Rem. calibre that was brought out in 1985 is a remarkable combination of the technology from both the Colt M-16 and the AK-47 rifles. This rifle is mainly exported to North America. The company plan to bring out a version in the Russian 7.62 x 39mm calibre: in 1997. Daewoo is not a newcomer to weapons manufacture and has made light arms for over fifteen years. Among their first models were the Max-1 and Max-2 in .223 Rem. Ca-libre. Max-1 has a telescopic sight, while Max-2 has a collapsible stock. All Daewoo weapons utilize the AR-15/Colt M-16 cartridge holders. The Daewoo AR-110 rifle in .223 Rem. calibre: was brought out in 1985.

Daewoo DR 200 rifle

TECHNICAL DETAILS

Calibre	: .223 Rem.
Cartridge capacity	: 5, 10, or 20 rounds AR-15 cartridge holders
Magazine catch	: right-hand side of mechanism housing
Action	: semi-automatic, gas-pressure (Colt system)
Locking	: Colt rotation locking
Weight	: 4.1kg (9lb)
Length	: 99.6cm (39¼in)
Barrel Length	: 46.5cm (18¼in)
Sight	: military optical sight and bead tunnel, mounting for telescopic sight available

External safety	: doubled-sided safety catch on mechanism housing above pistol grip
Internal safety	: locking

CHARACTERISTICS

• material	: steel and light metal
• finish	: matt black phosphate coated
• stock	: plastic with pistol grip and thumb-hole

The rifle is supplied without cartridge holders, but is suitable for all Colt and Armalite .223 Rem. cartridge holders.

Dakota

The way in which the Dakota firearms firm came into being is somewhat unusual. Its founder, American Don Allen, worked as a pilot with Northwest Airlines until 1984. He had been building rifles in his spare time, based upon the Winchester model 70. When he retired from the airline in 1984, he and his wife set up Dakota Arms Inc., based at Sturgis, South Dakota. The first gun that Allen put into production was the Dakota model 76 bolt-action rifle, that he introduced in 1987. Allen has developed six different rifle calibres for hunting medium-size to large game. These special calibres are described in the chapter on ammunition. Dakota seek to build their rifles so that a grouping of 5 rounds on target at 100m (109yds) is not greater than 38mm (1½in).

Dakota 10 Single Shot

TECHNICAL DETAILS

Calibre	: any calibre: requested
Cartridge capacity	: single shot
Magazine catch	: not applicable
Action	: trigger-guard lever-action
Locking	: drop-block locking
Weight	: 6lb (2.7kg)
Length	: 44in (118.8cm)
Barrel Length	: 23in (58.4cm)
Sight	: none, or fixed sight plus bead tunnel, suitable for mounting telescopic sight
External safety	: safety catch on back of stock near pistol grip
Internal safety	: locking

CHARACTERISTICS

• material	: steel
• finish	: blued
• stock	: walnut

Dakota model 22 Sporter

TECHNICAL DETAILS

Calibre	: .22 LR
Cartridge capacity	: 5-rounds cartridge holder
Magazine catch	: front of trigger guard
Action	: bolt-action
Locking	: 2-lugs locking
Weight	: 6lb 8oz (3kg)
Length	: 41in (104.1cm)
Barrel Length	: 22in (55.9cm)
Sight	: none, suitable for mounting telescopic sight
External safety	: winged safety catch behind bolt
Internal safety	: locking

CHARACTERISTICS

• material	: steel
• finish	: blued
• stock	: walnut

Dakota model 76 African Grade

TECHNICAL DETAILS

Calibre	: see below
Cartridge capacity	: 4 rounds
Magazine catch	: front of trigger guard
Action	: bolt-action
Locking	: 2-lugs locking
Weight	: 9lb 8oz (4.3kg)
Length	: 44in (118.8cm)
Barrel Length	: 24in (61cm)
Sight	: Express folding sight, suitable for mounting telescopic sight
External safety	: winged safety catch behind bolt
Internal safety	: locking

CHARACTERISTICS

• material	: steel
• finish	: blued
• stock	: specially selected walnut English stock

Calibres available (long Magnum bolt): .300 H & H Mag., .375 H & H Mag., .404 Jeffery, .416 Dakota, .416 Rigby, .416 Rem., .450 Dakota

Dakota model 76 Classic Grade

TECHNICAL DETAILS

Calibre	: see below
Cartridge capacity	: 3-5 rounds
Magazine catch	: front of trigger guard
Action	: bolt-action
Locking	: 2-lugs locking
Weight	: 7lb 8oz (3.4kg)
Length	: 41-43in (104.1-109.2cm)
Barrel Length	: 21-23in (53.3-58.4cm)
Sight	: none, suitable for mounting telescopic sight
External safety	: winged safety catch behind bolt
Internal safety	: locking

CHARACTERISTICS

• material	: steel
• finish	: blued
• stock	: specially selected walnut English stock

Calibres available (short bolt): .220 Swift, .22-250 Rem., .243 Win., 6mm Rem., .250-3000 Savage, .257 Roberts, 7mm-08 Rem., .308 Win; (standard bolt): .257 Roberts, .25-06 Rem., .270 Win., 7 x 57mm, .280 Rem., .30-06 Spr., .35 Whelen; (short Magnum bolt): 7mm Dakota, 7mm Rem. Mag., .300 Dakota, .300 Win. Mag., .330 Dakota, .338 Win. Mag., .375 Dakota, .458 Win. Mag.; (long Magnum bolt): .300 H & H Mag., .375 H & H Mag., .416 Rem.

Dakota model 76 Safari Grade

TECHNICAL DETAILS

Calibre	: see below
Cartridge capacity	: 3-5 rounds
Magazine catch	: front of trigger guard
Action	: bolt-action
Locking	: 2-lugs locking
Weight	: 8lb 8oz (3.9kg)
Length	: 43in (109.2cm)
Barrel Length	: 23in (58.4cm)
Sight	: fixed sight plus bead tunnel, suitable for mounting telescopic sight
External safety	: winged safety catch behind bolt
Internal safety	: locking

CHARACTERISTICS

• material	: steel
• finish	: blued
• stock	: specially selected walnut

Calibres available (short bolt): (standard bolt): .257 Roberts, .25-06 Rem., .270 Win., 7 x 57mm, .280 Rem., .30-06 Spr., .35 Whelen; (short Magnum bolt): 7mm Dakota, 7mm Rem. Mag., .300 Dakota, .300 Win. Mag., .330 Dakota, .338 Win. Mag., .375 Dakota, .458 Win. Mag.; (long Magnum bolt): .300 H & H Mag., .375 H & H Mag., .416 Rem.

Dakota model 76 Varmint Rifle

TECHNICAL DETAILS

Calibre : see below
Cartridge capacity : single shot
Magazine catch : not applicable
Action : bolt-action
Locking : 2-lugs locking
Weight : 8lb (3.6kg)
Length : 44in (118.8cm)
Barrel Length : 24in (61cm)
Sight : none, suitable for mounting telescopic sight
External safety : winged safety catch behind bolt
Internal safety : locking

CHARACTERISTICS

• material : steel receiver, chrome-molybdenum barrel
• finish : blued receiver, bare metal, untreated barrel
• stock : walnut

Available calibres (short bolt): .17 Rem., .22 PPC, .22 BR, .220 Swift, .222 Rem., 6mm PPS-Sako, 6mm BR, .223 Rem., .22-250 Rem.

Erma

The German Erma company (short for Erfurter Maschinenfabrik) is located at Dachau near Munich, in Bavaria. The company was founded in Erfurt in 1922 and was originally known as Erma-Werke B. Geipel GmbH after its founder.

A well-known product from the company is the Erma MP-40 machine-pistol. The factory was shut down by the allies at the end of the War in 1945. The present company was set up in 1949 and it moved to Dachau in 1952. In the early years of its existence, the company made firearm parts for the troops occupying Germany. When the new German army was created, the factory received orders to make armoured shields for fire-guidance systems. The company's business also flourished in the field of target shooting firearms. At first, the company only produced small-bore weapons of famous pistols, such as the Luger P08 and various small-calibre versions of the Walther PP and PPK. Their .22 LR calibre version of the famous .30-M1 Winchester carbine was a great commercial success. The company subsequently introduced a range of pistols with a style of their own, such as the Erma ESP-85.

In addition to the small-bore M1 carbine, Erma manufacture several lever-action repeating carbines.

Erma EG 712 carbine

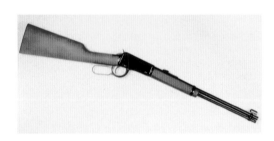

TECHNICAL DETAILS

Calibre : .22 LR
Cartridge capacity : 15 rounds
Magazine catch : not applicable, tubular magazine under barrel
Action : lever-action
Locking : lever-action
Weight : 2.4kg (5lb 5oz)
Length : 91cm (35⅞in)
Barrel Length : 47cm (18½in)
Sight : height adjustable sight plus bead tunnel, mounting for telescopic sight
External safety : none
Internal safety : locking, half-cock on hammer

CHARACTERISTICS

• material : steel barrel, light metal mechanism housing
• finish : blued
• stock : beech

Erma EG 712-Luxus carbine

TECHNICAL DETAILS

Calibre : .22 LR
Cartridge capacity : 15 rounds
Magazine catch : not applicable, tubular magazine under barrel

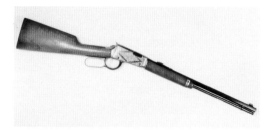

Action	: lever-action
Locking	: lever-action
Weight	: 2.4kg (5lb 5oz)
Length	: 91cm (35⅞in)
Barrel Length	: 47cm (18½in)
Sight	: height adjustable sight plus bead tunnel, mounting for telescopic sight
External safety	: none
Internal safety	: locking, half-cock on hammer

CHARACTERISTICS

- material : steel barrel, light metal mechanism housing
- finish : nickel-silver plated and engraved mechanism housing
- stock : walnut

Erma EG 712-MV carbine

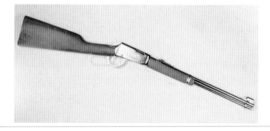

TECHNICAL DETAILS

Calibre	: .22 LR
Cartridge capacity	: 15 rounds
Magazine catch	: not applicable, tubular magazine under barrel
Action	: lever-action
Locking	: lever-action
Weight	: 2.4kg (5lb 5oz)
Length	: 91cm (35⅞in)
Barrel Length	: 47cm (18½in)
Sight	: height adjustable sight plus bead tunnel, mounting for telescopic sight
External safety	: none
Internal safety	: locking, half-cock on hammer

CHARACTERISTICS

- material : steel barrel, light metal mechanism housing

• finish	: matt nickel-plated (stainless-steel appearance)
• stock	: beech

Erma EG 722 carbine

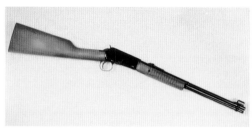

TECHNICAL DETAILS

Calibre	: .22 LR
Cartridge capacity	: 15 rounds
Magazine catch	: not applicable, tubular magazine under barrel
Action	: pump-action repeater
Locking	: horizontal slide
Weight	: 2.4kg (5lb 5oz)
Length	: 91cm (35⅞in)
Barrel Length	: 47cm (18½in)
Sight	: height adjustable sight plus bead tunnel, mounting for telescopic sight
External safety	: none
Internal safety	: locking, half-cock on hammer

CHARACTERISTICS

- material : steel barrel, light metal mechanism housing
- finish : blued
- stock : beech

Erma EGM-1 carbine

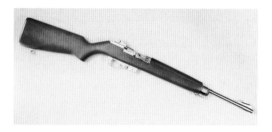

TECHNICAL DETAILS

Calibre	: .22 LR
Cartridge capacity	: 5,10, or15 rounds
Magazine catch	: in front of magazine aperture
Action	: semi-automatic

Locking	: inertia
Weight	: 2.9kg (6lb 14oz)
Length	: 90cm (35½in)
Barrel Length	: 45cm (17¾in)
Sight	: military optical sight, mounting for telescopic sight
External safety	: safety catch on right front of trigger guard (.30-M1 type)
Internal safety	: locking

CHARACTERISTICS

• material	: steel barrel, light metal mechanism housing
• finish	: matt nickel-plated (stainless-steel appearance)
• stock	: beech carbine stock

This carbine is a small-bore version of the Winchester .30-M1 carbine.

Erma EGM-1-Sport

TECHNICAL DETAILS

Calibre	: .22 LR
Cartridge capacity	: 2 or 5 rounds
Magazine catch	: in front of magazine aperture
Action	: semi-automatic
Locking	: inertia
Weight	: 3kg (6lb 10oz)
Length	: 94cm (37in)
Barrel Length	: 45cm (17¾in)
Sight	: adjustable military optical sight, mounting for telescopic sight
External safety	: safety catch on right front of trigger guard (.30-M1 type)
Internal safety	: locking

CHARACTERISTICS

• material	: steel barrel, light metal mechanism housing
• finish	: matt nickel-plated (stainless-steel appearance)
• stock	: laminated with thumb-hole and pistol grip

Erma EGM-1-Sport Special

TECHNICAL DETAILS

Calibre	: .22 LR
Cartridge capacity	: 2 or 5 rounds
Magazine catch	: in front of magazine aperture
Action	: semi-automatic
Locking	: inertia
Weight	: 3kg (6lb 10oz)
Length	: 94cm (37in)
Barrel Length	: 45cm (17¾in)
Sight	: mounting for telescopic sight, telescopic sight
External safety	: safety catch on right front of trigger guard (.30-M1 type)
Internal safety	: locking

CHARACTERISTICS

• material	: steel barrel, light metal mechanism housing
• finish	: matt nickel-plated (stainless-steel appearance)
• stock	: laminated with thumb-hole and pistol grip

Erma EM-1

TECHNICAL DETAILS

Calibre	: .22 LR
Cartridge capacity	: 5, 10, or 15 rounds
Magazine catch	: in front of magazine aperture
Action	: semi-automatic
Locking	: inertia
Weight	: 2.9kg (6lb 14oz)
Length	: 94cm (37in)
Barrel Length	: 45cm (17¾in)

Sight	: military optical sight, mounting for telescopic sight
External safety	: safety catch on right front of trigger guard (.30-M1 type)
Internal safety	: locking

CHARACTERISTICS

• material	: steel barrel, light metal mechanism housing
• finish	: blued
• stock	: beech carbine stock

Erma ESG-22

TECHNICAL DETAILS

Calibre	: .22 WMR
Cartridge capacity	: 2 or 5 rounds
Magazine catch	: in front of magazine aperture
Action	: semi-automatic
Locking	: inertia
Weight	: 3kg (6lb 10oz)
Length	: 94cm (37in)
Barrel Length	: 49cm (19¼in)
Sight	: military optical sight, mounting for telescopic sight
External safety	: safety catch on right front of trigger guard (.30-M1 type)
Internal safety	: locking

CHARACTERISTICS

• material	: steel barrel, light metal mechanism housing
• finish	: blued
• stock	: walnut

Erma SR 100 marksman's rifle

TECHNICAL DETAILS

| Calibre | : see below |
| Cartridge capacity | : 10, 8, or 5 rounds respectively |

Magazine catch	: at right in front of stock
Action	: bolt-action
Locking	: 3-lugs locking
Weight	: 6.4-6.9kg (14lb 6oz-15lb 3oz)
Length	: 126-136cm (49⅝in-53½in)
Barrel Length	: 65-75cm (25⅝-29½in)
Sight	: none, mounting for telescopic sight
External safety	: winged safety catch at rear of bolt
Internal safety	: locking, drop-out safety system

CHARACTERISTICS

• material	: steel, aluminium alloy breech
• finish	: blued matt
• stock	: special open-formed laminated stock, with bipod

Available calibres: .308 Win., .300 Win. Mag., .338 Lapua Mag.
This marksman's rifle has interchangeable barrels to change calibre. The trigger is fully adjustable.

Fanzoj

The area surrounding Ferlach in Austria has been renowned for making arms since the sixteenth century. Previously, military guns were mainly produced. For the past two hundred years, the emphasis has been on small-scale production and hand-crafted hunting rifles of very high quality. Fanzoj specialise in making rifles that are not in the ranges of other manufacturers. Their trio of rifles provide a rare specimen of craftsmanship. Close attention is given to every little detail and great care is taken in the quality of the finish which can withstand the most critical appraisal.

Fanzoj Carpathian rifle

TECHNICAL DETAILS

| Calibre | : 7 x 65R |
| Cartridge capacity | : single round |

Magazine catch	: not applicable
Action	: breech-action
Locking	: special double-sided breech lock with barrel catch
Weight	: 3.8kg (7lb 8oz)
Length	: 118cm (46½in)
Barrel Length	: 65cm (25½in)
Sight	: fixed sights, special clip-on mount for telescopic sight
External safety	: slider safety catch at rear of breech lock
Internal safety	: locking

CHARACTERISTICS

• material	: steel
• finish	: blued with engraved bare metal side panels
• stock	: walnut

This rifle is equipped with Holland & Holland type side locks.

Fanzoj Triple-Express rifle

TECHNICAL DETAILS

Calibre	: see below
Cartridge capacity	: 1 round per barrel
Magazine catch	: not applicable
Action	: breech-action
Locking	: special double-sided breech lock with barrel catch
Weight	: 4.5kg (10lb)
Length	: 107cm (42in)
Barrel Length	: 61cm (24in)
Sight	: fixed sights, special clip-on mount for telescopic sight

External safety	: slider safety catch at rear of breech lock; selector switch for choice of barrel
Internal safety	: locking

CHARACTERISTICS

• material	: steel
• finish	: blued with engraved bare metal side panels
• stock	: walnut

Calibres (top barrel): .22 Hornet; (centre barrel): 6.5 x 57R; (bottom barrel): 9.3 x 74R

The three barrels, placed above each other, can be clearly seen from the detailed illustration. At the top of the barrels block can be seen the double-sided robust locking lugs.

Fanzoj Double-Express rifle

TECHNICAL DETAILS

Calibre	: .470 Nitro Express
Cartridge capacity	: 1 round per barrel
Magazine catch	: not applicable
Action	: breech-action

Locking	: barrel catch and conical upper notch (doll's head)
Weight/Length	: 4.5kg (10lb)/107cm (42in)
Barrel Length	: 61cm (24in)
Sight	: Express folding sights
External safety	: slider safety catch at rear of breech lock
Internal safety	: locking

CHARACTERISTICS

• material	: steel
• finish	: blued with engraved bare metal side panels
• stock	: selected walnut

The detailed illustration shows the additional locking piece on the top of the barrels. The extended upper rim has a conical lug or doll's head. This engages precisely with the upper edge of the pivot breech. The precision required to machine this to fine tolerances is very costly.

Fanzoj Double-Express Side-Lock rifle

TECHNICAL DETAILS

Calibre	: 8 x 75RS

Cartridge capacity	: 1 round per barrel
Magazine catch	: not applicable
Action	: breech-action
Locking	: barrel catch and conical upper notch (doll's head)
Weight	: 4.5kg (10lb)
Length	: 107cm (42in)
Barrel Length	: 61cm (24in)
Sight	: Express folding sights
External safety	: slider safety catch at rear of breech lock
Internal safety	: locking

CHARACTERISTICS

• material	: steel
• finish	: blued with engraved bare metal side panels
• stock	: selected walnut

This rifle is equipped with the famous Holland & Holland side lock.

Fanzoj Ischl
Short-rifle or Carpathian rifle

TECHNICAL DETAILS

Calibre	: 6.5 x 57R, other calibres available on request
Cartridge capacity	: single shot
Magazine catch	: not applicable
Action	: breech-action
Locking	: barrel catch and conical top lug (doll's head)
Weight	: 2.7kg (4lb 7oz)
Length	: 103cm (40½in)
Barrel Length	: 60cm (23⅝in)
Sight	: none, special clip-on mounting for telescopic sight
External safety	: none
Internal safety	: locking, half-cock on external hammer

CHARACTERISTICS

• material	: steel
• finish	: blued, engraved bare metal side panels
• stock	: walnut stock runs through under barrel to muzzle

Feg

Hungary formed part of the Austrian empire until 1918. Famous firearms such as the Frommer-Stop pistol originate from this period.

After World War II, Hungary became a part of the eastern-block. The Hungarian weapon and machinery fac-tory of Feg is in Budapest. Feg stands for Fegyver es Gazkeszuelekgyara. The company pro-duced a range of pistols based on the FN-Browning High Power for many years.

The original design can be traced back to John Moses Browning but the Hungarian engineers have added modern improve-ments, such as a double-action trigger sys-tem. Feg is less well-known for rifles. They mainly manufacture rifles which bear other's names for foreign importers. During the time of the eastern block, Feg made Russian AK-47 rifles for the Warsaw pact forces, and also the Dragunov Rus-sian sniper's rifle.

Feg-KBI model SA-85M

TECHNICAL DETAILS

Calibre	: 7.62 x 39mm
Cartridge capacity	: 6 or 30 rounds cartridge hol-der
Magazine catch	: front of magazine aperture
Action	: semi-automatic, gas-pressure
Locking	: rotating slide
Weight	: 3.5kg (7lb 10oz)
Length	: 88.1cm (34¾in)
Barrel Length	: 41.4cm (16¼in)
Sight	: adjustable rack sight
External safety	: safety catch on right of mechanism housing
Internal safety	: locking

CHARACTERISTICS

• material	: steel
• finish	: blued
• stock	: light-coloured hardwood stock with pistol grip and thumb-hole

This rifle is a replica of the AK-47.

Feinwerkbau (FWB)

The German company Feinwerkbau, or FWB, was established in the nineteenth century. It too, in common with the other German armaments companies, was for-ced to shut down at the end of World War II but this was a major blow to the small town of Oberndorf am Neckar in Baden-Württemberg because suddenly almost everyone in the town became un-employed. The present company was re-started in 1948 by the engineers, Karl Westinger and Ernst Altenburger so the name was expanded to Feinwerkbau Wes-tinger & Altenburger GmbH. Initially, the new firm made office equipment and accountancy machines, adding machine-ry for the car and textile industries a little later. In 1959, they started to make air weapons and FWB air weapons have become a by-word in the target-shooting world. The first small-bore rifle was intro-duced in the late 1970s, leading to today's range of high-quality small-bore match rifles.

Feinwerkbau model 2602 Super Match

TECHNICAL DETAILS

Calibre	: .22 LR
Cartridge capacity	: single shot
Magazine catch	: not applicable
Action	: bolt-action
Locking	: 2-lugs bolt

Weight	: 6.3kg (13lb 14oz)
Length	: 124cm (48¾in)
Barrel Length	: 42.5cm (16¾in)
Sight	: optical sight and bead tunnel
External safety	: safety catch on right of receiver by bolt
Internal safety	: locking

CHARACTERISTICS

• material	: steel, light metal barrel cover
• finish	: blued
• stock	: special adjustable match stock with shoulder grip

◎

Feinwerkbau model 2602 Universal

TECHNICAL DETAILS

Calibre	: .22 LR
Cartridge capacity	: single shot
Magazine catch	: not applicable
Action	: bolt-action
Locking	: 2-lugs bolt
Weight	: 5kg (11lb)
Length	: 114cm (44⅞in)
Barrel Length	: 42.5cm (16¾in)
Sight	: optical sight and bead tunnel
External safety	: safety catch on right of receiver by bolt
Internal safety	: locking

CHARACTERISTICS

• material	: steel, light metal barrel cover
• finish	: blued
• stock	: special adjustable match stock with shoulder grip

◎

Frankonia

The German company Waffen-Frankonia was established by Nikolaus Hofmann in Würzburg in Bavaria in 1907. His son joined the business in 1939. The small rifle maker grew in the course of the years into a major armaments company. The firm was laid flat by bombing in 1945. In 1956, the business was restarted with eighty employees. Since that time, Frankonia has established itself through a large network of well-stocked gun shops throughout Germany. Many of these branches were acquired by taking over existing gun traders such as Jagerhuis in Darmstadt who were acquired in 1957. A second outlet was taken over in Munich in 1969, and in the 1970s the company changed its name to Frankonia-Jagd. Most of the shops have a small gunsmith's workshop where repairs and minor adaptations can be carried out. In the past decade, the company has started to expand elsewhere in Europe with subsidiaries in France, Denmark, Belgium, and the Czech Republic. The company also operates a large mail order business based in Würzburg dealing in weapons, ammunition, accessories, and everything for hunting and shooting, including clothing. The firm still has its own works making rifles that can customize rifles to a customer's requirements, including engraving. The company also trains new gunsmiths. With the Mauser 98 system at their heart, Frankonia produces an excellent range of rifles under the name Frankonia Favorit.

Frankonia Favorit de Luxe

TECHNICAL DETAILS

Calibre	: see below
Cartridge capacity	: 5 rounds (standard), 3 rounds (Magnum)
Magazine catch	: not applicable, fixed magazine
Action	: bolt-action
Locking	: 2-lugs bolt (Mauser 98)
Weight	: 3.3kg (7lb 5oz)
Length	: 113-118cm (44½-46½in)
Barrel Length	: 60-65cm (23⅝-25⅝in)
Sight	: adjustable sight
External safety	: winged safety catch at rear of bolt (Mauser system)
Internal safety	: locking

CHARACTERISTICS

- material : Action:steel, barrel: chrome-vanadium steel
- finish : blued
- stock : special walnut stock with pistol grip

Available calibres (standard): 6.5 x 57, 6 x 62 Fräres, 7 x 57, 7 x 64, 7.5 Swiss, 8 x 57 IS, .243 Win., .270 Win., .308 Win., .30-06 Spr., 9.3 x 62; (Magnum): 6.5 x 68, 7mm Rem. Mag., 8 x 68S, .300 Win. Mag.

Frankonia Favorit Drückjagd (driven game)

TECHNICAL DETAILS

Calibre:see below

Cartridge capacity	: 5 rounds (standard), 3 rounds (Magnum)
Magazine catch	: not applicable, fixed magazine
Action	: bolt-action
Locking	: 2-lugs bolt (Mauser 98)
Weight	: 3.1kg (6lb 13oz)
Length	: 104cm (41in)
Barrel Length	: 52cm (20½in)
Sight	: special sight for driven game and bead tunnel
External safety	: winged safety catch at rear of bolt (Mauser system)
Internal safety	: locking

CHARACTERISTICS

- material : Action:steel, barrel: chrome-vanadium steel
- finish : blued
- stock : walnut with pistol grip

Available calibres (standard): 7 x 64, .308 Win., .30-06 Spr., 8 x 57 IS, 9.3 x 62; (Magnum): .300 Win. Mag.

Frankonia Favorit Safari

TECHNICAL DETAILS

Calibre	: see below
Cartridge capacity	: 3 rounds
Magazine catch	: not applicable, fixed magazine
Action	: bolt-action
Locking	: 2-lugs bolt (Mauser 98)
Weight	: 3.6kg (7lb 14oz)
Length	: 118cm (46½in)
Barrel Length	: 65cm (25⅝in)
Sight	: adjustable sight
External safety	: winged safety catch at rear of bolt (Mauser system)
Internal safety	: locking

CHARACTERISTICS

- material : Action: steel, barrel:chrome-vanadium steel
- finish : blued
- stock : walnut with pistol grip

Available calibres 8 x 68 S, 9.3 x 64, .375 H & H, .338 Win. Mag., .458 Win. Mag.

Frankonia Favorit Standard

TECHNICAL DETAILS

Calibre	: see below
Cartridge capacity	: 5 rounds (standard), 3 rounds (Magnum)
Magazine catch	: not applicable, fixed magazine

Action	: bolt-action
Locking	: 2-lugs bolt (Mauser 98)
Weight	: 3.3kg (7lb 5oz)
Length	: 113-118cm (44½-46½in)
Barrel Length	: 60cm (23⅝in) standard;
	65cm (25⅝in) Magnum
Sight	: adjustable sight
External safety	: winged safety catch at rear
	of bolt (Mauser system)
Internal safety	: locking

CHARACTERISTICS

• material	: Action:steel, barrel: chrome-
	vanadium steel
• finish	: blued
• stock	: walnut with pistol grip

Available calibres (standard): 6.5 x 57, 6 x 62 Fräres, 7 x 57, 7 x 64, 7.5 Swiss, 8 x 57 IS, .243 Win., .270 Win., .308 Win., .30-06 Spr., 9.3 x 62; (Magnum): 6.5 x 68, 7mm Rem. Mag., 8 x 68S, .300 Win. Mag.

Frankonia Favorit Stützen (hunting carbine)

TECHNICAL DETAILS

Calibre	: see below
Cartridge capacity	: 5 rounds
Magazine catch	: not applicable,
	fixed magazine
Action	: bolt-action
Locking	: 2-lugs bolt (Mauser 98)
Weight	: 3.4kg (7lb 8oz)
Length	: 104cm (41in)
Barrel Length	: 52cm (20½in)
Sight	: adjustable sight
External safety	: winged safety catch at rear
	of bolt (Mauser system)
Internal safety	: locking

CHARACTERISTICS

• material	: Action:steel, barrel: chrome-
	vanadium steel
• finish	: blued
• stock	: walnut stock with pistol grip
	runs under barrel to muzzle

Available calibres (standard): 6.5 x 57, .243 Win., 7 x 57, 7 x 64, 8 x 57 IS, .308 Win., .30-06 Spr., 9.3 x 62; (Magnum): .300 Win. Mag.

Frankonia Favorit Super de Luxe

TECHNICAL DETAILS

Calibre	: see below
Cartridge capacity	: 5 rounds (standard),
	3 rounds (Magnum)
Magazine catch	: not applicable, fixed
	magazine
Action	: bolt-action
Locking	: 2-lugs bolt (Mauser 98)
Weight	: 3.3kg (7lb 5oz)
Length	: 113-118cm (44½-46½in)
Barrel Length	: 60cm-65cm (23⅝-25⅝in)
Sight	: adjustable sight and
	telescopic sight
External safety	: winged safety catch at rear
	of bolt (Mauser system)
Internal safety	: locking

CHARACTERISTICS

• material	: Action:steel, barrel: chrome-
	vanadium steel
• finish	: blued
• stock	: special walnut stock with
	pistol grip

This rifle can be customized to individual requirements, including engraving and choice of telescopic sight.

Gaucher Armes

The French armaments factory of Gaucher Armes was established in 1834 by Antoine Gaucher. The company is still based in the leading French munitions town of Saint-Etienne. Up to World War I, Gaucher produced heavy calibre double-barrelled Express rifles for hunting big game. After World War II, the firm started to make lighter weapons. The current range consists of double-barrelled Express rifles, shotguns, small-bore rifles, silenced rifles, and single-shot pistols for silhouette-target shooting.

Gaucher Bivouac Double-Express

TECHNICAL DETAILS

Calibre	: 9.3 x 74R, 8 x 57 JRS, or 7 x 65R
Cartridge capacity	: 1 round per barrel
Magazine catch	: not applicable
Action	: breech-action
Locking	: double-barrel catches, Webley & Scott transverse locking
Weight	: 3.1-3.4kg (6lb 12oz-7lb 8oz)
Length	: 105cm (41⅜in)
Barrel Length	: 60cm (23⅝in)
Sight	: Express folding sight, special mounting for telescopic sight
External safety	: sliding safety catch at rear locking key
Internal safety	: locking

CHARACTERISTICS

• material	: steel
• finish	: blued, engraved bare metal side plates; this weapon has no side-locks
• stock	: walnut

Gaucher Bivouac Double-Express

Gaucher Carbine RA

TECHNICAL DETAILS

Calibre	: .22 LR
Cartridge capacity	: 9-rounds cartridge holder
Magazine catch	: at front of magazine aperture
Action	: semi-automatic
Locking	: inertia
Weight	: 2.5kg (5lb 5oz)
Length	: 102cm (40⅛in)
Barrel Length	: 50cm (19¾in)
Sight	: rack sight and bead tunnel; mounting for telescopic sight
External safety	: cocking lever is held in position in receiver
Internal safety	: locking

CHARACTERISTICS

• material	: steel

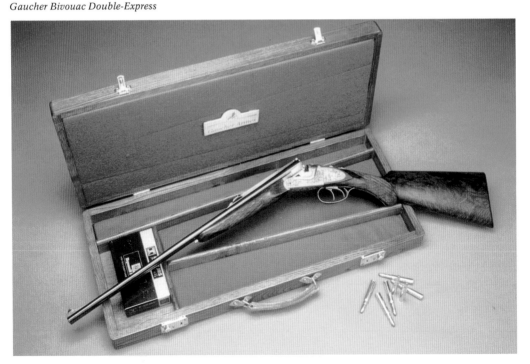

- finish : blued
- stock : hardwood

The muzzle is threaded to accept a silencer. It is unlawful to possess a silenced firearm in some countries.

Gaucher Colibri G3

TECHNICAL DETAILS

Calibre	: .22 LR
Cartridge capacity	: single shot
Magazine catch	: not applicable
Action	: bolt-action
Locking	: locking lever
Weight	: 2.2kg (4lb 14oz)
Length	: 107cm (42⅛in)
Barrel Length	: 55cm (21¾in)
Sight	: rack sight and bead tunnel; mounting for telescopic sight
External safety	: safety catch behind locking lever
Internal safety	: locking, load indicator at rear of bolt

CHARACTERISTICS

- material : steel
- finish : blued, nickel-plated bolt
- stock : hardwood

Gaucher Gazelle GR

TECHNICAL DETAILS

Calibre	: .22 LR
Cartridge capacity	: 9-rounds cartridge holder
Magazine catch	: at front of magazine aperture
Action	: bolt-action
Locking	: locking lever
Weight	: 2.5kg (5lb 8oz)
Length	: 107cm (42⅛in)
Barrel Length	: 55cm (21¾in)
Sight	: rack sight and bead tunnel; mounting for telescopic sight
External safety	: safety catch behind locking lever
Internal safety	: locking, load indicator at rear of bolt

CHARACTERISTICS

- material : steel
- finish : blued
- stock : hardwood

The muzzle is threaded to accept a silencer. It is unlawful to possess a silenced firearm in some countries.

Gaucher Gazelle GRN

TECHNICAL DETAILS

Calibre	: .22 LR
Cartridge capacity	: 9-rounds cartridge holder
Magazine catch	: at front of magazine aperture
Action	: bolt-action
Locking	: locking lever
Weight	: 2.5kg (5lb 8oz)
Length	: 107cm (42⅛in)
Barrel Length	: 55cm (21¾in)
Sight	: rack sight and bead tunnel; mounting for telescopic sight
External safety	: safety catch behind locking lever
Internal safety	: locking, load indicator at rear of bolt

CHARACTERISTICS
- material : steel
- finish : blued
- stock : hardwood

The muzzle is threaded to accept a silencer. It is unlawful to possess a silenced firearm in some countries.

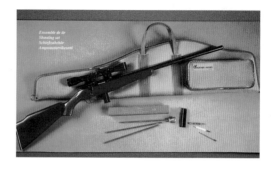

Gaucher Gazelle LSR

TECHNICAL DETAILS
Calibre : .22 LR
Cartridge capacity : 9-rounds cartridge holder
Magazine catch : at front of magazine aperture
Action : bolt-action
Locking : locking lever
Weight : 2.5kg (5lb 8oz)
Length : 107cm (42⅛in)
Barrel Length : 55cm (21¾in)
Sight : rack sight and bead tunnel; mounting for telescopic sight
External safety : safety catch behind locking lever
Internal safety : locking, load indicator at rear of bolt

CHARACTERISTICS
- material : steel
- finish : blued
- stock : hardwood stock runs full length of barrel to muzzle.

The muzzle is threaded to accept a silencer. It is unlawful to possess a silenced firearm in some countries.

Gaucher Phantom GR

TECHNICAL DETAILS
Calibre : .22 LR
Cartridge capacity : 9-rounds cartridge holder

Magazine catch : at front of magazine aperture
Action : bolt-action
Locking : locking lever
Weight : 2.5kg (5lb 8oz)
Length : 107cm (42⅛in)
Barrel Length : 58.4cm (23in)
Sight : none, supplied with 4 x 32 telescopic sight
External safety : safety catch behind locking lever
Internal safety : locking

CHARACTERISTICS
- material : steel
- finish : blued
- stock : hardwood

The muzzle is equipped with an integrated silencer. Factory data states that this reduces the sound of the shot to 47dB. It is unlawful to possess a silenced firearm in some countries.

Gaucher Star G

TECHNICAL DETAILS
Calibre : .22 LR
Cartridge capacity : single shot
Magazine catch : not applicable
Action : bolt-action
Locking : locking lever

Weight	: 2.2kg (4lb 14oz)
Length	: 107cm (42⅛in)
Barrel Length	: 55cm (21¾in)
Sight	: simple sight with height adjustment and bead tunnel, mounting for telescopic sight
External safety	: safety catch behind locking lever
Internal safety	: locking, load indicator at rear of bolt

CHARACTERISTICS

• material	: steel
• finish	: blued, nickel-plated bolt
• stock	: hardwood

The muzzle is threaded to accept a silencer. It is unlawful to possess a silenced firearm in some countries.

Gibbs

The Gibbs Rifle Company was started in 1991 by Val Foggett Jr. and it is based in Martinsburg, West Virginia in the USA. A 3,700 square metre (4,046 sq. yd) factory rose out of bare ground in under a year and the company acquired the rights to the famous Parker-Hale name from Birmingham, Great Britain, together with that of the Midland Gun Company. Gibbs started production of a range bearing both trade names. The Parker-Hale rifles are built around the Mauser 98 system while the Midland rifles are based on the 1903 Springfield. The company also makes the M-85 marksman's rifle that is used by Government organizations throughout the world. Much of the success of the company is founded on their trade in surplus army rifles, that the company refurbish before reselling.

Gibbs - Bell & Carlson Midland 1500S Survivor

TECHNICAL DETAILS

Calibre	: .308 Win
Cartridge capacity	: 5 rounds
Magazine catch	: in front of trigger guard
Action	: bolt-action
Locking	: 2-lugs locking
Weight	: 7lb (3.2kg)
Length	: 43in (109.2cm)
Barrel Length	: 22in (55.9cm)
Sight	: folding sight and bead tunnel, suitable for telescopic sight
External safety	: safety catch on right-hand side
Internal safety	: locking

CHARACTERISTICS

• material	: stainless-steel
• finish	: bare metal
• stock	: black Kevlar with pistol grip

This rifle is also available with 5-and 10-round cartridge holders like model 1500C

Gibbs Midland 2100

TECHNICAL DETAILS

Calibre	: see below
Cartridge capacity	: 5 rounds
Magazine catch	: in front of trigger guard
Action	: bolt-action
Locking	: 3-lugs locking
Weight	: 7lb (3.2kg)
Length	: 43in (109.2cm)
Barrel Length	: 22in (55.9cm) and 24in (61cm) for .22-250 Calibre
Sight	: folding sight and bead tunnel, suitable for telescopic sight
External safety	: winged safety catch on right-hand side
Internal safety	: locking

CHARACTERISTICS

• material	: steel
• finish	: blued
• stock	: walnut with pistol grip

Available calibres: .22-250 Rem. (only with 24in (61cm) barrel), .243 Win., 6mm Rem., .270 Win., 6.5 x 55mm, 7 x 57mm, 7 x 64mm, .308 Win., .30-06 Spr.

Gibbs Midland 2600

TECHNICAL DETAILS

Calibre:see below
Cartridge capacity : 5 rounds
Magazine catch : in front of trigger guard
Action : bolt-action
Locking : 3-lugs locking
Weight : 7lb (3.2kg)
Length : 43in (109.2cm)
Barrel Length : 22in (55.9cm) and 24in (61cm) for .22-250 Calibre
Sight : folding sight and bead tunnel, suitable for telescopic sight
External safety : winged safety catch on right-hand side
Internal safety : locking
CHARACTERISTICS
• material : steel
• finish : blued
• stock : hardwood with pistol grip

Available calibres: .22-250 Rem. (only with 24in (61cm) barrel), .243 Win., 6mm Rem., .270 Win., 6.5 x 55mm, 7 x 57mm, 7 x 64mm, .308 Win., .30-06 Spr.

Gibbs Midland 2700 Lightweight

TECHNICAL DETAILS

Calibre : see below
Cartridge capacity : 5 rounds

Magazine catch : in front of trigger guard
Action : bolt-action
Locking : 3-lugs locking
Weight : 6lb 8oz (3kg)
Length : 43in (109.2cm)
Barrel Length : 22in (55.9cm) and 24in (61cm) for .22-250 Calibre
Sight : folding sight and bead tunnel, suitable for telescopic sight
External safety : winged safety catch on right-hand side of bolt
Internal safety : locking
CHARACTERISTICS
• material : steel
• finish : blued
• stock : laminated with pistol grip

Available calibres: .22-250 Rem. (only with 24in (61cm) barrel), .243 Win., 6mm Rem., .270 Win., 6.5 x 55mm, 7 x 57mm, 7 x 64mm, .308 Win., .30-06 Spr.

Gibbs Midland 2800

TECHNICAL DETAILS

Calibre:see below
Cartridge capacity : 5 rounds
Magazine catch : in front of trigger guard
Action : bolt-action
Locking : 3-lugs locking
Weight : 7lb (3.2kg)
Length : 43in (109.2cm)
Barrel Length : 22in (55.9cm) and 24in (61cm) for .22-250 Calibre
Sight : folding sight and bead tunnel, suitable for telescopic sight
External safety : winged safety catch on right-hand side
Internal safety : locking
CHARACTERISTICS
• material : steel
• finish : blued
• stock : finely laminated beech with pistol grip

Available calibre:s: .22-250 Rem. (only with 24in (61cm) barrel), .243 Win.,

6mm Rem., .270 Win., 6.5 x 55mm, 7 x 57mm, 7 x 64mm, .308 Win., .30-06 Spr.

Gibbs Parker-Hale 1000 Standard

TECHNICAL DETAILS

Calibre	: see below
Cartridge capacity	: 5 rounds
Magazine catch	: in front of trigger guard
Action	: bolt-action
Locking	: 2-lugs locking (Mauser system)
Weight	: 7lb 4oz (3.3kg)
Length	: 43in (109.2cm)
Barrel Length	: 22in (55.9cm) and 24in (61cm) for .22-250 calibre
Sight	: adjustable folding sight and bead tunnel, suitable for telescopic sight
External safety	: safety catch on right behind bolt
Internal safety	: locking

CHARACTERISTICS

• material	: steel
• finish	: blued
• stock	: walnut with pistol grip

Available calibres: .22-250 Rem. (only with 24in (61cm)barrel), .243 Win., 6mm Rem., .270 Win., 6.5 x 55mm, 7 x 57mm, 7 x 64mm, .308 Win., .30-06 Spr.

Gibbs Parker-Hale 1100M African Magnum

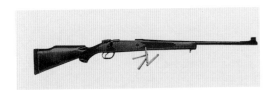

TECHNICAL DETAILS

Calibre	: .375 H & H Mag., .458 Win. Mag.

Cartridge capacity	: 4 rounds
Magazine catch	: in front of trigger guard
Action	: bolt-action
Locking	: 3-lugs locking
Weight	: 9lb 8oz (4.3kg)
Length	: 46in (116.8cm)
Barrel Length	: 24in (61cm)
Sight	: adjustable folding sight and bead tunnel, suitable for telescopic sight
External safety	: safety catch on right behind bolt
Internal safety	: locking

CHARACTERISTICS

• material	: steel
• finish	: blued
• stock	: walnut with pistol grip

Gibbs Parker-Hale 1100 Lightweight

TECHNICAL DETAILS

Calibre	: see below
Cartridge capacity	: 5 rounds
Magazine catch	: in front of trigger guard
Action	: bolt-action
Locking	: 2-lugs locking (Mauser system)
Weight	: 6lb 8oz (3kg)
Length	: 43in (109.2cm)
Barrel Length	: 22in (55.9cm) and 24in (61cm) for .22-250 Calibre
Sight	: adjustable folding sight and bead tunnel, suitable for telescopic sight
External safety	: safety catch on right behind bolt
Internal safety	: locking

CHARACTERISTICS

• material	: steel
• finish	: blued
• stock	: hardwood with pistol grip

Available calibres: .22-250 Rem. (only with 24in [61cm] barrel), .243 Win., 6mm Rem., .270 Win., 6.5 x 55mm, 7 x 57mm, 7 x 64mm, .308 Win., .30-06 Spr.

Gibbs Parker-Hale 1200 Super Clip

TECHNICAL DETAILS
Calibre : see below
Cartridge capacity : 5-rounds cartridge holder
Magazine catch : in front of trigger guard
Action : bolt-action
Locking : 2-lugs locking
Weight : 7lb 8oz (3.4kg)
Length : 44½in (113cm)
Barrel Length : 24in (61cm)
Sight : adjustable folding sight and bead tunnel, suitable for telescopic sight
External safety : safety catch on right behind bolt
Internal safety : locking

CHARACTERISTICS
• material : steel
• finish : blued
• stock : walnut with pistol grip

Available calibres: .22-250 Rem., .243 Win., 6mm Rem., .270 Win., 6.5 x 55mm, 7 x 64mm, .308 Win., .30-06 Spr.

Gibbs Parker-Hale 1300S Scout

TECHNICAL DETAILS
Calibre : .243 Win., .308 Win.
Cartridge capacity : 5 rounds (.308) or 10 rounds (.243)
Magazine catch : in front of trigger guard
Action : bolt-action (Mauser system)
Locking : 2-lugs locking
Weight : 8lb 8oz (3.9kg)
Length : 41in (104.1cm)
Barrel Length : 20in (50.8cm) including muzzle compensator
Sight : none, suitable for telescopic sight
External safety : safety catch on right behind bolt
Internal safety : locking

CHARACTERISTICS
• material : steel
• finish : blued
• stock : laminated beech with pistol grip

Gibbs Parker-Hale M81 African

TECHNICAL DETAILS
Calibre : .375 H & H Mag., 9.3 x 62mm
Cartridge capacity : 4 rounds
Magazine catch : in front of trigger guard
Action : bolt-action
Locking : 3-lugs locking
Weight : 9lb (4.1kg)
Length : 45in (114.3cm)
Barrel Length : 24in (61cm)
Sight : Express triple folding sight and bead tunnel, suitable for telescopic sight
External safety : safety catch on right behind bolt
Internal safety : locking

CHARACTERISTICS
• material : steel
• finish : blued
• stock : walnut with pistol grip

Gibbs Parker-Hale M-85 Sniper

TECHNICAL DETAILS

Calibre	: .308 Win.
Cartridge capacity	: 10 rounds
Magazine catch	: in front of trigger guard
Action	: bolt-action
Locking	: 3-lugs locking
Weight	: 12lb 10oz (5.7kg) including telescopic sight
Length	: 45in (114.3cm)
Barrel Length	: 24in (61cm)
Sight	: folding sight, suitable for telescopic sight
External safety	: safety catch on right behind bolt
Internal safety	: locking, load indicator (protruding pin) at rear of bolt

CHARACTERISTICS

• material	: steel
• finish	: blued
• stock	: glass-fibre McMillan stock with bipod in 6 different camouflage finishes (Nato green, desert, urban, black, jungle, Arctic)

Gibbs 98 Sporter

TECHNICAL DETAILS

Calibre	: see below
Cartridge capacity	: 5 rounds
Magazine catch	: not applicable, loading via breech
Action	: bolt-action
Locking	: 2-lugs locking
Weight	: 7lb 3oz (3.2kg)
Length	: 43¾in (111cm)
Barrel Length	: 22in (55.9cm)
Sight	: adjustable sight, suitable for telescopic sight
External safety	: Mauser winged safety catch at rear of bolt
Internal safety	: locking

CHARACTERISTICS

• material	: steel
• finish	: blued
• stock	: hardwood with pistol grip

Available calibres: .243 Win., .270 Win., .308 Win., .30-06 Spr.

GOL

The initial GOL stand for Gottfrieds Originelle Lösung, meaning Gottfried's original solution. The Gottfried is Gottfried Prechtl from Weinheim near Mannheim in Germany. Prechtl builds a range of precision and marksman's rifles that are based on the Mauser 98 system. His best-known rifle is the GOL Sniper that can be equipped with a wide range of different stocks. This .308 Win. calibre: rifle is capable of putting 10 rounds at 100m (109yds) within a grouping of 12-14mm (3/8-7/16in) diameter. Another famous GOL product is the StoCon skeleton stock of laminated wood. A further type of GOL rifle is the model "S" that is based on the Sako M591/L691 system. Since its introduction, one of the first three places at both national and international competitions often goes to a shooter using the Gol "S" Sniper.

GOL-Sniper Rifle
Standard Comp A model

TECHNICAL DETAILS

Calibre	: .308 Win.
Cartridge capacity	: 5 rounds
Magazine catch	: not applicable, fixed magazine
Action	: bolt-action
Locking	: 2-lugs Mauser bolt locking

Weight	: approx 5.5kg (12lb 1oz) including telescopic sight
Length	: approx 118.4cm (46⅝in)
Barrel Length	: 65cm (25⅝in) excluding muzzle compensator or flash reducer
Sight	: none, suitable for telescopic sight
External safety	: Timney trigger system with safety catch behind bolt
Internal safety	: locking

CHARACTERISTICS
- material : steel
- finish : blued
- stock : walnut with pistol grip

GOL-Rifle Standard Comp B model

TECHNICAL DETAILS

Calibre	: .308 Win.
Cartridge capacity	: 5 rounds
Magazine catch	: not applicable, fixed magazine
Action	: bolt-action
Locking	: 2-lugs Mauser bolt locking
Weight	: approx 5.5kg (12lb 1oz)
Length	: approx 118.4cm (46⅝in)
Barrel Length	: 65cm (25⅝in) excluding muzzle compensator or flash reducer
Sight	: none, suitable for telescopic sight
External safety	: Timney trigger system with safety catch behind bolt
Internal safety	: locking

CHARACTERISTICS
- material : steel

• finish	: blued
• stock	: walnut with pistol grip

GOL- Match model free rifle

TECHNICAL DETAILS

Calibre	: .308 Win.
Cartridge capacity	: 5 rounds
Magazine catch	: not applicable, fixed magazine
Action	: bolt-action
Locking	: 2-lugs Mauser bolt locking
Weight	: approx 5.5kg (12lb 1oz)
Length	: approx 118.4cm (46⅝in)
Barrel Length	: 65cm (25⅝in) excluding muzzle compensator or flash reducer
Sight	: none, suitable for telescopic sight
External safety	: Timney trigger system with safety catch behind bolt
Internal safety	: locking

CHARACTERISTICS
- material : steel
- finish : blued
- stock : laminated match stock with pistol grip and thumb-hole

GOL-Match model Comp A

TECHNICAL DETAILS

Calibre	: .308 Win.
Cartridge capacity	: single shot

Magazine catch	: not applicable
Action	: bolt-action
Locking	: 2-lugs Mauser bolt locking
Weight	: approx 5.4kg (11lb 14oz)
Length	: approx 118.4cm (46⅝in)
Barrel Length	: 65cm (25⅝in) excluding muzzle compensator or flash reducer
Sight	: none, suitable for telescopic sight
External safety	: Timney trigger system with safety catch behind bolt
Internal safety	: locking

CHARACTERISTICS

• material	: steel
• finish	: blued
• stock	: laminated match stock with pistol grip, thumb-hole, and bipod

Illustrated from top to bottom: Gol Match Comp A, Gol Match UIT, and Gol Match HV Comp B rifles.

GOL-Match UIT model

TECHNICAL DETAILS

Calibre	: .308 Win.
Cartridge capacity	: single shot
Magazine catch	: not applicable
Action	: bolt-action
Locking	: 2-lugs Mauser bolt locking
Weight	: approx 5.4kg (11lb 14oz)
Length	: approx 118.4cm (46⅝in)
Barrel Length	: 65cm (25⅝in) excluding muzzle compensator or flash reducer
Sight	: Hammerli optical sight and bead tunnel
External safety	: Timney trigger system with safety catch behind bolt
Internal safety	: locking

CHARACTERISTICS

• material	: steel
• finish	: blued

• stock	: laminated match stock with pistol grip, thumb-hole, and bipod

Illustrated from top to bottom: Gol Match Comp A, Gol Match UIT, and Gol Match HV Comp B rifles.

GOL-Match HV Comp B model

TECHNICAL DETAILS

Calibre	: .308 Win.
Cartridge capacity	: 5 rounds
Magazine catch	: not applicable, fixed magazine
Action	: bolt-action
Locking	: 2-lugs Mauser bolt locking
Weight	: approx 5.5kg (12lb 1oz) including telescopic sight
Length	: approx 118.4cm (46⅝in)
Barrel Length	: 65cm (25⅝in) excluding muzzle compensator or flash reducer
Sight	: none, suitable for telescopic sight
External safety	: Timney trigger system with safety catch behind bolt
Internal safety	: locking

CHARACTERISTICS

• material	: steel
• finish	: matt nickel-plated
• stock	: laminated match stock with pistol grip and thumb-hole

Illustrated from top to bottom: Gol Match A, Gol Match UIT, and Gol Match HV Comp B rifles.

GOL-Sniper Rifle Standard Synthetic

TECHNICAL DETAILS

Calibre	: .308 Win.
Cartridge capacity	: 5 rounds

Magazine catch	: not applicable, fixed magazine
Action	: bolt-action
Locking	: 2-lugs Mauser bolt locking
Weight	: approx 5.5kg (12lb 1oz)
Length	: approx 118.4cm (46⅝in)
Barrel Length	: 65cm (25⅝in) excluding muzzle compensator or flash reducer
Sight	: none, suitable for telescopic sight
External safety	: Timney trigger system with safety catch behind bolt
Internal safety	: locking

CHARACTERISTICS

• material	: steel
• finish	: blued
• stock	: black plastic with pistol grip

Magazine catch	: not applicable, fixed magazine
Action	: bolt-action
Locking	: 2-lugs Sako bolt locking
Weight	: approx 5.3kg (11lb 11oz) including telescopic sight
Length	: approx 118.4cm (46⅝in)
Barrel Length	: 65cm (25⅝in) excluding muzzle compensator or flash reducer
Sight	: none, suitable for telescopic sight
External safety	: Sako trigger system with safety catch behind bolt
Internal safety	: locking

CHARACTERISTICS

• material	: steel
• finish	: blued, nickel-plated barrel
• stock	: special open-form laminated stock with pistol grip and bipod

Tests have demonstrated that this rifle is capable of producing a group of 10 rounds on target within a diameter of 12-14mm (3/8-7/16in).
The GOL Sniper model S (Sako bolt). Top with the StoCon Duo-tone skeleton stock, below with a dark laminated wooden stock.

GOL-Sniper Rifle model S StoCon Duo-tone

GOL-Sniper Rifle model S Standard

TECHNICAL DETAILS

| Calibre | : .308 Win., .300 Win.
Mag., 6mm PPC |
| Cartridge capacity | : 5 rounds |

TECHNICAL DETAILS

Calibre	: .308 Win.
Cartridge capacity	: 5 rounds
Magazine catch	: not applicable, fixed magazine

Action	: bolt-action
Locking	: 2-lugs Sako bolt locking
Weight	: approx 5.5kg (12lb 1oz) including telescopic sight
Length	: approx 118.4cm (46⅝in)
Barrel Length	: 65cm (25⅝in) excluding muzzle compensator or flash reducer
Sight	: none, suitable for telescopic sight
External safety	: Sako trigger system with safety catch behind bolt
Internal safety	: locking

CHARACTERISTICS

• material	: steel
• finish	: blued
• stock	: laminated with pistol grip and bipod

Tests have demonstrated that this rifle is capable of producing a group of 10 rounds on target within a diameter of 12-14mm (3/8-7/16in).
The GOL Sniper model S (Sako bolt). Top with the StoCon Duo-tone skeleton stock, below with a dark laminated wooden stock.

Griffin & Howe

Griffin & Howe of New York was founded in 1923 and used to be part of the renowned Abercrombie & Fitch Company who outfitted the gentleman hunter with everything made-to-measure that he needed for a hunting safari in Africa. In the late 1920s, G & H brought out their own Magnum calibre, the .350 Griffin & Howe Magnum but it was not successful. The company is mainly a trading operation that acquires its rifles from the famous European gunsmiths. They have designed a special mounting for telescopic sights (see the illustration). The company also sell classic shotguns made by Arietta in Italy.

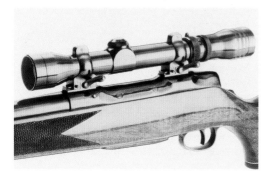

Griffin & Howe Magnum rifle

TECHNICAL DETAILS

Calibre	: .416 Rigby (other calibres available on request)
Cartridge capacity	: 4 rounds
Magazine catch	: at front of trigger guard
Action	: bolt-action
Locking	: 2-lugs locking (Mauser Magnum system)
Weight	: 10lb (4.5kg)
Length	: 43in (109.2cm)
Barrel Length	: 24in (61cm)
Sight	: fixed leaf sight or folding Express sight with bead tunnel, special Griffin & Howe mounting for telescopic sight
External safety	: at rear of bolt
Internal safety	: locking

CHARACTERISTICS

• material	: steel
• finish	: blued
• stock	: walnut with raised cheek and pistol grip

Grünig + Elmiger

The rifles from the Swiss gunmakers Grünig + Elmiger are legendary in shooting sports circles. The factory is close to Lucerne in Malters. These long-range weapons have a high degree of accuracy and are not based on any existing systems parts. The company has developed its own receiver and bolt mechanisms along principles of its own.
Marksmen equipped with Grünig + Elmiger rifles have achieved many victories in shooting matches and set world records.

Grünig + Elmiger Match Target rifle

TECHNICAL DETAILS

Calibre	: see below
Cartridge capacity	: single shot
Magazine catch	: not applicable

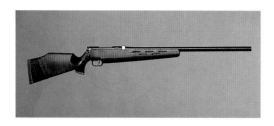

Action	: bolt-action
Locking	: 2-lugs bolt locking
Weight	: 3.8 or 4.8kg for heavy version (8lb 6oz or 10lb 10oz)
Length	: 106cm (41¾in)
Barrel Length	: 65cm (25⅝in)
Sight	: none, suitable for telescopic sight
External safety	: safety catch by trigger
Internal safety	: locking

CHARACTERISTICS

• material	: steel
• finish	: blued
• stock	: walnut with cooling vents in hand grip

Available calibres: .222 Rem., .223 Rem., (no military ammunition), 6.5 x 55mm, 7mm-08 Rem., 7.5mm Swiss., .308 Win., 8 x 57S

This rifle is equipped with double triggers. The front trigger prepares the weapon for use by cocking it. The rear trigger then requires the lightest touch to fire the weapon.

Grünig + Elmiger Prone Position rifle

TECHNICAL DETAILS

Calibre	: see below
Cartridge capacity	: single shot
Magazine catch	: not applicable
Action	: bolt-action
Locking	: 2-lugs bolt locking
Weight	: 5.5kg (12lb 1oz)
Length	: 106cm (41¾in)
Barrel Length	: 65cm (25⅝in)
Sight	: optical sight and bead tunnel
External safety	: safety catch next to bolt
Internal safety	: locking

CHARACTERISTICS

• material	: steel
• finish	: blued
• stock	: walnut with cooling vents in hand grip

Available calibres: .222 Rem., .223 Rem., (no military ammunition), 6.5 x 55mm, 7mm-08 Rem., 7.5mm Swiss., .308 Win.

This rifle is specially developed for prone firing at targets at a range of 300m (328yds).

Grünig + Elmiger Super Target 200/20 UIT/CISM

TECHNICAL DETAILS

Calibre	: see below
Cartridge capacity	: single shot
Magazine catch	: not applicable
Action	: bolt-action
Locking	: 3-lugs bolt locking
Weight	: 5.5kg (12lb 1oz)
Length	: 106cm (41¾in)
Barrel Length	: 65cm (25⅝in)
Sight	: optical sight and bead tunnel
External safety	: safety catch next to bolt
Internal safety	: locking

CHARACTERISTICS

• material	: steel
• finish	: blued
• stock	: walnut, hand-grip not connected to the barrel

Available calibres: .223 Rem., (no military ammunition), 6.5 x 55mm, 7mm-08 Rem., 7.5mm Swiss., .308 Win.

This rifle is specially developed for prone firing at targets at a range of 300m (328yds).

In the Super Target 200-CISM version, the rifle is equipped with a 10-round cartridge holder for 7.5mm Swiss and .308 Win. calibres.

Grünig + Elmiger Super Target 200/40 Free Rifle

TECHNICAL DETAILS

Calibre	: see below
Cartridge capacity	: single shot
Magazine catch	: not applicable
Action	: bolt-action
Locking	: 3-lugs bolt locking
Weight	: 6.5kg (14lb 5oz)
Length	: 106cm (41¾in)
Barrel Length	: 65cm (25⅝in)
Sight	: optical sight and bead tunnel
External safety	: safety catch on right next to bolt
Internal safety	: locking

CHARACTERISTICS

• material	: steel
• finish	: blued
• stock	: walnut, with shoulder grip and thumb-hole

Available calibres: .223 Rem., (no military ammunition), 6.5 x 55mm, 7mm-08 Rem., 7.5mm Swiss., .308 Win.

This rifle is specially developed for standing, kneeling, and prone firing at targets at a range of 300m (328yds).

Harrington & Richardson

The American weapon maker Harrington & Richardson was founded in 1871 by Gilbert Henderson Harrington and Franklin Wesson. Prior to this, Harrington worked for Ballard & Fairbanks who had a small-scale business making revolvers in Worcester, Massachusetts. Harrington had already designed the first self-ejecting revolver at the age of 26. Franklin Wesson was occupied with a small gunsmith's workshop where rifles were made. Ballard & Fairbanks decided in 1871 to cease making revolvers and in that same year Harrington determined to start up on his own, joining with his uncle Wesson in setting up their own business. Another Ballard & Fairbanks employee, William Augustus Richardson, became the technical manager. The single-shot Wesson & Harrington model 1871 rifle among others dates from this period. Uncle Wesson left the business in 1874 and it was continued by Harrington and Richardson. Their production was mainly of revolvers. Because of the major demand for double-barrelled shotguns, they decided to start making these. They entered into a licensing deal with the British company of Anson & Deely, however, the big increase in demand for H & R revolvers caused them to end this arrangement in 1886. In 1888 the company was significantly re-organized and renamed the Harrington & Richardson Arms Company. Both directors died soon after in 1897. The company continued under the triumvirate of Brooks, the former chief clerk and finance manager, Edwin C. Harrington, the 20-year-old son of the founder, and the daughter of the other later director, Mary A. Richardson. After being based for a long time in Worcester, the business moved to Garner in Massachusetts. The current range of H & R consists of a number of single-barrelled shotguns and rifles and revolvers. Their subsidiary company, New England Firearms, also makes a range of single-barrelled shotguns and rifles. The products from this company are still regarded for their great simplicity and reliability.

Harrington & Richardson 125th Anniversary

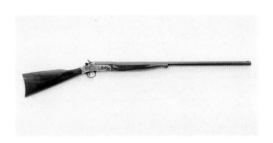

TECHNICAL DETAILS

Calibre : .45-70 Govt.
Cartridge capacity : single shot
Magazine catch : not applicable
Action : breech-action
Locking : barrel catch with breech
lock lever behind hammer
Weight : 8lb (3.6kg)
Length : 57¾in (146.5cm)
Barrel Length : 32in (81.3cm)
Sight : none, sight of customer's choice
External safety : none
Internal safety : locking

CHARACTERISTICS

• material : steel
• finish : blued
• stock : walnut

This rifle is a commemorative model that reproduces the Wesson & Harrington 1871 model.

Harrington & Richardson RMEF 1996 Commemorative

TECHNICAL DETAILS

Calibre : .35 Whelen
Cartridge capacity : single shot
Magazine catch : not applicable

Harrington & Richardson RMEF 1996 Commemorative

Action : breech-action
Locking : barrel catch with breech
lock lever behind hammer
Weight : 8lb (3.6kg)
Length : 45¼in (114.8cm)
Barrel Length : 26in (66cm)
Sight : none, suitable for telescopic
sight
External safety : none
Internal safety : locking

CHARACTERISTICS

• material : steel
• finish : blued
• stock : laminated wooden stock
with inlaid commemorative
plaque of the RMEF (Rocky
Mountain Elk Foundation)

Harrington & Richardson Ultra Varmint 22in

TECHNICAL DETAILS

Calibre : .223 Rem., .308 Win., .357
Rem. Max.
Cartridge capacity : single shot
Magazine catch : not applicable
Action : breech-action
Locking : barrel catch with breech
lock lever behind hammer

Weight   : 8lb (3.6kg)
Length   : 37⅛in (94.3cm)
Barrel Length   : 22in (55.9cm)
Sight   : none, suitable for telescopic
                       sight
External safety   : none
Internal safety   : locking

CHARACTERISTICS
• material   : steel
• finish   : blued
• stock   : laminated wood

Illustrated from top to bottom: Ultra Varmint 22, Ultra Varmint 26, and the Ultra Hunter.

Harrington & Richardson Ultra Varmint 26

TECHNICAL DETAILS
Calibre   : .223 Rem., .308 Win., .357
                       Rem. Max.
Cartridge capacity   : single shot
Magazine catch   : not applicable
Action   : breech-action

Locking   : barrel catch with breech
                       lock lever behind hammer
Weight   : 8lb (3.6kg)
Length   : 41⅛in (94.3cm)
Barrel Length   : 26in (66cm)
Sight   : none, suitable for mounting
                       telescopic sight
External safety   : none
Internal safety   : locking
• material   : steel
• finish   : blued
• stock   : laminated wood

Illustrated from top to bottom: Ultra Varmint 22, Ultra Varmint 26, and the Ultra Hunter.

Harrington & Richardson Ultra Hunter

TECHNICAL DETAILS
Calibre   : .357 Rem. Maximum
Cartridge capacity   : single shot
Magazine catch   : not applicable
Action   : breech-action
Locking   : barrel catch with breech
                       lock lever behind hammer
Weight   : 8lb (3.6kg)
Length   : 37⅛in (94.3cm)
Barrel Length   : 22in (55.9cm)
Sight   : adjustable rack sight
External safety   : none
Internal safety   : locking

CHARACTERISTICS
• material   : steel
• finish   : blued
• stock   : laminated wood

Illustrated from top to bottom: Ultra Varmint 22, Ultra Varmint 26, and the Ultra Hunter.

Harris Gunworks

The American firm of Harris Gunworks Inc. is situated in Phoenix, Arizona. The company mainly produces marksman's rifles in all manner of calibres for Government departments but also target shooting rifles. The Competition range is an example of this latter category, consisting of the National Match, the Target Bench-rest rifle, and the Long Range. These rifles have unusual polygon-section barrels. Harris guarantees that these rifles can achieve a group of three rounds on target with a diameter of 13mm (9/16in) at a range of 100yds (91.4m). The marksman's (or sniper's) rifles are designed for "clinical" operations at a range of more than 1,000m (1,090yds). The company also makes marksman's rifles in .50BMG (Browning Machine Gun) calibre for a range of 1,500m (1,640yds). Their multi-barrel marksman's rifle is another well-known product from Harris Gunworks. With this system, the rifle can have the calibre: of barrel changed with a quick turn of the hand. This provides barrels for .308 Win., .30-06 Spr., and .300 Win. Mag. The weapon can also be fitted with a silencer. There is even a .50 BMG weapon with a folding stock to make the weapon easier to carry.

Harris Target Benchrest

TECHNICAL DETAILS

Calibre	: to choice
Cartridge capacity	: single shot
Magazine catch	: not applicable
Action	: bolt-action
Locking	: 2-lugs bolt
Weight	: about 9lb 14oz (4.5kg) excluding telescopic sight
Length	: about 44½in (113cm)
Barrel Length	: about 26in (66cm)

Sight	: none, suitable for attaching a telescopic sight
External safety	: push-button behind trigger guard
Internal safety	: locking

CHARACTERISTICS

• material	: stainless-steel
• finish	: bare metal
• stock	: glass-fibre or wood

Illustrated from top to bottom are: the Harris Bench-rest and Harris Long Range rifles.

Harris Long Range

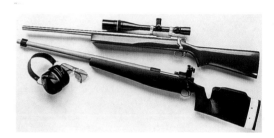

TECHNICAL DETAILS

Calibre	: .300 Win. Mag., or to choice
Cartridge capacity	: single shot
Magazine catch	: not applicable
Action	: bolt-action
Locking	: 2-lugs bolt
Weight	: about 11lb 8oz (5.2kg)
Length	: 44½in (113cm)
Barrel Length	: 26in (66cm)
Sight	: optical sight
External safety	: push-button behind trigger guard
Internal safety	: locking

CHARACTERISTICS

• material	: stainless-steel
• finish	: bare metal
• stock	: glass-fibre or wood

Illustrated from top to bottom are: the Harris Bench-rest and Harris Long Range rifles.

Harris Long Range Phoenix Sniper Rifle

TECHNICAL DETAILS

Calibre	: .300 Phoenix and other .30 Magnum calibres

Cartridge capacity : 5 rounds
Magazine catch : at front of trigger guard
Action : bolt-action
Locking : 2-lugs bolt
Weight : 12lb 10oz (5.7kg)
Length : 50in (127cm)
Barrel Length : 29in (73.7cm)
Sight : none, suitable for telescopic sight
External safety : safety catch on right, next to rear of bolt
Internal safety : locking

CHARACTERISTICS
• material : steel
• finish : matt black
• stock : glass-fibre

Harris National Match

TECHNICAL DETAILS
Calibre : .308 Win.
Cartridge capacity : single shot
Magazine catch : not applicable
Action : bolt-action
Locking : 2-lugs bolt
Weight : 11lb 14oz (5.4kg)
Length : 44½in (113cm)
Barrel Length : 26in (66cm)
Sight : optical sight, suitable for telescopic sight
External safety : safety catch on right behind bolt
Internal safety : locking

CHARACTERISTICS
• material : stainless-steel barrel, steel receiver

• finish : bare metal barrel, blued receiver
• stock : glass-fibre

Harris RBLP

TECHNICAL DETAILS
Calibre : .308 Win.
Cartridge capacity : single shot
Magazine catch : not applicable
Action : bolt-action
Locking : 2-lugs bolt
Weight : 11lb 11oz (5.3kg)
Length : 44½in (113cm)
Barrel Length : 26in (66cm)
Sight : telescopic sight of choice
External safety : safety catch on right behind bolt
Internal safety : locking

CHARACTERISTICS
• material : steel
• finish : blued
• stock : glass-fibre with pistol grip

The designation RBLP stands for Right Hand Bolt, Left side Port (ejector aperture) that is specially designed for long-range bench-rest and supported target shooting.

Harris Signature Classic

TECHNICAL DETAILS
Calibre	: any calibre required
Cartridge capacity	: dependent upon calibre
Magazine catch	: at front of trigger guard
Action	: bolt-action
Locking	: 2-lugs bolt
Weight	: 7lb 5oz (3.3kg) excluding telescopic sight
Length	: 52⅜in (133cm)
Barrel Length	: 26in (66cm)
Sight	: none, suitable for telescopic sight
External safety	: safety catch on right behind bolt
Internal safety	: locking

CHARACTERISTICS
• material	: steel
• finish	: blued
• stock	: choice of walnut, laminated wood, or plastic

Harris Signature Super Varminter

TECHNICAL DETAILS
Calibre	: All suitable calibres
Cartridge capacity	: dependent upon Calibre Magazine catch at front of trigger guard
Action	: bolt-action
Locking	: 2-lugs bolt
Weight	: 7lb 5oz (3.3kg)
Length	: 44½in (113cm)
Barrel Length	: 25in (63.5cm)
Sight	: telescopic sight of choice
External safety	: safety catch on right behind bolt
Internal safety	: locking

CHARACTERISTICS
• material	: steel
• finish	: matt black phosphate coating
• stock	: glass-fibre with pistol grip

Harris Talon Safari

TECHNICAL DETAILS
Calibre	: suitable .30 and .40 Magnum calibres, and .416 Rigby
Cartridge capacity	: 3-5 rounds
Magazine catch	: at front of trigger guard
Action	: bolt-action
Locking	: 2-lugs bolt
Weight	: 9lb (4.1kg)
Length	: 44½in (113cm)
Barrel Length	: 25in (63.5cm)
Sight	: adjustable folding sight, suitable for telescopic sight
External safety	: safety catch on right behind bolt
Internal safety	: locking

CHARACTERISTICS
• material	: steel
• finish	: blued
• stock	: glass-fibre, laminated wood, or walnut to choice

Harris Titanium Mountain rifle

TECHNICAL DETAILS
Calibre	: to choice

Cartridge capacity : 3-5 rounds
Magazine catch   : at front of trigger guard
Action   : bolt-action
Locking   : 2-lugs bolt
Weight   : 7lb 1oz (3.2kg)
Length   : 44½in (113cm)
Barrel Length   : 26in (66cm)
Sight   : none, suitable for telescopic
                    sight
External safety   : safety catch on right behind
                    bolt
Internal safety   : locking

CHARACTERISTICS
- material   : titanium receiver,
                     carbon-steel barrel
- finish   : matt black
- stock   : glass-fibre, with pistol grip

Harris M-86 Sniper rifle

TECHNICAL DETAILS
Calibre   : .308 Win., .300 Win. Mag.
Cartridge capacity : 5 or 10 rounds
Magazine catch   : at front of trigger guard
Action   : bolt-action
Locking   : 2-lugs bolt
Weight   : 13lb 7 oz (6.1 kg)
Length   : 41⅜in (105cm)
Barrel Length   : 24in (61cm)
Sight   : telescopic sight of choice
External safety   : safety catch on right behind
                    bolt
Internal safety   : locking

CHARACTERISTICS
- material   : steel
- finish   : matt black phosphate coated
- stock   : glass-fibre, with pistol grip

This rifle is also available in a single-shot
sporting version (M-87-M).

Harris M-87 Sniper rifle

TECHNICAL DETAILS
Calibre   : .50 BMG
Cartridge capacity : 5 rounds
Magazine catch   : at rear of magazine aperture
Action   : bolt-action
Locking   : heavy-duty 2-lugs bolt
Weight   : 21lb (9.5kg)
Length   : 53⅛in (135cm)
Barrel Length   : 29⅛in (74cm)
Sight   : telescopic sight of choice
External safety   : safety catch on right behind
                    bolt
Internal safety   : locking

CHARACTERISTICS
- material   : steel
- finish   : blued
- stock   : glass-fibre, with pistol grip
                     and thumb-hole

This weapon has been designed as a
marksman's rifle for ranges above
1,000yds/m. This rifle is also available in
a single-shot sporting version
(M-87-M).

Harris M-89 Sniper rifle

TECHNICAL DETAILS
Calibre   : .308 Win.
Cartridge capacity : 5, 10, or 20 rounds
Magazine catch   : at rear of magazine aperture
Action   : bolt-action

Locking : 2-lugs bolt
Weight : 15lb 7oz (7kg)
Length : 32⅞in (83.5cm)
Barrel Length : 18in (45.7cm)
Sight : telescopic sight of choice
External safety : safety catch on right behind bolt
Internal safety : locking

CHARACTERISTICS
• material : steel
• finish : blued
• stock : glass-fibre, with pistol grip

Harris M-89 Multi-Barrel Sniper rifle

TECHNICAL DETAILS
Calibre : .308 Win. and interchangeable barrels for .300 Win. Mag., and .30-06 Spr.
Cartridge capacity : 5, 10, or 20 rounds to choice
Magazine catch : at front of trigger guard
Action : bolt-action
Locking : 2-lugs bolt
Weight : 11lb 8oz (5.2kg)
Length : 38⅜in (97.4cm)
Barrel Length : 18/28in (45.7/71cm) longer length with recoil attenuator
Sight : none, suitable for telescopic sight
External safety : safety catch on right behind bolt
Internal safety : locking

CHARACTERISTICS
• material : steel
• finish : matt black
• stock : glass-fibre, with pistol grip

Harris M-89 Multi-Barrel Stainless Sniper rifle

TECHNICAL DETAILS
Calibre : .308 Win. and interchangeable barrels for .300 Win.

Mag., and .30-06 Spr.
Cartridge capacity : 5, 10, or 20 rounds to choice
Magazine catch : at front of trigger guard
Action : bolt-action
Locking : 2-lugs bolt
Weight : 11lb 8oz (5.2kg)
Length : 38⅜in (97.4cm)
Barrel Length : 18in (45.7cm)
Sight : none, suitable for telescopic sight
External safety : safety catch on right behind bolt
Internal safety : locking

CHARACTERISTICS
• material : stainless-steel
• finish : bare metal
• stock : glass-fibre

Harris M-93 Sniper

TECHNICAL DETAILS
Calibre : .50 BMG
Cartridge capacity : 10 or 20 rounds
Magazine catch : at front of trigger guard
Action : bolt-action
Locking : heavy-duty 2-lugs bolt
Weight : 21lb (9.5kg)
Length : 53in (134.7cm)
Barrel Length : 29in (73.7cm)

Sight	: none, suitable for telescopic sight
External safety	: safety catch on right behind bolt
Internal safety	: locking

CHARACTERISTICS
- material : steel
- finish : matt black
- stock : glass-fibre, with pistol grip. The stock folds down for carrying

This rifle is specially developed as a marksman's weapon for ranges exceeding 1,000yds/m.

Harris M-95 Ultra Light

TECHNICAL DETAILS
Calibre	: .50 BMG
Cartridge capacity	: 10 or 20 rounds
Magazine catch	: at front of trigger guard
Action	: bolt-action
Locking	: heavy-duty 2-lugs bolt
Weight	: 18lb (8.2kg)
Length	: 53⅛in (135cm)
Barrel Length	: 29in (73.7cm)
Sight	: none, suitable for telescopic sight
External safety	: safety catch on right behind bolt
Internal safety	: locking

CHARACTERISTICS
- material : titanium receiver, carbon-steel barrel
- finish : matt black
- stock : glass-fibre, with pistol grip

This rifle is specially developed as a marksman's weapon for ranges up to 2,000yds/m.

Heckler & Koch

The German company Heckler & Koch was set up in 1949. Once the German army was reformed in the 1950s, the company was asked to make the G-3 automatic army rifle in .308 Winchester Calibre. The rifle was equipped with the famous roller locking. Heckler & Koch were the first to use a polygon-section barrel. This type of barrel does not have the usual rifling, instead the many-sided internal section that has a specific twist to it, imparts spin on the bullet. Many technical innovations from military weapons can also be found on Heckler & Koch sporting and hunting rifles, such as their roller locking, specific range optical sights, and the polygonal barrels. Previously, H & K made a number of hunting rifles, such as the HK-270, HK-300, HK-770, HK-630, and HK-940 models. The present-day hunting range now comprises just the SL-6 and 7 rifles. The company also has a small range of marksman's rifles. During the 1980s, Heckler & Koch developed the G-11 special army rifle for case-less cartridges but the company ran into financial difficulties at the end of 1990 as a result of the lack of government orders. The choice by the US Army of the Beretta M-92 pistol instead of the Heckler & Koch P7-M13 was a considerable blow for them. There was also too little interest in the G-11 rifle project. The company was taken over in March 1991 by Royal Ordnance in Britain which is a subsidiary of British Aerospace. The company was acquired in 1995 by the German Wischo concern.

Heckler & Koch HK SL6

TECHNICAL DETAILS
Calibre	: .223 Rem.
Cartridge capacity	: 2 or 10 rounds
Magazine catch	: at front of trigger guard

Action : semi-automatic
Locking : HK roller locking
Weight : 3.9kg (8lb 10oz)
Length : 101.5cm (40in)
Barrel Length : 45cm (17¾in)
Sight : adjustable optical sight, suitable for telescopic sight
External safety : safety catch on left with indication on right
Internal safety : locking
CHARACTERISTICS
• material : steel
• finish : blued
• stock : wood

Illustrated: (top) Heckler & Koch SL6 and (below) SL7

Heckler & Koch HK SL7

TECHNICAL DETAILS
Calibre : .308 Win.
Cartridge capacity : 2 or 10 rounds
Magazine catch : at front of trigger guard
Action : semi-automatic
Locking : HK roller locking
Weight : 3.9kg (8lb 10oz)
Length : 101cm (39¾in)
Barrel Length : 43cm (1615/16in)

Sight : adjustable optical sight, suitable for telescopic sight
External safety : safety catch on left with indication on right
Internal safety : locking
CHARACTERISTICS
• material : steel
• finish : blued
• stock : wood

Illustrated: (top) Heckler & Koch SL6 and (below) SL7

HEGE/Zeughaus

The German firm of Zeughaus Hege GmbH is located at Überlingen on Lake Constance. The company was founded in 1959 by master gunsmith Friedrich Hebsacker. At that time, the company was based in Hall in Swabia. In 1974, the company managed to obtain the historic building that had been the arsenal of the once wealthy free town of öberlingen between 1471 and 1800. The building was extensively restored and the company moved its headquarters there. The company specializes in the production of replica black powder weapons, replica western weapons, and military weapons for collectors. They also sell the sporting weapons of Anschütz, Feinwerkbau, and Walther. The replica weapons are provided by makers such as Uberti, and Perdersoli, but in the main, they come from their own HEGE workshops. Beautifully crafted cases containing perfect replica HEGE-Manton flintlock duelling pistols or HEGE-Siber percussion duelling pistols are evidence of the company's quest for perfection. HEGE also make replicas of Remington percussion revolvers. The company's workshops also make many old-style percussion rifles, such as the HEGE-Whitney 1841 model and the Kentucky and Pennsylvania rifles.

HEGE-Henry 1860 model carbine

Gegen Erwerbsberechtigung

TECHNICAL DETAILS

Calibre	: .44-40
Cartridge capacity	: 9-rounds tubular magazine
Magazine catch	: loading aperture beneath mechanism housing
Action	: lever-action
Locking	: lever-action
Weight	: 3.6kg (7lb 14oz)
Length	: 95cm (37¾in)
Barrel Length	: 47.4cm (18¾in)
Sight	: adjustable rack sight
External safety	: none
Internal safety	: locking, half-cock on hammer

CHARACTERISTICS

- material : steel barrel, brass casing
- finish : bare metal
- stock : straight walnut stock

Inside the mechanism case of this carbine is inscribed "One of One Thousand." Only 1,000 of this very special model were produced.

Illustrated: 1. Henry 1860 model carbine and 2. Henry 1860 model rifle.

HEGE-Henry 1860 model rifle

TECHNICAL DETAILS

Calibre	: .44-40
Cartridge capacity	: 12-rounds tubular magazine
Magazine catch	: loading aperture beneath mechanism housing
Action	: lever-action
Locking	: lever-action
Weight	: 4kg (8lb 13oz)
Length	: 110cm (43¼in)
Barrel Length	: 61.4cm (24¼in)
Sight	: adjustable rack sight
External safety	: none
Internal safety	: locking, half-cock on hammer

CHARACTERISTICS

- material : steel
- finish : blued, tempered casing
- stock : straight walnut stock

Inside the mechanism casing of this carbine is inscribed "One of One Thousand." Only 1,000 of this very special model were produced.

Illustrated: 1. Henry 1860 model carbine and 2. Henry 1860 model rifle.

HEGE-Remington Rolling Block Long Range Creedmore rifle

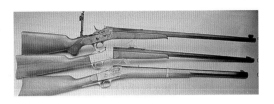

TECHNICAL DETAILS

Calibre	: .357 Mag., .45-70 Govt.
Cartridge capacity	: single shot
Magazine catch	: not applicable
Action	: roller block action
Locking	: roller block locking
Weight	: 5.5kg (12lb 1oz)
Length	: 119cm (46⅞in)
Barrel Length	: 76cm (29⅞in)
Sight	: adjustable rack sight and bead tunnel
External safety	: none
Internal safety	: locking

CHARACTERISTICS

- material : steel
- finish : blued, tempered casing
- stock : hardwood with pistol grip

Remington Rolling Block: 1. Long-Range Creedmore rifle, 2. Target rifle, and 3. carbine

HEGE-Remington Rolling Block Target rifle

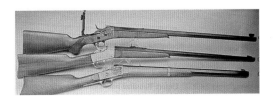

TECHNICAL DETAILS

Calibre	: .357 Mag., .45-70 Govt.
Cartridge capacity	: single shot
Magazine catch	: not applicable
Action	: roller block action
Locking	: roller block locking
Weight	: 4.4kg (9lb 11oz)
Length	: 119cm (46⅞in)
Barrel Length	: 76cm (29⅞in)
Sight	: adjustable height leaf sight
External safety	: none
Internal safety	: locking

CHARACTERISTICS

• material	: steel
• finish	: blued barrel, polished bare metal casing
• stock	: straight hardwood stock

Remington Rolling Block: 1. Long-Range Creedmore rifle, 2. Target rifle, and 3. carbine

HEGE-Remington Rolling Block carbine

TECHNICAL DETAILS

Calibre	: .357 Mag., .45-70 Govt.
Cartridge capacity	: single shot
Magazine catch	: not applicable
Action	: roller block action
Locking	: roller block locking
Weight	: 5.3kg (11lb 11oz)
Length	: 108cm (42½in)
Barrel Length	: 66cm (26in)
Sight	: sideways-adjustable leaf sight
External safety	: none
Internal safety	: locking

CHARACTERISTICS

• material	: steel
• finish	: blued barrel, tempered casing, brass trigger guard, and barrel band
• stock	: straight hardwood stock

Remington Rolling Block: 1. Long-Range Creedmore rifle, 2. Target rifle, and 3. carbine

HEGE-Uberti 1866 model Western rifle

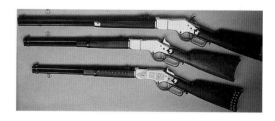

TECHNICAL DETAILS

Calibre	: .22 LR, .38 Spec., .44-40, .45 LC
Cartridge capacity	: 12-rounds tubular magazine
Magazine catch	: loading aperture in bottom of mechanism cover
Action	: lever-action
Locking	: lever-action locking
Weight	: 3.7kg (8lb 3oz)
Length	: 110cm (43¼in)
Barrel Length	: 61.6cm (24¼in)
Sight	: adjustable rack sight
External safety	: none
Internal safety	: locking, half-cock on hammer

CHARACTERISTICS

• material	: steel, brass
• finish	: blued barrel, brass casing
• stock	: straight hardwood stock with saddle ring

Hege-Ubert 1866 Western model: 1. 1866 rifle, 2. 1866 carbine, and 3.1866 Indian carbine.

HEGE-Uberti 1866 model Western carbine

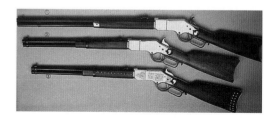

TECHNICAL DETAILS

Calibre	: .22 LR, .38 Spec., .44-40, .45 LC

Cartridge capacity	: 8-rounds tubular magazine
Magazine catch	: loading aperture in bottom of mechanism cover
Action	: lever-action
Locking	: lever-action locking
Weight	: 3.4kg (7lb 8oz)
Length	: 97cm (38¼in)
Barrel Length	: 46.5cm (18¼in)
Sight	: folding sight
External safety	: none
Internal safety	: locking, half-cock on hammer

CHARACTERISTICS
- material : steel, brass
- finish : blued barrel, brass casing
- stock : straight hardwood stock with saddle ring

Hege-Ubert 1866 Western model: 1. 1866 rifle, 2. 1866 carbine, and 3. 1866 Indian carbine.

HEGE-Uberti 1866 model Western Indian carbine

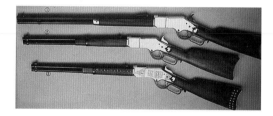

TECHNICAL DETAILS

Calibre	: .44-40
Cartridge capacity	: 8-rounds tubular magazine
Magazine catch	: loading aperture in bottom of mechanism cover
Action	: lever-action
Locking	: lever-action locking
Weight	: 3.4kg (7lb 8oz)
Length	: 97cm (38¼in)
Barrel Length	: 46.5cm (18¼in)
Sight	: folding sight
External safety	: none
Internal safety	: locking, half-cock on hammer

CHARACTERISTICS
- material : steel, brass
- finish : blued barrel, engraved brass casing
- stock : straight hardwood stock with embossing and saddle ring

Hege-Ubert 1866 Western model: 1. 1866 rifle, 2. 1866 carbine, and 3. 1866 Indian carbine.

HEGE 1873 model Western "One of One Thousand" rifle

TECHNICAL DETAILS

Calibre	: .357 Mag.
Cartridge capacity	: 12-rounds tubular magazine
Magazine catch	: loading aperture in bottom of mechanism cover
Action	: lever-action
Locking	: lever-action locking
Weight	: 3.5kg (7lb 11oz)
Length	: 109cm (42⅞in)
Barrel Length	: 61.8cm (24⅜in)
Sight	: adjustable rack sight
External safety	: none
Internal safety	: locking, half-cock on hammer

CHARACTERISTICS
- material : steel
- finish : blued
- stock : straight walnut stock

A limited edition of 1,000 of this replica rifle were produced. Each bears the inscription on the barrel "One of one Thousand."

Heym

The German weapon maker Friedrich Wilhelm Heym GmbH & Co KG is situated in Münnerstadt in northern Bavaria. The company was founded in 1865 when it acquired a patent for the first hammer-less triple-barrelled rifle. The son of the founder, Adolf Heym, took over the running of the business in 1912 and he in turn was followed by his son, August in 1920. During this time, the company produced Anson & Deeley triple-barrelled rifles. After World War II, when weapon manufacture was forbidden by the allies, the company was forced into making air guns and rifles. This lasted until 1952 when Heym was given permission to make firearms. The business was managed by August Heym and his son Rolf. Since then, Heym has become known for very high-quality rifles and shotguns. Only the highest quality Krupp steel is used in the manufacture of their guns. Each firearm is produced as a work of art. The company is unsurpassed in the quality of its engraving. Most of the production consists of breech-action rifles and shotguns and the triple-barrelled hunting guns that are synonymous with the company. These usually have one or two shotgun barrels, complemented by one or two rifled barrels. The high precision of their manufacture together with the time and care that goes into engraving them, means that Heym guns are rather expensive. The prices of these "Rolls-Royce" of guns vary from **2,000-3,000 or $3,200-11,000 for "off the shelf" models.

Heym model SR 20 N

TECHNICAL DETAILS

Calibre	: see below
Cartridge capacity	: 3-5 rounds
Magazine catch	: at front of trigger guard
Action	: bolt-action
Locking	: locking lugs
Weight	: 3.2-3.8kg (7-7lb 8oz)
Length	: 113-118cm (44½-46½in)
Barrel Length	: 60-65cm (23½-25½in)
Sight	: folding sight, suitable for telescopic sight
External safety	: safety catch behind bolt handle
Internal safety	: locking, half-cock on hammer

CHARACTERISTICS
- material : steel
- finish : blued
- stock : walnut

Available calibres: .22-250 Rem., .243 Win., .270 Win., .308 Win., .30-06 Spr., 6 x 62 Fräres, 6.5 x 55mm, 6.5 x 57mm,

6.5 x 64mm, 6.5 x 65mm, 6.5 x 68mm, 7 x 57mm, 7 x 64mm, 8 x 57mm, 8 x 68S, 9.3 x 62mm, 9.3 x 64mm, 10.3 x 60R, 7mm Rem. Mag., .300 Win. Mag., .338 Win Mag., .375 H & H Mag.

Heym model 44 B

TECHNICAL DETAILS

Calibre	: see below
Cartridge capacity	: single shot
Magazine catch	: not applicable
Action	: breech-action
Locking	: breech-lock beneath barrel
Weight	: 2.7kg (6lb)
Length	: 103cm (40½in)
Barrel Length	: 60cm (23½in)
Sight	: folding sight, suitable for telescopic sight
External safety	: safety catch behind breech lock
Internal safety	: locking

CHARACTERISTICS
- material : steel
- finish : blued
- stock : walnut

Available calibres: .22 Hornet, .222 Rem., .222 Rem. Mag., .22-250 Rem., .243 Win., .308 Win., .30-06 Spr., .30R Blaser, 5.6 x 50R Mag., 5.6 x 52R, 5.6 x 57R, 6 x 62 Fräres, 6.5 x 55mm, 6.5 x 57R, 6.5 x 65R, 7 x 57R, 7 x 65R, 8 x 57mm, 8 x 75R, 9.3 x 74R, 10.3 x 60R

Heym model 55 BS double-barrelled mountain carbine (Bergstutzen)

TECHNICAL DETAILS

Calibre	: see below
Cartridge capacity	: 1 round per barrel

Magazine catch	: not applicable
Action	: breech-action
Locking	: central lock with breech lock on top of breech pivot
Weight	: 3.5kg (7lb 12oz)
Length	: 106cm (41¾in)
Barrel Length	: 63.5cm (25in)
Sight	: fixed sight, suitable for telescopic sight
External safety	: safety catch on neck of stock behind breech lock
Internal safety	: locking

CHARACTERISTICS

• material	: steel
• finish	: blued, breech pivot is engraved bare metal
• stock	: walnut

Available calibres (standard, upper barrel): .22 Hornet, .222 Rem., .222 Rem. Mag., 5.6 x 50R Mag., 5.6 x 52R; (standard, lower barrel): .308 Win., .30-06 Spr., .30R Blaser, 7 x 65R, 8 x 57 Mauser, 8 x 75RS, 9.3 x 74R; (Magnum, upper barrel): .243 Win., 6.5 x 55mm, 6.5 x 57R, 6.5 x 65R, 7 x 65R, .308 Win., .30-06 Spr., .30 Blaser; (Magnum, lower barrel): .300 Win. Mag., .375 H& H Mag., .416 Rigby, .458 Win. Mag., .470 NE

This through-and-through hunting rifle for big game is equipped with one trigger per barrel for firing with second trigger for each of them to make the weapon ready to fire.

Heym model 80B double-barrelled

TECHNICAL DETAILS

Calibre	: see below
Cartridge capacity	: 1 round per barrel
Magazine catch	: not applicable
Action	: breech-action

Locking	: breech lock lever under barrel with catch on top of breech pivot
Weight	: 3.2kg (7lb 1oz)
Length	: 103cm (40⅝in)
Barrel Length	: 60cm (23⅝in)
Sight	: fixed sight, suitable for telescopic sight
External safety	: safety catch on neck of stock behind breech lock
Internal safety	: locking

CHARACTERISTICS

• material	: steel
• finish	: blued, breech pivot is engraved bare metal
• stock	: walnut

Available calibres: .30-06 Spr., .30 Blaser, 7 x 65R, 8 x 57 Mauser, 8 x 75RS, 9.3 x 74R

Heym model 88 B/BSS double-barrelled

TECHNICAL DETAILS

| Calibre | : see below |

Cartridge capacity	: 1 round per barrel
Magazine catch	: not applicable
Action	: breech-action
Locking	: central lock with breech lock on top of breech pivot
Weight	: 3.6kg (8lb)
Length	: 107cm (42in)
Barrel Length	: 63.5cm (25in)
Sight	: fixed sight, suitable for telescopic sight
External safety	: safety catch on neck of stock behind breech lock
Internal safety	: locking

CHARACTERISTICS

• material	: steel
• finish	: blued, breech pivot is engraved bare metal
• stock	: walnut

Available calibres .30-06 Spr., .30R Blaser, 7 x 65R, 8 x 57 Mauser, 8 x 75RS, 9.3 x 74R, .375 H & H Mag.

This through-and-through hunting rifle for big game is equipped with one trigger per barrel for firing with second trigger for each of them to make the weapon ready to fire.

Heym model 88 B/Safari double-barrelled

TECHNICAL DETAILS

Calibre	: see below
Cartridge capacity	: 1 round per barrel
Magazine catch	: not applicable
Action	: breech-action
Locking	: central lock with breech lock on top of breech pivot
Weight	: 4.5kg (10lb)
Length	: 107cm (42in)
Barrel Length	: 61cm (24in)

Sight	: Express folding sight, suitable for telescopic sight
External safety	: sliding catch on neck of stock behind breech lock
Internal safety	: locking

CHARACTERISTICS

• material	: steel
• finish	: blued, breech pivot is engraved bare metal
• stock	: walnut

Available calibres .375 H & H Mag., .458 Win. Mag., .470 NE, .500 NE, .600 NE (NE = Nitro Express)

This through-and-through hunting rifle for big game is equipped with one trigger per barrel.

Heym Express model

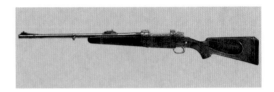

TECHNICAL DETAILS

Calibre	: see below
Cartridge capacity	: 3-5 rounds
Magazine catch	: at front of trigger guard
Action	: bolt-action
Locking	: 2-lugs Mauser Magnum system
Weight	: 4.5kg (10lb)
Length	: 115cm (41¼in)
Barrel Length	: 55.9-61cm (22-24in)
Sight	: Express folding sight, suitable for telescopic sight
External safety	: safety catch behind breech lock
Internal safety	: locking

CHARACTERISTICS

• material	: steel
• finish	: blued, receiver is engraved bare metal
• stock	: walnut

Available calibres .338 Lap. Mag., .375 H & H Mag., .378 Wby. Mag., .404 Jeffery, .425 Express, .416 Rigby, .460 Wby. Mag., .500 A-Square, .600 NE

Howa

The weapon manufacturer Howa Machinery Company Ltd. is established in the Japanese city of Nagoya, on the Isewan or Ise bay in a direct line between Tokyo and Osaka. The car town of Toyota is on Nagoya's outskirts. Apart from the manufacture of their own brand of rifles, the company is known for the complete receivers with barrels it makes for the Mark V Weatherby rifles. The Howa rifle has a 3-lugs locking system that ensures positive engagement and secure locking. The rifle is also equipped with a plastic stock made by Butler Creek. Howa rifles are imported into North America by the trading company Interarms. The make is unfortunately less well-known in Europe.

Howa Lightning

TECHNICAL DETAILS

Calibre	: see below
Cartridge capacity	: up to 5 rounds
Magazine catch	: at front of trigger guard
Action	: bolt-action
Locking	: 3 lugs locking
Weight	: 3.6kg (8lb)
Length	: 121cm (47⅜in)
Barrel Length	: 61cm (24in)
Sight	: none , suitable for telescopic sight
External safety	: safety catch on right behind bolt
Internal safety	: locking

CHARACTERISTICS

- material : steel
- finish : blued
- stock : black plastic

Available calibres (standard): .223 Rem., .22-250 Rem., .243 Win., .270 Win., .308 Win., .30-06 Spr.; (Magnum): .300 Win. Mag., .338 Win. Mag., 7mm Rem. Mag.

I.M.I. (Israel Military Industries)

Israel gained its independence on 14 May 1948. This led almost immediately to war with the neighbouring Arab states. Because Israel was politically isolated, and had to cope with limited resources, it was forced to fend for and supply itself. The new country had supplies of the British Sten sub-machine gun but there was an urgent need for more weapons. An Israeli Colonel, Uziel Gal designed the famous Uzi sub-machine gun that was widely adopted by the Israeli Army in 1951. The design was so good that the Uzi has seen service with the armies of many countries. It is built under licence in some countries, including the FN factory at Herstal, near Liege, Belgium, and at the Dutch Hembrug plant. The Uzi has even become an official NATO weapon. After the Israeli-Arab war of 1967, the Israeli Army decided to develop a light rifle as a riposte to the Russian AK-47 with which the Arab forces were equipped. For practical reasons, they decided to incorporate the gas-pressure system of the AK-47 with the NATO .223 Remington Calibre. Because of the urgency, a large supply of weapon parts were acquired in Finland from the Valmet model 62 army rifle, that was adapted in Israel to the Galil rifle. Currently there is considerable foreign interest in the Galil rifle, which delivers considerable foreign exchange to Israel, with the result that much of the Israeli Army is equipped with Colt M-16 rifles. The I.M.I. company also produces ammunition under the brand names of Uzi and Samson

I.M.I. Galil SASR: Semi-Automatic Sniper Rifle

TECHNICAL DETAILS

Calibre	: .308 Win.
Cartridge capacity	: 25 rounds
Magazine catch	: at front of trigger guard

Action	: semi-automatic, gas-pressure
Locking	: rotating slide
Weight	: 6.4kg (14lb 1oz)
Length	: 111.2cm (43¾in)
Barrel Length	: 50.8cm (20in)
Sight	: optical sight, suitable for telescopic sight
External safety	: double-sided safety catch on mechanism housing
Internal safety	: locking

CHARACTERISTICS

• material	: steel
• finish	: matt black phosphate coating
• stock	: wooden folding stock

Jarrett

The keyword for the US family firm of Jarrett Rifles Inc., is precision. This company, based in Jackson, South Carolina, builds rifles of the highest quality around Remington model 700 receivers. The Jarrett firm prefers McMillan plastic stocks because they do not "work" in the way that wood does and are not susceptible to either damp or drying out. The barrels are cold-tempered stainless-steel ones from either Hart or Schneider. Each rifle is extensively tested. A grouping in excess of 3/4in (19mm) at a range of 100yds (91.4m) is not accepted. The tests are performed on the company's own range at distances of up to 1,000 yds (914m). Prior to 1979, the founder of the company, Kenneth Jarrett, worked on his uncle's farm growing soya beans. In his spare time, he occupied himself making his own custom-built rifles with which he broke six world records. Since then, marksmen have gained a further nine world records with his rifles. Jarrett has also developed his own calibres like the .300 Jarrett, .338 Jarrett, and the .416 Jarrett. It goes without saying that these hand-made or modified-by-hand Jarrett rifles are expensive. The price for a standard rifle is about $3,000.

Jarrett Custom rifle

TECHNICAL DETAILS

Calibre	: see below
Cartridge capacity	: 3-5 rounds internal magazine
Magazine catch	: at front of trigger guard
Action	: bolt-action

Locking	: 2-lugs Remington model 7 bolt
Weight	: 7lb 8oz-9lb 8oz (3.4-4.3kg)
Length	: about 45in (114.3cm)
Barrel Length	: 21-26in (53.3-66cm)
Sight	: none, suitable for telescopic sight
External safety	: safety catch on right behind bolt
Internal safety	: locking

CHARACTERISTICS

• material	: steel
• finish	: blued or matt black
• stock	: plastic or walnut with pistol grip

Available calibres: any calibre: requested from .22 LR to .458 Win. Mag., including many unusual and wildcat calibre:s, such as: .17 Javelina, .22 Snipe, .220 Coyote, .220 Jaybird, 6mm Snipe, .240 Coyote, .243 Ackley Improved, .243 Catbird, .264 Jarrett, .270 Jarrett, 7mm STW, .308 Bluebird, .30-06 Ackley Improved, .300 Jarrett, .338-06 Ackley Improved, .338-378 Kubla Kahn, .338 Jarrett, .358 STA, .416 Taylor, .416 Jarrett.

KBI

KBI Inc. of Harrisburg, Pennsylvania in the USA, imports Armscor rifles into North America and semi-automatic AK-47 rifles made by FEG in Hungary. The company also import original Russian Dragunov sniper's rifles. The Dragunov is supplied complete with an original set of accessories such as the PSO-4X telescopic sight and case, four cartridge holders, an ammunition pouch, and an original bayonet. The official name of this rifle is Snayperskaya Vintovka Dragunova (SVD). The weapon was developed by Eugeni Fjodorowits Dragonov and entered service with the Red Army in 1963 and soon after was also made available for the other Warsaw Pact armies. It replaced the old Moisin-Nagant M1891/30 sniper's rifle used in World War II. The system of the Dragunov is based upon that of the AK-47 and although intended for use with telescopic sights, it also has other simple sights. This rifle is also made in China and is exported by the Chinese as the NDM-86. The rifle is also manufactured by some of the former East Block countries under licence.

This Dragunov rifle is an original of Russian manufacture.

Keppeler

The Keppeler & Fritz company was set up by Dieter Keppeler in Fichtenberg, Bavaria, in Germany. This German arms manufacturer is one of the few custom rifle makers in Europe. The company has also developed two special muzzle compensators that act as recoil suppressors. Keppeler rifles are extremely accurate and a grouping of 3 shots on target within a 70mm (2¾in) radius at 300m (328yds) using standard production ammunition (.338 Lapua Magnum) is nothing exceptional.

Keppeler 300 metre full-bore prone rifle

TECHNICAL DETAILS
Calibre	: see below
Cartridge capacity	: single shot
Magazine catch	: not applicable
Action	: bolt-action
Locking	: 9-lugs bolt
Weight	: 5.3kg (11lb 12oz)
Length	: 121.5cm (47¾in)
Barrel Length	: 65cm (25⅝in)
Sight	: Anschütz optical sight and bead tunnel
External safety	: none
Internal safety	: locking

CHARACTERISTICS
• material	: steel
• finish	: blued
• stock	: special match stock with thumb-hole

Available calibres (system 1): .243 Win., 7mm-08 Rem., 7.5mm Swiss, .308 Win., 8 x 57JS; (system 2): .222 Rem., .223 Rem.

KBI-Dragunov model SVD

TECHNICAL DETAILS
Calibre:7.62 x 54R
Cartridge capacity	: 10-rounds cartridge holder
Magazine catch	: at front of magazine aperture
Action	: semi-automatic, gas-pressure
Locking	: rotating slide
Weight	: 3.5kg (7lb 13oz)
Length	: 122.6cm (48¼in)
Barrel Length	: 68.6cm (27in)
Sight	: adjustable rack, special telescopic sight (PSO) with illuminated cross-hairs and infra-red imaging
External safety	: safety catch on right of mechanism housing
Internal safety	: locking

CHARACTERISTICS
• material	: steel
• finish	: blued
• stock	: laminated hardwood with pistol grip

Keppeler 300 metre full-bore standard rifle

TECHNICAL DETAILS
Calibre   : see below
Cartridge capacity : single shot
Magazine catch   : not applicable
Action   : bolt-action
Locking   : 9-lugs bolt
Weight   : 5.3kg (11lb 12oz)
Length   : 121.5cm (47¼in)
Barrel Length   : 65cm (25⅝in)
Sight   : Anschütz optical sight and bead tunnel
External safety   : none
Internal safety   : locking

CHARACTERISTICS
• material   : steel
• finish   : blued
• stock   : special match stock with thumb-hole

Available calibres (system 1): .243 Win., 7mm-08 Rem., 7.5mm Swiss, .308 Win., 8 x 57JS; (system 2): .222 Rem., .223 Rem.

Keppeler 300 metre full-bore UIT-CISM standard rifle

TECHNICAL DETAILS
Calibre   : see below
Cartridge capacity : 10-rounds cartridge holder
Magazine catch   : at rear of magazine aperture
Action   : bolt-action
Locking   : 9-lugs bolt

Weight   : 5.2kg (11lb 8oz)
Length   : 123.5cm (48⅝in)
Barrel Length   : 67cm (26⅝in)
Sight   : Anschütz optical sight and bead tunnel
External safety   : none
Internal safety   : locking

CHARACTERISTICS
• material   : steel
• finish   : blued
• stock   : special match stock with thumb-hole

Available calibres: .243 Win., 7mm-08 Rem., 7.5mm Swiss, .308 Win., 8 x 57JS.

Keppeler 300 metre full-bore free rifle

TECHNICAL DETAILS
Calibre   : see below
Cartridge capacity : single shot
Magazine catch   : not applicable
Action   : bolt-action
Locking   : 9-lugs bolt
Weight   : 6.4kg (14lb 1oz)
Length   : 121.5cm (47¼in)
Barrel Length   : 65cm (25⅝in)
Sight   : Anschütz optical sight and bead tunnel
External safety   : none
Internal safety   : locking

CHARACTERISTICS
• material   : steel
• finish   : blued
• stock   : special match stock with thumb-hole, adjustable shoulder grip, cheek plate, and hand-grip

Available calibres (system 1): .243 Win., 7mm-08 Rem., 7.5mm Swiss, .308 Win., 8 x 57JS; (system 2): .222 Rem., .223 Rem.

Keppeler KS III Bullpup Sniper

TECHNICAL DETAILS
Calibre	: see below
Cartridge capacity	: 3-5 rounds
Magazine catch	: not applicable
Action	: bolt-action
Locking	: 9-lugs bolt
Weight	: 5kg (11lb) excluding telescopic sight
Length	: 110cm (43¼in)
Barrel Length	: 65cm (25⅝in) including muzzle compensator
Sight	: none, suitable for telescopic sight
External safety	: safety catch on left of mechanism housing behind pistol grip
Internal safety	: locking, drop-out safety system

CHARACTERISTICS
- material : steel
- finish : blued matt
- stock : special skeleton stock

Available calibres .308 Win., .300 Win. Mag., .338 Lapua Mag.

Keppeler Long Range rifle

TECHNICAL DETAILS
Calibre	: .308 Win.
Cartridge capacity	: single shot
Magazine catch	: not applicable
Action	: bolt-action

(continued)
Locking	: 9-lugs bolt
Weight	: 5.2kg (11lb 8oz)
Length	: 128.9cm (50¾in)
Barrel Length	: 76.2cm (30in)
Sight	: none, suitable for telescopic sight
External safety	: none
Internal safety	: locking

CHARACTERISTICS
- material : steel
- finish : blued
- stock : match stock with thumb-hole

Keppeler Sport rifle

TECHNICAL DETAILS
Calibre	: .308 Win.
Cartridge capacity	: single shot
Magazine catch	: not applicable
Action	: bolt-action
Locking	: 9-lugs bolt
Weight	: 5.3kg (11lb 11oz)
Length	: 119.9cm (47¼in)
Barrel Length	: 62cm (243/8in)
Sight	: none, suitable for telescopic sight
External safety	: none
Internal safety	: locking

CHARACTERISTICS
- material : steel
- finish : blued
- stock : match stock with thumb-hole

Krico

Krico is the trade mark of the German company A. Kriegeskorte GmbH. The company is based in Fürth-Stadeln, close to Neurenberg in Bavaria. The company's history stretches back to 1878, when Robert Kriegeskorte founded Junghans &

Kriegeskorte. That company was based in Esslingen amZollberg. At first, the company were wholesalers in gunpowder, dynamite, munitions, and weapons. The son of the founder, Max, took over the running of the business in 1918. Production of weapons became difficult following World War I so that between 1918 and 1928, the company made cycle frames. At the end of World War II, the company had renewed problems because the allies banned the production of weapons. Kriegeskorte directed their attention to making consumer goods. It was not until 1950 that the company was permitted to make air rifles and a year later allowed to make small-bore rifles. The company did not begin making hunting rifles in .22 Hornet and .222 Remington using the 400 system until 1954. In 1963, the 600 and 700 systems were developed for larger calibres.

Krico model 260

TECHNICAL DETAILS

Calibre	: .22 LR
Cartridge capacity	: 2, 5, or 10 rounds
Magazine catch	: at rear of magazine aperture
Action	: semi-automatic
Locking	: inertia
Weight	: 3kg (6lb 10oz)
Length	: 99cm (39in)
Barrel Length	: 50cm (19¾in)
Sight	: adjustable rack and bead tunnel
External safety	: safety catch on right of receiver
Internal safety	: locking, repeating mechanism can be disengaged

CHARACTERISTICS

• material	: steel
• finish	: blued
• stock	: beech

Krico model 300

TECHNICAL DETAILS

Calibre	: .22 LR, .22 WMR., or .22 Hornet
Cartridge capacity	: 5 or 10 rounds (.22 Hornet: 5)
Magazine catch	: at rear of magazine aperture
Action	: bolt-action
Locking	: 2 locking lugs
Weight	: 2.9-3kg (6lb 6oz-6lb 10oz)
Length	: 98-109cm (38⅝in-42⅞in)
Barrel Length	: 50-60cm (19¾-23⅝in)
Sight	: adjustable rack and bead tunnel, mounting for telescopic sight
External safety	: safety catch on right of receiver
Internal safety	: locking, load indicator (protruding pin)

CHARACTERISTICS

• material	: steel
• finish	: blued
• stock	: beech

The rifle is equipped with a German pressure-point trigger mechanism (Stecher).

Krico model 300-Luxus

TECHNICAL DETAILS

Calibre	: .22 LR, .22 WMR., or .22 Hornet
Cartridge capacity	: 5 or 10 rounds (.22 Hornet: 5)
Magazine catch	: at rear of magazine aperture
Action	: bolt-action

Locking	: 2 locking lugs
Weight	: 2.9-3kg (6lb 6oz-6lb 10oz)
Length	: 98-109cm (38⅝-42⅞in)
Barrel Length	: 50-60cm (19¾-23⅝in)
Sight	: adjustable rack and bead tunnel, mounting for telescopic sight
External safety	: safety catch on right of receiver
Internal safety	: locking, load indicator (protruding pin)

CHARACTERISTICS
- material : steel
- finish : blued
- stock : walnut

The rifle is equipped with a German pressure-point trigger mechanism (Stecher).

Krico model 300-SA (Sound Absorber)

TECHNICAL DETAILS

Calibre	: .22 LR
Cartridge capacity	: 5 or 10 rounds cartridge holder
Magazine catch	: at rear of magazine aperture
Action	: bolt-action
Locking	: 2 locking lugs
Weight	: 2.8kg (6lb 3oz)
Length	: 108cm (42½in)
Barrel Length	: 28cm (11in); 57.5cm (22⅝in) with integrated silencer
Sight	: none, mounting for telescopic sight
External safety	: safety catch on right behind bolt
Internal safety	: locking, load indicator

CHARACTERISTICS
- material : steel
- finish : blued
- stock : hardwood with pistol grip

The use of silencers on weapons is not permitted in some countries.

Krico model 300-carbine

TECHNICAL DETAILS

Calibre	: .22 LR, .22 WMR., or .22 Hornet
Cartridge capacity	: 5 or 10 rounds (.22 Hornet: 5)
Magazine catch	: at rear of magazine aperture
Action	: bolt-action
Locking	: 2 locking lugs
Weight	: 3kg (6lb 10oz)
Length	: 98cm (38⅝in)
Barrel Length	: 50cm (19¾in)
Sight	: adjustable rack and bead tunnel, mounting for telescopic sight
External safety	: safety catch on right of receiver
Internal safety	: locking, load indicator (protruding pin)

CHARACTERISTICS
- material : steel
- finish : blued
- stock : walnut stocks runs through under barrel to muzzle

The rifle is equipped with a German pressure-point trigger mechanism (Stecher).

Krico Biathlon 360 SII

TECHNICAL DETAILS

Calibre	: .22 LR
Cartridge capacity	: 10-rounds cartridge holder
Magazine catch	: in magazine aperture
Action	: bolt-action
Locking	: bolt
Weight	: 4.4kg (9lb 11oz)
Length	: 103cm (40½in)
Barrel Length	: 54cm (21¼in)

Sight	: none, mounting for optical sight
External safety	: none
Internal safety	: locking

CHARACTERISTICS
- material : steel
- finish : blued
- stock : hardwood biathlon stock with space for extra cartridges, with adjustable pistol grip

Krico model 400 single shot

TECHNICAL DETAILS
Calibre	: .22 Hornet
Cartridge capacity	: single shot
Magazine catch	: not applicable
Action	: bolt-action
Locking	: 2 locking lugs on bolt
Weight	: 3.8kg (8lb 6oz)
Length	: 105cm (413/8in)
Barrel Length	: 60cm (23⅝in)
Sight	: none, mounting for telescopic sight
External safety	: safety catch on right of receiver
Internal safety	: locking, load indicator (protruding pin)

CHARACTERISTICS
- material : steel
- finish : blued
- stock : walnut

The rifle is equipped with a German pressure-point trigger mechanism (Stecher) (see illustration), or match trigger.

Krico model 400 match

TECHNICAL DETAILS
Calibre	: .22 LR, .22 Hornet
Cartridge capacity	: 5 or 10 rounds
Magazine catch	: at rear of magazine aperture

Action	: bolt-action
Locking	: 2 locking lugs on bolt
Weight	: 4kg (8lb 13oz)
Length	: 107cm (42⅛in) or 108cm (42½in) for .22 Hornet
Barrel Length	: 50cm (19 ¾in) or 60cm (23⅝in) for .22 Hornet
Sight	: none, mounting for telescopic sight
External safety	: safety catch on right of receiver
Internal safety	: locking, load indicator (protruding pin)

CHARACTERISTICS
- material : steel
- finish : blued
- stock : walnut

The rifle is equipped with a German pressure-point trigger mechanism (Stecher) (see illustration), or match trigger.

Krico model 530 S Krico-Tronic

TECHNICAL DETAILS
Calibre	: .22 LR, .22 Hornet, or .222 Rem.
Cartridge capacity	: single shot
Magazine catch	: not applicable
Action	: bolt-action
Locking	: 2 locking lugs on bolt
Weight	: 4.3-4.5kg (9lb 8oz-9lb 14oz)
Length	: 107cm (42⅛in) or 116cm (45¾in)
Barrel Length	: 60-69 cm (23⅝-27⅛in)

Sight	: none, mounting for telescopic or optical sight	
External safety	: safety catch on right front of bolt	
Internal safety	: locking, on/off switch for electronic firing	

CHARACTERISTICS
- material : steel
- finish : blued
- stock : walnut with adjustable cheek plate and butt

This rifle has electronic firing instead of a mechanical firing pin. The cartridge is fired electronically by means of a ceramic rod. The built-in rechargeable battery has a capacity of 250 rounds.

Krico model 600-Match (DJV)

TECHNICAL DETAILS

Calibre	: see below
Cartridge capacity	: 3-6 rounds
Magazine catch	: push-button on left of magazine aperture
Action	: bolt-action
Locking	: 2 locking lugs on bolt
Weight	: 4kg (8lb 13oz)
Length	: 110cm (43¼in)
Barrel Length	: 60cm (23⅝in)
Sight	: none, mounting for telescopic sight
External safety	: safety catch on right of receiver
Internal safety	: locking, load indicator (protruding pin)

CHARACTERISTICS
- material : steel
- finish : blued
- stock : walnut

Available calibres: .222 Rem., .223 Rem., .22-250 Rem., .243 Win., .308 Win.

This rifle is equipped with an immediate trigger, pressure point (German Stecher) trigger, a match trigger, or a Super-Match

trigger. The abbreviation DJV stands for Deutsches Jagd Verband, meaning the German hunter's association.

Krico model 600-Jagdmatch (hunting/match)

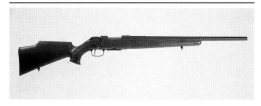

TECHNICAL DETAILS

Calibre	: see below
Cartridge capacity	: 3-6 rounds
Magazine catch	: push-button on left of magazine aperture
Action	: bolt-action
Locking	: 2 locking lugs on bolt
Weight	: 3.6kg (7lb 14oz)
Length	: 111cm (43¾in)
Barrel Length	: 60cm (23⅝in)
Sight	: none, mounting for telescopic sight
External safety	: safety catch on right of receiver
Internal safety	: locking, load indicator (protruding pin)

CHARACTERISTICS
- material : steel
- finish : blued
- stock : walnut

Available calibres: .222 Rem., .223 Rem., .22-250 Rem., .243 Win., .308 Win.

This rifle is equipped with an immediate trigger, pressure point (German Stecher) trigger, a match trigger, or a Super-Match trigger.

Krico model 600- Match Single-shot

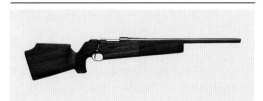

TECHNICAL DETAILS

Calibre : see below
Cartridge capacity : single shot
Magazine catch : not applicable
Action : bolt-action
Locking : 2 locking lugs on bolt
Weight : 4.5kg (9lb 14oz)
Length : 110cm (43¼in)
Barrel Length : 60cm (23⅝in)
Sight : none, mounting for telescopic sight
External safety : safety catch on right of receiver
Internal safety : locking, load indicator (protruding pin)

CHARACTERISTICS

• material : steel
• finish : blued
• stock : walnut

Available calibres: .222 Rem., .223 Rem., .22-250 Rem., .243 Win., .308 Win.

This rifle is equipped with an immediate trigger, pressure point (German Stecher) trigger, a match trigger, or a Super-Match trigger.

Krico model 600 Sniper

TECHNICAL DETAILS

Calibre : see below
Cartridge capacity : 3-6 rounds
Magazine catch : on left of magazine aperture
Action : bolt-action
Locking : 2 locking lugs on bolt
Weight : 4.2kg (9lb 5oz)
Length : 115cm (45¼in)
Barrel Length : 60cm (23⅝in)
Sight : none, mounting for telescopic sight
External safety : safety catch on right of receiver
Internal safety : locking, load indicator (protruding pin)

CHARACTERISTICS

• material : steel
• finish : blued

• stock : walnut

Available calibres: .222 Rem., .223 Rem., .22-250 Rem., .243 Win., .308 Win.

This rifle is equipped with an immediate trigger, pressure point (German Stecher) trigger, a match trigger, or a Super-Match trigger.

Krico model 700

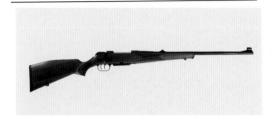

TECHNICAL DETAILS

Calibre : see below
Cartridge capacity : 3-6 rounds
Magazine catch : push-button on left of magazine aperture
Action : bolt-action
Locking : 2 locking lugs on bolt
Weight : 4.2kg (9lb 5oz)
Length : 110-117cm (43¼-46in)
Barrel Length : 60-65cm (23⅝-25⅝in)
Sight : folding sight and bead tunnel, mounting for telescopic sight
External safety : safety catch on right of receiver
Internal safety : locking, load indicator (protruding pin)

CHARACTERISTICS

• material : steel
• finish : blued
• stock : walnut

This rifle is equipped with an immediate trigger, pressure point (German Stecher) trigger, a match trigger, or a Super-Match trigger. Calibres (group I): .17 Rem., .222 Rem., .222 Rem. Mag., .223 Rem., 5.6 x 50 Mag., .243 Win., .308 Win., 5.6 x 57 RWS, .22-250 Rem.: (group II): 6.5 x 55, 6.5 x 57, 7 x 57, .270 Win., 7 x 64, .30-06, 9.3 x 62; (group III): 6.5 x 68, 7mm Rem. Mag., .300 Win.Mag., 8 x 68 S, 7.5 Swiss, 9.3 x 64, 6 x 62 Frères

Krico model 700 Economy

TECHNICAL DETAILS

Calibre	: see below
Cartridge capacity	: 3-6 rounds
Magazine catch	: push-button on left of magazine aperture
Action	: bolt-action
Locking	: 2 locking lugs on bolt
Weight	: 3.2-3.3kg (7lb 1oz-7lb 5oz)
Length	: 110-117cm (43¼-46in)
Barrel Length	: 60-65cm (23⅝-25⅝in)
Sight	: folding sight, mounting for telescopic sight
External safety	: safety catch on right of receiver
Internal safety	: locking, load indicator (protruding pin)

CHARACTERISTICS
- material : steel
- finish : blued
- stock : walnut

This rifle is equipped with an immediate trigger, pressure point (German Stecher) trigger.
Calibres (group I): .17 Rem., .222 Rem., .222 Rem. Mag., .223 Rem., 5.6 x 50 Mag., .243 Win., .308 Win., 5.6 x 57 RWS, .22-250 Rem.: (group II): 6.5 x 55, 6.5 x 57, 7 x 57, .270 Win., 7 x 64, .30-06, 9.3 x 62; (group III): 6.5 x 68, 7mm Rem. Mag., .300 Win.Mag., 8 x 68 S, 7.5 Swiss, 9.3 x 64, 6 x 62 Frères

Krico model 700 Luxus

TECHNICAL DETAILS

Calibre	: see below

Cartridge capacity	: 3-6 rounds
Magazine catch	: push-button on left of magazine aperture
Action	: bolt-action
Locking	: 2 locking lugs on bolt
Weight	: 3.3-3.5kg (7lb 5oz-7lb 11oz)
Length	: 111-118cm (43¾-46½in)
Barrel Length	: 60-65cm (23⅝-25⅝in)
Sight	: folding sight and bead tunnel, mounting for telescopic sight
External safety	: safety catch on right of receiver
Internal safety	: locking, load indicator (protruding pin)

CHARACTERISTICS
- material : steel
- finish : blued
- stock : walnut

This rifle is equipped with an immediate trigger, pressure point (German Stecher) trigger, a match trigger, or a Super-Match trigger. Calibres (group I): .17 Rem., .222 Rem., .222 Rem. Mag., .223 Rem., 5.6 x 50 Mag., .243 Win., .308 Win., 5.6 x 57 RWS: (group II): 6.5 x 55, 6.5 x 57, 7 x 57, .270 Win., 7 x 64, .30-06, 9.3 x 62; (group III): 6.5 x 68, 7mm Rem. Mag., .300 Win.Mag., 8 x 68 S, 7.5 Swiss, 9.3 x 64, 6 x 62 Frères

Krico model 700 Luxus-S

TECHNICAL DETAILS

Calibre	: see below
Cartridge capacity	: 3-6 rounds
Magazine catch	: push-button on left of magazine aperture
Action	: bolt-action
Locking	: 2 locking lugs on bolt
Weight	: 3.4-3.6kg (7lb 8oz-7lb 14oz)
Length	: 111-118cm (43¾-46½in)
Barrel Length	: 60-65cm (23⅝-25⅝in)
Sight	: folding sight and bead tunnel, mounting for telescopic sight

| External safety | : weapon is always in un-cocked mode, cocking lever on rear of pistol grip |
| Internal safety | : locking, load indicator (protruding pin) |

CHARACTERISTICS

• material	: steel
• finish	: blued
• stock	: walnut

This rifle is equipped with a pressure point trigger mechanism with a single trigger. Calibres (group I): .17 Rem., .222 Rem., .222 Rem. Mag., .223 Rem., 5.6 x 50 Mag., .243 Win., .308 Win., 5.6 x 57 RWS, .22-250 Rem.; (group II): 6.5 x 55, 6.5 x 57, 7 x 57, .270 Win., 7 x 64, .30-06, 9.3 x 62; (group III): 6.5 x 68, 7mm Rem. Mag., .300 Win. Mag., 8 x 68 S, 7.5 Swiss, 9.3 x 64, 6 x 62 Frères

Krico model 700 Luxus carbine

TECHNICAL DETAILS

Calibre	: see below
Cartridge capacity	: 3-6 rounds
Magazine catch	: push-button on left of maga-zine aperture
Action	: bolt-action
Locking	: 2 locking lugs on bolt
Weight	: 3.4-3.6kg (7lb 8oz-7lb 14oz)
Length	: 111-118cm (43¾-46½in)
Barrel Length	: 60-65cm (23⅝-25⅝in)
Sight	: folding sight and bead tunnel, mounting for teles-copic sight
External safety	: weapon is always in uncoc-ked mode, cocking lever on rear of pistol grip
Internal safety	: locking, load indicator (protruding pin)

CHARACTERISTICS

• material	: steel
• finish	: blued
• stock	: walnut stock continues under barrel to muzzle

This rifle is equipped with an immediate trigger, pressure point (German Stecher) trigger, a match trigger, or a Super-Match

trigger. Calibres (group I): .17 Rem., .222 Rem., .222 Rem. Mag., .223 Rem., 5.6 x 50 Mag., .243 Win., .308 Win., 5.6 x 57 RWS, .22-250 Rem.: (group II): 6.5 x 55, 6.5 x 57, 7 x 57, .270 Win., 7 x 64, .30-06, 9.3 x 62; (group III): .300 Win.Mag.

Krico model 900-MC

TECHNICAL DETAILS

Calibre	: from .308 Win. to .375 H & H
Cartridge capacity	: 3 rounds
Magazine catch	: push-button on left of magazine aperture
Action	: bolt-action
Locking	: 3 locking lugs on bolt
Weight	: 3.1kg (6lb 13oz)
Length	: 108cm (42½in)
Barrel Length	: 57cm (22½in)
Sight	: folding sight and bead tunnel, mounting for telescopic sight
External safety	: safety catch on right of receiver
Internal safety	: locking, load indicator (protruding pin)

CHARACTERISTICS

• material	: steel
• finish	: blued
• stock	: special Monte Carlo walnut stock

Lakefield

Lakefield is a Canadian arms manufacturer of small-bore rifles in .22 LR and .22 WMR calibres. The business is based at Lakefield, Ontario. Lakefield's range divides into two main groups: sporting rifles and carbines for leisure and hunting, and a small range of match rifles including an unusual biathlon rifle. One unique point is that all models are available in left-hand versions as well as the more usual right-hand versions. The company was taken over at the end of 1995 by the US company Savage Arms Inc. and it has changed its name to

Savage Arms Canada Inc. The European importer of Lakefield rifles is the German trading house Akah (Albrecht Kind GmbH) in Gummersbach-Hunsting.

Illustrated: Lakefield Mark I- Youth (above) and Mark I (below)

Lakefield Mark I

TECHNICAL DETAILS

Calibre	: .22 Short, .22 Long, and .22 LR
Cartridge capacity	: single shot
Magazine catch	: not applicable
Action	: bolt-action
Locking	: by bolt
Weight	: 5lb 8oz (2.5kg)
Length	: 39½in (100.3cm)
Barrel Length	: 20¾in (52.7cm)
Sight	: adjustable leaf sight, mounting for telescopic sight
External safety	: safety catch on right behind bolt
Internal safety	: locking

CHARACTERISTICS

• material	: steel
• finish	: blued
• stock	: hardwood

This rifle is also available in a left-hand version.

Lakefield Mark I en I-Youth

Lakefield Mark I-Youth

TECHNICAL DETAILS

Calibre	: .22 Short, .22 Long, and .22 LR
Cartridge capacity	: single shot
Magazine catch	: not applicable
Action	: bolt-action
Locking	: by bolt
Weight	: 5lb (2.3kg)
Length	: 37in (94cm)

Barrel Length	: 19in (48.3cm)
Sight	: adjustable leaf sight, mounting for telescopic sight
External safety	: safety catch on right behind bolt
Internal safety	: locking

CHARACTERISTICS

- material : steel
- finish : blued
- stock : hardwood

This rifle is also available in a left-hand version.

Illustrated: Lakefield Mark I- Youth (above) and Mark I (below)

Lakefield Mark II

TECHNICAL DETAILS

Calibre	: .22 LR
Cartridge capacity	: 10-rounds cartridge holder
Magazine catch	: at front of magazine aperture
Action	: bolt-action
Locking	: by bolt
Weight	: 5lb 8oz (2.5kg)
Length	: 39½in (100.3cm)
Barrel Length	: 20¾in (52.7cm)
Sight	: adjustable leaf sight, mounting for telescopic sight
External safety	: safety catch on right behind bolt
Internal safety	: locking

CHARACTERISTICS

- material : steel
- finish : blued
- stock : hardwood

Illustrated from top to bottom: Lakefield Mark II-Youth, the Lakefield II left-hand version and the right-hand Mark II

Lakefield Mark II-Youth

TECHNICAL DETAILS

Calibre	: .22 LR
Cartridge capacity	: 10-rounds cartridge holder
Magazine catch	: at front of magazine aperture
Action	: bolt-action
Locking	: by bolt
Weight	: 5lb (2.3kg)
Length	: 37in (94cm)
Barrel Length	: 19in (48.3cm)
Sight	: adjustable leaf sight, mounting for telescopic sight
External safety	: safety catch on right behind bolt
Internal safety	: locking

CHARACTERISTICS

- material : steel
- finish : blued
- stock : hardwood

Illustrated from top to bottom: Lakefield Mark II-Youth, the Lakefield II left-hand version and the right-hand Mark II

Lakefield model 64B

TECHNICAL DETAILS

| Calibre | : .22 LR |

Cartridge capacity : 10-rounds cartridge holder
Magazine catch : at front of magazine apertu-
re
Action : semi-automatic
Locking : inertia
Weight : 5lb 8oz (2.5kg)
Length : 40in (101.6cm)
Barrel Length : 20¼in (51.4cm)
Sight : adjustable leaf sight, moun-
ting for telescopic sight
External safety : safety catch on right of
mechanism housing
Internal safety : locking

CHARACTERISTICS
• material : steel
• finish : blued
• stock : hardwood

Lakefield model 90B-Biathlon

TECHNICAL DETAILS
Calibre : .22 LR
Cartridge capacity : 5-rounds cartridge holder
Magazine catch : at front of magazine
aperture
Action : bolt-action
Locking : bolt locking
Weight : 8lb 4oz (3.7kg)
Length : 39⅝in (100.6cm)
Barrel Length : 21in (53.3cm) with snow
guard
Sight : optical sight and bead
tunnel
External safety : safety catch on right of bolt
Internal safety : locking

CHARACTERISTICS
• material : steel
• finish : blued
• stock : beech

The left hand version (lower of the two) is also shown in the illustration.

Lakefield model 91T

TECHNICAL DETAILS
Calibre : .22 Short, .22 Long, or .22
LR
Cartridge capacity : single shot
Magazine catch : not applicable
Action : bolt-action
Locking : bolt locking
Weight : 8lb (3.6kg)
Length : 43⅝in (110.7cm)
Barrel Length : 25in (63.5cm)
Sight : optical sight and bead
tunnel
External safety : safety catch on right, behind
bolt
Internal safety : locking

CHARACTERISTICS
• material : steel
• finish : blued
• stock : hardwood

This rifle can also be delivered in a left-hand version.

Lakefield model 91TR

TECHNICAL DETAILS
Calibre : .22 LR
Cartridge capacity : 5-rounds cartridge holder

Magazine catch	: front of magazine aperture
Action	: bolt-action
Locking	: bolt locking
Weight	: 8lb (3.6kg)
Length	: 43⅝in (110.7cm)
Barrel Length	: 25in (63.5cm)
Sight	: optical sight and bead tunnel
External safety	: safety catch on right, behind bolt
Internal safety	: locking

CHARACTERISTICS
- material : steel
- finish : blued
- stock : hardwood

This rifle can also be delivered in a left-hand version.

Illustrated (from top to bottom): Lakefield models 91TR Target and model 92S-Silhouette

Lakefield model 92S-Silhouette

TECHNICAL DETAILS
Calibre	: .22 LR
Cartridge capacity	: 5-rounds cartridge holder
Magazine catch	: front of magazine aperture
Action	: bolt-action
Locking	: bolt locking
Weight	: 8lb (3.6kg)
Length	: 39⅝in (100.6cm)
Barrel Length	: 21in (53.3cm)
Sight	: none, special mounting for telescopic sight
External safety	: safety catch on right, behind bolt
Internal safety	: locking

CHARACTERISTICS
- material : steel
- finish : blued

• stock : hardwood

This rifle can also be delivered in a left-hand version.

Illustrated (from top to bottom): Lakefield models 91TR Target and model 92S-Silhouette

Lakefield model 93 Magnum

TECHNICAL DETAILS
Calibre	: .22 WMR
Cartridge capacity	: 5-rounds cartridge holder
Magazine catch	: front of magazine aperture
Action	: bolt-action
Locking	: bolt locking
Weight	: 5lb 12oz (2.6kg)
Length	: 39½in (100.3cm)
Barrel Length	: 20¼in (52.7cm)
Sight	: adjustable leaf sight, special mounting for telescopic sight
External safety	: safety catch on right, behind bolt
Internal safety	: locking

CHARACTERISTICS
- material : steel
- finish : blued
- stock : hardwood

L.A.R.

The American L.A.R. Manufacturing Inc. is best known for its .44 Magnum, .45 Winchester Grizzly Magnum, and even .50 Magnum (Action Express) pistols. The company is based at West Jordan, Utah where it was founded in 1968 as a supplier of parts for other weapon manufacturers. L.A.R makes gun mounts for various types of machine-gun for the US armed forces and also parts for the M-16 army rifle. Because of the considerable interest in heavy long-range rifles in .50 BMG (Browning Machine Gun) calibre, the company decided to bring out such a weapon: the Big Bore Competitor.

The initial interest for this type of rifle came from the US Army. During the Gulf War in particular, there was a need for a marksman's rifle with a range capability up to 3,000 yds (2,743m). This type of weapon was subsequently also available for the civilian market. Target shooting competitions for this calibre are no longer unusual in North and South America.

LAR Grizzly 50 Big Bore

TECHNICAL DETAILS

Calibre	: .50 BMG
Cartridge capacity	: single shot
Magazine catch	: not applicable
Action	: bolt-action
Locking	: 2 heavy-duty lugs
Weight	: 28lb 6oz (12.9kg)
Length	: 45½in (115.6cm)
Barrel Length	: 36in (91.4cm)
Sight	: none, suitable for telescopic sight
External safety	: safety catch on left of pistol grip
Internal safety	: locking

CHARACTERISTICS

• material	: steel
• finish	: matt black phosphate coating
• stock	: steel with rubber butt plate

This rifle has an effective range of 3,000 yds (almost 3,000m).

LAR Grizzly 50 Big Bore Competitor rifle

TECHNICAL DETAILS

Calibre	: .50 BMG
Cartridge capacity	: single shot
Magazine catch	: not applicable
Action	: bolt-action
Locking	: 2 heavy-duty lugs
Weight	: 30lb 6oz (13.8kg)
Length	: 45½in (115.6cm) including muzzle compensator
Barrel Length	: 36in (91.4cm)
Sight	: none, suitable for telescopic sight
External safety	: double-sided safety catch on pistol grip
Internal safety	: locking

CHARACTERISTICS

• material	: steel
• finish	: matt black phosphate coating
• stock	: steel with rubber butt plate and bipod

This rifle has an effective range of 3,000 yds (almost 3,000m). The considerable weight of the weapon together with the muzzle compensator considerably reduces the heavy recoil.

Magnum Research

The American company Magnum Research Inc. is based in Minneapolis, Minnesota. It is mainly engaged in the development and import of weapons made by the Israeli weapon producer Israel Military Industries (I.M.I.). This includes several versions of the Jericho 941 pistol sold in North America under the name

Baby Eagle. The company also has a single-shot silhouette target rifle in its range, called the Lone Eagle, together with the larger Desert Eagle and Galil army rifle and sporting rifle. Their hunting rifle is the Mountain Eagle bolt-action rifle that has a glass-fibre stock. The receiver and bolt of this rifle origi-nate from Sako in Finland with the barrel coming from the well-known Krieger factory.

Magnum Research Mountain Eagle

TECHNICAL DETAILS

Calibre	: see below
Cartridge capacity	: 5 (long) or 4 (Magnum)
Magazine catch	: in front of trigger guard
Action	: bolt-action
Locking	: 3 lugs locking
Weight	: 7lb 2oz (3.2kg)
Length	: 44in (112cm)
Barrel Length	: 24in (61cm)
Sight	: none, suitable for telescopic sight
External safety	: safety catch on right of receiver
Internal safety	: locking, load indicator on left of receiver

CHARACTERISTICS

• material	: steel
• finish	: blued
• stock	: glass-reinforced polyester

Available calibres (long bolt): .270 Win., .280 Rem., .30-06; (Magnum): .300 Win. Mag., .338 Win. Mag., 7mm Rem. Mag.

The receiver and bolt of this rifle are made in Finland by Sako.

MagTech

MagTech is the brand name of the Brazilian weapons and munitions manufacturer Companhia Brasileira de Cartuchos (CBC) based in São Paulo.
The company was set up in 1926 by a family of Italian immigrants called Mata-razzo, under the name Companhia Brasileira Cartucheria. In those days it mainly made shotgun cartridges for the domestic market. The company developed in a few decades into a major company with exports of munitions to many countries. From 1936 to 1979, the company was jointly owned by the American Remington Arms Company and ICI (Imperial Chemical Industries) from Britain). The company was taken over in 1979 by the Arbi and Imbel groups, two major Brazilian corporations involved in tourism, the steel industry, and manufacture of munitions. This is when the name was changed to Companhia Brasileira de Cartuchos (CBC). The brass cartridge cases for ammunition are produced by a subsidiary company S.A. Marvin of Nova Iguaçu near Rio de Janeiro. The company underwent major reorganization in 1991 and 1992. Under the management of the well-known munitions specialist Charles von Helle and with help from several German technological institutes, the production of munitions was totally modernized and automated with an investment of about $3,000,000. The company has a number of 400m (437yds) testing ranges. About 80 percent of the company's output is exported to countries throughout the world. The company makes two small-bore rifles and a range of pump-action shotguns. The range of ammunitions consists of various pistol and rifle calibres and 20mm and 30mm cannon shells.

Mag Tech MT 122

TECHNICAL DETAILS

Calibre	: .22 LR
Cartridge capacity	: 10-rounds cartridge holder
Magazine catch	: at rear of magazine aperture
Action	: bolt-action
Locking	: locking lugs
Weight	: 2.5kg (5lb 8oz)
Length	: 92.5cm (363/8in)
Barrel Length	: 54cm (21¼in)

Sight	: adjustable sight, mounting for telescopic sight
External safety	: safety catch on right of receiver, behind bolt
Internal safety	: locking, load indicator behind bolt

CHARACTERISTICS
- material : steel
- finish : blued
- stock : hardwood

Mag Tech MT 122-2 ML

TECHNICAL DETAILS

Calibre	: .22 LR .22 LR
Cartridge capacity	: 10-rounds cartridge holder
Magazine catch	: at rear of magazine aperture
Action	: bolt-action
Locking	: locking lugs
Weight	: 3kg (6lb 8oz)
Length	: 109cm (43in)
Barrel Length	: 61cm (24in)
Sight	: micrometer sight, mounting for telescopic sight
External safety	: safety catch on right of receiver, behind bolt
Internal safety	: locking, load indicator behind bolt

CHARACTERISTICS
- material : steel
- finish : blued
- stock : hardwood

Marlin

John Mahlon Marlin was born in Connecticut in 1836. Before the American Civil War of 1861 to 1865, he studied as an apprentice toolmaker and foundryman. During the Civil War he worked in the Colt plant at Hertford. In 1870, he set-up his own business in New Haven, Connecticut and his early successes were with his 1891 and 1893 model rifles that today are Marlin's models 39 and 336. His company also made a range of revolvers, pistols, and derringers between 1870 and 1899. The company was strengthened in 1873 by the addition of Charles Daly. He was the designer of the famous Ballard match rifle that was subsequently produced in diverse calibres by Marlin. Daly sold his share in the company back to Marlin in 1893. With Winchester having started with a very successful range of lever-action rifles in about 1870, John Marlin wanted to win a share of this new market so he brought out his model 1881 in that year in .45-70 Government calibre. This was a popular calibre at this time because the US Army had used this cartridge in their 1873 Springfield Trapdoor rifles. In order to strengthen the construction of the lever-action, Marlin developed a receiver and mechanism housing that ejected the spent cartridge at the side instead of at the customary opening at the top. Marlin has since adhered to this principle. In 1893, Marlin brought out lever-action rifles for .32-40, and .38-55 calibres.

When a new smokeless cartridge, the .30-30 Winchester, was introduced, he immediately brought out an appropriate range of rifles for it. Famous models from those times are his 1891 and 1897 rifles that were used by Annie Oakley and "Buffalo Bill" Cody in their Wild West shows. John Marlin died in 1901 and the business was carried on by his two sons. In that same year, they took over the Ideal Manufacturing Company that they sold again in 1925 to Lyman. During that time they also made other products, such as shoe-horns and handcuffs. Early in World War I, in 1915, Marlin was purchased by a New York trading company which changed the company name to the Marlin Rockwell Corporation. Production of sporting and hunting rifles dwindled significantly and the main activity was the manufacture of the Colt-Browning M1895 machine-gun for the US Army. After the war, Rockwell had no interest in sporting and hunting rifles so Marlin-Rockwell continued as an independent concern until 1923.

Financial difficulties led to the business having to be sold in 1924. Because of a lack of interest, the company came into the hands of a lawyer, Frank Kenna, for $100, who had to take over the $100,000 company loan. Since then the business has remained in the Kenna family. It was taken over by Roger Kenna in 1947 following his father's death that year. In 1953, the company introduced its Micro-Groove system. The machining of rifling in barrels had been a long-winded and costly process but Marlin's engineers developed a process in which a large number of small and shallow grooves could be cut in one procedure.

Roger Kenna was succeeded by his son Frank in 1959, and in 1969 the business moved to an entirely new factory in North Haven, Connecticut. In commemoration of the 125th anniversary, in 1990, of the company's founding, during which time 25,000,000 rifles have been made and sold, a special model M1894CL was brought out.

Marlin model 15YN "Little Buckarro"

TECHNICAL DETAILS

Calibre	: .22 LR
.22 LR, .22 Long, .22 Short	
Cartridge capacity	: single shot
Magazine catch	: not applicable
Action	: bolt-action
Locking	: locking lugs
Weight	: 4lb 4oz (1.9kg)
Length	: 33¼in (84.5cm)
Barrel Length	: 16¼in (41.3cm) with 16 Micro-Grooves
Sight	: adjustable sight, mounting for telescopic sight
External safety	: safety catch on right of receiver, behind bolt
Internal safety	: locking, load indicator behind bolt

CHARACTERISTICS
- material : steel
- finish : blued
- stock : hardwood

Marlin model 1894 Century Limited

TECHNICAL DETAILS

Calibre	: .44-40
Cartridge capacity	: 12-rounds tubular magazine
Magazine catch	: not applicable, loading port in right of receiver
Action	: lever-action
Locking	: lever-locking
Weight	: 6lb 8oz (2.95kg)
Length	: 40³⁄₈in (103.5cm)
Barrel Length	: 24in (61cm)
Sight	: adjustable folding sight, suitable for telescopic sight
External safety	: safety catch on right of casing, beneath hammer
Internal safety	: locking, firing-pin safety system, trigger block when lever not fully closed, half-cock hammer safety

CHARACTERISTICS
- material : steel
- finish : blued, engraved casing with inlay of gold
- stock : walnut

This model was produced in limited quantities in 1994 to celebrate 100 years of the Marlin company's existence.

Marlin model 1894 CL

TECHNICAL DETAILS

Calibre	: .25-20 Win., .32-20 Win.

Cartridge capacity	: 6-rounds tubular magazine
Magazine catch	: not applicable, loading port in right of receiver
Action	: lever-action
Locking	: lever-locking
Weight	: 6lb 4oz (2.8kg)
Length	: 38¾in (98.4cm)
Barrel Length	: 22in (55.9cm)
Sight	: adjustable folding sight, suitable for telescopic sight
External safety	: safety catch on right of casing, beneath hammer
Internal safety	: locking, firing-pin safety system, trigger block when lever not fully closed, half-cock hammer safety

CHARACTERISTICS
- material : steel
- finish : blued
- stock : walnut

Marlin model 1894 Cowboy

TECHNICAL DETAILS

Calibre	: .45 Long Colt
Cartridge capacity	: 10-rounds tubular magazine
Magazine catch	: not applicable, loading port in right of receiver
Action	: lever-action
Locking	: lever-locking
Weight	: 7lb 8oz (3.4kg)
Length	: 41½in (105.4cm)
Barrel Length	: 24in (61cm)
Sight	: adjustable folding sight, suitable for telescopic sight
External safety	: safety catch on right of casing, beneath hammer
Internal safety	: locking, firing-pin safety system, trigger block when lever not fully closed, half-cock hammer safety

CHARACTERISTICS
- material : steel

• finish	: blued
• stock	: walnut

Marlin model 1894CS

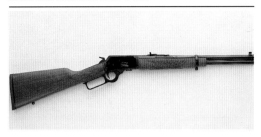

TECHNICAL DETAILS

Calibre	: .357 Magnum/ .38 Special
Cartridge capacity	: 9-rounds tubular magazine
Magazine catch	: not applicable, loading port in right of receiver
Action	: lever-action
Locking	: lever-locking
Weight	: 6lb (2.7kg)
Length	: 36in (91.4cm)
Barrel Length	: 18½in (47cm) with 12 Micro-Grooves
Sight	: adjustable folding sight, suitable for telescopic sight
External safety	: safety catch on right of casing, beneath hammer
Internal safety	: locking, firing-pin safety system, trigger block when lever not fully closed, half-cock hammer safety

CHARACTERISTICS
- material : steel
- finish : blued
- stock : walnut

Marlin model 1894S

TECHNICAL DETAILS

Calibre : .44 Mag./.44 Spec.
Cartridge capacity : 10-rounds tubular magazine
Magazine catch : not applicable, loading port in right of receiver
Action : lever-action
Locking : lever-locking
Weight : 6lb (2.7kg)
Length : 37½in (95.3cm)
Barrel Length : 20in (50.8cm) with 12 Micro-Grooves
Sight : adjustable folding sight, suitable for telescopic sight
External safety : safety catch on right of casing, beneath hammer
Internal safety : locking, firing-pin safety system, trigger block when lever not fully closed, half-cock hammer safety

CHARACTERISTICS

• material : steel
• finish : blued
• stock : walnut

Marlin model 1895SS

TECHNICAL DETAILS

Calibre : .45-70 Govt.
Cartridge capacity : 4-rounds tubular magazine
Magazine catch : not applicable, loading port in right of receiver
Action : lever-action
Locking : lever-locking
Weight : 7lb 8oz (3.4kg)
Length : 40½in (102.9cm)
Barrel Length : 22in (55.9cm) with 12 Micro-Grooves
Sight : adjustable folding sight, suitable for telescopic sight
External safety : safety catch on right of casing, beneath hammer
Internal safety : locking, firing-pin safety system, trigger block when lever not fully closed, half-cock hammer safety

CHARACTERISTICS

• material : steel
• finish : blued
• stock : walnut with pistol grip

Marlin model 2000L

TECHNICAL DETAILS

Calibre : .22 LR
Cartridge capacity : single shot
Magazine catch : not applicable
Action : bolt-action
Locking : locking lugs
Weight : 8lb (3.6kg)
Length : 41in (104.1cm)
Barrel Length : 22in (55.9cm) with Micro-Grooves
Sight : optical sight and bead tunnel
External safety : safety catch on right behind bolt
Internal safety : locking, load indicator at rear of bolt

CHARACTERISTICS

• material : steel
• finish : blued
• stock : laminated wood

This rifle is also available with a blue-finished Kevlar stock and a conversion kit to adapt it to accept a 5-rounds magazine is also available.

Marlin model 25MN

TECHNICAL DETAILS

Calibre : .22 WMR
Cartridge capacity : 7-rounds cartridge holder
Magazine catch : at rear of magazine aperture
Action : bolt-action
Locking : locking lugs
Weight : 6lb (2.7kg)
Length : 41in (104.1cm)
Barrel Length : 22in (55.9cm) with 20 Micro-Grooves
Sight : adjustable sight, mounting for telescopic sight
External safety : safety catch on right behind bolt
Internal safety : locking, load indicator at rear of bolt

CHARACTERISTICS

• material : steel
• finish : blued
• stock : hardwood

Marlin model 25N

TECHNICAL DETAILS

Calibre : .22 LR
Cartridge capacity : 7-rounds cartridge holder
Magazine catch : at rear of magazine aperture
Action : bolt-action
Locking : locking lugs
Weight : 5lb 8oz (2.5kg)
Length : 41in (104.1cm)
Barrel Length : 22in (55.9cm) with 16 Micro-Grooves
Sight : adjustable sight, mounting for telescopic sight
External safety : safety catch on right behind bolt
Internal safety : locking, load indicator at rear of bolt

CHARACTERISTICS

• material : steel
• finish : blued
• stock : hardwood

Marlin model 30AS

TECHNICAL DETAILS

Calibre : .30-30 Win.
Cartridge capacity : 6-rounds tubular magazine
Magazine catch : not applicable, loading port at rear of casing
Action : lever-action
Locking : lever-locking
Weight : 7lb (3.2kg)
Length : 38¼in (97.2cm)
Barrel Length : 20in (50.8cm) with 12 Micro-Grooves
Sight : adjustable folding sight, mounting for telescopic sight
External safety : safety catch on right of casing beneath hammer
Internal safety : locking, firing-pin safety system, trigger block when lever not fully closed, half-cock hammer safety

CHARACTERISTICS

• material : steel
• finish : blued
• stock : beech with pistol grip

Marlin model 336CS

TECHNICAL DETAILS

Calibre : .30-30 Win., .35 Rem.
Cartridge capacity : 6-rounds tubular magazine
Magazine catch : not applicable, loading port at rear of casing
Action : lever-action
Locking : lever-locking
Weight : 7lb (3.2kg)
Length : 38½in (97.8cm)

Barrel Length	: 20in (50.8cm) with 12 Micro-Grooves
Sight	: adjustable folding sight and bead tunnel, suitable for telescopic sight
External safety	: safety catch on right of casing beneath hammer
Internal safety	: locking, firing-pin safety system, trigger block when lever not fully closed, half-cock hammer safety

CHARACTERISTICS
- material : steel
- finish : blued
- stock : walnut with pistol grip

Marlin model 39AS

TECHNICAL DETAILS

Calibre	: .22 LR, .22 Long, .22 Short
Cartridge capacity	: tubular magazine for 19, 21, or 26 rounds respectively
Magazine catch	: not applicable, loading port in centre of casing
Action	: lever-action
Locking	: lever-locking
Weight	: 6lb 8oz (3kg)
Length	: 40in (101.6cm)
Barrel Length	: 24in (61cm) with 16 Micro-Grooves
Sight	: adjustable folding sight and bead tunnel, suitable for telescopic sight
External safety	: safety catch on right of casing beneath hammer
Internal safety	: locking

CHARACTERISTICS
- material : steel
- finish : blued
- stock : walnut with pistol grip

A large screw on the right of the mechanism housing can be unscrewed with a coin to split the rifle into two parts for carrying.

Marlin model 39TDS

TECHNICAL DETAILS

Calibre	: .22 LR, .22 Long, .22 Short
Cartridge capacity	: tubular magazine for 11, 12, or 16 rounds respectively
Magazine catch	: not applicable, loading port in centre of magazine
Action	: lever-action
Locking	: lever-locking
Weight	: 5lb 4oz (2.4kg)
Length	: 32½in (82.6cm)
Barrel Length	: 16½in (41.9cm) with 16 Micro-Grooves
Sight	: adjustable folding sight and bead tunnel, suitable for telescopic sight
External safety	: safety catch on right of casing beneath hammer
Internal safety	: locking

CHARACTERISTICS
- material : steel
- finish : blued
- stock : walnut with pistol grip

This weapon is the carbine version of model 39AS. A large screw on the right of the mechanism housing can be unscrewed with a coin to split the rifle into two parts for carrying.

Marlin model 444SS

TECHNICAL DETAILS

Calibre	: .444 Marlin
Cartridge capacity	: 5-rounds tubular magazine
Magazine catch	: not applicable, loading port on right of casing

Action : lever-action
Locking : lever-locking
Weight : 7lb 8oz (3.4kg)
Length : 40½in (102.9cm)
Barrel Length : 22in (55.9cm) with 12
Micro-Grooves
Sight : adjustable folding sight and
bead tunnel, suitable for
telescopic sight
External safety : safety catch on right of
casing beneath hammer
Internal safety : locking, firing-pin safety
system, trigger block when
lever not fully closed,
half-cock hammer safety

CHARACTERISTICS
• material : steel
• finish : blued
• stock : walnut with pistol grip

Marlin model 45

TECHNICAL DETAILS
Calibre : .45 ACP
Cartridge capacity : 7-rounds cartridge holder
Magazine catch : push-button on right of
magazine
Action : semi-automatic
Locking : inertia
Weight : 6lb 12oz (3.1kg)
Length : 35½in (90.2cm)
Barrel Length : 16½in (41.9cm)
12 Micro-Grooves
Sight : adjustable sight, suitable for
telescopic sight

External safety : safety catch in front of
trigger guard
Internal safety : locking, load indicator,
magazine safety system

CHARACTERISTICS
• material : steel
• finish : blued
• stock : beech with pistol grip

Marlin model 60-Blue

TECHNICAL DETAILS
Calibre : .22 LR
Cartridge capacity : 17-rounds tubular magazine
Magazine catch : not applicable, loading port
mid-way along tubular
magazine
Action : semi-automatic
Locking : inertia
Weight : 5lb 8oz (2.5kg)
Length : 40½in (102.9cm)
Barrel Length : 22in (55.9cm) with
16 Micro-Grooves
Sight : adjustable sight and bead
tunnel, mounting for
telescopic sight
External safety : doubled-sided push-button
safety catch
Internal safety : locking

CHARACTERISTICS
• material : steel
• finish : blued
• stock : hardwood

Marlin model 60SS

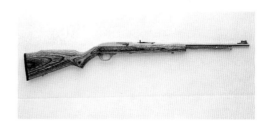

TECHNICAL DETAILS

Calibre	: .22 LR
Cartridge capacity	: 17-rounds tubular magazine
Magazine catch	: not applicable, loading port mid-way along tubular magazine
Action	: semi-automatic
Locking	: inertia
Weight	: 5lb 8oz (2.5kg)
Length	: 40½in (102.9cm)
Barrel Length	: 22in (55.9cm) with 16 Micro-Grooves
Sight	: adjustable sight and bead tunnel, mounting for telescopic sight
External safety	: doubled-sided push-button safety catch
Internal safety	: locking

CHARACTERISTICS

• material	: stainless-steel
• finish	: bare metal
• stock	: laminated wood or hard-wood

Marlin model 70HC

TECHNICAL DETAILS

Calibre	: .22 LR
Cartridge capacity	: 15-rounds cartridge holder
Magazine catch	: catch at rear of magazine aperture
Action	: semi-automatic
Locking	: inertia
Weight	: 5lb (2.3kg)
Length	: 36¾in (93.4cm)
Barrel Length	: 18in (45.7cm) with 16 Micro-Grooves
Sight	: adjustable sight, mounting for telescopic sight
External safety	: push-button safety catch in rear of trigger guard
Internal safety	: locking

CHARACTERISTICS

• material	: steel
• finish	: blued
• stock	: hardwood with pistol grip

Marlin model 70-P "Papoose"

TECHNICAL DETAILS

Calibre	: .22 LR
Cartridge capacity	: 7-rounds cartridge holder
Magazine catch	: at front of magazine aperture
Action	: semi-automatic
Locking	: inertia
Weight	: 3lb 4oz (1.5kg)
Length	: 35¼in (89.5cm)
Barrel Length	: 16¼in (41.3cm) with 16 Micro-Grooves
Sight	: adjustable sight, mounting for telescopic sight
External safety	: doubled-sided push-button safety catch in trigger guard
Internal safety	: locking

CHARACTERISTICS

• material	: steel
• finish	: blued
• stock	: hardwood

The rifle can be taken apart by unscrewing the barrel crew. The name "Papoose" is derived from a native American word for the way in which a baby was carried in a bundle on a squaw's back. The intention is to suggest the ease with which this rifle can be carried on long treks. Other makers call this type of rifle a "back packer."

Marlin model 70-PSS "Papoose Stainless"

TECHNICAL DETAILS

Calibre	: .22 LR

Cartridge capacity	: 7-rounds cartridge holder
Magazine catch	: at front of magazine aperture
Action	: semi-automatic
Locking	: inertia
Weight	: 3lb 4oz (1.5kg)
Length	: 35¼in (89.5cm)
Barrel Length	: 16¼in (41.3cm) with 16 Micro-Grooves
Sight	: adjustable sight and bead tunnel, mounting for telescopic sight
External safety	: doubled-sided push-button safety catch in trigger guard
Internal safety	: locking

CHARACTERISTICS

• material	: stainless-steel
• finish	: bare metal
• stock	: black glass reinforced polyester

This rifle can be taken apart by means of the barrel screw.

Marlin model 75C

TECHNICAL DETAILS

Calibre	: .22 LR
Cartridge capacity	: 13-rounds tubular magazine
Magazine catch	: not applicable, loading port half-way along tubular magazine

Action	: semi-automatic
Locking	: inertia
Weight	: 5lb (2.3kg)
Length	: 36½in (92.7cm)
Barrel Length	: 18in (45.7cm) with 16 Micro-Grooves
Sight	: adjustable sight, mounting for telescopic sight
External safety	: doubled-sided push-button safety catch in trigger guard
Internal safety	: locking

CHARACTERISTICS

• material	: steel
• finish	: blued
• stock	: hardwood

This is the carbine version of Marlin model 60.

Marlin model 880 Blue

TECHNICAL DETAILS

Calibre	: .22 LR
Cartridge capacity	: 7-rounds cartridge holder
Magazine catch	: at rear of magazine aperture
Action	: bolt-action
Locking	: locking lugs
Weight	: 5lb 8oz (2.5kg)
Length	: 41in (104.1cm)
Barrel Length	: 22in (55.9cm) with 16 Micro-Grooves
Sight	: adjustable sight and bead tunnel, mounting for telescopic sight
External safety	: safety catch on right of receiver, behind bolt
Internal safety	: locking, load indicator at rear of bolt

CHARACTERISTICS

• material	: steel
• finish	: blued
• stock	: walnut with pistol grip

Marlin model 880SQ

TECHNICAL DETAILS

Calibre	: .22 LR
Cartridge capacity	: 7-rounds cartridge holder
Magazine catch	: at rear of magazine aperture
Action	: bolt-action
Locking	: locking lugs
Weight	: 5lb 8oz (2.5kg)
Length	: 41in (104.1cm)
Barrel Length	: 22in (55.9cm) with 16 Micro-Grooves
Sight	: none, mounting for telescopic sight
External safety	: safety catch on right of receiver, behind bolt
Internal safety	: locking, load indicator at rear of bolt

CHARACTERISTICS

- material : steel
- finish : matt black phosphate coating
- stock : black plastic with pistol grip

This rifle is supplied without a telescopic sight

Marlin model 880SS

TECHNICAL DETAILS

Calibre	: .22 LR
Cartridge capacity	: 7-rounds cartridge holder
Magazine catch	: at rear of magazine aperture
Action	: bolt-action
Locking	: locking lugs
Weight	: 5lb 8oz (2.5kg)
Length	: 41in (104.1cm)
Barrel Length	: 22in (55.9cm) with

Sight	16 Micro-Grooves : adjustable sight and bead tunnel, mounting for telescopic sight
External safety	: safety catch on right of receiver, behind bolt
Internal safety	: locking, load indicator at rear of bolt

CHARACTERISTICS

- material : stainless-steel
- finish : bare metal
- stock : black Kevlar with pistol grip

Marlin model 881

TECHNICAL DETAILS

Calibre	: .22 LR, .22 Short, .22 Long
Cartridge capacity	: tubular magazine for 17, 19, and 25 rounds respectively
Magazine catch	: not applicable
Action	: bolt-action
Locking	: locking lugs
Weight	: 6lb (2.7kg)
Length	: 41in (104.1cm)
Barrel Length	: 22in (55.9cm) with 16 Micro-Grooves
Sight	: adjustable leaf sight and bead tunnel, mounting for telescopic sight
External safety	: safety catch on right of receiver, behind bolt
Internal safety	: locking, load indicator at rear of bolt

CHARACTERISTICS

- material : steel
- finish : blued
- stock : walnut with pistol grip

Marlin model 882 Blue

TECHNICAL DETAILS

Calibre	: .22 WMR
Cartridge capacity	: 7-rounds cartridge holder

Magazine catch : at front of magazine
                 aperture
Action   : bolt-action
Locking   : locking lugs
Weight   : 6lb (2.7kg)
Length   : 41in (104.1cm)
Barrel Length : 22in (55.9cm) with
                 20 Micro-Grooves
Sight   : adjustable leaf sight and
                 bead tunnel, mounting for
                 telescopic sight
External safety : safety catch on right of
                  receiver, behind bolt
Internal safety : locking, load indicator at
                  rear of bolt

CHARACTERISTICS
• material   : steel
• finish   : blued
• stock   : walnut with pistol grip

Marlin model 882L

TECHNICAL DETAILS
Calibre   : .22 WMR
Cartridge capacity : 7-rounds cartridge holder
Magazine catch   : at front of magazine apertu-
                     re
Action   : bolt-action
Locking   : locking lugs
Weight   : 6lb (2.7kg)
Length   : 41in (104.1cm)
Barrel Length   : 22in (55.9cm) with
                     20 Micro-Grooves
Sight   : adjustable sight and bead
                     tunnel, mounting for
                     telescopic sight
External safety   : safety catch on right of
                     receiver, behind bolt

Internal safety : locking, load indicator at
                  rear of bolt

CHARACTERISTICS
• material   : steel
• finish   : blued
• stock   : laminated wood

Marlin model 882SS

TECHNICAL DETAILS
Calibre   : .22 WMR
Cartridge capacity : 7-rounds cartridge holder
Magazine catch   : at front of magazine
                     aperture
Action   : bolt-action
Locking   : locking lugs
Weight   : 6lb (2.7kg)
Length   : 41in (104.1cm)
Barrel Length   : 22in (55.9cm) with
                     20 Micro-Grooves
Sight   : adjustable sight and bead
                     tunnel, mounting for
                     telescopic sight
External safety   : safety catch on right of
                     receiver, behind bolt
Internal safety   : locking, load indicator at
                     rear of bolt

CHARACTERISTICS
• material   : stainless-steel
• finish   : bare metal
• stock   : black Kevlar

Marlin model 883 Blue

TECHNICAL DETAILS
Calibre   : .22 WMR

Cartridge capacity : 12-rounds tubular magazine
Magazine catch : not applicable
Action : bolt-action
Locking : locking lugs
Weight : 6lb (2.7kg)
Length : 41in (104.1cm)
Barrel Length : 22in (55.9cm) with
20 Micro-Grooves
Sight : adjustable sight and bead
tunnel, mounting for
telescopic sight
External safety : safety catch on right of
receiver, behind bolt
Internal safety : locking, load indicator at
rear of bolt

CHARACTERISTICS
• material : steel
• finish : blued
• stock : walnut with pistol grip

Marlin model 883 Nickel

TECHNICAL DETAILS
Calibre : .22 WMR
Cartridge capacity : 12-rounds tubular magazine
Magazine catch : not applicable
Action : bolt-action
Locking : locking lugs
Weight : 6lb (2.7kg)
Length : 41in (104.1cm)
Barrel Length : 22in (55.9cm) with
20 Micro-Grooves
Sight : adjustable sight and orange
bead and bead tunnel,
mounting for telescopic
sight
External safety : safety catch on right of
receiver, behind bolt
Internal safety : locking, load indicator at
rear of bolt

CHARACTERISTICS
• material : steel
• finish : nickel-plated
• stock : walnut with pistol grip

Marlin model 883SS

TECHNICAL DETAILS
Calibre : .22 WMR
Cartridge capacity : 7-rounds cartridge holder
Magazine catch : at front of magazine
aperture
Action : bolt-action
Locking : locking lugs
Weight : 6lb (2.7kg)
Length : 41in (104.1cm)
Barrel Length : 22in (55.9cm) with
20 Micro-Grooves
Sight : adjustable sight and bead
tunnel, mounting for
telescopic sight
External safety : safety catch on right of
receiver, behind bolt
Internal safety : locking, load indicator at
rear of bolt

CHARACTERISTICS
• material : stainless-steel
• finish : bare metal
• stock : laminated wood

Marlin model 9

TECHNICAL DETAILS
Calibre : 9mm Para.
Cartridge capacity : 10-rounds cartridge holder
Magazine catch : push-button on right of
magazine housing
Action : semi-automatic
Locking : inertia
Weight : 6lb 12oz (3.1kg)
Length : 35½in (90.2cm)
Barrel Length : 16½in (41.9cm)
with 12 Micro-Grooves

Sight	: adjustable sight, suitable for telescopic sight
External safety	: safety catch at front of trigger guard
Internal safety	: locking, load indicator magazine safety system

CHARACTERISTICS
- material : steel
- finish : blued or nickel-plated
- stock : beech with pistol grip

Marlin model 922 Magnum

TECHNICAL DETAILS
Calibre	: .22 WMR
Cartridge capacity	: 7-rounds cartridge holder
Magazine catch	: catch at rear of magazine aperture
Action	: semi-automatic
Locking	: inertia
Weight	: 6lb 8oz (3kg)
Length	: 39¼in (101cm)
Barrel Length	: 20½in (52.1cm) with 20 Micro-Grooves
Sight	: adjustable sight and bead tunnel, suitable for telescopic sight
External safety	: safety catch at front of trigger guard
Internal safety	: locking, magazine safety system

CHARACTERISTICS
- material : steel
- finish : blued
- stock : walnut with pistol grip

Marlin model 995

TECHNICAL DETAILS
Calibre	: .22 LR
Cartridge capacity	: 7-rounds cartridge holder
Magazine catch	: catch at rear of magazine aperture
Action	: semi-automatic

Locking	: inertia
Weight	: 5lb (2.3kg)
Length	: 36¼in (93.4cm)
Barrel Length	: 18in (45.7cm) with 16 Micro-Grooves
Sight	: adjustable sight, mounting for telescopic sight
External safety	: push-button safety catch in rear of trigger guard
Internal safety	: locking

CHARACTERISTICS
- material : steel
- finish : blued
- stock : walnut with pistol grip

Marlin model 995SS-Stainless

TECHNICAL DETAILS
Calibre	: .22 LR
Cartridge capacity	: 7-rounds cartridge holder
Magazine catch	: catch at rear of magazine aperture
Action	: semi-automatic
Locking	: inertia
Weight	: 5lb (2.3kg)
Length	: 37in (94cm)
Barrel Length	: 18in (45.7cm) with 16 Micro-Grooves
Sight	: adjustable sight, mounting for telescopic sight
External safety	: push-button safety catch in rear of trigger guard
Internal safety	: locking

CHARACTERISTICS
- material : stainless-steel
- finish : bare metal, nickel-plated cartridge holder

- stock : black plastic with pistol grip

Marlin MR-7

TECHNICAL DETAILS

Calibre	: .270 Win., .30-06 Spr.
Cartridge capacity	: 4-rounds cartridge holder
Magazine catch	: at front of trigger guard
Action	: bolt-action
Locking	: 2 locking lugs
Weight	: 7lb 8oz (3.4kg)
Length	: 43in (109.2cm)
Barrel Length	: 22in (55.9cm)
Sight	: adjustable Williams sight or none, suitable for telescopic sight
External safety	: winged safety catch on right behind bolt
Internal safety	: locking

CHARACTERISTICS

• material	: steel
• finish	: blued
• stock	: walnut with pistol grip

Mauser

Peter Paul Mauser, the founder of the world-famous Mauser arms company, was born in 1838 in Oberndorf am Neckar in Baden-Württemberg, Germany.

His father, Franz Andreas Mauser, worked as a master gunsmith for the state arsenal in that town. Peter Paul Mauser was required to do military service in 1859 and was recruited to the artillery. His first invention was for a rear breech-loading cannon but the military saw no value in it. In 1865, he developed his first bolt-action rifle with a sprung firing pin that was only driven from the bolt by means of a tumbler in the trigger mechanism. This was a great advantage over other designs with protruding firing pins because loaded cartridges were known from time to time to be fired accidentally before the weapon was fully locked. On the basis of his prototype, Mauser was granted a development credit by the government for machines and materials. This led to the formation of the first Mauser company, with his brother Wilhelm taking care of commercial management. One problem though was that neither his own country or those surrounding Prussia had any interest in a new army rifle.

The Mauser brothers had contact in 1866 with Samuel Norris from the American Remington Arms Company, who saw a commercial future for the Mauser design. The rifles would be made at a factory in Liege, Belgium, and also in the United States. In this manner, the Mauser-Norris rifle came to be introduced in 1867. Norris hoped to sell the rifle to the French army which wanted to replace their Chassepot rifles but, unfortunately, the French chose a weapon of French origin. On top of this, the Remington board was not prepared support the project. With hindsight, Remington must have regretted this decision enormously. The Prussian army did adopt the rifle in 1871 giving it the designation M71. The rifle had a calibre of 11mm and used a blackpowder cartridge of 11.15 x 60R.

The state arsenal in Oberndorf was sold to the Mauser brothers company, Mauser & Cie, in 1873, giving them access to manufacturing facilities. The rifles were also made in Erfurt, Spandau, Amberg, and Danzig, plus at Steyr in Austria. Wilhelm Mauser died in 1882 and the company was changed into Waffenfabrik Mauser AG.

That same year, a new type of M71 was developed with a tubular magazine for 8 cartridges, known as the M71/84. This was followed in 1887 by the M87 model in 9.5mm calibre for the Turkish army. In 1888 the company made the Gewehr 88 (rifle 88) or Kommissions-Gewehr (officially procured rifle) in 7.92 calibre because the army was not satisfied with the M71 rifle with its tubular magazine. The Belgian army decided to switch to the Mauser rifle in 1889 and these were made under licence by the FN factory in 7.65 Mauser calibre. The Spanish army too wanted the weapon but in 7mm calibre

(7 x 57mm). This weapon appeared to be so exceptional for its time that it gave the Americans considerable trouble during the Spanish-American War in 1898. The US Army decided to develop a similar weapon, which led to the Springfield M1903. This rifle was identical to the Mauser design so that the US government was forced to pay $200,000 for infringing patent rights to the Mauser company. The German army decided in 1889 to adopt the rifle as Gewehr 98 in 7.92 Mauser calibre. Shorter versions were designated Kar-98a in 1904, Kar-98b (after World War I), and Kar-98k in 1935. Military Mauser rifles are produced in many countries along with countless sporting and hunting versions in 8 x 57mm calibre. The rifle is also made in many different calibres ranging from 9.3 x 57mm to 6.5 x 54mm. Paul Mauser died in 1914 and the company's name was changed in 1922 to Mauser-Werke AG. After the ban on weapons production following World War II, the company was restarted as Mauser-Werke Oberndorf Waffensysteme GmbH. The numerous versions, modifications, and types of Mauser rifles are so numerous that it is impossible to cover them fully within this book.

Sight	: adjustable leaf sight and bead tunnel, special mounting for telescopic sight
External safety	: safety catch to block firing-pin and bolt with protection against accidentally moving safety catch
Internal safety	: locking

CHARACTERISTICS

• material	: steel
• finish	: blued
• stock	: various walnut stocks with pistol grip. Custom engraving of stock/ and or receiver (see illustration)

Available calibres (standard): .243 Win., 6.5 x 57mm, .270 Win., 7 x 64mm, .30-06 Spr.,.308 Win., 9.3 x 62mm; (Magnum): 6.5 x 68mm, 7mm Rem. Mag., 8 x 68S, .300 Win. Mag., .300 Wby Mag., 9.3 x 64mm; (carbine): .243 Win., 6.5 x 57mm, .270 Win., 7 x 64mm, .30-06 Spr., 9.3 x 62mm; (big game): .375 H & H Mag., .458 Win. Mag.

Within this range of calibres, changeable barrels are available for this rifle.

Mauser model 66S

TECHNICAL DETAILS

Calibre	: see below
Cartridge capacity	: 3-rounds internal magazine
Magazine catch	: not applicable, loaded via breech
Action	: bolt-action
Locking	: 2 locking lugs
Weight	: 3.3-4.2kg (7lb 5oz-9lb 5oz)
Length	: 108-112cm (42½-44⅛in)
Barrel Length	: 60-65cm (23⅝-25⅝in)

Mauser model 66 SP Sniper

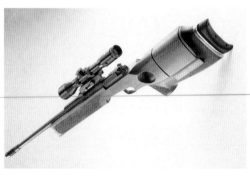

TECHNICAL DETAILS

Calibre	: .308 Win
Cartridge capacity	: 3-rounds internal magazine
Magazine catch	: not applicable, loaded via breech
Action	: bolt-action
Locking	: 2 locking lugs
Weight	: 5.4kg (12lb) excluding telescopic sight
Length	: 133cm (523/8in)
Barrel Length	: 75cm (29½in) including muzzle attenuator

Sight   : none, special mounting for
                        telescopic sight, or optical
                        sight with bead tunnel
External safety   : safety catch on rear of bolt
Internal safety   : locking

CHARACTERISTICS
- material   : steel
- finish   : matt blued
- stock   : walnut with thumb-hole and
                        pistol grip

Mauser model 83 Sport

TECHNICAL DETAILS
Calibre   : .308 Win
Cartridge capacity   : single shot
Magazine catch   : not applicable
Action   : bolt-action
Locking   : 2 locking lugs
Weight   : 4.8kg (10lb 10oz)
Length   : 116cm (45¼in)
Barrel Length   : 65cm (25⅜in)
Sight   : Anschütz optical sight and
                        bead tunnel
External safety   : winged safety catch at rear
                        of bolt
Internal safety   : locking

CHARACTERISTICS
- material   : steel
- finish   : blued
- stock   : special match stock with
                        thumb-hole and pistol grip

This rifle is also available in a UIT-free
rifle version or CISM standard rifle with
a 10-rounds cartridge holder.

Mauser model 86/86SR (Sniper rifle)

TECHNICAL DETAILS
Calibre   : .308 Win
Cartridge capacity   : 9-rounds cartridge holder
Magazine catch   : right-hand side of magazine
                        aperture
Action   : bolt-action

Locking   : 2 locking lugs
Weight   : 4.9kg (10lb 13oz)
Length   : 124cm (48¼in)
Barrel Length   : 75cm (29½in) including
                        muzzle attenuator
Sight   : none, special mounting for
                        telescopic sight or optical
                        sight and bead tunnel
External safety   : winged safety catch at rear
                        of bolt
Internal safety   : locking

CHARACTERISTICS
- material   : steel
- finish   : matt blued
- stock   : laminated wood stock with
                        thumb-hole and pistol grip
                        or special camouflage stock;
                        fitting for attaching bipod or
                        shooting sling

Mauser model SR 93 Sniper

TECHNICAL DETAILS
Calibre   : .308 Win., .300 Win. Mag.
Cartridge capacity   : 3-rounds magazine
Magazine catch   : not applicable
Action   : bolt-action
Locking   : 2 locking lugs
Weight   : 8kg (17lb 10oz)
Length   : 123.5cm (48⅝in)
Barrel Length   : 65cm (25⅜in) excluding
                        muzzle attenuator
Sight   : none, special mounting for
                        telescopic sight or optical
                        sight and bead tunnel

External safety   : winged safety catch at rear
                      of bolt
Internal safety   : locking
CHARACTERISTICS
• material   : steel
• finish   : matt blued
• stock   : special stock with thumb-
                      hole, pistol grip, and bipod

Mauser M94

TECHNICAL DETAILS
Calibre   : see below
Cartridge capacity : standard:4 rounds;
                      Magnum: 3 rounds
Magazine catch   : at front of magazine
                      aperture
Action   : bolt-action
Locking   : 6 locking lugs
Weight   : 3.3kg (7lb 5oz)
Length   : 108cm (42½in) standard;
                      113cm (44½in) Magnum
Barrel Length   : 56cm (22in) standard; 61cm
                      (24in) Magnum
Sight   : side adjustment leaf sight
External safety   : safety catch on right of
                      receiver
Internal safety   : locking
CHARACTERISTICS
• material   : steel
• finish   : blued
• stock   : walnut with pistol grip

Calibres available (standard): .243 Win.,
.270 Win., 7 x 64, .308 Win., .30-06 Spr.,
9.3 x 62; (Magnum): 7mm Rem. Mag.,
.300 Win. Mag., 8 x 68S.

Mauser M96

TECHNICAL DETAILS
Calibre   : .270 Win., .30-06 Spr.
Cartridge capacity : 5 rounds
Magazine catch   : not applicable, loading via
                      breech
Action   : horizontally-acting bolt
Locking   : 16 locking lugs

Weight   : 2.8kg (6lb 4oz)
Length   : 106.7cm (42in)
Barrel Length   : 55.9cm (22in)
Sight   : none, suitable for telescopic
                      sight
External safety   : sliding safety catch on top of
                      pistol grip
Internal safety   : locking, disengagement of
                      firing pin when bolt is
                      opened
CHARACTERISTICS
• material   : steel
• finish   : blued
• stock   : walnut with pistol grip

Mauser M98 Original

TECHNICAL DETAILS
Calibre   : .243 Win., 6.5 x 57, .308
                      Win., .30-06 Spr., 8 x 57IS,
                      9.3 x 62
Cartridge capacity : 5 rounds
Magazine catch   : not applicable, loading via
                      breech
Action   : bolt-action
Locking   : 2 locking lugs
Weight   : 3.2kg (7lb 1oz)
Length   : 111cm (43¼in)
Barrel Length   : 56cm (22in)

Sight	: adjustable leaf sight, special mount for telescopic sight
External safety	: Mauser winged safety catch on rear of bolt
Internal safety	: locking

CHARACTERISTICS
- material : steel
- finish : blued
- stock : walnut with pistol grip

Illustrated from top to bottom: the Mauser M98 Original and M98 carbine.

Mauser M98 carbine

TECHNICAL DETAILS

Calibre	: .243 Win., 6.5 x 57, .308 Win., .30-06 Spr., 8 x 57IS, 9.3 x 62
Cartridge capacity	: 5 rounds
Magazine catch	: not applicable, loading via breech
Action	: bolt-action
Locking	: 2 locking lugs
Weight	: 3.4kg (7lb 8oz)
Length	: 111cm (43¾in)
Barrel Length	: 56cm (22in)
Sight	: adjustable leaf sight, special mount for telescopic sight
External safety	: Mauser winged safety catch on rear of bolt
Internal safety	: locking

CHARACTERISTICS
- material : steel
- finish : blued
- stock : walnut with pistol grip runs full length under barrel to muzzle

Mauser model 105

TECHNICAL DETAILS

| Calibre | : .22 LR |
| Cartridge capacity | : 5, 8, or 15-rounds cartridge holder |

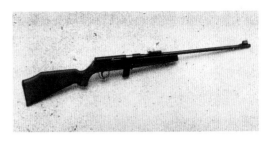

Magazine catch	: at front of magazine aperture
Action	: semi-automatic
Locking	: inertia
Weight	: 2.3kg (5lb 1oz)
Length	: 105cm (413/8in)
Barrel Length	: 55cm (21¾in)
Sight	: adjustable rack sight, mounting for telescopic sight
External safety	: receiver can be locked by means of cocking lever
Internal safety	: locking

CHARACTERISTICS
- material : steel
- finish : blued
- stock : beech with pistol grip

Mauser model 107

TECHNICAL DETAILS

Calibre	: .22 LR
Cartridge capacity	: 5, or 8-rounds cartridge holder
Magazine catch	: at front of magazine aperture
Action	: bolt-action
Locking	: bolt locking
Weight	: 2.3kg (5lb 1oz)
Length	: 102cm (40⅛in)
Barrel Length	: 55cm (21¾in)
Sight	: adjustable rack sight, mounting for telescopic sight
External safety	: safety catch at rear of bolt
Internal safety	: locking

CHARACTERISTICS

- material : steel
- finish : blued
- stock : beech with pistol grip

Mauser model 201-Luxus

TECHNICAL DETAILS

Calibre : .22 LR or .22 WMR
Cartridge capacity : 5-rounds cartridge holder
Magazine catch : at front of magazine
  aperture
Action : bolt-action
Locking : 2 locking lugs
Weight : 2.8kg (6lb 3oz)
Length : 102cm (40⅛in)
Barrel Length : 55cm (21¾in)
Sight : side adjusting leaf sight,
  mounting for telescopic
  sight
External safety : safety catch at rear of bolt
Internal safety : locking

CHARACTERISTICS

- material : steel
- finish : blued
- stock : walnut with pistol grip

The same rifle is available with a beech stock as Model 201.

Mauser model 225 Standard

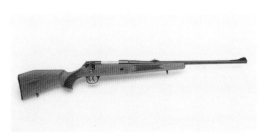

TECHNICAL DETAILS

Calibre : see below
Cartridge capacity : 3-5 rounds cartridge holder
Magazine catch : at front of magazine
  aperture
Action : bolt-action
Locking : 2 locking lugs
Weight : 3.7-4kg (8lb 3oz-8lb 13oz)
Length : 113-117cm (44½-46in)
Barrel Length : 60-65cm (23⅝-25⅝in)
Sight : side adjusting leaf sight,
  suitable for telescopic sight
External safety : safety catch at rear of bolt
Internal safety : locking, load indicator with
  protruding pin at rear of bolt

CHARACTERISTICS

- material : steel
- finish : blued; double trigger
- stock : walnut with pistol grip

Calibres available (standard): .270 Win., 7 x 64mm, 30.06 Spr., .308 Win., 9.3 x 62mm; (Magnum): 6.5 x 68mm, 7mm Rem. Mag., 8 x 68S, .300 Win. Mag., .300 Wby. Mag., .375 H & H Mag.

Merkel

The German town of Suhl in Thuringia has been renowned for its armourers for more than five hundred years. The finest weapons from the area bear names such as Merkel, Simson, and Haenel. Suhl is mainly known for its hand-made rifles and outstandingly fine engraving on so many weapons.

Merkel is the best-known of the names. The company mainly produces breech-action shotguns, combined shotguns and rifles, double-barrelled rifles, and triple-barrelled guns that have at least one rifled barrel. After World War II, Thuringia fell within the Russian zone and formed part of East Germany as it then was or the DDR.
Weapons from Suhl brought in much needed foreign currency during those years although some western countries were not permitted to import such weapons from "behind the Iron Curtain."

When the two German republics were reunified after the fall of the Berlin wall, the factories in Suhl once again gained access to a world market. In terms of their quality and superlative finish, Merkel rifles are among the best there are in the world.

Merkel model 140

TECHNICAL DETAILS

Calibre	: see below
Cartridge capacity	: 1 round per barrel
Magazine catch	: not applicable
Action	: breech-action
Locking	: locking lever on upper side of pivot breech
Weight	: 3.5kg (7lb 11oz)
Length	: 103cm (40½in)
Barrel Length	: 60cm (23⅝in)
Sight	: fixed leaf sight, suitable for telescopic sight
External safety	: sliding safety catch on back of pistol grip
Internal safety	: locking, automatic safety when breech is broken

CHARACTERISTICS

• material	: steel
• finish	: blued; tempered breech
• stock	: specially selected walnut

Available calibres: 7 x 57R, 7 x 65R, .30-06 Spr., .30R Blaser, 8 x 57mm, 8 x 75RS, .308 Win., 9.3 x 74R

Merkel model 160 Luxus

TECHNICAL DETAILS

Calibre	: see below
Cartridge capacity	: 1 round per barrel
Magazine catch	: not applicable
Action	: breech-action
Locking	: locking lever on upper side of pivot breech

Weight	: 3.5kg (7lb 11oz)
Length	: 103cm (40½in)
Barrel Length	: 60cm (23⅝in)
Sight	: fixed leaf sight, special mounting for telescopic sight
External safety	: sliding safety catch on back of pistol grip
Internal safety	: locking, automatic safety when breech is broken

CHARACTERISTICS

• material	: steel
• finish	: blued; engraved bare metal breech casing
• stock	: specially selected walnut

Available calibres: 7 x 57R, 7 x 65R, .30-06 Spr., .30R Blaser, 8 x 57mm, 8 x 75RS, .308 Win., 9.3 x 74R

Merkel 221 E BDB double-barrel

TECHNICAL DETAILS

Calibre	: 7 x 57R, 7 x 65R
Cartridge capacity	: 1 round per barrel
Magazine catch	: not applicable
Action	: breech-action
Locking	: locking lever on upper side of pivot breech
Weight	: 3.2kg (7lb 1oz)
Length	: 103cm (40½in)
Barrel Length	: 63cm (24¾in)
Sight	: folding sight, special mounting for telescopic sight
External safety	: sliding safety catch on back of pistol grip

| Internal safety | : locking, automatic safety when breech is broken |

CHARACTERISTICS
- material : steel
- finish : blued; engraved bare metal breech casing
- stock : specially selected walnut

Merkel 323 Luxus BDB double-barrel

TECHNICAL DETAILS

Calibre	: .308 Win., .30-06 Spr.
Cartridge capacity	: 1 round per barrel
Magazine catch	: not applicable
Action	: breech-action
Locking	: locking lever on upper side of pivot breech
Weight	: 3.8kg (8lb 6oz)
Length	: 103cm (40½in)
Barrel Length	: 63cm (24¾in)
Sight	: folding sight, special mounting for telescopic sight
External safety	: sliding safety catch on back of pistol grip
Internal safety	: locking, automatic safety when breech is broken

CHARACTERISTICS
- material : steel
- finish : blued; engraved bare metal breech casing with gold inlay
- stock : specially selected walnut

Mitchell Arms Inc.

The American firm of Mitchell Arms was started in 1984 by John Mitchell after the bankruptcy in 1984 of the High Standard Arms concern, of which he had been a director. Mitchell Arms is based in Santa Ana, California. At first the new company directed its efforts towards making military-style weapons in .22 LR calibre,

such as the Colt M16, Kalashnikov AK-47, and French MAS assault rifle. Mitchell Arms also made replicas of the Colt Single Action Army (Peacemaker) in .44 Magnum and .45 Long Colt calibres and traded in a range of replicas of large calibre blackpowder revolvers originally made by Colt and Remington. These were produced by the famous Uberti arms factory in Italy. Mitchell produces a number of models of carbines that externally resemble sub-machine guns which used to be manufactured by the American firm, Feather, as AT-22 and AT-9.

Mitchell model 20/22 carbine

TECHNICAL DETAILS

Calibre	: .22 LR
Cartridge capacity	: 10-rounds cartridge holder
Magazine catch	: at rear of magazine aperture
Action	: semi-automatic
Locking	: inertia
Weight	: 6lb 4oz (2.8kg)
Length	: 37½in (95.3cm)
Barrel Length	: 20½in (52.1cm)
Sight	: adjustable sight, mounting for telescopic sight
External safety	: safety catch on right
Internal safety	: locking

CHARACTERISTICS
- material : steel
- finish : blued
- stock : walnut

Three versions of the model 20/22 are illustrated. They are (from top to bottom): carbine, Deluxe, and Special.

Mitchell model 9303

TECHNICAL DETAILS

Calibre	: .22 LR or .22 WMR
Cartridge capacity	: 5- or 10-rounds cartridge holder
Magazine catch	: at front of trigger guard

Action	: bolt-action
Locking	: bolt-locking
Weight	: 6lb 8oz (3kg)
Length	: 40¾in (103.5cm)
Barrel Length	: 22½in (57.2cm)
Sight	: adjustable sight, mounting for telescopic sight
External safety	: safety catch on right behind bolt
Internal safety	: locking

CHARACTERISTICS
- material : steel
- finish : blued
- stock : walnut

Model 9303 is .22 LR calibre; models 9302 and 9304 are .22 WMR calibre.

Mitchell Guardian Angel LW-22 Lightweight rifle

TECHNICAL DETAILS
Calibre	: .22 LR
Cartridge capacity	: 20 rounds
Magazine catch	: at front of magazine
Action	: semi-automatic
Locking	: inertia
Weight	: 3lb 4oz (1.5kg)
Length	: 347/8in (88.6cm) with metal stock extended
Barrel Length	: 17in (43.2cm)
Sight	: military optical sight and ring bead

| External safety | : safety catch at front of trigger guard |
| Internal safety | : locking |

CHARACTERISTICS
- material : steel and light-metal
- finish : matt black
- stock : pull-out metal or black plastic

Mitchell Guardian Angel LW-9 Lightweight rifle

TECHNICAL DETAILS
Calibre	: 9mm Para.
Cartridge capacity	: 25 rounds
Magazine catch	: at front of magazine
Action	: semi-automatic
Locking	: inertia
Weight	: 5lb (2.3kg)
Length	: 347/8in (88.6cm) with metal stock extended
Barrel Length	: 17in (43.2cm)
Sight	: military optical sight and ring bead,
External safety	: safety catch at front of trigger guard
Internal safety	: locking

CHARACTERISTICS
- material : steel and light-metal
- finish : matt black
- stock : pull-out metal or black plastic

Musgrave

The South African firm of Musgrave is part of Denel (Pty) Ltd. Musgrave was established in 1951 in Bloemfontein in the Orange Free State. The company has a long history in the arms business. During the Boer War of 1899-1902, between Britain and the Orange Free State and the Transvaal, the Afrikaners were forced to find weapons supplies. The republic of the Orange Free State and the Transvaal bought 38,000 Mauser 96 rifles and their ruling council acquired a further 12,000 Mauser sporting rifles in 1899. These were sold to the Afrikaner "farmers" for the sum of £5 in order to create a civilian militia or people's army to fight the British. The Boer's armoury, where weapons were repaired and maintained, eventually came into the hands of Musgrave. The company still build an excellent range of sporting and hunting rifles based on the Mauser K98, including the main local match rifle. These are made in a large number of different popular calibres. The Mauser system has also been adapted for use with heavier calibres such as .375 Holland & Holland Magnum. Other Musgrave products include golf clubs, car parts, and car alarms. During the recent past, products from South Africa were boycotted because of the then government's Apartheid regime. Since the changes in that country, which began at the beginning of the 1990s, leading to Nelson Mandela becoming president, arms and munitions such as Vektor pistols and Swartklip cartridges are being exported all over the world.

Musgrave African rifle

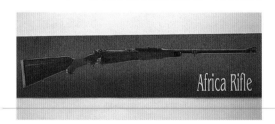

TECHNICAL DETAILS

Calibre	: see below
Cartridge capacity	: 3-5 rounds
Magazine catch	: internal magazine, catch for bottom plate at front of trigger guard
Action	: bolt-action
Locking	: 2 locking lugs (Mauser system)
Weight	: 9lb 15oz (4.5kg)
Length	: 43⅛in (109.6cm)
Barrel Length	: 24in (61cm)
Sight	: 3-leaves Express folding sight; suitable for telescopic sight
External safety	: winged safety catch at rear of bolt
Internal safety	: locking

CHARACTERISTICS

• material	: steel
• finish	: blued
• stock	: walnut with pistol grip

Calibres available: .300 Win. Mag., 7mm Rem. Mag., .308 Norma Mag., .375 H & H Mag., .30-06 Spr., .270 Win., 7 x 64mm

Musgrave K-98 rifle

TECHNICAL DETAILS

Calibre	: see below
Cartridge capacity	: 4 rounds (internal magazine)
Magazine catch	: not applicable
Action	: bolt-action
Locking	: 2 locking lugs (Mauser system)
Weight	: 7lb 15oz (3.6kg)
Length	: 43in (109cm)
Barrel Length	: 24in (61cm)
Sight	: adjustable leaf sight and bead tunnel; suitable for telescopic sight
External safety	: winged safety catch at rear of bolt
Internal safety	: locking

CHARACTERISTICS

• material	: steel
• finish	: blued
• stock	: walnut Monte Carlo stock with pistol grip

Calibres available: .243 Win., .270 Win., .308 Win., .30-06 Spr., 7 x 57mm, 7 x 64mm

Musgrave Magnum rifle

TECHNICAL DETAILS

Calibre	: see below
Cartridge capacity	: 3 rounds (internal magazine)

Magazine catch	: not applicable
Action	: bolt-action
Locking	: 2 locking lugs (Mauser system)
Weight	: 8lb 3oz (3.7kg)
Length	: 43¼in (110cm)
Barrel Length	: 24in (61cm)
Sight	: adjustable leaf sight and bead tunnel; suitable for telescopic sight
External safety	: winged safety catch at rear of bolt
Internal safety	: locking

CHARACTERISTICS
- material : steel
- finish : blued
- stock : walnut with pistol grip

Calibres available: .375 H & H Mag., .300 Win. Mag., 7mm Rem. Mag., .308 Norma Mag.

Musgrave Match rifle

TECHNICAL DETAILS

Calibre	: .308 Win.
Cartridge capacity	: single shot
Magazine catch	: not applicable
Action	: bolt-action
Locking	: 2 locking lugs (Mauser system)
Weight	: 11lb 10oz (5.25kg)
Length	: 45⅛in (114.6cm)
Barrel Length	: 26½in (67.5cm)
Sight	: optical sight and bead tunnel

External safety	: safety catch at rear of bolt
Internal safety	: locking

CHARACTERISTICS
- material : steel
- finish : blued
- stock : walnut with pistol grip

Musgrave Mauser Magnum rifle

TECHNICAL DETAILS

Calibre	: see below
Cartridge capacity	: 3 rounds (internal magazine)
Magazine catch	: not applicable
Action	: bolt-action
Locking	: 2 locking lugs (Mauser system)
Weight	: 8lb 3oz (3.7kg)
Length	: 43¼in (110cm)
Barrel Length	: 24in (61cm)
Sight	: adjustable leaf sight and bead tunnel; suitable for telescopic sight
External safety	: winged safety catch at rear of bolt
Internal safety	: locking

CHARACTERISTICS
- material : steel
- finish : blued
- stock : walnut Monte Carlo stock with pistol grip

Calibres available: .375 H & H Mag., .300 Win. Mag., 7mm Rem. Mag., .308 Norma Mag.

Musgrave model 2000

TECHNICAL DETAILS

Calibre	: see below
Cartridge capacity	: 4 rounds
Magazine catch	: front of trigger guard
Action	: bolt-action

Locking	: 2 locking lugs (Mauser system)
Weight	: 9lb 5oz (4.2kg)
Length	: 43¼in (110cm)
Barrel Length	: 24in (61cm)
Sight	: adjustable leaf sight and bead tunnel; suitable for telescopic sight
External safety	: winged safety catch at rear of bolt
Internal safety	: locking

CHARACTERISTICS
- material : steel
- finish : blued
- stock : walnut with pistol grip

Available calibres: .243 Win., .270 Win., .308 Win., .30-06 Spr., 7 x 57mm, 7 x 64mm

Musgrave model 90

TECHNICAL DETAILS

Calibre	: see below
Cartridge capacity	: 4 rounds (internal magazine)
Magazine catch	: at front of trigger guard
Action	: bolt-action
Locking	: 2 locking lugs (Mauser system)
Weight	: 9lb 5oz (4.2kg)
Length	: 43¼in (110cm)
Barrel Length	: 24in (61cm)
Sight	: adjustable leaf sight and bead tunnel; suitable for telescopic sight
External safety	: winged safety catch at rear of bolt

Internal safety	: locking

CHARACTERISTICS
- material : steel
- finish : blued
- stock : walnut stock with pistol grip

Calibres available: .243 Win., .270 Win.,.308 Win., .30-06 Spr., 7 x 57mm, 7 x 64mm

Musgrave Mini 90 model

TECHNICAL DETAILS

Calibre	: .222 Rem., .223 Rem., .22-250 Rem.
Cartridge capacity	: 4-5 rounds (internal magazine)
Magazine catch	: at front of trigger guard
Action	: bolt-action
Locking	: 2 locking lugs (Mauser system)
Weight	: 7lb 5oz (3.3kg)
Length	: 40⅛in (102cm)
Barrel Length	: 22in (56cm)
Sight	: adjustable leaf sight and bead tunnel; suitable for telescopic sight
External safety	: winged safety catch at rear of bolt
Internal safety	: locking

CHARACTERISTICS
- material : steel
- finish : blued
- stock : walnut stock with pistol grip

Musgrave RSA Standard

TECHNICAL DETAILS

Calibre	: .308 Win.
Cartridge capacity	: single shot
Magazine catch	: not applicable
Action	: bolt-action

Locking   : 2 locking lugs
                     (Mauser system)
Weight   : 11lb 10oz (5.25kg)
Length   : 45¼in (115cm)
Barrel Length   : 26¾in (68cm)
Sight   : optical sight and bead
                     tunnel
External safety   : safety catch at rear of bolt
Internal safety   : locking

CHARACTERISTICS
• material   : steel
• finish   : blued
• stock   : walnut stock with pistol grip

Musgrave Scout rifle

TECHNICAL DETAILS
Calibre   : see below
Cartridge capacity : 4 rounds (internal magazine)
Magazine catch   : not applicable
Action   : bolt-action
Locking   : 2 locking lugs
                     (Mauser system)
Weight   : 6lb 10oz (3kg)
Length   : 39in (99cm)
Barrel Length   : 20⅛in (51cm)
Sight   : none, mounting for
                     telescopic sight
External safety   : winged safety catch at rear
                     of bolt
Internal safety   : locking

CHARACTERISTICS
• material   : steel
• finish   : blued

• stock   : walnut stock with pistol
                     grip

Calibres available: .243 Win., .270 in.,.308
Win., .30-06 Spr., 7 x 57mm, 7 x 64mm

Musgrave RSA Thumbhole

TECHNICAL DETAILS
Calibre   : .308 Win.
Cartridge capacity : single shot
Magazine catch   : not applicable
Action   : bolt-action
Locking   : 2 locking lugs
                     (Mauser system)
Weight   : 11lb 11oz (5.3kg)
Length   : 45¼in (115cm)
Barrel Length   : 26¾in (68cm)
Sight   : optical sight and bead
                     tunnel
External safety   : safety catch at rear of bolt
Internal safety   : locking

CHARACTERISTICS
• material   : steel
• finish   : blued
• stock   : walnut stock with pistol grip
                     and thumb-hole

Navy Arms

The American firm Navy Arms Co. is
based in Ridgefield, New Jersey. The
owner of the company, Val Foggett, set up
Service Armament Co. in 1957. This company specialises in buying and selling surplus weapons from around the world that
can be used for sporting purposes.
In his spare time, Val Foggett became a
keen blackpowder shooter which led to
him becoming involved with an association that re-enacts and studies the
American Civil War known as the North-
South Skirmish Association. This group
use antique weapons and uniforms for

their shooting matches. Since weapons from this period are very costly, he decided to get replicas made of them. For this purpose he travelled to Europe in order to visit many different weapon manufacturers. Finally in 1960, he selected several Italian makers that were prepared to make these weapons to order for him. His first replica was the Colt 1851 Navy. A new company was formed for this purpose called Navy Arms which has been extremely successful.

The popularity of these replicas is demonstrated by the fact that he has produced a greater number of originals than all the weapons used in the Civil War.

CHARACTERISTICS

• material	: steel barrel, brass casing
• finish	: blued, polished casing
• stock	: straight walnut stock

Illustrated (from left to right):
1. 1866 model Yellowboy rifle
2. 1866 model Yellowboy carbine
3. 1873 model Winchester-style rifle
4. 1873 model Winchester-style sporting rifle
5. 1873 model Winchester-style carbine

Navy Arms 1866 model Yellowboy carbine

Navy Arms 1866 model Yellowboy rifle

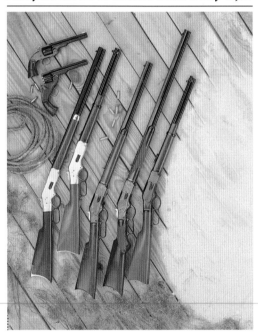

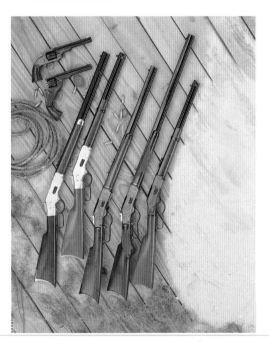

TECHNICAL DETAILS

Calibre	: .44-40
Cartridge capacity	: 13-rounds in tubular magazine
Magazine catch	: not applicable, loading port in right of casing
Action	: lever-action
Locking	: lever-locking
Weight	: 8lb 13oz (4kg)
Length	: 42½in (108cm)
Barrel Length	: 24in (61cm)
Sight	: adjustable rack
External safety	: none
Internal safety	: locking, trigger blocked when lever not fully closed

TECHNICAL DETAILS

Calibre	: .44-40
Cartridge capacity	: 10-rounds in tubular magazine
Magazine catch	: not applicable, loading port in right of casing
Action	: lever-action
Locking	: lever-locking
Weight	: 7lb 6oz (3.4kg)
Length	: 38¼in (97.2cm)
Barrel Length	: 19in (48.3cm)
Sight	: adjustable rack
External safety	: none
Internal safety	: locking, trigger blocked when lever not fully closed

CHARACTERISTICS

• material	: steel barrel, brass casing

- finish   : blued, polished casing
- stock   : straight walnut stock

Illustrated (from left to right):
1. 1866 model Yellowboy rifle
2. 1866 model Yellowboy carbine
3. 1873 model Winchester-style rifle
4. 1873 model Winchester-style sporting rifle
5. 1873 model Winchester-style carbine

Navy Arms 1873 model Winchester-style rifle

TECHNICAL DETAILS

Calibre	: .44-40, .45 LC
Cartridge capacity	: 13-rounds in tubular magazine
Magazine catch	: not applicable, loading port in right of casing
Action	: lever-locking
Locking	: lever-action
Weight	: 8lb 3oz (3.8kg)
Length	: 43in (109.2cm)
Barrel Length	: 24in (61cm)
Sight	: adjustable rack
External safety	: none
Internal safety	: locking, trigger blocked when lever not fully closed

CHARACTERISTICS

- material   : steel barrel
- finish   : blued, tempered casing
- stock   : straight walnut stock

Illustrated (from left to right):
1. 1866 model Yellowboy rifle
2. 1866 model Yellowboy carbine
3. 1873 model Winchester-style rifle
4. 1873 model Winchester-style sporting rifle
5. 1873 model Winchester-style carbine

Navy Arms 1873 model Winchester-style sporting rifle

TECHNICAL DETAILS

Calibre	: .44-40, .45 LC
Cartridge capacity	: 15 rounds in tubular magazine
Magazine catch	: not applicable, loading port in right of casing
Action	: lever-action
Locking	: lever-locking
Weight	: 8lb 3oz (3.7kg)
Length	: 48¾in (123.8cm)
Barrel Length	: 30in (76.2cm)
Sight	: adjustable rack

External safety	: none
Internal safety	: locking, trigger blocked when lever not fully closed

CHARACTERISTICS
- material : steel
- finish : blued, tempered casing
- stock : walnut with pistol grip

Illustrated (from left to right):
1. 1866 model Yellowboy rifle
2. 1866 model Yellowboy carbine
3. 1873 model Winchester-style rifle
4. 1873 model Winchester-style sporting rifle
5. 1873 model Winchester-style carbine

Weight	: 7lb 6oz (3.4kg)
Length	: 38¼in (97.2cm)
Barrel Length	: 19in (48.3cm)
Sight	: adjustable rack
External safety	: none
Internal safety	: locking, trigger blocked when lever not fully closed

CHARACTERISTICS
- material : steel
- finish : blued
- stock : straight walnut stock

Illustrated (from left to right):
1. 1866 model Yellowboy rifle
2. 1866 model Yellowboy carbine
3. 1873 model Winchester-style rifle
4. 1873 model Winchester-style sporting rifle
5. 1873 model Winchester-style carbine

Navy Arms 1873 model Winchester-style carbine

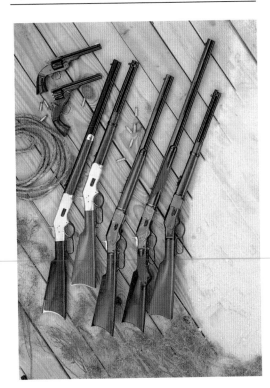

Navy Arms 1874 model Sharps infantry rifle

TECHNICAL DETAILS

Calibre	: .44-40, .45 LC
Cartridge capacity	: 10-rounds in tubular magazine
Magazine catch	: not applicable, loading port in right of casing
Action	: lever-action
Locking	: lever-locking

TECHNICAL DETAILS

Calibre	: .45-70 Govt.
Cartridge capacity	: single shot
Magazine catch	: not applicable

Action	: lever-action
Locking	: drop-block locking
Weight	: 8lb 13oz (4kg)
Length	: 46¾in (118.8cm)
Barrel Length	: 30in (76.2cm)
Sight	: adjustable rack
External safety	: none
Internal safety	: locking, trigger blocked when lever not fully closed

CHARACTERISTICS
- material : steel
- finish : blued, tempered casing
- stock : straight walnut stock

Illustrated (from left to right):
1. 1874 model Sharps infantry rifle
2. 1874 model Sharps cavalry carbine
3. 1873 model Springfield cavalry carbine (Trapdoor)

Navy Arms 1874 model Sharps cavalry carbine

TECHNICAL DETAILS

Calibre	: .45-70 Govt.
Cartridge capacity	: single shot
Magazine catch	: not applicable
Action	: lever-action

Locking	: drop-block locking
Weight	: 7lb 2oz (3.3kg)
Length	: 39in (99.1cm)
Barrel Length	: 22in (55.9cm)
Sight	: adjustable rack
External safety	: none
Internal safety	: locking, trigger blocked when lever not fully closed

CHARACTERISTICS
- material : steel
- finish : blued, tempered casing
- stock : straight walnut stock

Illustrated (from left to right):
1. 1874 model Sharps infantry rifle
2. 1874 model Sharps cavalry carbine
3. 1873 model Springfield cavalry carbine (Trapdoor)

Navy Arms 1873 model Springfield cavalry carbine "Trapdoor"

TECHNICAL DETAILS

Calibre	: .45-70 Govt.
Cartridge capacity	: single shot
Magazine catch	: not applicable
Action	: hinged

Locking	: hinged locking
Weight	: 7lb (3.2kg)
Length	: 40½in (102.9cm)
Barrel Length	: 22in (55.9cm)
Sight	: adjustable rack
External safety	: none
Internal safety	: locking knob for hinged locking

CHARACTERISTICS
* material : steel
* finish : blued
* stock : straight walnut stock with saddle-ring

Illustrated (from left to right):
1. 1874 model Sharps infantry rifle
2. 1874 model Sharps cavalry carbine
3. 1873 model Springfield cavalry carbine (Trapdoor)

Navy Arms Kodiak Mark IV double-rifle

TECHNICAL DETAILS

Calibre	: .45-70 Govt.
Cartridge capacity	: 2-rounds double-barrel
Magazine catch	: not applicable
Action	: barrel catch on back of pistol grip
Locking	: barrel catch
Weight	: 10lb (4.5kg)
Length	: 39¾in (101cm)
Barrel Length	: 24in (61cm)
Sight	: folding sight with four leaves for different ranges
External safety	: none
Internal safety	: locking

CHARACTERISTICS
* material : steel
* finish : blued
* stock : walnut stock with pistol grip

This rifle has twin triggers so that each barrel can be discharged independently.

Illustrated (from left to right):
1. Kodiak Mark IV double-rifle
2. Sharps plains long range rifle
3. Sharps buffalo rifle

Navy Arms Sharps plains long-range rifle

TECHNICAL DETAILS

Calibre	: .45-70 Govt.
Cartridge capacity	: single-shot
Magazine catch	: not applicable
Action	: lever-action
Locking	: drop-block locking
Weight	: 9lb 13oz (4.5kg)
Length	: 49in (124.5cm)
Barrel Length	: 32in (81.3cm)
Sight	: adjustable rack sight
External safety	: none
Internal safety	: locking, trigger blocked when cocking lever not fully closed

CHARACTERISTICS
* material : steel
* finish : blued, tempered casing
* stock : straight walnut stock

Illustrated (from left to right):
1. Kodiak Mark IV double-rifle
2. Sharps plains long range rifle
3. Sharps buffalo rifle

Navy Arms Sharps buffalo rifle

TECHNICAL DETAILS

Calibre	: .45-70 Govt., .45-90
Cartridge capacity	: single-shot
Magazine catch	: not applicable
Action	: lever-action
Locking	: drop-block locking
Weight	: 10lb 1oz (4.6kg)
Length	: 46in (116.8cm)
Barrel Length	: 28in (71.1cm)
Sight	: special optical ladder sight on back of stock
External safety	: none
Internal safety	: locking, trigger blocked when cocking lever not fully closed

CHARACTERISTICS

• material	: steel
• finish	: blued, tempered casing
• stock	: straight walnut stock

Illustrated (from left to right):
1. Kodiak Mark IV double-rifle
2. Sharps Plains long range rifle
3. Sharps buffalo rifle

NEF - New England Firearms

New England Firearms is a subsidiary of the well-known Harrington & Richardson 1871 Inc. Both concerns are based at Gardner in the northern part of Massachusetts. The entire area is known for the various weapons manufacturers based locally. The products made by NEF are very similar to those of Harrington & Richardson. For more information about the history of the company see under Harrington & Richardson.

NEF Handi-Rifle type A

TECHNICAL DETAILS

Calibre	: .22 Hornet, .30-30 Win.
Cartridge capacity	: single-shot
Magazine catch	: not applicable
Action	: breech-action
Locking	: barrel lock with uncocking lever behind hammer
Weight	: 7lb (3.2kg)
Length	: 40in (101.6cm)
Barrel Length	: 22in (55.9cm)

Sight	: adjustable ladder sight, drilled and tapped for telescopic sight
External safety	: none
Internal safety	: locking, transfer lever

CHARACTERISTICS

• material	: steel
• finish	: matt blued
• stock	: hardwood with pistol grip

NEF Handi-Rifle type B

TECHNICAL DETAILS

Calibre	: .223 Rem., .243 Win., .270 Win., .280 Rem., .30-06 Spr.
Cartridge capacity	: single-shot
Magazine catch	: not applicable
Action	: breech-action
Locking	: barrel lock with uncocking lever behind hammer
Weight	: 7lb (3.2kg)
Length	: 44in (111.8cm)
Barrel Length	: 26in (66cm)
Sight	: none, mounting for telescopic sight
External safety	: none
Internal safety	: locking, transfer lever

CHARACTERISTICS

• material	: steel
• finish	: matt blued
• stock	: hardwood with pistol grip

NEF Handi-Rifle type C

TECHNICAL DETAILS

Calibre	: .45-70 Govt., .44 Mag.
Cartridge capacity	: single-shot
Magazine catch	: not applicable

Action	: breech-action
Locking	: barrel lock with uncocking lever behind hammer
Weight	: 7lb (3.2kg)
Length	: 40in (101.6cm)
Barrel Length	: 22in (55.9cm)
Sight	: adjustable ladder sight, drilled and tapped for telescopic sight
External safety	: none
Internal safety	: locking, transfer lever

CHARACTERISTICS

• material	: steel
• finish	: matt blued
• stock	: hardwood with pistol grip

NEF Handi-Rifle type D Varmint

TECHNICAL DETAILS

Calibre	: .223 Rem.
Cartridge capacity	: single-shot
Magazine catch	: not applicable
Action	: breech-action
Locking	: barrel lock with uncocking lever behind hammer
Weight	: 7lb (3.2kg)
Length	: 40in (101.6cm)
Barrel Length	: 22in (55.9cm)
Sight	: none, mounting for telescopic sight
External safety	: none
Internal safety	: locking, transfer lever

CHARACTERISTICS

• material	: steel
• finish	: matt blued
• stock	: hardwood with pistol grip

NEF Survivor 223-REM

TECHNICAL DETAILS

Calibre : .223 Rem.
Cartridge capacity : single-shot
Magazine catch : not applicable
Action : breech-action
Locking : barrel lock with uncocking
lever behind hammer
Weight : 6lb (2.7kg)
Length : 36in (91.4cm)
Barrel Length : 22in (55.9cm)
Sight : none, mounting for
telescopic sight
External safety : none
Internal safety : locking, transfer lever

CHARACTERISTICS

• material : steel
• finish : matt blued
• stock : plastic with pistol grip;
storage space in rear of
stock for ammunition

NEF Survivor 357-MAG

TECHNICAL DETAILS

Calibre : .357 Magnum/ .38 Special
Cartridge capacity : single-shot
Magazine catch : not applicable
Action : breech-action
Locking : barrel lock with uncocking
lever behind hammer
Weight : 6lb (2.7kg)
Length : 36in (91.4cm)
Barrel Length : 22in (55.9cm)
Sight : adjustable rack sight,
suitable for telescopic sight
External safety : none

Internal safety : locking, transfer lever

CHARACTERISTICS

• material : steel
• finish : matt blued
• stock : plastic with pistol grip; storage space in rear of stock
for ammunition

Norinco

Norinco is the state export company for
the Chinese weapon industry. Norinco
trades on behalf of several state
enterprises such as the small-bore
weapons of Golden Arrow, that are made
in the Zhongzhou Machinery Plant in He
Nan. The military rifles come from Plant
66 in Beijing. Norinco keeps a sharp eye
on the success of weapons and where
there is demand for a particular model, it
produces and sells them for very low
prices. For instance they make a
Chinese version of the Dragunov sniper's
rifle under the type name NDM-86 that is
available not only in the original
7.62 x 54R calibre, but also in .308
Winchester. The same is true of "replicas" of the well-known Kalashnikov SKS
rifle that are available from them in the
original 7.62 x 39mm and .223 Remington
calibres. The Chinese also make the
renowned AK-47 in both calibres, known
as type 84S-AK. This is not all, for they
also produce the Makarov pistol (type 59)
but in 9mm Para., the Czech CZ-75 pistol
(NZ-75), and an imitation of the Colt
1911 (M1911), plus a copy of the famous
French Famas army rifle (type 86S). There
are no fewer than five different versions of
the Russian AK-47 rifle. In 1992, Norinco even brought out their version of the
Mauser (K98) KKW Wehrsport .22 LR
rifle.
Norinco is represented in Europe by Nor-
conia in Rottendorf, Germany, and in
North America, by Interarms and Century International Arms.

Norinco JW15A

TECHNICAL DETAILS

Calibre : .22 LR
Cartridge capacity : 5 rounds
Magazine catch : catch in front of magazine
aperture

This rifle can be broken into two parts (stock and barrel) by loosening the locking screw in front of the trigger guard

Norinco JW21

Action	: bolt-action
Locking	: 2 locking lugs
Weight	: 2.8kg (6lb 3oz)
Length	: 104cm (41in)
Barrel Length	: 58.5cm (23in)
Sight	: sight adjustable for height with bead tunnel, mounting for telescopic sight
External safety	: winged safety catch at rear of bolt
Internal safety	: locking

CHARACTERISTICS
- material : steel
- finish : blued
- stock : hardwood

Norinco JW20

TECHNICAL DETAILS
Calibre	: .22 LR
Cartridge capacity	: 10-rounds tubular magazine
Magazine catch	: not applicable, loading port on right of stock
Action	: semi-automatic
Locking	: inertia
Weight	: 2.1kg (4lb 10oz)
Length	: 93cm (36⅝in)
Barrel Length	: 49cm (19¼in)
Sight	: sight adjustable for height
External safety	: push-button safety catch in front of trigger guard
Internal safety	: locking

CHARACTERISTICS
- material : steel
- finish : blued
- stock : walnut

TECHNICAL DETAILS
Calibre	: .22 LR
Cartridge capacity	: 19-rounds tubular magazine
Magazine catch	: not applicable, loading port in centre of magazine
Action	: lever-action
Locking	: lever-locking
Weight	: 3.1kg (6lb 13oz)
Length	: 102cm (40⅛in)
Barrel Length	: 61cm (24in)
Sight	: sight adjustable for height, suitable for telescopic sight
External safety	: safety catch on back of pistol grip
Internal safety	: locking

CHARACTERISTICS
- material : steel
- finish : blued
- stock : walnut with pistol grip

Norinco JW25A

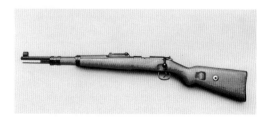

TECHNICAL DETAILS
Calibre	: .22 LR
Cartridge capacity	: 5-or 10-rounds cartridge holder

Magazine catch	: catch at front of magazine aperture
Action	: bolt-action
Locking	: 2 locking lugs
Weight	: 3.1kg (6lb 13oz)
Length	: 96cm (37¾in)
Barrel Length	: 52cm (20½in)
Sight	: adjustable rack sight
External safety	: safety catch at rear of bolt
Internal safety	: locking

CHARACTERISTICS

• material	: steel
• finish	: blued
• stock	: walnut

This carbine is an exact copy of the Mauser G33/40 small-bore training rifle. Extra cartridge holders are available from the German weapons dealers Frankonia, and original telescopic sights and rifle slings are also available from them.

Remington

Eliphalet Remington II, who founded the Remington Arms Company, lived from 1793 to 1861. Remington Senior was a gunsmith and Remington Junior made his first flintlock rifle in his father's workshop in 1816. Father and son established E. Remington & Son in Illion, New York State, in 1825 and nephew Philo Remington joined the company in 1844, followed by Samuel and Eliphalet III the founder's son. The company's name was changed to E. Remington & Sons. The company was taken over in 1888 by Hartley and Graham when the name was changed to Remington Arms Company. In 1902, the company merged with the Union Cartridge Company.
Today, the business is based in Bridgeport, Connecticut, and it forms part of the Du-Pont group. In the early days, Remington was mainly known for his model 1863 blackpowder Army revolver.
That same year, Remington introduced a breech-loading rifle using roller locking. This rifle was based on patents from 1863 of Leonard Geiger and Joseph Rider. The US government entered into a contract with Remington for 14,999 rolling block carbines in .56-50 rimfire calibre. This type of ·rifle was also sold to Sweden among others. Remington did not have much success in his own country be-

cause the big government orders were reserved for the state arsenal at Springfield Armory. Remington was able to pick up a few "crumbs" as supplier of parts. For this reason, the company directed most attention to the civilian market. During World War I, the company was used by the government to make model 1917 Enfield rifles. During World War II Remington made large numbers of Colt model 1911-A1 .45 ACP pistols for the US forces. Not until 1966 did the company again succeed in the military market. Military tests for a new marksman's rifle chose the Remington model 700 as the best contender and it entered service with the Marine Corps as Sniper rifle M40. This led to many police force special units buying the rifle for their marksmen. The origins of the model 700 date back to 1948, when the company brought out bolt-action repeating rifles in models 721 for the larger calibres and model 722 for smaller calibres.
These were replaced in 1962 by the standard model 700. This bolt-action repeating rifle forms the core of Remington's range and there are many variations on this theme. In 1995, there were 29 different versions from the .17 Remington of the Model Seven Lightweight to the .458 Winchester Magnum of the Model 700 Safari. The action, or receiver and bolt of the model 700 is widely used by custom rifle makers throughout the world to make their own creations. Even the extra-heavy rifles of A-Square in .500 A-Square calibre are equipped with Remington 700 locking systems. This speaks volumes for the quality of the system. From the introduction of this model, it has been equipped with the adjustable Williams sight.

Remington model 700-ADL

TECHNICAL DETAILS

Calibre	: see below
Cartridge capacity	: 3 (Magnum) to 4 rounds
Magazine catch	: internal magazine
Action	: bolt-action

Locking	: 2 locking lugs
Weight	: 7lb 4oz (3.3kg)
Length	: 41½-44½in
	(105.4-113cm)
Barrel Length	: 22-24in (55.9-61cm)
	(larger size for Magnum)
Sight	: adjustable Williams leaf
	sight, drilled and tapped for
	telescopic sight
External safety	: safety catch at rear of bolt
Internal safety	: locking

CHARACTERISTICS
- material : steel
- finish : blued
- stock : walnut with pistol grip

Available calibres: .243 Win., .270 Win.,
7mm Rem. Mag., .30-06 Spr., .308 Win.

Remington model 700-APR (African Plains Rifle)

TECHNICAL DETAILS
Calibre	: see below
Cartridge capacity	: 3 rounds
Magazine catch	: internal magazine, catch at
	front of trigger guard for
	bottom plate
Action	: bolt-action
Locking	: 2 locking lugs
Weight	: 7lb 12oz (3.5kg)
Length	: 46½in (118.1cm)
Barrel Length	: 26in (66cm)
Sight	: none, drilled and tapped for
	telescopic sight
External safety	: safety catch at rear of bolt
Internal safety	: locking

CHARACTERISTICS
- material : steel
- finish : blued
- stock : laminated hardwood with
  pistol grip

Available calibres: 7mm Rem. Mag., .300
Win. Mag., .300 Wby. Mag., .338 Win.
Mag., .375 H & H Mag.

This rifle is a special model from Remington's custom workshop.

Remington model 700-AWR (Alaskan Wilderness Rifle)

TECHNICAL DETAILS
Calibre	: see below
Cartridge capacity	: 3 rounds
Magazine catch	: internal magazine, catch at
	front of trigger guard for
	bottom plate
Action	: bolt-action
Locking	: 2 locking lugs
Weight	: 6lb 12oz (3.1kg)
Length	: 44½in (113cm)
Barrel Length	: 24in (61cm)
Sight	: none, drilled and tapped for
	telescopic sight
External safety	: safety catch at rear of
	bolt
Internal safety	: locking

CHARACTERISTICS
- material : steel
- finish : blued
- stock : black Kevlar with pistol grip

Available calibres: 7mm Rem. Mag., .300
Win. Mag., .300 Wby. Mag., .338 Win.
Mag., .375 H & H Mag.

This rifle is a special model from
Remington's custom workshop.

Remington model 700-BDL

TECHNICAL DETAILS
Calibre	: see below
Cartridge capacity	: 3-5 rounds
Magazine catch	: internal magazine, catch at
	front of trigger guard for
	bottom plate
Action	: bolt-action
Locking	: 2 locking lugs
Weight	: 7lb 4oz-7lb 12oz (3.3-3.5kg)
Length	: 41½-44½in (105.4-113cm)

Barrel Length	: 22-24in (55.9-61cm)Sight : adjustable Williams leaf sight, drilled and tapped for telescopic sight
External safety	: safety catch at rear of bolt
Internal safety	: locking

CHARACTERISTICS
- material : steel
- finish : blued
- stock : classic walnut Monte Carlo stock with pistol grip

Available calibres: .17 Rem., .222 Rem., .22-250 Rem., .223 Rem., .243 Win., .25-06 Rem., .270 Win., .280 Rem., 7mm Rem. Mag., .300 Win. Mag., .30-06 Spr., .308 Win., .338 Win. Mag.

Remington model 700-BDL DM (Detachable Magazine)

TECHNICAL DETAILS

Calibre	: see below
Cartridge capacity	: 3-4 rounds cartridge holder
Magazine catch	: catch on right of cartridge holder
Action	: bolt-action
Locking	: 2 locking lugs
Weight	: 7lb 4oz-7lb 12oz (3.3-3.5kg)
Length	: 41¾-44½in (106.1-113cm)
Barrel Length	: 22-24in (55.9-61cm)
Sight	: adjustable Williams leaf sight with bead tunnel, drilled and tapped for telescopic sight
External safety	: safety catch at rear of bolt
Internal safety	: locking

CHARACTERISTICS
- material : steel
- finish : blued
- stock : classic walnut Monte Carlo stock with pistol grip

Available calibres: 6mm Rem., .243 Win., .25-06 Rem., .270 Win., .280 Rem., 7mm-08 Rem., 7mm Rem. Mag., .300 Win. Mag., .30-06 Spr., .308 Win., .338 Win. Mag.

Remington model 700-BDL DM-LH (Detachable Magazine left-handed)

TECHNICAL DETAILS

Calibre	: see below
Cartridge capacity	: 3-4 rounds cartridge holder
Magazine catch	: catch on right of cartridge holder
Action	: bolt-action
Locking	: 2 locking lugs
Weight	: 7lb 4oz-7lb 12oz (3.3-3.5kg)
Length	: 41¾-44½in (106.1-113cm)
Barrel Length	: 22-24in (55.9-61cm)
Sight	: adjustable Williams leaf sight with bead tunnel, drilled and tapped for telescopic sight
External safety	: safety catch on left at rear of bolt
Internal safety	: locking

CHARACTERISTICS
- material : steel
- finish : blued
- stock : classic walnut Monte Carlo stock with pistol grip

Available calibres: .243 Win., .270 Win., 7mm-08 Rem., 7mm Rem. Mag., .300 Win. Mag., .30-06 Spr.

The model 700-BDL DM-LH has a left-handed bolt and safety catch for left-handed shooters.

Remington model 700-BDL SS-DM (Detachable Magazine) Stainless

TECHNICAL DETAILS
Calibre	: see below
Cartridge capacity	: 3-4 rounds cartridge holder
Magazine catch	: catch on right of cartridge holder
Action	: bolt-action
Locking	: 2 locking lugs
Weight	: 7lb-7lb 8oz (3.2-3.4kg)
Length	: 43½-44½in (110.5-113cm)
Barrel Length	: 24in (61cm)
Sight	: none, drilled and tapped for telescopic sight
External safety	: safety catch at rear of bolt
Internal safety	: locking

CHARACTERISTICS
• material	: stainless-steel
• finish	: bare metal
• stock	: black plastic with pistol grip

Available calibres: 6mm Rem., .243 Win., .25-06 Rem., .270 Win., .280 Rem., 7mm-08 Rem., 7mm Rem. Mag., .300 Win. Mag., .300 Wby. Mag., .30-06 Spr., .308 Win., .338 Win. Mag.

Remington model 700-BDL-LH (left-handed)

TECHNICAL DETAILS
Calibre	: see below
Cartridge capacity	: 3-5 rounds
Magazine catch	: internal magazine, catch in front of trigger guard for bottom plate
Action	: bolt-action
Locking	: 2 locking lugs

Weight	: 7lb 4oz-7lb 8oz (3.3-3.4kg)
Length	: 41½-44½in (105.4-113cm)
Barrel Length	: 22-24in (55.9-61cm)
Sight	: adjustable Williams leaf sight, drilled and tapped for telescopic sight
External safety	: safety catch at rear of bolt
Internal safety	: locking

CHARACTERISTICS
• material	: steel
• finish	: blued
• stock	: classic walnut Monte Carlo stock with pistol grip

Available calibres: .22-250 Rem., .243 Win. .270 Win., 7mm Rem. Mag., .30-06 Spr.

This rifle has a left-hand bolt for left-handed shooters.

Remington model 700-BDL Stainless Synthetic

TECHNICAL DETAILS
Calibre	: see below
Cartridge capacity	: 3-4 rounds
Magazine catch	: internal magazine, catch in front of trigger guard for bottom plate
Action	: bolt-action
Locking	: 2 locking lugs
Weight	: 7lb 4oz-7lb 8oz (3.3-3.4kg)
Length	: 42½-44½in (108-113cm)
Barrel Length	: 24in (61cm)
Sight	: none, drilled and tapped for telescopic sight
External safety	: safety catch at rear of bolt
Internal safety	: locking

CHARACTERISTICS
• material	: stainless-steel
• finish	: bare metal
• stock	: black plastic with pistol grip

Available calibres: .270 Win., .280 Rem.,

7mm Rem. Mag., .300 Win. Mag., .300
Wby. Mag., .30-06 Spr., .338 Win. Mag.

Remington model 700-BDL Varmint (VLS: Varmint Laminated Stock)

TECHNICAL DETAILS

Calibre	: see below
Cartridge capacity	: 4-5 rounds
Magazine catch	: internal magazine
Action	: bolt-action
Locking	: 2 locking lugs
Weight	: 9lb 6oz (4.3kg)
Length	: 45½in (115.6cm)
Barrel Length	: 26in (66cm)
Sight	: none, drilled and tapped for telescopic sight
External safety	: safety catch at rear of bolt
Internal safety	: locking

CHARACTERISTICS

- material : steel
- finish : blued
- stock : laminated hardwood Monte Carlo stock with pistol grip

Available calibres: .222 Rem., .22-250
Rem., .223 Rem., .243 Win., .25-06 Rem.,
.308 Win.

Remington model 700-Classic

TECHNICAL DETAILS

Calibre	: .300 Win. Mag.
Cartridge capacity	: 3 rounds
Magazine catch	: internal magazine, catch at front of trigger guard for bottom plate
Action	: bolt-action

Locking	: 2 locking lugs
Weight	: 7lb 4oz (3.3kg)
Length	: 44½in (113cm)
Barrel Length	: 24in (61cm)
Sight	: none, drilled and tapped for telescopic sight
External safety	: safety catch at rear of bolt
Internal safety	: locking

CHARACTERISTICS

- material : steel
- finish : blued
- stock : walnut with pistol grip

Remington model 700-Mountain Custom KS

TECHNICAL DETAILS

Calibre	: see below
Cartridge capacity	: 3-4 rounds
Magazine catch	: not applicable, internal magazine
Action	: bolt-action
Locking	: 2 locking lugs
Weight	: 6lb 8oz-6lb 12oz (3-3.1kg)
Length	: 44½in (113cm)
Barrel Length	: 24in (61cm)
Sight	: none, drilled and tapped for telescopic sight
External safety	: safety catch at rear of bolt
Internal safety	: locking

CHARACTERISTICS

- material : steel
- finish : blued
- stock : black Kevlar with pistol grip

Available calibres: .270 Win., .280 Rem.,
.30-06 Spr., 7mm Rem. Mag., .300 Win.
Mag., .300 Wby. Mag.,.338 Win. Mag.,
8mm Rem. Mag., .35 Whelen, .375 H & H
Mag.

This rifle is a special from the Remington
custom workshop.

Remington model 700-Mountain Custom KS LH (left-handed)

TECHNICAL DETAILS

Calibre : see below
Cartridge capacity : 3-4 rounds
Magazine catch : not applicable, internal magazine
Action : bolt-action
Locking : 2 locking lugs
Weight : 6lb 8oz-6lb 12oz (3-3.1kg)
Length : 44½in (113cm)
Barrel Length : 24in (61cm)
Sight : none, drilled and tapped for telescopic sight
External safety : safety catch at rear of bolt
Internal safety : locking

CHARACTERISTICS

• material : steel
• finish : matt black
• stock : black Kevlar with pistol grip

Available calibres: .270 Win., .280 Rem., .30-06 Spr., 7mm Rem. Mag., .300 Win. Mag., .300 Wby. Mag.,.338 Win. Mag., 8mm Rem. Mag., .35 Whelen, .375 H & H Mag.

This rifle has a left-handed bolt for left-handed shooters. It is a special from the Remington custom workshop.

Remington model 700-Mountain Rifle Custom KS-Stainless

TECHNICAL DETAILS

Calibre : see below
Cartridge capacity : 3-4 rounds
Magazine catch : not applicable, internal magazine
Action : bolt-action
Locking : 2 locking lugs

Weight : 6lb 8oz-6lb 12oz (3-3.1kg)
Length : 44½in (113cm)
Barrel Length : 24in (61cm)
Sight : none, drilled and tapped for telescopic sight
External safety : safety catch at rear of bolt
Internal safety : locking

CHARACTERISTICS

• material : stainless-steel
• finish : bare metal
• stock : black Kevlar with pistol grip

Available calibres: .270 Win., .280 Rem., .30-06 Spr., 7mm Rem. Mag., .300 Win. Mag., .300 Wby. Mag.,.338 Win. Mag., .35 Whelen, .375 H & H Mag.

This rifle is a special from the Remington custom workshop.

Remington model 700-Mountain Rifle DM (Detachable Magazine)

TECHNICAL DETAILS

Calibre : see below
Cartridge capacity : 3-4 rounds
Magazine catch : not applicable, internal magazine
Action : bolt-action
Locking : 2 locking lugs
Weight : 6lb 8oz (3kg)
Length : 42½in (108cm)
Barrel Length : 22in (55.9cm)
Sight : none, drilled and tapped for telescopic sight
External safety : safety catch at rear of bolt
Internal safety : locking

CHARACTERISTICS

• material : steel
• finish : blued
• stock : walnut with pistol grip

Available calibres: . 243 Win., .25-06 Rem., .270 Win., .280 Rem., 7mm-08 Rem., .30-06 Spr.

Remington model 700-Safari Classic

TECHNICAL DETAILS

Calibre	: see below
Cartridge capacity	: 3 rounds
Magazine catch	: internal magazine, catch at front of trigger guard for bottom plate
Action	: bolt-action
Locking	: 2 locking lugs
Weight	: 9lb (4.1kg)
Length	: 44½in (113cm)
Barrel Length	: 24in (61cm)
Sight	: adjustable Williams leaf sight, drilled and tapped for telescopic sight
External safety	: safety catch at rear of bolt
Internal safety	: locking

CHARACTERISTICS

• material	: steel
• finish	: blued
• stock	: walnut with pistol grip

Available calibres: 8mm Rem. Mag., .375 H & H Mag., .416 Rem. Mag., .458 Win. Mag.

This rifle is a special from Remington's custom workshop.

Remington model 700-Safari Classic LH (left-handed)

TECHNICAL DETAILS

Calibre	: see below
Cartridge capacity	: 3 rounds

Magazine catch	: internal magazine, catch at front of trigger guard for bottom plate
Action	: bolt-action
Locking	: 2 locking lugs
Weight	: 9lb (4.1kg)
Length	: 44½in (113cm)
Barrel Length	: 24in (61cm)
Sight	: adjustable Williams leaf sight, drilled and tapped for telescopic sight
External safety	: safety catch at rear of bolt
Internal safety	: locking

CHARACTERISTICS

• material	: steel
• finish	: blued
• stock	: walnut with pistol grip

Available calibres: 8mm Rem. Mag., .375 H & H Mag., .416 Rem. Mag., .458 Win. Mag.

This rifle is a special from Remington's custom workshop. It has a left-handed bolt for left-handed shooters.

Remington model 700-Safari KS-Kevlar

TECHNICAL DETAILS

Calibre	: see below
Cartridge capacity	: 3 rounds
Magazine catch	: internal magazine, catch at front of trigger guard for bottom plate
Action	: bolt-action
Locking	: 2 locking lugs
Weight	: 9lb (4.1kg)
Length	: 42½in (108cm)
Barrel Length	: 22in (55.9cm)
Sight	: adjustable Williams leaf sight, drilled and tapped for telescopic sight
External safety	: safety catch at rear of bolt
Internal safety	: locking

CHARACTERISTICS
- material   : steel
- finish   : blued
- stock   : dark grey Kevlar stock with pistol grip

Available calibres: 8mm Rem. Mag., .375 H & H Mag., .416 Rem. Mag., .458 Win. Mag.

This rifle is a special from Remington's custom workshop.

Remington model 700-Safari KS-Kevlar LH (left-handed)

TECHNICAL DETAILS
Calibre	: see below
Cartridge capacity	: 3 rounds
Magazine catch	: internal magazine, catch at front of trigger guard for bottom plate
Action	: bolt-action
Locking	: 2 locking lugs
Weight	: 9lb (4.1kg)
Length	: 42½in (108cm)
Barrel Length	: 22in (55.9cm)
Sight	: adjustable Williams leaf sight, drilled and tapped for telescopic sight
External safety	: safety catch on left at rear of bolt
Internal safety	: locking

CHARACTERISTICS
- material   : steel
- finish   : blued
- stock   : dark grey Kevlar stock with pistol grip

Available calibres: 8mm Rem. Mag., .375 H & H Mag., .416 Rem. Mag., .458 Win. Mag.

This rifle is a special from Remington's custom workshop and it is equipped with a left-handed bolt for left-handed shooters.

Remington model 700-Safari KS-Kevlar Stainless

TECHNICAL DETAILS
Calibre	: see below
Cartridge capacity	: 3 rounds
Magazine catch	: internal magazine, catch at front of trigger guard for bottom plate
Action	: bolt-action
Locking	: 2 locking lugs
Weight	: 9lb (4.1kg)
Length	: 44½in (113cm)
Barrel Length	: 22in (55.9cm)
Sight	: adjustable Williams leaf sight, drilled and tapped for telescopic sight
External safety	: safety catch at rear of bolt
Internal safety	: locking

CHARACTERISTICS
- material   : stainless-steel
- finish   : bare metal
- stock   : black Kevlar stock with pistol grip

Available calibres: .375 H & H Mag., .416 Rem. Mag., .458 Win. Mag.

This rifle is a special from Remington's custom workshop

Remington model 700-Safari Monte Carlo

TECHNICAL DETAILS
Calibre	: see below
Cartridge capacity	: 3 rounds
Magazine catch	: internal magazine, catch at front of trigger guard for bottom plate
Action	: bolt-action

Locking   : 2 locking lugs
Weight   : 9lb (4.1kg)
Length   : 44½in (113cm)
Barrel Length   : 24in (61cm)
Sight   : adjustable Williams leaf
                    sight, drilled and tapped for
                    telescopic sight
External safety   : safety catch at rear of bolt
Internal safety   : locking

CHARACTERISTICS

• material   : steel
• finish   : blued
• stock   : specially selected walnut
                      Monte Carlo stock with
                      pistol grip

Available calibres: 8mm Rem. Mag., .375 H & H Mag., .416 Rem. Mag., .458 Win. Mag.

This rifle is a special from Remington's custom workshop

Remington model 700-Sendero

TECHNICAL DETAILS

Calibre   : see below
Cartridge capacity : 3-4 rounds
Magazine catch   : internal magazine, catch at
                     front of trigger guard for
                     bottom plate
Action   : bolt-action
Locking   : 2 locking lugs
Weight   : 9lb (4.1kg)
Length   : 45¾in (116.2cm)
Barrel Length   : 26in (66cm)
Sight   : none, drilled and tapped for
                     telescopic sight
External safety   : safety catch at rear of
                     bolt
Internal safety   : locking

CHARACTERISTICS

• material   : steel
• finish   : matt black
• stock   : black Kevlar with grey
                      veining with pistol
                      grip

Available calibres: .25-06 Rem., .270 Win., 7mm Rem. Mag., .300 Win. Mag.

Remington model 700 Varmint Synthetic

TECHNICAL DETAILS

Calibre   : see below
Cartridge capacity : 4-5 rounds
Magazine catch   : internal magazine
Action   : bolt-action
Locking   : 2 locking lugs
Weight   : 9lb (4.1kg)
Length   : 45¾in (116.2cm)
Barrel Length   : 26in (66cm)
Sight   : none, drilled and tapped for
                     telescopic sight
External safety   : safety catch at rear of bolt
Internal safety   : locking

CHARACTERISTICS

• material   : steel
• finish   : matt black
• stock   : black Kevlar with grey
                      veining with pistol grip

Available calibres: .220 Swift, .22-250 Rem., .223 Rem., .308 Win.

Remington model 700 Varmint Synthetic-Stainless

TECHNICAL DETAILS

Calibre   : see below
Cartridge capacity : 4-5 rounds
Magazine catch   : internal magazine, hinged
                     bottom plate with catch at
                     front of magazine aperture
Action   : bolt-action
Locking   : 2 locking lugs

Weight   : 8lb 8oz (3.9kg)
Length   : 45¾in (116.2cm)
Barrel Length   : 26in (66cm)
Sight   : none, drilled and tapped for
                  telescopic sight
External safety : safety catch at rear of bolt
Internal safety : locking
CHARACTERISTICS
- material : stainless-steel
- finish   : bare metal
- stock   : black Kevlar with grey
             veining with pistol grip

Available calibres: .220 Swift, .22-250 Rem., .223 Rem., .308 Win.

This rifle has a special stainless steel varmint barrel with longitudinal grooves for additional cooling.

Remington model Seven carbine

TECHNICAL DETAILS
Calibre   : see below
Cartridge capacity : 3-5 rounds
Magazine catch   : internal magazine, hinged
                    bottom plate with catch at
                    front of trigger guard
Action   : bolt-action
Locking   : 2 locking lugs
Weight   : 6lb 4oz (2.8kg)
Length   : 37¾in (95.9cm)
Barrel Length   : 18½in (47cm)
Sight   : adjustable Williams sight,
                    drilled and tapped for
                    telescopic sight
External safety   : safety catch on right at rear
                    of bolt
Internal safety   : locking
CHARACTERISTICS
- material : steel
- finish   : blued
- stock   : hardwood with pistol grip

Available calibres: .17 Rem., .223 Rem., .243 Win., 6mm Rem., 7mm-08 Rem., .308 Win.

Remington model Seven Custom-KS carbine

TECHNICAL DETAILS
Calibre   : see below
Cartridge capacity : 3-4 rounds
Magazine catch   : internal magazine, catch at
                    front of trigger guard
Action   : bolt-action
Locking   : 2 locking lugs
Weight   : 5lb 12oz (2.6kg)
Length   : 39-39½in (99.1-100.3cm)
Barrel Length   : 20in (50.8cm)
Sight   : adjustable Williams sight,
                    drilled and tapped for
                    telescopic sight
External safety   : safety catch on right at rear
                    of bolt
Internal safety   : locking
CHARACTERISTICS
- material : steel
- finish   : matt black
- stock   : plastic stock in camouflage
             colours with pistol grip

Available calibres: .223 Rem., 7mm-08 Rem., .308 Win., .35 Rem., .350 Rem. Mag.

This rifle is a special from the Remington Custom workshop.

Remington model Seven MS carbine (Mannlicher Stock)

TECHNICAL DETAILS
Calibre   : see below
Cartridge capacity : 3-5 rounds
Magazine catch   : internal magazine, hinged
                    bottom plate with catch at
                    front of trigger guard
Action   : bolt-action
Locking   : 2 locking lugs
Weight   : 6lb 8oz (3kg)
Length   : 39in (99.1cm)

Barrel Length	: 20in (50.8cm)
Sight	: adjustable Williams sight, drilled and tapped for telescopic sight
External safety	: safety catch on right at rear of bolt
Internal safety	: locking

CHARACTERISTICS

• material	: steel
• finish	: blued
• stock	: laminated hardwood stock runs under barrel to muzzle, with pistol grip

Available calibres: .222 Rem., .223 Rem., .22-250 Rem., .243 Win., 6mm Rem., .250 Savage, .257 Roberts, 7mm-08 Rem., .308 Win., .35 Rem., .350 Rem. Mag.

This is a special from the Remington Custom workshop.

Remington model Seven Stainless- Synthetic carbine

TECHNICAL DETAILS

Calibre	: see below
Cartridge capacity	: 4 rounds
Magazine catch	: internal magazine
Action	: bolt-action
Locking	: 2 locking lugs
Weight	: 6lb 4oz (2.8kg)
Length	: 39¼in (99.7cm)
Barrel Length	: 20in (50.8cm)
Sight	: none, drilled and tapped for telescopic sight
External safety	: safety catch on right at rear of bolt
Internal safety	: locking

CHARACTERISTICS

• material	: stainless-steel
• finish	: matt bare metal
• stock	: black plastic with pistol grip

Available calibres: .243 Win., 7mm-08 Rem., .308 Win.

Remington model Seven Youth carbine

TECHNICAL DETAILS

Calibre	: see below
Cartridge capacity	: 4 rounds
Magazine catch	: internal magazine, catch for bottom plate at front of trigger guard
Action	: bolt-action
Locking	: 2 locking lugs
Weight	: 6lb (2.7kg)
Length	: 36¼in (93.4cm)
Barrel Length	: 18½in (47cm)
Sight	: adjustable Williams sight, drilled and tapped for telescopic sight
External safety	: safety catch on right at rear of bolt
Internal safety	: locking

CHARACTERISTICS

• material	: steel
• finish	: blued
• stock	: hardwood with pistol grip

Available calibres: .243 Win., 7mm-08 Rem.

Rhöner
The Rhöner Sportwaffenfabrik GmbH is situated in Oberelsbach-Weisbach in Germany. The firm was set up in 1959 by Walter Maier and remains a family concern. Initially the company made only starting pistols in the 8mm blank calibre.
Since 1966, the company has directed its efforts more towards hunting and sporting weapons.

Rhöner-SM model 69A

TECHNICAL DETAILS

Calibre	: .22 LR
Cartridge capacity	: single shot
Magazine catch	: not applicable
Action	: bolt-action
Locking	: bolt locking
Weight	: 2.3kg (5lb 2oz)
Length	: 100cm (393/8in)
Barrel Length	: 60cm (23⅝in)

Locking	: bolt locking
Weight	: 3.2kg (7lb 1oz)
Length	: 102.5cm (403/8in)
Barrel Length	: 60cm (23⅝in)
Sight	: optical sight and bead tunnel
External safety	: safety catch on receiver
Internal safety	: locking

CHARACTERISTICS
- material : steel
- finish : blued
- stock : beech match stock

Rhöner-SM model 75

TECHNICAL DETAILS

Calibre	. : .22 Hornet, .22 WMR
Cartridge capacity	: single shot
Magazine catch	: not applicable
Action	: breech-action
Locking	: lever locking beside trigger
Weight	: 2.95kg (6lb 8oz)
Length	: 100cm (393/8in)
Barrel Length	: 60cm (23⅝in)
Sight	: folding sight, mounting for telescopic sight
External safety	: safety catch on receiver
Internal safety	: locking, half-cock on hammer

CHARACTERISTICS
- material : steel
- finish : blued
- stock : beech

Sight	: folding sight and bead tunnel, mounting for telescopic sight
External safety	: safety catch on receiver
Internal safety	: locking, load indicator through rear of bolt

CHARACTERISTICS
- material : steel
- finish : blued
- stock : beech with pistol grip

Rhöner-SM model 69 Match

TECHNICAL DETAILS

Calibre	: .22 LR
Cartridge capacity	: single shot
Magazine catch	: not applicable
Action	: bolt-action

Rhöner-SM model 75-L

TECHNICAL DETAILS

Calibre	: .22 Hornet, .22 WMR
Cartridge capacity	: single shot
Magazine catch	: not applicable
Action	: breech-action

Rhöner-SM model R-81

TECHNICAL DETAILS

Calibre : .22 Hornet, .222 Rem.,
5.6 x 50R Mag.
Cartridge capacity : single shot
Magazine catch : not applicable
Action : breech-action
Locking : lever locking beside trigger
Weight : 2.9-3.1kg (6lb 8oz-6lb 13oz)
Length : 99cm (39in)
Barrel Length : 60cm (23⅝in)
Sight : folding sight, mounting for
telescopic sight
External safety : safety catch on receiver
Internal safety : locking, half-cock on ham-
mer

CHARACTERISTICS
• material : steel
• finish : blued
• stock : walnut

Locking : lever locking beside trigger
Weight : 2.95kg (6lb 8oz)
Length : 100cm (393/8in)
Barrel Length : 60cm (23⅝in)
Sight : folding sight, mounting for
telescopic sight
External safety : safety catch on receiver
Internal safety : locking, half-cock on
hammer

CHARACTERISTICS
• material : steel
• finish : blued, engraved bare metal
breech plates
• stock : walnut

Rhöner-SM Model R-81

Rhöner-SM model R-81-S

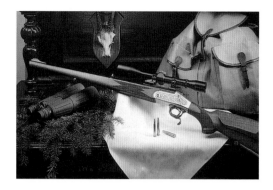

TECHNICAL DETAILS

Calibre	: .22 Hornet, .222 Rem., 5.6 x 50R Mag.
Cartridge capacity	: single shot
Magazine catch	: not applicable
Action	: breech-action
Locking	: lever locking beside trigger
Weight	: 2.9-3.1kg (6lb 8oz-6lb 13oz)
Length	: 99cm (39in)
Barrel Length	: 60cm (23⅝in)
Sight	: folding sight, mounting for telescopic sight
External safety	: safety catch on receiver
Internal safety	: locking, half-cock on hammer

CHARACTERISTICS

• material	: steel
• finish	: blued, engraved bare metal breech plates
• stock	: walnut stock with storage for 4 cartridges

Rhöner-SM model R-81-Z

TECHNICAL DETAILS

Calibre	: .22 Hornet, .222 Rem., 5.6 x 50R Mag.
Cartridge capacity	: single shot
Magazine catch	: not applicable
Action	: breech-action
Locking	: lever locking beside trigger
Weight	: 2.9-3.1kg (6lb 8oz-6lb 13oz)
Length	: 99cm (39in)
Barrel Length	: 60cm (23⅝in)
Sight	: folding sight, mounting for telescopic sight
External safety	: safety catch on receiver
Internal safety	: locking, half-cock on hammer

CHARACTERISTICS

• material	: steel
• finish	: blued, engraved bare metal breech plates; stock and barrel can be taken down for carrying
• stock	: walnut stock with storage for 4 cartridges

Robar

Robar Companies Inc. is a "custom-shop", in other words it makes a rifle to a customer's specific requirements, such as receiver and bolt, and choice of other parts. The resulting rifles are not produced in series and therefore those shown here are merely representative. The business was started by Robert A. Barrkman, an enthusiastic hunter and sports shooter and is based in Phoenix, Arizona, USA. Robar started at the time when many competitive shooters wanted to have their pistols adapted to their specific preferences. This is less common now because the major manufacturers have themselves filled this "gap in the market" with special models and versions. If a customer sent Robar a Colt Government Mark IV, for example, it could be converted to a Thunder Ranch pistol incorporating the latest technical wizardry. Subsequently the business has concentrated on all kinds of different unusual hunting weapons and marksman's rifles up to the Robar .50 BMG. For its non-wooden stocks, Robar solely uses glass-reinforced polyester ones by McMillan. Robar can also carry out modifications to the finish of weapons such as blueing or nickel-plating of steel, black finish for stainless-steel (to avoid reflection for sniper's rifles), and "parkerizing". This is a chemical process which applies a layer of manganese or zinc-phosphate to a weapon to protect it against rusting. The firm uses a process it developed itself known as the Roguard finish for all blued weapons which provides the metal with an extremely hard polymer coating.

A further new process for surface treating steel developed by Robar is NP3. This coats the weapon with a layer of plastic polytetra-fluorethylene in conjunction with nickel-plating.

Robar Custom Hunter

TECHNICAL DETAILS

Calibre	: any calibre required
Cartridge capacity	: dependent upon the system and calibre
Magazine catch	: at front of trigger guard
Action	: bolt-action
Locking	: locking lugs (depending on system chosen)
Weight	: about 10lb (4.5kg)
Length	: about 44in (111.8cm)
Barrel Length	: about 24in (61cm)
Sight	: leaf sight, drilled and tapped for telescopic sight
External safety	: winged safety catch on right behind bolt
Internal safety	: locking, half-cock on hammer

CHARACTERISTICS

• material	: steel or stainless-steel
• finish	: blued, bare metal, or matt black
• stock	: walnut with pistol grip or McMillan glass-fibre

The rifle illustrated is merely an example. The Robar Custom Hunter is made to order to a customer's specific requirements.

Robar QR2
(Quick Reaction) - marksman's rifle

TECHNICAL DETAILS

Calibre	: any calibre required
Cartridge capacity	: dependent upon calibre
Magazine catch	: at front of trigger guard
Action	: bolt-action
Locking	: 2 locking lugs (Remington 700 or Ruger M77)
Weight	: 7-9lb (3.2-4.1kg)
Length	: 44in (111.8cm)
Barrel Length	: 24in (61cm)
Sight	: none, standard telescopic sight
External safety	: safety catch on right behind bolt
Internal safety	: locking

CHARACTERISTICS

• material	:stainless-steel
• finish	: matt black with NP3 coating
• stock	: black or grey McMillan glass-fibre stock with pistol grip

The special stainless-steel match barrel has additional longitudinal cooling grooves. This marksman's rifle is designed for police and army units but it is an effective hunting firearm. The precision of the rifle guarantees a grouping of 3 rounds on target of ½in (13mm) diameter at a range of 100yds (91.4m).

Robar RC-50

TECHNICAL DETAILS

Calibre	: .50 BMG
Cartridge capacity	: 5 rounds
Magazine catch	: at front of trigger guard
Action	: bolt-action
Locking	: locking lugs
Weight	: 25lb (11.3kg)
Length	: 55in (139.7cm)
Barrel Length	: 29in (73.7cm) excluding muzzle compensator
Sight	: none, special mount for telescopic sight
External safety	: safety catch on right behind bolt
Internal safety	: locking

CHARACTERISTICS

• material	: chrome-molybdenum steel
• finish	: NP3 coating
• stock	: McMillan glass-fibre stock with pistol grip and bipod

This marksman's rifle is designed for military units and for target shooters on ranges longer than 300yds/m. This type of rifle was used during the Gulf War at ranges between 1-2,000m (1,093-2,187yds).

Robar SR60 - marksman's rifle

TECHNICAL DETAILS

Calibre	: .308 Win., .300 Win. Mag.
Cartridge capacity	: 5 or 4 rounds respectively
Magazine catch	: at front of trigger guard
Action	: bolt-action
Locking	: 2 locking lugs (Remington 700-BDL)
Weight	: 9lb 7oz (4.3kg)
Length	: 44in (111.8cm)
Barrel Length	: 24in (61cm)
Sight	: none, standard telescopic sight
External safety	: safety catch on right behind bolt
Internal safety	: locking

CHARACTERISTICS

• material	: stainless-steel

• finish	: matt black with NP3 coating
• stock	: black or grey McMillan glass-fibre stock with pistol grip

The special stainless-steel match barrel has additional longitudinal cooling grooves. This marksman's rifle is designed for police and army units. The precision of the rifle guarantees a grouping of 3 rounds on target of 1/2in (13mm) diameter at a range of 100yds (91.4m).

 ## Robar SR90 - marksman's rifle

TECHNICAL DETAILS

Calibre	: .308 Win., .300 Win. Mag.
Cartridge capacity	: 5 or 4 rounds respectively
Magazine catch	: at front of trigger guard
Action	: bolt-action
Locking	: 2 locking lugs (Remington 700-BDL)
Weight	: 10lb 7oz (4.7kg)
Length	: 44in (111.8cm)
Barrel Length	: 24in (61cm)
Sight	: none, standard telescopic sight
External safety	: safety catch on right behind bolt
Internal safety	: locking

CHARACTERISTICS

• material	: stainless-steel
• finish	: matt black with NP3 coating
• stock	: black or grey McMillan glass-fibre stock with pistol grip, adjustable cheek, butt plate and bipod

The special stainless-steel match barrel has additional longitudinal cooling grooves. This marksman's rifle was used by special forces during the Gulf War. The precision of the rifle guarantees a grouping of 3 rounds on target of 1/2in (13mm) diameter at a range of 100yds (91.4m).

TECHNICAL DETAILS

Calibre	: any calibre required
Cartridge capacity	: dependent upon calibre
Magazine catch	: at front of trigger guard
Action	: bolt-action
Locking	: 2 locking lugs (Remington 700-BDL)
Weight	: 8lb 8oz (3.9kg)
Length	: 44in (111.8cm)
Barrel Length	: 24in (61cm)
Sight	: none, standard telescopic sight
External safety	: safety catch on right behind bolt
Internal safety	: locking

CHARACTERISTICS

• material	: stainless-steel
• finish	: matt black with NP3 coating
• stock	: McMillan glass-fibre stock with pistol grip and bipod; choice of colour

The special stainless-steel match barrel has additional longitudinal cooling grooves.

Ruger

Sturm, Ruger & Company Inc. was started in 1948 by William Batterman Ruger and Alexander M. Sturm. Between them, they rented a shed in Southport, Connecticut, and established a modest workshop for small-weapons. Ruger had gained his experience at the state arsenal, the Springfield Armory and at the armaments manufacturer Auto-Ordnance which made the Tommy-gun submachine gun. Their first product was a small-calibre pistol that was introduced in 1949. After the death of Sturm in an aircraft crash, William (Bill) Ruger continued in business on his own. In memory of his dead friend and partner, he changed the company logo from red to black. Up to 1959, Ruger produced a large number of revolvers. The first design of rifle was not introduced until 1959. It was a semi-automatic carbine in .44 Magnum calibre. The growth of the business made extending the works essential. In 1964 the company built a new factory in Newport, New Hampshire.

The Ruger No. 1 single-shot rifle went into production in 1967. Until this time, single-shot weapons were rather looked down upon. Those available were mainly inexpensive breech-pivot firearms for hunting small game. Ruger himself was an admirer of heavy single-shot English rifles such as those of Alexander Henry. He considered that such a concept was also suitable for the North American market. The respected maker of stocks, Leonard Brownell, was taken on to design attractive stocks for this type of rifle and he became the technical manager of the Newport factory. The No. 1 rifle was a great success. A subsequent rifle was the model 77 introduced in 1968. This was a bolt-action repeating rifle with a stock designed by Brownell. The classic rifle was most unusual for its time. In 1974, Ruger developed an automatic carbine, the Mini-14 for .223 Rem. calibre that was followed the next year by a civilian version. At first glance, the Mini-14 looks like a cross between the M1-Garand rifle and the Winchester .30-M1 carbine. The M77 rifle was succeeded in 1992 by the M77-Mark II rifle. The Mark II had a better cartridge ejector that gripped the cartridge after it had been removed from the chamber by the bolt. The receiver is made of stainless-steel.

Ruger model 10/22 DSP (Deluxe Sporter)

TECHNICAL DETAILS

Calibre	: .22 LR
Cartridge capacity	: 5- or 10-rounds rotating cartridge holder
Magazine catch	: front of trigger guard
Action	: semi-automatic
Locking	: inertia

Weight	: 5lb (2.3kg)
Length	: 37¼in (94.6cm)
Barrel Length	: 18½in (47cm)
Sight	: height adjustable folding sight, suitable for telescopic sight
External safety	: push-button safety catch at front of trigger guard
Internal safety	: locking

CHARACTERISTICS

• material	: steel barrel, light metal receiver
• finish	: blued
• stock	: walnut

Ruger model 10/22 RB (Standard)

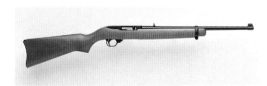

TECHNICAL DETAILS

Calibre	: .22 LR
Cartridge capacity	: 5- or 10-rounds rotating cartridge holder
Magazine catch	: front of trigger guard
Action	: semi-automatic
Locking	: inertia
Weight	: 5lb (2.3kg)
Length	: 37¼in (94.6cm)
Barrel Length	: 18½in (47cm)
Sight	: height adjustable folding sight, suitable for telescopic sight
External safety	: push-button safety catch at front of trigger guard
Internal safety	: locking

CHARACTERISTICS

• material	: steel barrel, light metal receiver
• finish	: blued
• stock	: hardwood

Ruger model 10/22 RBI (International)

TECHNICAL DETAILS

Calibre	: .22 LR
Cartridge capacity	: 5- or 10-rounds rotating cartridge holder

Magazine catch	: front of trigger guard
Action	: semi-automatic
Locking	: inertia
Weight	: 5lb (2.3kg)
Length	: 37¼in (94.6cm)
Barrel Length	: 18½in (47cm)
Sight	: height adjustable folding sight, suitable for telescopic sight
External safety	: push-button safety catch at front of trigger guard
Internal safety	: locking

CHARACTERISTICS

• material	: steel barrel, light metal receiver
• finish	: blued
• stock	: hardwood stock runs under barrel to muzzle

Ruger model K10/22 RB (Standard Stainless)

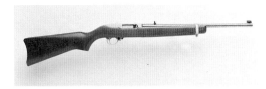

TECHNICAL DETAILS

Calibre	: .22 LR
Cartridge capacity	: 5- or 10-rounds rotating cartridge holder
Magazine catch	: front of trigger guard
Action	: semi-automatic
Locking	: inertia
Weight	: 5lb (2.3kg)
Length	: 37¼in (94.6cm)
Barrel Length	: 18½in (47cm)
Sight	: height adjustable folding sight, suitable for telescopic sight
External safety	: push-button safety catch at front of trigger guard
Internal safety	: locking

CHARACTERISTICS

• material	: stainless-steel barrel, light metal receiver

- finish : bare metal
- stock : hardwood

Ruger model K10/22 RBI (International-Stainless)

TECHNICAL DETAILS

Calibre : .22 LR
Cartridge capacity : 5- or 10-rounds rotating cartridge holder
Magazine catch : front of trigger guard
Action : semi-automatic
Locking : inertia
Weight : 5lb (2.3kg)
Length : 37¼in (94.6cm)
Barrel Length : 18½in (47cm)
Sight : height adjustable folding sight, suitable for telescopic sight
External safety : push-button safety catch at front of trigger guard
Internal safety : locking

CHARACTERISTICS

- material : stainless-steel barrel, light metal receiver
- finish : bare metal
- stock : hardwood stock runs under barrel to muzzle

Ruger model 10/22 T (Target)

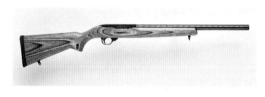

TECHNICAL DETAILS

Calibre : .22 LR
Cartridge capacity : 5- or 10-rounds rotating cartridge holder
Magazine catch : front of trigger guard
Action : semi-automatic

Locking : inertia
Weight : 7lb 4oz (3.3kg)
Length : 38½in (98cm)
Barrel Length : 20in (51cm) special heavy barrel
Sight : none, suitable for telescopic sight
External safety : push-button safety catch at front of trigger guard
Internal safety : locking

CHARACTERISTICS

- material : steel barrel, light metal receiver
- finish : blued
- stock : laminated hardwood

Ruger model 77/22R

TECHNICAL DETAILS

Calibre : .22 LR
Cartridge capacity : 5- or 10-rounds rotating cartridge holder
Magazine catch : front of trigger guard
Action : bolt-action
Locking : locking lugs
Weight : 6lb (2.7kg)
Length : 39¼in (99.7cm)
Barrel Length : 20in (51cm)
Sight : none, mounting for telescopic sight
External safety : winged safety catch at rear of bolt
Internal safety : locking

CHARACTERISTICS

- material : steel
- finish : blued
- stock : walnut with pistol grip

Ruger model 77/22RH

TECHNICAL DETAILS

Calibre : .22 Hornet
Cartridge capacity : 6-rounds rotating cartridge holder
Magazine catch : front of trigger guard
Action : bolt-action

Locking	: locking lugs
Weight	: 6lb (2.7kg)
Length	: 40in (102cm)
Barrel Length	: 20in (51cm)
Sight	: none, mounting for telescopic sight
External safety	: winged safety catch at rear of bolt
Internal safety	: locking

CHARACTERISTICS
- material : steel
- finish : blued
- stock : walnut with pistol grip

Ruger model K77/22RHVBZ

TECHNICAL DETAILS

Calibre	: .22 Hornet
Cartridge capacity	: 6-rounds rotating cartridge holder
Magazine catch	: front of trigger guard
Action	: bolt-action
Locking	: locking lugs
Weight	: 6lb (2.7kg)
Length	: 40in (102cm)
Barrel Length	: 20in (51cm)
Sight	: none, mounting for telescopic sight
External safety	: winged safety catch at rear of bolt
Internal safety	: locking

CHARACTERISTICS
- material : stainless-steel
- finish : matt grey
- stock : laminated hardwood with pistol grip

Ruger model 77/22RM

TECHNICAL DETAILS

Calibre	: .22 WMR
Cartridge capacity	: 5- or 9-rounds rotating cartridge holder
Magazine catch	: front of trigger guard
Action	: bolt-action
Locking	: locking lugs
Weight	: 6lb (2.7kg)
Length	: 39¼in (99.7cm)
Barrel Length	: 20in (51cm)
Sight	: none, mounting for telescopic sight
External safety	: winged safety catch at rear of bolt
Internal safety	: locking

CHARACTERISTICS
- material : steel
- finish : blued
- stock : walnut with pistol grip

Ruger model K77/22RMP All-Weather

TECHNICAL DETAILS

Calibre	: .22 WMR
Cartridge capacity	: 5- or 9-rounds rotating cartridge holder
Magazine catch	: front of trigger guard
Action	: bolt-action
Locking	: locking lugs
Weight	: 6lb (2.7kg)
Length	: 39¼in (99.7cm)
Barrel Length	: 20in (51cm)
Sight	: none, mounting for telescopic sight
External safety	: winged safety catch at rear of bolt
Internal safety	: locking

CHARACTERISTICS
- material : stainless-steel
- finish : bare metal
- stock : black plastic Zytel stock
  with pistol grip

Ruger model K77/22RP All-Weather

TECHNICAL DETAILS
Calibre : .22 LR
Cartridge capacity : 5- or 10-rounds rotating
cartridge holder
Magazine catch : front of trigger guard
Action : bolt-action
Locking : locking lugs
Weight : 6lb (2.7kg)
Length : 39¼in (99.7cm)
Barrel Length : 20in (51cm)
Sight : none, mounting for
telescopic sight
External safety : winged safety catch at rear
of bolt
Internal safety : locking
CHARACTERISTICS
- material : stainless-steel
- finish : bare metal
- stock : black plastic Zytel stock
  with pistol grip

Ruger model 77/22RS

TECHNICAL DETAILS
Calibre : .22 LR
Cartridge capacity : 5- or 10-rounds rotating car-
tridge holder
Magazine catch : front of trigger guard
Action : bolt-action
Locking : locking lugs
Weight : 6lb (2.7kg)
Length : 39¼in (99.7cm)
Barrel Length : 20in (51cm)

Sight : adjustable folding sight,
mounting for telescopic
sight
External safety : winged safety catch at rear
of bolt
Internal safety : locking
CHARACTERISTICS
- material : steel
- finish : blued
- stock : walnut with pistol grip

Ruger model 77/22RSM

TECHNICAL DETAILS
Calibre : .22 WMR
Cartridge capacity : 5- or 9-rounds rotating
cartridge holder
Magazine catch : front of trigger guard
Action : bolt-action
Locking : locking lugs
Weight : 6lb (2.7kg)
Length : 39¼in (99.7cm)
Barrel Length : 20in (51cm)
Sight : adjustable folding sight,
mounting for telescopic
sight
External safety : winged safety catch at rear
of bolt
Internal safety : locking
CHARACTERISTICS
- material : steel
- finish : blued
- stock : walnut with pistol grip

Ruger model K77/22RSMP
All-Weather

TECHNICAL DETAILS
Calibre : .22 WMR

Cartridge capacity	: 5- or 9-rounds rotating cartridge holder
Magazine catch	: front of trigger guard
Action	: bolt-action
Locking	: locking lugs
Weight	: 6lb (2.7kg)
Length	: 39¼in (99.7cm)
Barrel Length	: 20in (51cm)
Sight	: adjustable folding sight, mounting for telescopic sight
External safety	: winged safety catch at rear of bolt
Internal safety	: locking

CHARACTERISTICS
- material : stainless-steel
- finish : bare metal
- stock : black plastic Zytel stock with pistol grip

Ruger model K77/22RSP

Magazine catch	: front of trigger guard
Action	: bolt-action
Locking	: locking lugs
Weight	: 7lb 5oz (3.3kg)
Length	: 43¼in (110cm)
Barrel Length	: 24in (61cm)
Sight	: none, mounting for telescopic sight
External safety	: winged safety catch at rear of bolt
Internal safety	: locking

CHARACTERISTICS
- material : stainless-steel
- finish : matt grey
- stock : laminated hardwood with pistol grip

Ruger model K77/22VMBZ

TECHNICAL DETAILS

Calibre	: .22 LR
Cartridge capacity	: 5- or 10-rounds rotating cartridge holder
Magazine catch	: front of trigger guard
Action	: bolt-action
Locking	: locking lugs
Weight	: 6lb (2.7kg)
Length	: 39¼in (99.7cm)
Barrel Length	: 20in (51cm)
Sight	: adjustable folding sight, mounting for telescopic sight
External safety	: winged safety catch at front of trigger guard
Internal safety	: locking

CHARACTERISTICS
- material : stainless-steel
- finish : bare metal
- stock : black plastic Zytel stock with pistol grip

Ruger model K77/22VBZ

TECHNICAL DETAILS

Calibre	: .22 LR
Cartridge capacity	: 5- or 10-rounds rotating cartridge holder

TECHNICAL DETAILS

Calibre	: .22 WMR
Cartridge capacity	: 5- or 9-rounds rotating cartridge holder
Magazine catch	: front of trigger guard
Action	: bolt-action
Locking	: locking lugs
Weight	: 7lb 5oz (3.3kg)
Length	: 43¼in (110cm)
Barrel Length	: 24in (61cm)
Sight	: none, mounting for telescopic sight
External safety	: winged safety catch at rear of bolt
Internal safety	: locking

CHARACTERISTICS
- material : stainless-steel
- finish : matt grey
- stock : laminated hardwood with pistol grip

Ruger M77LR Mark II
Left-handed rifle

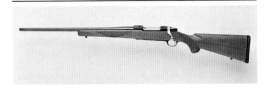

TECHNICAL DETAILS

Calibre	: see below
Cartridge capacity	: 4 rounds (3 for Magnum)
Magazine catch	: front of magazine aperture
Action	: bolt-action
Locking	: 2 locking lugs (on left of receiver)
Weight	: 7lb 5oz (3.3kg)
Length	: 39¾-41¾in (101-106cm) longer length for Magnum
Barrel Length	: 22-24in (56-61cm)
Sight	: none, mounting rail and rings for telescopic sight
External safety	: winged safety catch at rear of bolt
Internal safety	: locking

CHARACTERISTICS

• material	: steel
• finish	: blued
• stock	: left-handed walnut stock with pistol grip

Available calibres: .270 Win., 7mm Rem. Mag., .30-06 Spr., .300 Win. Mag.

Ruger M77R Mark II rifle

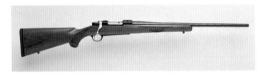

TECHNICAL DETAILS

Calibre	: see below
Cartridge capacity	: 4 rounds (3 for Magnum)
Magazine catch	: front of magazine aperture
Action	: bolt-action
Locking	: 2 locking lugs
Weight	: 7lb 5oz (3.3kg)
Length	: 39¾-41¾in (101-106cm) longer length for Magnum
Barrel Length	: 22-24in (56-61cm)

Sight	: none, mounting rail and rings for telescopic sight
External safety	: winged safety catch at rear of bolt
Internal safety	: locking

CHARACTERISTICS

• material	: steel
• finish	: blued
• stock	: walnut with pistol grip

Available calibres: .223 Rem., .22-250, 6mm Rem., .243 Win., .257 Roberts, .25-06, 6.5 x 55, .270 Win., 7 x 57mm, .280 Rem., 7mm Rem. Mag., .30-06 Spr., .308 Win., .300 Win. Mag., .338 Win. Mag.

Ruger M77RL Mark II
Ultra-Light rifle

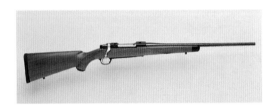

TECHNICAL DETAILS

Calibre	: see below
Cartridge capacity	: 4 rounds (3 for Magnum)
Magazine catch	: front of magazine aperture
Action	: bolt-action
Locking	: 2 locking lugs
Weight	: 6lb (2.7kg)
Length	: 37¾in (96cm)
Barrel Length	: 20in (51cm)
Sight	: none, mounting rail and rings for telescopic sight
External safety	: winged safety catch at rear of bolt
Internal safety	: locking

CHARACTERISTICS

• material	: steel
• finish	: blued
• stock	: walnut with pistol grip

Available calibres: .223 Rem., .243 Win., .257 Roberts, .270 Win., .30-06 Spr., .308 Win.

Ruger KM77RP Mark II All-Weather rifle

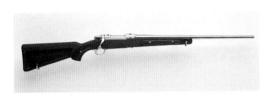

TECHNICAL DETAILS
Calibre : see below
Cartridge capacity : 4 rounds (3 for Magnum)
Magazine catch : front of magazine aperture
Action : bolt-action
Locking : 2 locking lugs
Weight : 7lb 5oz (3.3kg)
Length : 39¾-41¾in (101-106cm) longer length for Magnum
Barrel Length : 22-24in (56-61cm)
Sight : none, mounting rail and rings for telescopic sight
External safety : winged safety catch at rear of bolt
Internal safety : locking

CHARACTERISTICS
• material : stainless-steel
• finish : bare metal
• stock : plastic Zytel stock with pistol grip

Available calibres: .223 Rem., .22-250, .243 Win., .270 Win. .280 Rem., 7mm Rem. Mag., .30-06 Spr., .308 Win., .300 Win. Mag., .338 Win. Mag.

Ruger M77RS Mark II rifle

TECHNICAL DETAILS
Calibre : see below
Cartridge capacity : 4 rounds (3 for Magnum)
Magazine catch : front of magazine aperture
Action : bolt-action
Locking : 2 locking lugs
Weight : 7lb 5oz (3.3kg)

Length : 39¾-41¾in (101-106cm) longer length for Magnum
Barrel Length : 22-24in (56-61cm)
Sight : folding sight, mounting rail and rings for telescopic sight
External safety : winged safety catch at rear of bolt
Internal safety : locking

CHARACTERISTICS
• material : steel
• finish : blued
• stock : walnut with pistol grip

Available calibres: .243 Win., .25-06, .270 Win. 7mm Rem. Mag., .30-06 Spr., .308 Win., .300 Win. Mag., .338 Win. Mag., .458 Win. Mag.

Ruger M77RSEXP Mark II Express rifle

TECHNICAL DETAILS
Calibre : see below
Cartridge capacity : 4 rounds (3 for Magnum)
Magazine catch : front of magazine aperture
Action : bolt-action
Locking : 2 locking lugs
Weight : 7lb 8oz (3.4kg)
Length : 42⅛in (107cm)
Barrel Length : 22-24in (56-61cm) longer length for Magnum
Sight : adjustable folding sight, mounting rail and rings for telescopic sight
External safety : winged safety catch at rear of bolt
Internal safety : locking

CHARACTERISTICS
• material : steel
• finish : blued
• stock : specially selected walnut stock with pistol grip

Available calibres: .270 Win. .30-06 Spr., 7mm Rem. Mag., .300 Win. Mag., .338 Win. Mag.

Ruger M77RSI Mark II International rifle

TECHNICAL DETAILS
Calibre	: see below
Cartridge capacity	: 4 rounds
Magazine catch	: front of magazine aperture
Action	: bolt-action
Locking	: 2 locking lugs
Weight	: 7lb 1oz (3.2kg)
Length	: 38¼in (97cm)
Barrel Length	: 18½in (47cm)
Sight	: adjustable folding sight, mounting rail and rings for telescopic sight
External safety	: winged safety catch at rear of bolt
Internal safety	: locking

CHARACTERISTICS
- material : steel
- finish : blued
- stock : specially selected walnut stock with pistol grip runs full-length under barrel to muzzle

Available calibres: .243 Win., .30-06 Spr., .308 Win.

Ruger M77RSM Mark II Magnum rifle

TECHNICAL DETAILS
Calibre	: see below
Cartridge capacity	: 4 rounds (.375./.404)
	3 rounds (.416/.458)
Magazine catch	: front of magazine aperture
Action	: bolt-action
Locking	: 2 locking lugs
Weight	: 9lb 5oz-10lb 5oz (4.2-4.65kg)
Length	: 447/8in (114cm)

Barrel Length	: 24in (61cm)
Sight	: adjustable folding sight, mounting rail and rings for telescopic sight
External safety	: winged safety catch at rear of bolt
Internal safety	: locking

CHARACTERISTICS
- material : steel
- finish : blued
- stock : specially selected walnut stock with pistol grip

Available calibres: .375 H & H Mag., .404 Jeffery, .416 Rigby, .458 Win. Mag.

Ruger KM77RSP Mark II All-Weather rifle

TECHNICAL DETAILS
Calibre	: see below
Cartridge capacity	: 4 rounds (3 for Magnum)
Magazine catch	: front of magazine aperture
Action	: bolt-action
Locking	: 2 locking lugs
Weight	: 7lb 5oz (3.3kg)
Length	: 39¾-41¾in (101-106cm) longer length for Magnum
Barrel Length	: 22-24in (56-61cm)
Sight	: folding sight, mounting rail and rings for telescopic sight
External safety	: winged safety catch at rear of bolt
Internal safety	: locking

CHARACTERISTICS
- material : stainless-steel
- finish : bare metal
- stock : plastic Zytel stock with pistol grip

Available calibres: .243 Win., .270 Win., 7mm Rem. Mag., .30-06 Spr., .300 Win. Mag., .338 Win. Mag.

Ruger KM77VT Mark II Target rifle

TECHNICAL DETAILS
Calibre   : see below
Cartridge capacity : 4 rounds
Magazine catch   : front of magazine aperture
Action   : bolt-action
Locking   : 2 locking lugs
Weight   : 9lb 5oz (4.2kg)
Length   : 46½in (118cm)
Barrel Length   : 26in (66cm)
Sight   : none, mounting rail and
                          rings for telescopic sight
External safety   : winged safety catch at rear
                          of bolt
Internal safety   : locking

CHARACTERISTICS
• material   : stainless-steel
• finish   : matt grey
• stock   : laminated hardwood stock
                       with pistol grip

Available calibres: .223 Rem., .22 PPC, .22-250, .22 Swift, 6mm PPC, .243 Win., .25-06, .308 Win.

Ruger Mini-14/5R Ranch Rifle

TECHNICAL DETAILS
Calibre   : .223 Rem.
Cartridge capacity : 5-, 20-, or 30-rounds cartrid-
                       ge holder
Magazine catch   : front of magazine aperture
Action   : semi-automatic, gas-pressure
Locking   : rotating slide
Weight   : 6lb 9oz (3kg)
Length   : 37⅛in (94.3cm)
Barrel Length   : 18½in (47cm)
Sight   : folding optical sight and
                       mounting for telescopic
                       sight

External safety   : safety catch at front of trig-
                       ger guard (Garand-style)
Internal safety   : locking

CHARACTERISTICS
• material   : steel
• finish   : blued
• stock   : hardwood

Ruger Mini-14/5R Ranch Rifle Stainless

TECHNICAL DETAILS
Calibre   : .223 Rem.
Cartridge capacity : 5-, 20-, or 30-rounds
                       cartridge holder
Magazine catch   : front of magazine aperture
Action   : semi-automatic, gas-pressure
Locking   : rotating slide
Weight   : 6lb 9oz (3kg)
Length   : 37⅛in (94.3cm)
Barrel Length   : 18½in (47cm)
Sight   : folding optical sight and
                       mounting for telescopic
                       sight
External safety   : safety catch at front of
                       trigger guard (Garand-style)
Internal safety   : locking

CHARACTERISTICS
• material   : stainless-steel
• finish   : bare metal
• stock   : hardwood stock with pistol
                       grip and black plastic hand
                       grip

Ruger Government Mini-14/20GB

TECHNICAL DETAILS
Calibre   : .223 Rem.
Cartridge capacity : 5-, 20-, or 30-rounds
                       cartridge holder

Magazine catch	: front of magazine aperture
Action	: semi-automatic, gas-pressure
Locking	: rotating slide
Weight	: 6lb 13oz (3.1kg)
Length	: 38¾in (98.4cm)
Barrel Length	: 18½in (47cm) with flash reducer
Sight	: adjustable optical sight
External safety	: safety catch at front of trigger guard (Garand-style)
Internal safety	: locking

CHARACTERISTICS

• material	: steel
• finish	: blued
• stock	: hardwood stock with black plastic hand grip

Ruger Mini-Thirty

TECHNICAL DETAILS

Calibre	: 7.62 x 39mm
Cartridge capacity	: 5-rounds cartridge holder
Magazine catch	: front of magazine aperture
Action	: semi-automatic, gas-pressure
Locking	: rotating slide
Weight	: 6lb 15oz (3.1kg)
Length	: 37⅛in (94.3cm)
Barrel Length	: 18½in (47cm)
Sight	: folding optical sight and mounting for telescopic sight
External safety	: safety catch at front of trigger guard (Garand-style)
Internal safety	: locking

CHARACTERISTICS

• material	: steel
• finish	: blued
• stock	: hardwood stock with black plastic hand grip

Ruger Mini-Thirty Stainless

TECHNICAL DETAILS

Calibre	: 7.62 x 39mm
Cartridge capacity	: 5-rounds cartridge holder
Magazine catch	: front of magazine aperture

Action	: semi-automatic, gas-pressure
Locking	: rotating slide
Weight	: 6lb 15oz (3.1kg)
Length	: 37⅛in (94.3cm)
Barrel Length	: 18½in (47cm)
Sight	: folding optical sight and mounting for telescopic sight
External safety	: safety catch at front of trigger guard (Garand-style)
Internal safety	: locking

CHARACTERISTICS

• material	: stainless-steel
• finish	: bare metal
• stock	: hardwood stock with black plastic hand grip

Ruger No. 1-A Light Sporter

TECHNICAL DETAILS

Calibre	: see below
Cartridge capacity	: single-shot
Magazine catch	: not applicable
Action	: trigger-guard lever-action
Locking	: drop-block locking
Weight	: 7lb 3oz (3.2kg)
Length	: 39¾in (101cm)
Barrel Length	: 22in (56cm)
Sight	: folding sight and mounting for telescopic sight
External safety	: safety catch on back of stock by pistol grip
Internal safety	: locking

CHARACTERISTICS

• material	: steel
• finish	: blued
• stock	: walnut with pistol grip

Available calibres: .243 Win., .270 Win., 7 x 57, .30-06 Spr.

Ruger No. 1-B Standard

TECHNICAL DETAILS
Calibre : see below
Cartridge capacity : single-shot
Magazine catch : not applicable
Action : trigger-guard lever-action
Locking : drop-block locking
Weight : 8lb (3.6kg)
Length : 43¾in (111cm)
Barrel Length : 26in (66cm)
Sight : none, mounting for telescopic sight
External safety : safety catch on back of stock by pistol grip
Internal safety : locking
CHARACTERISTICS
• material : steel
• finish : blued
• stock : walnut with pistol grip

Available calibres: .218 Bee, .22 Hornet, .223 Rem., .22-250, .220 Swift, 6mm Rem, .243 Win., .257 Roberts, .25-06, .270 Win., .270 Wby. Mag., .280 Rem., 7mm Rem. Mag., .30-06 Spr., .300 Win. Mag., .300 Wby. Mag., .338 Win. Mag.

Ruger No. 1-H Tropical

TECHNICAL DETAILS
Calibre : see below
Cartridge capacity : single-shot
Magazine catch : not applicable
Action : trigger-guard lever-action
Locking : drop-block locking
Weight : 9lb (4.1kg)
Length : 41¾in (106cm)
Barrel Length : 24in (61cm)
Sight : folding sight and mounting for telescopic sight

External safety : safety catch on back of stock by pistol grip
Internal safety : locking
CHARACTERISTICS
• material : steel
• finish : blued
• stock : walnut with pistol grip

Available calibres: .375 H& H Mag., .404 Jeffery, .416 Rigby, .416 Rem. Mag., .458 Win. Mag.

Ruger No. 1-RSI International carbine

TECHNICAL DETAILS
Calibre : see below
Cartridge capacity : single-shot
Magazine catch : not applicable
Action : trigger-guard lever-action
Locking : drop-block locking
Weight : 7lb 5oz (3.3kg)
Length : 37¾in (96cm)
Barrel Length : 20in (51cm)
Sight : folding sight and mounting for telescopic sight
External safety : safety catch on back of stock by pistol grip
Internal safety : locking
CHARACTERISTICS
• material : steel
• finish : blued
• stock : walnut stock with pistol grip runs under barrel to muzzle

Available calibres: .243 Win., .270 Win., 7 x 57, .30-06 Spr.

Ruger No. 1-S Medium Sporter

TECHNICAL DETAILS

Calibre	: see below
Cartridge capacity	: single-shot
Magazine catch	: not applicable
Action	: trigger-guard lever-action
Locking	: drop-block locking
Weight	: 7lb 5oz (3.3kg)
Length	: 43¾in (111cm)
Barrel Length	: 26in (66cm) .45-70 is 22in (56cm)
Sight	: folding sight and mounting for telescopic sight
External safety	: safety catch on back of stock by pistol grip
Internal safety	: locking

CHARACTERISTICS

• material	: steel
• finish	: blued
• stock	: walnut stock with pistol grip

Available calibres: .218 Bee, 7mm Rem. Mag., .300 Win. Mag., .338 Win. Mag., .45-70 Govt.

Ruger No. 1-V Special Varminter

TECHNICAL DETAILS

Calibre	: see below
Cartridge capacity	: single-shot
Magazine catch	: not applicable
Action	: trigger-guard lever-action
Locking	: drop-block locking
Weight	: 9lb (4.1kg)
Length	: 41¾in (106cm)
Barrel Length	: 24in (61cm) .220 Swift is 26in. (66cm)
Sight	: none, Ruger mounting for telescopic sight
External safety	: safety catch on back of stock by pistol grip
Internal safety	: locking

CHARACTERISTICS

• material	: steel
• finish	: blued
• stock	: walnut stock with pistol grip

Available calibres: .223 Rem., .22 PPC, .22-250, .220 Swift, 6mm Rem., 6mm PPC, .25-06.

Sako

The Finnish weapon firm Sako was established immediately after World War I as a repair and modification facility for the military rifles of the time. Many of these weapons were adapted for hunting use. The Sako factory is situated at Riihimäki in southern Finland. In common with many companies in the field, the business suffered greatly during the great depression of the Thirties. The business virtually disappeared during World War II and had to be rebuilt from almost nothing in 1946. In those years too, Sako occupied itself with converting military rifles into hunting and sporting fire-arms. Early in the 1950s, the company developed its own range of hunting and precision rifles based upon three different receivers and bolts: the short bolt designated S491, the medium bolt - M591, and the long and Magnum bolt - the L691. Towards the end of the 1980s, Sako developed a sniper's rifle with a very different locking mechanism known as the TRG series. This rifle is also available in a hunting version. Sako also produces separate receivers with bolts because many custom rifle makers choose to use the Sako action as the basis for their weapons.

Sako also makes military firearms with auto-matic rifles inspired by the AK-47, such as the Sako RK-95 in .223 Rem. or 7.62 x 39mm calibres. The Sako concern includes a munitions factory which makes cartridges ranging from .22 Hornet to .375 H & H Magnum. This ammunition is equipped with special bullet tips with names such as Hammerhead, Powerhead, and Speedhead. The company also makes a range of ammu-nition for hand guns including a special poli-ce cartridge, the 9mm Para KPO.

Sako Battue (rifle for driven game)

TECHNICAL DETAILS

Calibre	: see below
Cartridge capacity	: magazine for 4 or 5 rounds
Magazine catch	: catch for magazine bottom plate in front of trigger
Action	: bolt-action

Locking	: 3 locking lugs
Weight	: 3.1-3.3kg (6lb 13oz-8lb 10oz)
Length	: 99.5-101.5cm (39⅛-40in)
Barrel Length	: 49cm (19¼)in
Sight	: special driven game sight with height adjustment, bead tunnel, mounting for telescopic sight
External safety	: safety catch on right behind bolt
Internal safety	: locking

CHARACTERISTICS

• material	: steel
• finish	: blued
• stock	: walnut stock with pistol grip

Available calibres (M591 medium bolt): .22-250 Rem., .243 Win., 7mm-08 Rem., .308 Win.; (M691 long bolt): .25-06 Rem., 6.5 x 55mm, .270 Win., 7 x 64mm, .280 Rem., .30-06 Spr., 9.3 x 62mm; (M691 Magnum): 7mm Rem. Mag., .300 Win. Mag., .300 Wby. Mag., .338 Win. Mag., .375 H & H Mag.

This rifle is also available in a stainless-steel version.

Sako Hunting Carbine

TECHNICAL DETAILS

Calibre	: see below
Cartridge capacity	: magazine for 4 or 5 rounds
Magazine catch	: catch for magazine bottom plate in front of trigger
Action	: bolt-action
Locking	: 3 locking lugs
Weight	: 3.2-3.4kg (7lb-7lb 8oz)
Length	: 99.5-101.5cm (39⅛-40in)
Barrel Length	: 49cm (19¼in)
Sight	: side-adjustable leaf sight and bead tunnel, mounting for telescopic sight
External safety	: safety catch on right behind bolt
Internal safety	: locking

CHARACTERISTICS

• material	: steel

• finish	: blued
• stock	: walnut stock with pistol grip

Available calibres (M591 medium bolt): .22-250 Rem., .243 Win., 7mm-08 Rem., .308 Win.; (M691 long bolt): .25-06 Rem., 6.5 x 55mm, .270 Win., 7 x 64mm, .280 Rem., .30-06 Spr., 9.3 x 62mm; (M691 Magnum): 7mm Rem. Mag., .300 Win. Mag., .300 Wby. Mag., .338 Win. Mag., .375 H & H Mag.

This rifle is also available in a stainless-steel version

Sako Deluxe

TECHNICAL DETAILS

Calibre	: see below
Cartridge capacity	: magazine for 4-, 5-, or 6-rounds
Magazine catch	: catch for magazine bottom plate in front of trigger
Action	: bolt-action
Locking	: 3 locking lugs
Weight	: 3.1-3.9kg (6lb 13oz-8lb 10oz)
Length	: 106-114.5cm (41¾-45in)
Barrel Length	: 57-62cm (22½-24½in)
Sight	: side-adjustable leaf sight and bead tunnel, mounting for telescopic sight
External safety	: safety catch on right behind bolt
Internal safety	: locking

CHARACTERISTICS

• material	: steel
• finish	: blued
• stock	: walnut stock with pistol grip

Available calibres (S491 short bolt): .17 Rem., .222 Rem., .223 Rem., .22 PPCV, 6mm PPC; (M591 medium bolt): .22-250 Rem., .243 Win., 7mm-08 Rem., .308 Win.; (M691 long bolt): .25-06 Rem., 6.5 x 55mm, .270 Win., 7 x 64mm, .280 Rem., .30-06 Spr., 9.3 x 62mm;

(M691 Magnum): 7mm Rem. Mag., .300 Win. Mag., .300 Wby. Mag., .338 Win. Mag., .375 H & H Mag., .416 Rem. Mag.

This rifle is also available in a stainless-steel version.

Sako Euro

TECHNICAL DETAILS

Calibre	: see below
Cartridge capacity	: magazine for 4-, 5-, or 6-rounds
Magazine catch	: catch for magazine bottom plate in front of trigger
Action	: bolt-action
Locking	: 3 locking lugs
Weight	: 3.1-3.9kg (6lb 13oz-8lb 10oz)
Length	: 106-114.5cm (41¾-45in)
Barrel Length	: 57-62cm (22½-24½in)
Sight	: side-adjustable leaf sight and bead tunnel, mounting for telescopic sight
External safety	: safety catch on right behind bolt
Internal safety	: locking

CHARACTERISTICS

• material	: steel
• finish	: blued
• stock	: walnut stock with pistol grip

Available calibres (S491 short bolt): .17 Rem., .222 Rem., .223 Rem., .22 PPCV, 6mm PPC; (M591 medium bolt): .22-250 Rem., .243 Win., 7mm-08 Rem., .308 Win.; (M691 long bolt): .25-06 Rem., 6.5 x 55mm, .270 Win., 7 x 64mm, .280 Rem., .30-06 Spr., 9.3 x 62mm; (M691 Magnum): 7mm Rem. Mag., .300 Win. Mag., .300 Wby. Mag., .338 Win. Mag., .375 H & H Mag.

This rifle is also available in a stainless-steel version.

Sako Finnfire (P94S)

TECHNICAL DETAILS

Calibre	: .22 LR
Cartridge capacity	: 5- or 10-rounds cartridge holder
Magazine catch	: at front of magazine aperture
Action	: bolt-action
Locking	: 2 locking lugs
Weight	: 2.6kg (5lb 11oz)
Length	: 100cm (39½in)
Barrel Length	: 56cm (22in)
Sight	: side-adjustable leaf sight and bead tunnel, mounting for telescopic sight
External safety	: safety catch on right behind bolt
Internal safety	: locking

CHARACTERISTICS

• material	: steel
• finish	: blued
• stock	: walnut stock with pistol grip

Sako Finnfire Varmint

TECHNICAL DETAILS

Calibre	: .22 LR
Cartridge capacity	: 5- or 10-rounds cartridge holder
Magazine catch	: at front of magazine aperture
Action	: bolt-action
Locking	: 2 locking lugs
Weight	: 3.3kg (7lb 5oz)
Length	: 102.5cm (40½in)
Barrel Length	: 58.5cm (23in)
Sight	: none, mounting for telescopic sight
External safety	: safety catch on right behind bolt
Internal safety	: locking

CHARACTERISTICS

• material	: steel

- finish : blued
- stock : walnut stock with pistol grip

Sako Hunter

TECHNICAL DETAILS
Calibre : see below
Cartridge capacity : 4-, 5-, or 6-rounds magazine
Magazine catch : catch for hinged bottom plate at front of trigger guard
Action : bolt-action
Locking : 3 locking lugs
Weight : 3.1-3.9kg (6lb 13oz-8lb 10oz)
Length : 106-114.5cm (41¾-45in)
Barrel Length : 57-62cm (22½-24½in)
Sight : side adjustable leaf sight and bead tunnel, mounting for telescopic sight
External safety : safety catch on right behind bolt
Internal safety : locking
CHARACTERISTICS
- material : steel
- finish : blued
- stock : walnut stock with pistol grip

Available calibres (S491 short bolt): .17 Rem., .222 Rem., .223 Rem., .22 PPCV, 6mm PPC; (M591 medium bolt): .22-250 Rem., .243 Win., 7mm-08 Rem., .308 Win.; (M691 long bolt): .25-06 Rem., 6.5 x 55mm, .270 Win., 7 x 64mm, .280 Rem., .30-06 Spr., 9.3 x 62mm; (M691 Magnum): 7mm Rem. Mag., .300 Win. Mag., .300 Wby. Mag., .338 Win. Mag., .375 H & H Mag., .416 Rem. Mag.

This rifle is also available in a stainless-steel version.

Sako Safari

TECHNICAL DETAILS
Calibre : see below
Cartridge capacity : 5-rounds magazine

Magazine catch : catch for magazine bottom plate at front of trigger
Action : bolt-action
Locking : 3 locking lugs
Weight : 4.2kg (9lb 5oz)
Length : 114.5cm (45in)
Barrel Length : 62cm (24½in)
Sight : side adjustable leaf sight and bead tunnel, mounting for telescopic sight
External safety : safety catch on right behind bolt
Internal safety : locking
CHARACTERISTICS
- material : steel
- finish : blued
- stock : straight walnut stock with pistol grip

Available calibres: .338 Win. Mag., .375 H & H Mag., .416 Rem. Mag.

Sako Super Deluxe

TECHNICAL DETAILS
Calibre : see below
Cartridge capacity : 4-, 5-, or 6-rounds magazine
Magazine catch : catch for magazine bottom plate at front of trigger
Action : bolt-action
Locking : 3 locking lugs
Weight : 3.1-3.9kg (6lb 13oz-8lb 10oz)
Length : 106-114.5cm (41¾-45in)
Barrel Length : 57-62cm (22½-24½in)
Sight : side adjustable leaf sight and bead tunnel, mounting for telescopic sight
External safety : safety catch on right behind bolt
Internal safety : locking

CHARACTERISTICS
- material : steel
- finish : blued
- stock : specially engraved walnut stock with pistol grip

Available calibres (S491 short bolt): .17 Rem., .222 Rem., .223 Rem., .22 PPCV, 6mm PPC; (M591 medium bolt): .22-250 Rem., .243 Win., 7mm-08 Rem., .308 Win.; (M691 long bolt): .25-06 Rem., 6.5 x 55mm, .270 Win., 7 x 64mm, .280 Rem., .30-06 Spr., 9.3 x 62mm; (M691 Magnum): 7mm Rem. Mag., .300 Win. Mag., .300 Wby. Mag., .338 Win. Mag., .375 H & H Mag., .416 Rem. Mag.

This rifle is also available in a stainless-steel version.

Sako TRG-21

TECHNICAL DETAILS
Calibre : 6mm PPC, .308 Win.
Cartridge capacity : 10-rounds cartridge holder
Magazine catch : at front of cartridge holder
Action : bolt-action
Locking : 3 locking lugs
Weight : 4.7kg (10lb 4oz)
Length : 115cm (45¼in)
Barrel Length : 66cm (26in)
Sight : none, mounting for telescopic sight
External safety : safety catch in trigger guard
Internal safety : locking
CHARACTERISTICS
- material : stainless-steel barrel, aluminium front grip, plastic stock
- finish : bare metal barrel, matt black receiver
- stock : aluminium front grip, plastic stock with pistol grip, adjustable cheek and butt-plate

The finish of the sniper version is matt black.

Sako TRG-21/TRG-41 Sniper

TECHNICAL DETAILS
Calibre : .308 Win., (TRG-21) or .338 Lapua Mag., (TRG-41)
Cartridge capacity : 10 rounds (TRG-21) or 5 rounds (TRG-41)
Magazine catch : at front of cartridge holder
Action : bolt-action
Locking : 3 locking lugs
Weight : 4.7 or 5.1kg (10lb 4oz or 11lb 3oz) excluding telescopic sight
Length : 115 or 120cm (45¼ or 47¾in)
Barrel Length : 66 or 69cm (26 or 27¼in)
Sight : none, mounting for telescopic sight
External safety : safety catch on right behind bolt
Internal safety : locking, load indicator at rear of bolt
CHARACTERISTICS
- material : steel barrel, aluminium front grip, plastic stock
- finish : matt black
- stock : aluminium front grip, plastic stock with pistol grip, adjustable cheek and butt-plate

Sako TRG-S

TECHNICAL DETAILS
Calibre : see below
Cartridge capacity : 3-, 4-, or 5-rounds cartridge holder
Magazine catch : at front of magazine aperture
Action : bolt-action
Locking : 3 locking lugs
Weight : 3.3-3.6kg (7lb 4oz-7lb 12oz)

Length	: 112-116cm (44-45½in)
Barrel Length	: 58-62cm (22¾-24½in)
Sight	: side adjustable leaf sight and bead tunnel, mounting for telescopic sight
External safety	: safety catch on right behind bolt
Internal safety	: locking

CHARACTERISTICS

- material : steel
- finish : blued
- stock : black plastic with pistol grip

Available calibres (M995 bolt): .308 Win., .25-06 Rem., 6.5 x 55mm, .270 Win., 7 x 64mm, .280 Rem., .30-06 Spr., 9.3 x 62mm, 7mm Rem. Mag., .300 Win. Mag., .300 Wby. Mag., .338 Win. Mag., .375 H & H Mag., .338 Lapua Mag.

This rifle is also available in a stainless-steel version.

Sako Varmint

TECHNICAL DETAILS

Calibre	: see below
Cartridge capacity	: 5- or 6-rounds magazine
Magazine catch	: catch for hinged magazine bottom plate at front of trigger
Action	: bolt-action
Locking	: 3 locking lugs
Weight	: 3.8-4.1kg (8lb 7oz-9lb)
Length	: 109-112.5cm (43-44¼in)
Barrel Length	: 60cm (23⅝in)
Sight	: none, mounting for telescopic sight
External safety	: safety catch on right behind bolt
Internal safety	: locking, load indicator at rear of bolt

CHARACTERISTICS

- material : steel
- finish : blued
- stock : black plastic with pistol grip

Available calibres (S491 short bolt): .17 Rem., .222 Rem., .223 Rem., .22 PPC,

6mm PPC; (M591 medium bolt): .22-250 Rem., .243 Win., 7mm-08 Rem., .308 Win. This rifle is also available in a stainless-steel version.

Sako Varmint Stainless Single-Shot

TECHNICAL DETAILS

Calibre	: see below
Cartridge capacity	: single-shot
Magazine catch	: not applicable
Action	: bolt-action
Locking	: 3 locking lugs
Weight	: 3.6-3.7kg (7lb 15oz-8lb 3oz)
Length	: 109-110.5cm (43-43½in)
Barrel Length	: 60cm (23⅝in)
Sight	: none, mounting for telescopic sight
External safety	: safety catch on right behind bolt
Internal safety	: locking, load indicator at rear of bolt

CHARACTERISTICS

- material : stainless-steel
- finish : bare metal
- stock : laminated wood with pistol grip

Available calibres (S491 short bolt): .17 Rem., .222 Rem., .223 Rem., .22 PPC, 6mm PPC; (M591 medium bolt): .22-250 Rem., .243 Win., 7mm-08 Rem., .308 Win.

Sako Vixen Laminate

TECHNICAL DETAILS

| Calibre | : see below |

Cartridge capacity	: 4-, 5-, or 6-rounds magazine
Magazine catch	: catch for hinged magazine bottom plate at front of trigger
Action	: bolt-action
Locking	: 3 locking lugs
Weight	: 3.1-3.6kg (6lb 13oz-7lb 15oz)
Length	: 106-114.5cm (41¼-45in)
Barrel Length	: 57-62cm (22½-24½in)
Sight	: none, mounting for telescopic sight
External safety	: safety catch on right behind bolt
Internal safety	: locking, load indicator at rear of bolt

CHARACTERISTICS

• material	: steel
• finish	: blued
• stock	: laminated wood with pistol grip

Available calibres (S491 short bolt): .17 Rem., .222 Rem., .223 Rem., .22 PPCV, 6mm PPC; (M591 medium bolt): .22-250 Rem., .243 Win., 7mm-08 Rem., .308 Win.; (M691 long bolt): .25-06 Rem., 6.5 x 55mm, .270 Win., 7 x 64mm, .280 Rem., .30-06 Spr., 9.3 x 62mm; (M691 Magnum): 7mm Rem. Mag., .300 Win. Mag., .300 Wby. Mag., .338 Win. Mag., .375 H & H Mag.

Savage

Savage Arms Inc. has a long history of making arms. In 1966, the business had been in existence 133 years. This American company was founded by Arthur William Savage in Westfield, Massachusetts, where it is still based today, in the weapon industry enclave surrounding the town of Springfield. Prior to 1960, the company was mainly known for its range of lever-action repeating rifles. Since that time, Savage has developed an extensive range of bolt-action rifles. The company's logo - an Indian head - was first used at the beginning of the twentieth century. In 1901, Savage decided to go-ahead with a request to supply weapons to Cheyenne Indians for them to use for hunting in their Wyoming reservation. In exchange, the Indians wanted to promote Savage rifles at Indian shows that were very popular at that time. After World War II a great proportion of the German Mauser rifles were converted to sporting and hunting rifles, leading to greater interest in bolt-action rifles. Various American producers

did not want to get left behind so they developed their own designs for bolt rifles in order to win a share of the market. Savage was the first, in 1920, to introduce a rifle for the .250-3000 and .300 Savage calibres. The second of these was specially developed for the company by Charles Newton; the rifle was the 1920 model Hi-Power. The model 1920 was followed in 1928 by models 40 and 45 in .30-06 Springfield and .30-30 Winchester calibres. In about 1930, a young weapon designer called Nick Brewer joined a subsidiary of Savage - Stevens Arms & Tool Company. He designed a number of different rifles such as the Stevens model 15 small-bore and the Savage M-340 and M-987 rifles. His greatest achievement was with the model 110 rifle introduced in 1958.

During World War II, the production of sporting arms more or less stopped. Virtually the entire capacity of Savage was given over to making Browning machine-guns. Since its introduction, the model 110 underwent a number of modifications, particularly in 1966 by the engineer Bob Greenleaf. These particular modifications led to a "new" model, that was largely based on the old M-110 rifle.

During the 1970s, the company, which had become part of the Emhart Corporation, ran into difficulties due to labour disputes. These became so serious that the Emhart Corp. offered the business for sale. The model 99 has been the most successful Savage model since it was first made and it is produced in a wide range of calibres and different versions, indicated by different letters following the model number. In 1995, the special 99CE Centennial rifle was brought out to commemorate 100 years since the rifle was introduced in 1895. Only 1,000 examples were made of this rifle. Savage takes gun-safety seriously. Since 1991, all rifles are supplied with a safety pack that includes a lock for the rifle, ear-defenders, a target disc, and shooting safety glasses.

Savage Mark I-GY Youth

TECHNICAL DETAILS

Calibre	: .22 LR

Cartridge capacity : 10-rounds cartridge holder
Magazine catch : at front of magazine
aperture
Action : bolt-action
Locking : bolt-locking
Weight : 5lb (2.3kg)
Length : 37in (94cm)
Barrel Length : 19in (48.3cm)
Sight : adjustable sight, mounting
for telescopic sight
External safety : safety catch on right behind
bolt
Internal safety : locking

CHARACTERISTICS
• material : steel
• finish : blued
• stock : hardwood

Savage Mark II-GXP

TECHNICAL DETAILS
Calibre : .22 LR
Cartridge capacity : 10-rounds cartridge holder
Magazine catch : at front of magazine apertu-
re
Action : bolt-action
Locking : bolt-locking
Weight : 5lb 8oz (2.5kg)
Length : 39½in (100.3cm)
Barrel Length : 20¾in (52.7cm)
Sight : adjustable sight and 4 x
15mm telescopic sight
External safety : safety catch on right behind
bolt
Internal safety : locking

CHARACTERISTICS
• material : steel
• finish : blued
• stock : hardwood

Savage model 99-C

TECHNICAL DETAILS
Calibre : .243 Win., .308 Win.
Cartridge capacity : 4-rounds cartridge holder
Magazine catch : push-button at front of
locking casing
Action : lever-action
Locking : lever-locking
Weight : 7lb 12oz (3.5kg)
Length : 45½in (115.6cm)
Barrel Length : 22in (55.9cm)
Sight : adjustable sight, suitable for
telescopic sight
External safety : safety catch on top of
receiver
Internal safety : locking, load indication by
pin on safety catch

CHARACTERISTICS
• material : steel
• finish : blued
• stock : walnut with pistol grip

Savage model 99-CE Centennial Edition

TECHNICAL DETAILS
Calibre : .300 Savage
Cartridge capacity : 4-rounds cartridge holder
Magazine catch : push-button at front of loc-
king casing
Action : lever-action
Locking : lever-locking
Weight : 7lb 12oz (3.5kg)
Length : 45½in (115.6cm)
Barrel Length : 22in (55.9cm)
Sight : adjustable sight, suitable for
telescopic sight
External safety : safety catch on top of recei-
ver
Internal safety : locking, load indication by
pin in front of safety catch

CHARACTERISTICS
• material : steel
• finish : blued
• stock : specially selected walnut
stock with pistol grip

Only 1,000 examples were made of this
Savage Jubilee model. The trigger

and safety catch are inlaid with 24 carat gold. There is also engraving of figures on the action casing.

Savage model 110-B

TECHNICAL DETAILS
Calibre : see below
Cartridge capacity : 4-rounds
(internal magazine)
Magazine catch : not applicable
Action : bolt-action
Locking : 2 locking lugs
Weight : 8lb (3.6kg)
Length : 45½in (115.6cm)
Barrel Length : 24in (61cm)
Sight : adjustable sight, suitable for telescopic sight
External safety : safety catch on right in front of bolt
Internal safety : locking
CHARACTERISTICS
• material : steel
• finish : blued
• stock : laminated wood

Available calibres: 7mm Rem. Mag., .300 Win. Mag., .338 Win. Mag.

Savage model 110-F

TECHNICAL DETAILS
Calibre : .308 Win., .30-06 Spr., .270 Win.
Cartridge capacity : 5 rounds (internal magazine)
Magazine catch : not applicable
Action : bolt-action
Locking : 2 locking lugs
Weight : 7lb 8oz (3.4kg)

Length : 43½in (110.5cm)
Barrel Length : 22in (55.9cm)
Sight : adjustable sight, suitable for telescopic sight
External safety : safety catch on right in front of bolt
Internal safety : locking
CHARACTERISTICS
• material : steel
• finish : blued
• stock : black plastic (Rynite)

Savage model 110-G

TECHNICAL DETAILS
Calibre : .22-250 Rem., .223 Rem., .243 Win.
Cartridge capacity : 5 rounds (internal magazine)
Magazine catch : not applicable
Action : bolt-action
Locking : 2 locking lugs
Weight : 7lb 8oz (3.4kg)
Length : 43½in (110.5cm)
Barrel Length : 22in (55.9cm)
Sight : adjustable sight, suitable for telescopic sight
External safety : safety catch on right in front of bolt
Internal safety : locking
CHARACTERISTICS
• material : steel
• finish : blued
• stock : hardwood

Savage model 111-FCXP3 rifle

TECHNICAL DETAILS
Calibre : see below

Cartridge capacity	: 4-rounds cartridge holder (3 rounds for Magnum)
Magazine catch	: push-button in right of front grip
Action	: bolt-action
Locking	: 2 locking lugs
Weight	: 7lb 8oz (3.4kg)
Length	: 45½in (115.6cm)
Barrel Length	: 22-24in (55.9-61cm)
Sight	: none, suitable for telescopic sight
External safety	: safety catch on right in front of bolt
Internal safety	: locking

CHARACTERISTICS

- material : steel
- finish : blued
- stock : black plastic with pistol grip

Available calibres .270 Win., .30-06 Spr.,: 7mm Rem. Mag., .300 Win. Mag.

Savage model 112-BVSS Long Range rifle

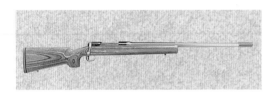

TECHNICAL DETAILS

Calibre	: see below
Cartridge capacity	: 4-rounds cartridge holder (3 rounds for Magnum)
Magazine catch	: push-button in right of front grip
Action	: bolt-action
Locking	: 2 locking lugs
Weight	: 10lb 8oz (4.8kg)
Length	: 47½in (120.7cm)
Barrel Length	: 26in (66cm)
Sight	: none, suitable for telescopic sight
External safety	: safety catch on right in front of bolt
Internal safety	: locking

CHARACTERISTICS

- material : stainless-steel
- finish : bare metal
- stock : laminated hardwood with pistol grip

Available calibres .223 Rem., .22-250 Rem., .25-06 Rem., .30-06 Spr., .308 Win., 7mm Rem. Mag., .300 Win. Mag.

The barrel of this rifle has longitudinal grooves for improved cooling.

Savage model 114-CE Classic European rifle

TECHNICAL DETAILS

Calibre	: see below
Cartridge capacity	: 4-rounds cartridge holder (3 rounds for Magnum)
Magazine catch	: push-button in right of front grip
Action	: bolt-action
Locking	: 2 locking lugs
Weight	: 7lb 3oz (3.3kg)
Length	: 43½-45½in (110.5-115.6cm)
Barrel Length	: 22-24in (55.9-61cm)
Sight	: adjustable, suitable for telescopic sight
External safety	: safety catch on right in front of bolt
Internal safety	: locking

CHARACTERISTICS

- material : steel
- finish : blued
- stock : walnut with pistol grip

Available calibres .270 Win., .30-06 Spr.,: 7mm Rem. Mag., .300 Win. Mag.

Savage model 116-US Ultra Stainless

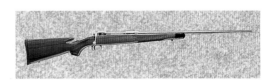

TECHNICAL DETAILS

Calibre	: see below
Cartridge capacity	: 4-rounds cartridge holder (3 rounds for Magnum)
Magazine catch	: push-button in right of front grip
Action	: bolt-action
Locking	: 2 locking lugs
Weight	: 7lb 3oz (3.3kg)
Length	: 43½-45½in (110.5-115.6cm)
Barrel Length	: 22-24in (55.9-61cm)
Sight	: adjustable, suitable for telescopic sight
External safety	: safety catch on right in front of bolt
Internal safety	: locking

CHARACTERISTICS

• material	: stainless-steel
• finish	: bare metal
• stock	: walnut with pistol grip

Available calibres .270 Win., .30-06 Spr.,: 7mm Rem. Mag., .300 Win. Mag.

Seehuber

Target shooting at a range of 300m (328yds) is a sport that is growing in popularity. This has led to a wider range of rifles being introduced that are suitable for this activity. The smaller makers have been particularly active in this area.

An example of this is the master gunsmith and target shooter Franz Seehuber, with his firm of the same name based in Überlingen in Germany. The company makes its own receivers and bolts but the barrels are supplied by several different makers. Seehuber's preference is for barrels from the Belgian maker Delcour but American barrels are also used when the client requests them.

The triggermechanisms and range of different stocks come from Anschütz. The action, together with the barrel is bedded in to the stock with plastic to create a perfect union between the system and the stock. The optical sights from Anschütz are also used with Seehuber's rifles. Many custom makers use actions from different manufacturers such as Sako, Remington, or Winchester. Seehuber preferred to develop his own system which includes a number of technical innovations, such as a funnel-shaped feed for the cartridges into the chamber to prevent any damage

to the bullet tip. This is specially important when soft-point rounds are used.

The Seehuber rifles are a 300m-standard rifle and a 300m-free rifle. The quality of the rifles can only be judged by their accuracy. Most custom makers guarantee a grouping of about 13mm (1/2in) with 3 shots on target at 100m (109yds). Seehuber surpasses this with a 10-rounds grouping of 13mm (1/2in) using Norma-or MEN-standard cartridges.

Seehuber 300-metre standard rifle

TECHNICAL DETAILS

Calibre	: .308 Win., 7mm-08 Rem., .222 Rem.
Cartridge capacity	: single shot
Magazine catch	: not applicable
Action	: bolt-action
Locking	: 2 locking lugs
Weight	: 5.5kg (12lb 1oz)
Length	: 116cm (45¾in)
Barrel Length	: 65cm (25⅝in)
Sight	: optical sight and bead tunnel, mounting for telescopic sight
External safety	: safety catch on left of receiver
Internal safety	: locking

CHARACTERISTICS

• material	: steel
• finish	: blued
• stock	: adjustable Anschütz beech stock

This rifle can be ordered in any calibre required.

Seehuber 300-metre free-standard rifle

TECHNICAL DETAILS

Calibre	: .308 Win., 7mm-08 Rem., .222 Rem.
Cartridge capacity	: single shot

Magazine catch	: not applicable
Action	: bolt-action
Locking	: 2 locking lugs
Weight	: 5.5kg (12lb 1oz)
Length	: 116cm (45¼in)
Barrel Length	: 65cm (25⅝in)
Sight	: optical sight and bead tunnel, mounting for telescopic sight
External safety	: safety catch on left of receiver
Internal safety	: locking

CHARACTERISTICS
- material : steel
- finish : blued
- stock : adjustable Anschütz walnut stock

This rifle can be ordered in any calibre required.

Seehuber 300-metre free rifle Supermatch

TECHNICAL DETAILS
Calibre	: .308 Win., 7mm-08 Rem., .222 Rem.
Cartridge capacity	: single shot
Magazine catch	: not applicable
Action	: bolt-action
Locking	: 2 locking lugs
Weight	: 6-7kg (13lb 3oz-15lb 7oz)
Length	: 116cm (45¼in)
Barrel Length	: 65cm (25⅝in)
Sight	: optical sight and bead tunnel, mounting for telescopic sight
External safety	: safety catch on left of receiver
Internal safety	: locking

CHARACTERISTICS
- material : steel
- finish : blued
- stock : special adjustable Anschütz beech stock with shoulder grip

This rifle can be ordered in any calibre required.

SIG

The Schweizerische Waggons Fabrik was founded in 1853 by watch-maker Heinrich Moser, politician Friedrich Peyer im Hof, and Swiss army officer Conrad Neher-Stokar.

Initially the company set up a railway works in Schaffhausen but at the request of the Swiss army, they began to produce weapons in 1860. In 1865, the weapon factory, as a separate company, was put under the management of Friedrich Vetterli, who was responsible for developing the military rifle, the Vetterli model 1869. Since then, the company has developed many weapons. Up to 1877, some 140,000 Vetterli rifles were made by the company that was now the independent Schweizer Waffenfabrik. Soon afterwards, the company became the Schweizerische Industrie Gesellschaft, Neuhausen am Rheinfall, more easily known as SIG. In the years from 1908 to 1911, the first semi-automatic gas-pressure rifle was produced, known as the Mondragon carbine. It was based on a design by a Mexican general, Manuel Mondragon. In 1920, large numbers of Bergmann sub-machine guns were made and exported to Japan, Finland, China, and other countries. In 1927, the first SIG machine-gun was brought-out as the KE-7. This weapon was supplied to Chile, China, Colombia, Finland, and Peru. In 1938, SIG had an export ban imposed, with weapons being permitted to be exported only with specific government permission. This still applies for the whole of Europe. During World War II, when Switzerland remained neutral, large quantities of weapons were made for the Swiss army, including the MP41 sub-machine gun, followed by types 44, 45, 46, and 48. The company made a semi-automatic pistol that was commissioned by the Swiss army in 1947. It entered service as the model SP-47/8. This designation was changed to SIG P210 for the civilian market. During the 1950s, the firm received a government order to develop and produce an automatic rifle. This resulted in the Sturmgewehr 57 (assault rifle) of which 700,000 were supplied to the Swiss army alone. In 1971, SIG took over the sporting guns maker Hämmerli and in 1974, the German arms maker Sauer & Sohn from Eckenfïrde was added to the group. This latter co-operation resulted in a complete range of SIG pistols. SIG developed a new rifle in 1984, which also led to a new range known as SG 550/551.

SIG-Sauer 205

TECHNICAL DETAILS

Calibre	: 7.5mm Swiss, .308 Win.
Cartridge capacity	: 10 rounds
Magazine catch	: in front of trigger
Action	: bolt-action
Locking	: 6 locking lugs
Weight	: 5.4kg (11lb 15oz)
Length	: 115cm (45¼in)
Barrel Length	: 66cm (26in)

SIG-Sauer 205

Sight	: adjustable optical sight and bead tunnel
External safety	: safety catch on receiver
Internal safety	: locking

CHARACTERISTICS

• material	: steel
• finish	: matt black
• stock	: laminated hardwood

This match rifle for the range of 300m (328yds) is of modular construction, consisting of stock, bolt-action, barrel, and front grip.

SIG-SSG 3000 Sniper

TECHNICAL DETAILS

Calibre	: .308 Win.
Cartridge capacity	: 5-rounds cartridge holder
Magazine catch	: in front of trigger
Action	: bolt-action
Locking	: 6 locking lugs
Weight	: 6.2kg (13lb 11oz)
Length	: 118cm (46½in)

Barrel Length   : 61cm (24in) without flash
                       reducer
Sight   : mounting for telescopic
                       sight
External safety   : safety catch beside bolt,
                       release knob in trigger guard
Internal safety   : locking, load indicator at
                       rear of bolt

CHARACTERISTICS
- material   : steel
- finish   : matt black phosphate
                       coating
- stock   : black laminated wood with
                       pistol grip

A special telescopic sight by
Zeiss/Hensoldt (1.5-6x24 BL) has been
developed for this sniper's rifle.

SIG SG 550 Sniper

TECHNICAL DETAILS
Calibre   : .223 Rem.
Cartridge capacity : 5-, 20-, or 30-rounds
                     cartridge holder
Magazine catch   : in front of trigger
Action   : semi-automatic, gas-pressure
Locking   : rotating slide
Weight   : 7.02kg (15lb 8oz)
Length   : 108cm (42½in)
Barrel Length   : 61cm (24in) with flash
                     reducer
Sight   : only with telescopic sight
External safety   : double-sided safety catch
                     above pistol grip

Internal safety   : locking
CHARACTERISTICS
- material   : steel
- finish   : matt black phosphate
                       coating
- stock   : plastic stock and hand guard

Simson-Suhl

The master gunsmith Franz Jäger from
Suhl in Germany was granted a patent in
1906 on a new type of pivot-breech
action. Until World War II, a number of
different rifles were made using this
action, under the name Simson-Jäger.
After the war, the system was improved
and eventually utilized in the Simson K1
rifle. An unusual feature of this rifle is
that it remains uncocked when it has been
opened, loaded and re-closed. Cocking
of the firing pin and trigger tumbler does
not occur until a cocking lever on the
neck of the stock is operated. If no shot
is fired, the weapon can be uncocked
again silently by moving the sliding lever
forwards again. The trigger-pressure can
be adjusted in three steps between 250-
500g (9-171/2oz) with the help of an
adjuster in the front of the trigger guard.
The Simson K1 is made in Standard, Pre-
mium, Jagd, Jena, Weimar, Erfurt, and
Suhl versions.

Simson K1-rifle

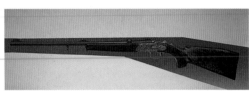

TECHNICAL DETAILS
Calibre   : see below
Cartridge capacity : single shot
Magazine catch   : not applicable
Action   : breech-action
Locking   : cocking lever on top of pivot
                     breech
Weight   : 2.3-2.8kg (5lb 1oz-6lb 3oz)
Length   : 100cm (393/8in)
Barrel Length   : 60cm (23⅝in)
Sight   : leaf sight, special mounting
                     for telescopic sight
External safety   : safety catch and uncocking
                     lever on back of pistol grip

Internal safety : locking

CHARACTERISTICS
- material : steel
- finish : blued, engraved bare metal breech action
- stock : specially selected walnut

Available calibres: .222 Rem., 5.6 x 50 Mag., 5.6 x 52R, .243 Win., 6 x 62R Frères, 6.5 x 57R, 6.5 x 65R, 6.5 x 68R, 7 x 57R, 7 x 65R, .308 Win., .30-06 Spr., .30R Blaser, 7mm Rem. Mag., .300 Win. Mag., 8 x 57mm, 8 x 57 RS, 9.3 x 74R.

The trigger-pressure of this rifle can be adjusted by pressing a selector (black button) in the rear of the trigger guard from 250-500g (9-171/2oz).

Springfield

The original Springfield Armory factory, which was the US Government Arsenal, was based in Massachusetts and had been in existence since 1777.
The state enterprise made countless weapons for the US armed forces during its existence. Famous models from the past include the 1873 model "Trapdoor" rifle and the Springfield M1903. In 1968 the business was closed down by the then minister of defence, Robert S. MacNamarra. Three years later, a businessman from Texas planned to buy the use of the name and the patent rights that belonged to Springfield but this attempt failed in 1974. Three years later another purchaser appeared in the form of Robert Reese who had wide experience as a weapons wholesale trader.
He saw business opportunities in the old company and moved it to Genesco in Illinois where it was based in a former cow shed. He and his three sons set to work, initially producing a range of M1A weapons and a civilian version of the US Army M14. The current Springfield programme consists of a range of pistols based on the Colt Government, the M1A National Match .308 Win. rifle, the M6 Scout
Survival carbine (a double-barrelled carbine in .22 Long Rifle and .410 shotgun), the famous M1 Garand .30-06 rifle (also in .308 Win., and .270 Win), the building under licence of Beretta BM-59 army rifles in .308 Win. and SAR-

48, and a copy of the FN-FAL in .308 Win. Springfield has a number of weapons made for it by, for instance, the Brazilian factory of Imbel from Itajuba. Examples of these are the Colt M1911-A1 pistol and the SAR-48 rifle. Springfield also make adaptations of the "old" Colt 1911 concept, often with in-built or add-on compensators for use as competition models. Springfield Armory had to cease trading in 1992 because of financial difficulties but the business did not go bankrupt.
The business was restructured in a slimmed-down form as Springfield Inc. The tremendous success of their products in great measure led to the difficulties. The business grew too quickly and there were a number of costly mistakes with projects. For instance, the Linkless 10mm pistol project never got off the ground, and the company introduced the Omega pistol, that was made by Peters Stahl in Germany, to North America but this did not catch on. A third failed project was the SASS conversion project which sought to provide a conversion kit for Colt 1911 pistols so that rifle cartridges could be fired. Finally, the company suffered financially from a deal with the Israeli company IMI whereby it was to import Uzi sub-machine guns and Uzi semi-automatic carbines into North America. Through the introduction of a new law, the Federal Assault Rifle Ban, it became illegal to sell this type of weapon in the United States. Since these problems, Springfield has bounced back and business is flourishing as never before.

Springfield M1A Bush rifle

TECHNICAL DETAILS

Calibre : .308 Win.
Cartridge capacity : 5,10, or 20-rounds cartridge holder
Magazine catch : at rear of magazine aperture
Action : semi-automatic, gas-pressure
Locking : rotating slide

Weight	: 8lb 12oz (4kg)
Length	: 40½in (102.9cm)
Barrel Length	: 18in (45.7cm)
Sight	: military optical sight
External safety	: safety catch at front of trigger guard
Internal safety	: locking

CHARACTERISTICS
- material : steel
- finish : matt black
- stock : walnut with brown plastic hand guard

Springfield M1A Bush rifle Synthetic

TECHNICAL DETAILS
Calibre	: .308 Win.
Cartridge capacity	: 5-,10-, or 20-rounds cartridge holder
Magazine catch	: at rear of magazine aperture
Action	: semi-automatic, gas-pressure
Locking	: rotating slide
Weight	: 8lb 12oz (4kg)
Length	: 40½in (102.9cm)
Barrel Length	: 18in (45.7cm)
Sight	: military optical sight
External safety	: safety catch at front of trigger guard
Internal safety	: locking

CHARACTERISTICS
- material : steel
- finish : matt black
- stock : black glass-fibre with plastic hand guard

Springfield M1A National Match

TECHNICAL DETAILS
Calibre	: .308 Win.
Cartridge capacity	: 5-,10-, or 20-rounds cartridge holder
Magazine catch	: at rear of magazine aperture
Action	: semi-automatic, gas-pressure
Locking	: rotating slide
Weight	: 10lb (4.5kg)
Length	: 44¼in (112.6cm)
Barrel Length	: 22in (55.9cm)
Sight	: military optical sight
External safety	: safety catch at front of trigger guard
Internal safety	: locking

CHARACTERISTICS
- material : steel
- finish : matt black
- stock : walnut with plastic hand guard

Springfield M1A National Match Government

TECHNICAL DETAILS
Calibre	: .308 Win.
Cartridge capacity	: 5-,10-, or 20-rounds cartridge holder
Magazine catch	: at rear of magazine aperture
Action	: semi-automatic, gas-pressure
Locking	: rotating slide
Weight	: 10lb (4.5kg)
Length	: 44¼in (112.6cm)
Barrel Length	: 22in (55.9cm)
Sight	: military optical sight and telescopic sight
External safety	: safety catch at front of trigger guard
Internal safety	: locking

CHARACTERISTICS
- material : steel
- finish : matt black
- stock : walnut with plastic hand guard

This special match rifle is equipped with a bipod, a special mounting for telescopic sight, and a telescopic sight with range-finder.

Springfield M6 Scout

TECHNICAL DETAILS

Calibre	: .22 LR or .22 Hornet and .410 shotgun
Cartridge capacity	: single shot per barrel
Magazine catch	: not applicable
Action	: breech-action
Locking	: barrel lock on top of breech
Weight	: 4lb (1.8kg)
Length	: 32in (81.3cm)
Barrel Length	: 18¼in (46.4cm)
Sight	: folding sight, suitable for telescopic sight
External safety	: safety catch on hammer
Internal safety	: locking

CHARACTERISTICS

• material	: steel
• finish	: matt black
• stock	: steel skeleton with storage for cartridges

This carbine is based on the US Air Force M6 Survival rifle and it is made for Springfield by the Czech company CZ

Springfield M6 Scout Stainless

TECHNICAL DETAILS

Calibre	: .22 LR or .22 Hornet and .410 shotgun
Cartridge capacity	: single shot per barrel
Magazine catch	: not applicable
Action	: breech-action
Locking	: barrel lock on top of breech
Weight	: 4lb (1.8kg)
Length	: 32in (81.3cm)
Barrel Length	: 18¼in (46.4cm)
Sight	: folding sight, suitable for telescopic sight
External safety	: safety catch on hammer
Internal safety	: locking

CHARACTERISTICS

• material	: stainless-steel
• finish	: matt-finish
• stock	: steel skeleton with storage for cartridges

This carbine is based on the US Air Force M6 Survival rifle and it is made for Springfield by the Czech company CZ

Springfield SAR-4800 rifle

TECHNICAL DETAILS

Calibre	: .308 Win.
Cartridge capacity	: 20-rounds cartridge holder
Magazine catch	: at rear of magazine aperture
Action	: semi-automatic, adjustable gas-pressure
Locking	: slide with locking lugs
Weight	: 9lb 8oz (4.3kg)
Length	: 43¼in (110cm)
Barrel Length	: 21in (53.3cm)
Sight	: military optical sight
External safety	: safety catch on left of housing
Internal safety	: locking

CHARACTERISTICS

• material	: steel
• finish	: matt black
• stock	: plastic skeleton with pistol grip and metal hand guard

This rifle is made for Springfield in Brazil under licence from Fabrique Nationale (FN) in Belgium.

Springfield SAR-8 rifle

TECHNICAL DETAILS

Calibre : .308 Win.
Cartridge capacity : 20-rounds cartridge holder
Magazine catch : on right of magazine aperture
Action : semi-automatic, adjustable gas-pressure
Locking : roller locking (Heckler & Koch system)
Weight : 8lb 11oz (4kg)
Length : 403/8in (102.6cm)
Barrel Length : 18in (45.7cm)
Sight : military optical sight and bead tunnel
External safety : safety catch on left of housing
Internal safety : locking

CHARACTERISTICS

• material : steel
• finish : matt black
• stock : plastic skeleton with pistol grip and metal hand guard

This rifle is made for Springfield in Brazil under licence from Heckler & Koch (Heckler & Koch G-3/HK-91).

Steyr

The history of the Steyr company starts really with the birth of Josef Werndl in 1831 in Steyr in Austria. His father, Leopold Werndl was the proprietor of a business that made spare rifle parts for the Viennese weapon industry. After a period of study in Vienna and Prague, Josef joined his father's business but he was impatient with the conservative methods of production. In 1849, he decided to do military service and because of his experience, he was set to work with a Viennese rifle maker where he was introduced to modern American machines for mass production.
His father used his influence to get his son discharged from military service and he returned to work with him but father and son

clashed once more. Josef wanted to modernize production but his father was too conservative for his ideas. In 1852, Josef departed for Thuringia in Germany where he worked for several arms makers until he left for America. In the United States, he worked for Remington and Colt in Hartford.
Full of ideas, he returned to Austria in 1853 and set up his own workshop in Wehrgraben. His father died in a cholera epidemic in 1855 and his mother convinced her son of the necessity of continuing the family business.
The business was drastically modernized, after which Werndl directed all his attention to developing a rear-loading rifle. For this purpose he undertook two study trips to America together with his chief developer, Karel Holub. In 1866, Josef set up in business with his brother as Josef and Frank Werndl & Company of Steyr. In 1866, Werndl attempted to persuade the minister of defence to equip the army with his Werndl-Holub rear-loading rifles. After extensive army testing, Werndl received an order for 100,000 rifles of rifle model 1867. The business in Steyr was expanded and a subsidiary was set up in Budapest. All this expansion meant that operating capital was scarce and Werndl decided to strengthen the company by issuing shares. For this purpose, the business became österreichische Waffenfabrik-Gesellschaft with Vienna as the place of registration. In 1873, Werndl received an order from the Royal Prussian army to make at least 500,000 Mauser model 1871 rifles. Following this, Werndl was overwhelmed with government orders from France, Persia (present-day Iran), Rumania, Greece, China, and Chile. The tide turned in 1882. All the European armies were now equipped with rear-loading rifles so there were no more big orders. In this crisis situation, Wendl decided to adapt his production capacity in order to make other products. Examples of the time were dynamos, electrical motors, and incandescent lamps. Steyr was the first European town with electric street-lighting in 1884. A new design of rifle went into production in 1885. It was a rear-loader with a magazine for five cartridges using the Mannlicher system. This led to orders for 87,000. Josef Werndl died of a lung infection in 1899. The business continued in the control of a four-man committee of management until Otto Schönauer took over control in 1896. The business had by this time grown into a large concern with many factories and about 10,000 employees. At the turn of the nineteenth and twentieth

centuries, the business made a wide range of products including cycles, followed in 1919 by cars and trucks. Following World War II the company suffered greatly and was only given permission by the allies to make firearms in 1950. Since then the company has principally made hunting rifles under the name Mannlicher-Schönauer. The company was merged into Steyr-Daimler-Puch AG in 1987 and the weapons manufacture became a separate subsidiary, Steyr-Mannlicher AG. Today's Steyr concern makes hunting and sporting rifles such as Steyr-Mannlichers and also military weapons such as the futuristic Steyr AUG (Armee Universal Gewehr) or universal army rifle.

Steyr AUG-Police

TECHNICAL DETAILS

Calibre	: 9mm Para.
Cartridge capacity	: 32 rounds
Magazine catch	: at rear of magazine chamber
Action	: semi-automatic
Locking	: inertia
Weight	: 3.3kg (7lb 5oz)
Length	: 66.5cm (26¼in)
Barrel Length	: 42cm (16½in)
Sight	: standard optical sight
External safety	: push-button safety catch behind trigger
Internal safety	: locking

CHARACTERISTICS

- material : aluminium, steel, and plastic
- finish : matt black or stock in different colours
- stock : integrated stock and front support

Steyr AUG-SA

TECHNICAL DETAILS

Calibre	: .223 Rem.
Cartridge capacity	: 40 rounds
Magazine catch	: push-button at rear of magazine chamber
Action	: semi-automatic
Locking	: rotating slide
Weight	: 3.3kg (7lb 5oz)
Length	: 69cm (27¼in)
Barrel Length	: 40.6cm (16in)
Sight	: standard optical sight
External safety	: push-button safety catch behind trigger
Internal safety	: locking

CHARACTERISTICS

- material : aluminium, steel, and plastic
- finish : matt black or stock in different colours
- stock : integrated stock and front support

Steyr AUG-SA Standard

TECHNICAL DETAILS

Calibre	: .223 Rem.
Cartridge capacity	: 40 rounds
Magazine catch	: push-button on side of cartridge holder
Action	: semi-automatic
Locking	: rotating slide
Weight	: 3.6kg (8lb)
Length	: 79cm (31⅛in)
Barrel Length	: 50.8cm (20in)

Sight	: side-adjusting military optical sight in carrying handle and adjustable height bead tunnel
External safety	: push-button safety catch behind trigger
Internal safety	: locking

CHARACTERISTICS
- material : aluminium, steel, and plastic
- finish : matt black or stock in different colours
- stock : integrated stock and front support

Steyr-Mannlicher model L (light calibre)

TECHNICAL DETAILS
Calibre	: .243 Win., .308 Win.
Cartridge capacity	: 5-rounds rotating cartridge holder
Magazine catch	: at both sides of cartridge holder
Action	: bolt-action
Locking	: 6 locking lugs at rear of bolt
Weight	: 2.8kg (6lb 3oz)
Length	: 99cm (39in)
Barrel Length	: 50.8cm (20in)
Sight	: side-adjusting sight, drilled and tapped for telescopic sight
External safety	: safety catch on right of receiver behind bolt
Internal safety	: locking, load indicator at rear of bolt

CHARACTERISTICS
- material : steel
- finish : blued
- stock : walnut with pistol grip

Steyr-Mannlicher model L-Long (light calibre)

TECHNICAL DETAILS
| Calibre | : .243 Win., .308 Win. |

Cartridge capacity	: 5-rounds rotating cartridge holder
Magazine catch	: at both sides of cartridge holder
Action	: bolt-action
Locking	: 6 locking lugs at rear of bolt
Weight	: 2.85kg (6lb 5oz)
Length	: 108cm (42½in)
Barrel Length	: 60cm (23⅝in)
Sight	: side-adjusting sight, drilled and tapped for telescopic sight
External safety	: safety catch on right of receiver behind bolt
Internal safety	: locking, load indicator at rear of bolt

CHARACTERISTICS
- material : steel
- finish : blued
- stock : walnut with pistol grip

Steyr-Mannlicher model L-Stutzen (hunting carbine)

TECHNICAL DETAILS
Calibre	: .243 Win., .308 Win.
Cartridge capacity	: 5-rounds rotating cartridge holder
Magazine catch	: at both sides of cartridge holder
Action	: bolt-action
Locking	: 6 locking lugs at rear of bolt
Weight	: 2.8kg (6lb 3oz)
Length	: 99cm (39in)
Barrel Length	: 50.8cm (20in)

Sight	: side-adjusting sight, drilled and tapped for telescopic sight
External safety	: safety catch on right of receiver behind bolt
Internal safety	: locking, load indicator at rear of bolt

CHARACTERISTICS

• material	: steel
• finish	: blued
• stock	: walnut stock with pistol grip runs through under barrel to muzzle

Steyr-Mannlicher model M (medium calibre)

TECHNICAL DETAILS

Calibre	: see below
Cartridge capacity	: 5-rounds rotating cartridge holder
Magazine catch	: at both sides of cartridge holder
Action	: bolt-action
Locking	: 6 locking lugs at rear of bolt
Weight	: 3.1kg (6lb 13oz)
Length	: 101cm (39¾in)
Barrel Length	: 50.8cm (20in)
Sight	: side-adjusting sight, drilled and tapped for telescopic sight
External safety	: safety catch on right of receiver behind bolt
Internal safety	: locking, load indicator at rear of bolt

CHARACTERISTICS

• material	: steel
• finish	: blued
• stock	: walnut with pistol grip

Available calibres: 6.5 x 57mm, .270 Win., 7 x 64mm, .30-06 Spr., 9.3 x 62mm; to order: 6.5 x 55mm, 7.5 Swiss, 8 x 57mm.

Steyr-Mannlicher model M-Long (medium calibre)

TECHNICAL DETAILS

Calibre	: see below
Cartridge capacity	: 5-rounds rotating cartridge holder
Magazine catch	: at both sides of cartridge holder
Action	: bolt-action
Locking	: 6 locking lugs at rear of bolt
Weight	: 3.15kg (6lb 15oz)
Length	: 110cm (43¼in)
Barrel Length	: 60cm (23⅝in)
Sight	: side-adjusting sight, drilled and tapped for telescopic sight
External safety	: safety catch on right of receiver behind bolt
Internal safety	: locking, load indicator at rear of bolt

CHARACTERISTICS

• material	: steel
• finish	: blued
• stock	: walnut with pistol grip

Available calibres: 6.5 x 57mm, .270 Win., 7 x 64mm, .30-06 Spr., 9.3 x 62mm; to order: 6.5 x 55mm, 7.5 Swiss, 8 x 57mm.

Steyr-Mannlicher model M (medium calibre) left-hand version

TECHNICAL DETAILS

Calibre : 7 x 64mm, .30-06 Spr.
Cartridge capacity : 5-rounds rotating cartridge holder
Magazine catch : at both sides of cartridge holder
Action : bolt-action
Locking : 6 locking lugs at rear of bolt
Weight : 3.15kg (6lb 15oz)
Length : 110cm (43¼in)
Barrel Length : 60cm (23⅜in)
Sight : side-adjusting sight, drilled and tapped for telescopic sight
External safety : safety catch on right of receiver behind bolt
Internal safety : locking, load indicator at rear of bolt

CHARACTERISTICS

• material : steel
• finish : blued, left-handed bolt
• stock : walnut with pistol grip

Steyr-Mannlicher model M Professional

TECHNICAL DETAILS

Calibre : see below
Cartridge capacity : 5-rounds rotating cartridge holder
Magazine catch : at both sides of cartridge holder
Action : bolt-action
Locking : 6 locking lugs at rear of bolt
Weight : 3.9kg (8lb 10oz)
Length : 113cm (44½in)
Barrel Length : 65cm (25⅝in)
Sight : side-adjusting sight, drilled and tapped for telescopic sight
External safety : safety catch on right of receiver behind bolt

Internal safety : locking, load indicator at rear of bolt

CHARACTERISTICS

• material : steel
• finish : blued, pressure-point trigger system (Stecher)
• stock : brown plastic with pistol grip

Available calibres: 6.5 x 57mm, .270 Win., 7 x 64mm, .30-06 Spr., 9.3 x 62mm; to order: 6.5 x 55mm, 7.5 Swiss, 8 x 57mm.

Steyr-Mannlicher model M-Stutzen (hunting carbine)

TECHNICAL DETAILS

Calibre : see below
Cartridge capacity : 5-rounds rotating cartridge holder
Magazine catch : at both sides of cartridge holder
Action : bolt-action
Locking : 6 locking lugs at rear of bolt
Weight : 3.1kg (6lb 13oz)
Length : 101cm (39¾in)
Barrel Length : 50.8cm (20in)
Sight : side-adjusting sight, drilled and tapped for telescopic sight
External safety : safety catch on right of receiver behind bolt
Internal safety : locking, load indicator at rear of bolt

CHARACTERISTICS

• material : steel
• finish : blued
• stock : walnut stock with pistol grip runs beneath barrel to muzzle

Available calibres: 6.5 x 57mm, .270 Win., 7 x 64mm, .30-06 Spr., 9.3 x 62mm; to order: 6.5 x 55mm, 7.5 Swiss, 8 x 57mm.

Steyr-Mannlicher model Police SSG

TECHNICAL DETAILS

Calibre	: .243 Win., .308 Win.
Cartridge capacity	: 5-rounds rotating cartridge holder
Magazine catch	: at both sides of cartridge holder
Action	: bolt-action
Locking	: 6 locking lugs at rear of bolt
Weight	: 3.9kg (8lb 10oz)
Length	: 113cm (44½in)
Barrel Length	: 65cm (25⅝in)
Sight	: none, drilled and tapped for telescopic sight
External safety	: safety catch on right of receiver behind bolt
Internal safety	: locking, load indicator at rear of bolt

CHARACTERISTICS

• material	: steel
• finish	: matt black
• stock	: black plastic with pistol grip

Steyr-Mannlicher model Police SSG-PI

TECHNICAL DETAILS

Calibre	: .308 Win.
Cartridge capacity	: 5-rounds rotating cartridge holder

Magazine catch	: at both sides of cartridge holder
Action	: bolt-action
Locking	: 6 locking lugs at rear of bolt
Weight	: 4.1kg (9lb)
Length	: 113cm (44½in)
Barrel Length	: 65cm (25⅝in)
Sight	: none, drilled and tapped for telescopic sight
External safety	: safety catch on right of receiver behind bolt
Internal safety	: locking, load indicator at rear of bolt

CHARACTERISTICS

• material	: steel
• finish	: matt black
• stock	: black plastic with pistol grip

The models illustrated are (top) Steyr Police SSG-PII (fixed emergency sights are optional) and (below) Steyr Police SSG-PI (with two-stage trigger).

Steyr-Mannlicher model Police SSG-PII

TECHNICAL DETAILS

Calibre	: .308 Win.
Cartridge capacity	: 5-rounds rotating cartridge holder
Magazine catch	: at both sides of cartridge holder
Action	: bolt-action
Locking	: 6 locking lugs at rear of bolt
Weight	: 4.3kg (9lb 10oz)
Length	: 113cm (44½in)
Barrel Length	: 65cm (25⅝in)
Sight	: none, drilled and tapped for telescopic sight

| External safety | : safety catch on right of receiver behind bolt |
| Internal safety | : locking, load indicator at rear of bolt |

CHARACTERISTICS
- material : steel
- finish : matt black
- stock : black plastic with pistol grip

The models illustrated are (top) Steyr Police SSG-PII (fixed emergency sights are optional) and (below) Steyr Police SSG-PI (with two-stage trigger).

Steyr-Mannlicher model Police SSG-PIV SD

TECHNICAL DETAILS

Calibre	: .308 Win.
Cartridge capacity	: 5-rounds rotating cartridge holder
Magazine catch	: at both sides of cartridge holder
Action	: bolt-action
Locking	: 6 locking lugs at rear of bolt
Weight	: 3.8kg (8lb 10oz)
Length	: 100.3cm (39½in)
Barrel Length	: 40.7cm (16in) excluding flash reducer
Sight	: none, drilled and tapped for telescopic sight
External safety	: safety catch on right of receiver behind bolt
Internal safety	: locking, load indicator at rear of bolt

CHARACTERISTICS
- material : steel
- finish : matt black
- stock : black plastic with pistol grip

Steyr-Mannlicher model S (heavy calibre)

TECHNICAL DETAILS

Calibre	: see below
Cartridge capacity	: 4-rounds rotating cartridge holder
Magazine catch	: at both sides of cartridge holder
Action	: bolt-action
Locking	: 6 locking lugs at rear of bolt
Weight	: 3.8kg (8lb 7oz)
Length	: 110cm (43¼in)
Barrel Length	: 60cm (23⅝in) excluding flash reducer
Sight	: side-adjustable sight, drilled and tapped for telescopic sight
External safety	: safety catch on right of receiver behind bolt
Internal safety	: locking, load indicator at rear of bolt

CHARACTERISTICS
- material : steel
- finish : blued
- stock : walnut with pistol grip

Available calibres: 6.5 x 68mm, 7mm Rem. Mag., .300 Win. Mag., 8 x 68S, .375 H & H Mag.

Steyr-Mannlicher model SL (very light calibre)

TECHNICAL DETAILS

Calibre	: .222 Rem., .223 Rem., 5.6 x 50 Mag.
Cartridge capacity	: 5-rounds rotating cartridge holder
Magazine catch	: at both sides of cartridge holder

Action	: bolt-action
Locking	: 6 locking lugs at rear of bolt
Weight	: 2.85kg (6lb 5oz)
Length	: 108cm (42½in)
Barrel Length	: 60cm (23⅝in)
Sight	: side-adjustable sight, drilled and tapped for telescopic sight
External safety	: safety catch on right of receiver behind bolt
Internal safety	: locking, load indicator at rear of bolt

CHARACTERISTICS

• material	: steel
• finish	: blued, with pressure-point trigger (Stecher)
• stock	: walnut with pistol grip

Steyr-Mannlicher model SL-Stutzen (hunting carbine)

TECHNICAL DETAILS

Calibre	: .222 Rem., .223 Rem., 5.6 x 50 Mag.
Cartridge capacity	: 5-rounds rotating cartridge holder
Magazine catch	: at both sides of cartridge holder
Action	: bolt-action
Locking	: 6 locking lugs at rear of bolt
Weight	: 2.85kg (6lb 5oz)
Length	: 99cm (39in)
Barrel Length	: 50.8cm (20in)
Sight	: side-adjustable sight, drilled and tapped for telescopic sight
External safety	: safety catch on right of receiver behind bolt
Internal safety	: locking, load indicator at rear of bolt

CHARACTERISTICS

• material	: steel
• finish	: blued, with pressure-point trigger (Stecher)
• stock	: walnut stock with pistol grip runs under barrel to muzzle

Steyr-Mannlicher Sport

TECHNICAL DETAILS

Calibre	: .243 Win., .308 Win.
Cartridge capacity	: 5-rounds rotating cartridge holder
Magazine catch	: at both sides of cartridge holder
Action	: bolt-action
Locking	: 6 locking lugs at rear of bolt
Weight	: 3.9kg (8lb 10oz)
Length	: 113cm (44½in)
Barrel Length	: 65cm (25⅝in)
Sight	: adjustable leaf sight and bead tunnel, drilled and tapped for telescopic sight
External safety	: safety catch on right of receiver behind bolt
Internal safety	: locking, load indicator at rear of bolt

CHARACTERISTICS

• material	: steel
• finish	: matt black
• stock	: brown or green plastic pistol grip

Steyr SPP-Police carbine

TECHNICAL DETAILS

| Calibre | : 9mm Para. |

Trigger Action	: double-action
Cartridge capacity	: 15- or 30- rounds cartridge holder
Magazine catch	: at both sides of cartridge holder
Action	: semi-automatic
Locking	: rotating slide
Weight	: 1.75kg (3lb 14oz)
Length	: 59.8cm (23½in)
Barrel Length	: 13cm (5⅛in)
Sight	: side adjustment micrometer sight, adjustable height bead
External safety	: push-button safety catch above trigger guard
Internal safety	: locking, automatic trigger tumbler locking

CHARACTERISTICS

• material	: plastic casing, steel barrel and breech
• finish	: matt black
• stock	: plastic casing

Stoner

Knight's Manufacturing Company was set up in Vero Beach, Florida, USA by C. Reed Knight, an orange grower who founded an arms company as a hobby. The hobby got out of hand, since a business employing seventy people can hardly be considered a hobby. Knight contacted the renowned weapon designer Eugene Stoner, famous for the many weapons he has designed, such as the AR-10,, the Stoner-63, but most of all for the AR-15/M-16 army rifle. The Stoner SR-25 rifle is based on the AR-10 design. Stoner designed this advanced army rifle in 1954 when he worked for the Armalite division of Fairchild Aircraft Company. This rifle was the predecessor of the AR-15 rifle. In contrast to the AR-15, there was no interest by the army in the AR-10.The AR-10 was produced in small quantities in the Netherlands by the Artillery Establishment in Zaandam. None of the NATO partners was interested in the weapon. The United States chose the AR-15/M-16 concept in .223 Remington calibre and Europe mainly chose the FN-FAL in 7.62 x 51mm NATO calibre (or .308 Winchester). The AR-10 rifles that were made in the Netherlands were sold to Portugal, the Sudan, and Burma. Reed Knight was himself interested in another of Stoner's designs, the Stoner-63, a semi-automatic rifle in .308 Win. calibre. Because the Pentagon had chosen the AR-15 concept, the Stoner-63 was not selected. Only a small section of the US Navy, the Navy Seals use a fully-automatic version of this weapon. The Stoner SR-25 (Sniper Rifle) is a mixture of AR-10, the AR-15, and the Stoner-63.

A number of parts are therefore interchangeable with those of the AR-15 rifle. The special cold-forged barrel of the SR-25 comes from Remington, which uses this barrel in that company's military M-24 sniper's rifle. This barrel has 5R grooves to act as rifling. These do not have sharp edges but are rounded off according to a new concept. This system improves accuracy and increases the life of the barrel. The precision of the SR-25 is guaranteed to deliver a grouping of 5 rounds on target at a range of 100m (109yds) of 1in (25mm). This is extremely good for a semi-automatic weapon. The experiences of target shooters has demonstrated that better results than this can be achieved. Once the rifle is well settled in after about 2,000 rounds, results of 94 out of 100 points were achieved at 100m (109yds). This weapon is the best imaginable tool for a competitive target shooter who wishes to use a semi-automatic rifle. It has only one disadvantage: it is rather expensive.

Stoner SR-25 Match

TECHNICAL DETAILS

Calibre	: .308 Win.
Cartridge capacity	: 5-, 10-, or 20-rounds cartridge holder
Magazine catch	: at right of mechanism housing
Action	: semi-automatic, gas-pressure
Locking	: rotating slide
Weight	: 10lb 12oz (4.9kg)

Length	: 44in (111.8cm)
Barrel Length	:24in (61cm)
Sight	: none, special mount for telescopic sight
External safety	: safety turn-catch on left of mechanism housing
Internal safety	: locking

CHARACTERISTICS

• material	: steel, light metal mechanism housing
• finish	: matt black
• stock	: black plastic with pistol grip

Thompson/Center

The origins of the Thompson/Center Arms Company Inc. were established in 1964. Warren Center, who developed the Thompson/Center Contender pistol, already had a major background as a weapons specialist.

During his military service at the time of World War II, he worked in Ordnance, which is a government department that manages the government procurement of weapons. After the war, he was a gunsmith in Dallas, Texas but he suddenly decided to return to the area where he was born in Massachusetts, where he set up his own weapons workshop. In 1954, he was employed by the Iver Johnson weapon factory for which he developed several revolvers. In 1959, he started his own business with Elton Whiting, making single-shot pistols. In 1963, he was head of development of the well-known firm of Harrington & Richardson and in that year, he developed a prototype pivot-breech single-shot pistol for which his employer had no interest. In 1964, he came into contact with Kenneth William Thompson. Together, they decided to produce this pistol.

He became a director of the K. W. Thompson Tool Company and in 1965 both directors established the Thompson/Center Arms Company. The Thompson/Center pistol was introduced in 1967. It was not until 1985 that the company brought out a arbine version of the Thompson/Center pistol in 9 different calibres. A new rifle, the Encore, is to be

Thompson Contender Carbine

introduced in 1997. All Thompson/Center weapons are equipped with a unique safety switch on the head of the hammer. This permits the firing pin to be switched between centre- or rimfire but it also allows the firing pin to be completely withdrawn so that the weapon cannot be fired.

Thompson Contender Carbine

TECHNICAL DETAILS

Calibre	: see below
Cartridge capacity	: single round
Magazine catch	: not applicable
Action	: breech-action
Locking	: barrel catch on bottom of breech
Weight	: 5lb 5oz (2.4kg)
Length	: 34¾in (88.3cm)
Barrel Length	: 21in (53.3cm)
Sight	: adjustable rack sight, suitable for telescopic sight
External safety	: firing pin point on hammer can be withdrawn
Internal safety	: locking, trigger blocked when breech is opened

CHARACTERISTICS
- material : steel
- finish : blued
- stock : walnut with pistol grip

Available calibres: .22 LR, .17 Rem., .22 Hornet, .223 Rem., 7mm-30 Waters, .30-30 Win., .375 Win.

Thompson Contender SST Carbine All Weather

TECHNICAL DETAILS

Calibre	: see below
Cartridge capacity	: single round
Magazine catch	: not applicable
Action	: breech-action
Locking	: barrel catch on bottom of breech
Weight	: 5lb 5oz (2.4kg)
Length	: 34¾in (88.3cm)
Barrel Length	: 21in (53.3cm)
Sight	: adjustable rack sight, suitable for telescopic sight
External safety	: firing pin point on hammer can be withdrawn
Internal safety	: locking, trigger blocked when breech is opened

CHARACTERISTICS
- material : stainless-steel
- finish : bare metal
- stock : black plastic

Available calibres: .22 LR, .22 Hornet, .223 Rem., 7mm-30 Waters, .30-30 Win., .375 Win.

Thompson Contender Youth Carbine

TECHNICAL DETAILS

Calibre	: .22 LR, .223 Rem.
Cartridge capacity	: single round
Magazine catch	: not applicable
Action	: breech-action
Locking	: barrel catch on bottom of breech
Weight	: 5lb 1oz (2.3kg)
Length	: 30in (76.2cm)
Barrel Length	: 16¼in (41.3cm)
Sight	: adjustable rack sight, suitable for telescopic sight
External safety	: firing pin point on hammer can be withdrawn
Internal safety	: locking, trigger blocked when breech is opened

CHARACTERISTICS
- material : steel
- finish : blued
- stock : walnut with pistol grip

An exchange shotgun barrel for .410 cartridges is available for this youth rifle.

Thompson Encore Rifle

TECHNICAL DETAILS

Calibre	: see below
Cartridge capacity	: single round
Magazine catch	: not applicable
Action	: breech-action
Locking	: barrel catch on bottom of breech
Weight	: 5lb 11oz (2.6kg)
Length	: 37¾in (95.9cm)
Barrel Length	: 24in (61cm)
Sight	: none, mounting for telescopic sight or adjustable rack sight
External safety	: firing pin point on hammer can be withdrawn
Internal safety	: locking, trigger blocked when breech is opened

CHARACTERISTICS

• material	: steel
• finish	: blued
• stock	: walnut with pistol grip

Available calibres: .22-250 Rem., 7mm-08 Rem., .308 Win., .30-06 Spr.

The Thompson Encore rifle was introduced in 1997 in the above calibres. The number of calibres is likely to be expanded and a stainless-steel version is likely to follow.

Tikka

The Finnish company Tikka dates back to 1893. The company's full name was Tikkakoski O/Y and it made machines and engines. It was based in Sakara. The company did not start to make firearms until 1918 at the time of the Finnish war of independence with Russia. During World War II, the company's production capacity was given over to making the Suomi sub-machine gun. Following the war, the company switched over to making consumer appliances such as vacuum cleaners and sewing machines. From 1965, the company made a range of both shotguns and rifles and exported large numbers of them to the United States. The weapon makers Ithaca in the US put these on the market as the Ithica LSA-55 and LSA-65. The company merged with another Finnish arms maker, Sako, in 1983 to become Sako-Tikka with production being concentrated in the Sako factory at Riihimaki.

Both companies were shortly afterwards taken over by the huge Finnish Nokia concern (telecommunications and defence systems), of which the Valmet arms factory is also a part.

Tikka Master

TECHNICAL DETAILS

Calibre	: see below
Cartridge capacity	: 3-rounds cartridge holder (optional 5 rounds)
Magazine catch	: in right of front grip by magazine aperture
Action	: bolt-action
Locking	: 2 locking lugs
Weight	: 3.2-3.4kg (7-7lb 8oz)
Length	: 107-113cm (42⅛-44½in)
Barrel Length	: 57-62cm (22½-24½in)
Sight	: side-adjustable leaf sight with bead tunnel, mounting for telescopic sight
External safety	: safety catch on right of receiver behind bolt
Internal safety	: locking

CHARACTERISTICS

• material	: steel
• finish	: blued
• stock	: walnut with pistol grip

Available calibres (M595 short bolt): .17 Rem., .222 Rem., .223 Rem., .22-250 Rem., .243 Win., .308 Win.;(M695 long bolt): .25-06 Rem., 6.5 x 55mm, .270 Win., 7 x 64mm, .30-06 Spr., 9.3 x 62mm;(M695M bolt, Magnum): 7mm Rem. Mag., .300 Win. Mag., .338 Win. Mag.

Tikka Master Battue (driven game rifle)

TECHNICAL DETAILS

Calibre	: see below
Cartridge capacity	: 3-rounds cartridge holder (optional 5 rounds)
Magazine catch	: in right of front grip by magazine aperture
Action	: bolt-action
Locking	: 2 locking lugs
Weight	: 3.1-3.2kg (6lb 13oz-7lb)
Length	: 102.5-103.5cm (403/8-40¾in)
Barrel Length	: 52.5cm (20¾in)
Sight	: special driven game sight with bead tunnel, mounting and drilled and tapped for telescopic sight
External safety	: safety catch on right of receiver behind bolt
Internal safety	: locking

CHARACTERISTICS

• material	: steel
• finish	: blued
• stock	: walnut with pistol grip

Available calibres (M595 short bolt): .17 Rem., .222 Rem., .223 Rem., .22-250 Rem., .243 Win., .308 Win.; (M695 long bolt): .25-06 Rem., 6.5 x 55mm, .270 Win., 7 x 64mm, .30-06 Spr., 9.3 x 62mm; (M695M bolt, Magnum): 7mm Rem. Mag., .300 Win. Mag., .338 Win. Mag.

Tikka Master Continental

TECHNICAL DETAILS

Calibre	: see below
Cartridge capacity	: 3-rounds cartridge holder (optional 5 rounds)
Magazine catch	: in right of front grip by magazine aperture
Action	: bolt-action
Locking	: 2 locking lugs
Weight	: 3.7-3.8kg (8lb 3oz-8lb 6oz)
Length	: 111-112cm (43¾-44in)
Barrel Length	: 60cm (23⅝in)
Sight	: none, mounting and drilled and tapped for telescopic sight
External safety	: safety catch on right of receiver behind bolt
Internal safety	: locking

CHARACTERISTICS

• material	: steel
• finish	: blued
• stock	: walnut stock with extra wide front grip and pistol grip

Available calibres (M595 short bolt): .17 Rem., .222 Rem., .223 Rem., .22-250 Rem., .243 Win., .308 Win.; (M695 long bolt): .25-06 Rem., 6.5 x 55mm, .270 Win., 7 x 64mm, .30-06 Spr., 9.3 x 62mm; (M695M bolt, Magnum): 7mm Rem. Mag., .300 Win. Mag., .338 Win. Mag.

Tikka Master Deluxe

TECHNICAL DETAILS

Calibre	: see below
Cartridge capacity	: 3-rounds cartridge holder (optional 5 rounds)
Magazine catch	: in right of front grip by magazine aperture
Action	: bolt-action
Locking	: 2 locking lugs
Weight	: 3.2-3.4kg (7lb-7lb 8oz)
Length	: 107-113cm (42⅛-44½in)
Barrel Length	: 57-62cm (22½-24½in)
Sight	: side-adjustable leaf sight with bead tunnel, mounting and drilled and tapped for telescopic sight
External safety	: safety catch on right of receiver behind bolt

Internal safety   : locking
CHARACTERISTICS
- material   : steel
- finish   : blued
- stock   : walnut with pistol grip

Available calibres (M595 short bolt): .17
Rem., .222 Rem., .223 Rem., .22-250
Rem., .243 Win., .308 Win.; (M695 long
bolt): .25-06 Rem., 6.5 x 55mm, .270 Win.,
7 x 64mm, .30-06 Spr., 9.3 x 62mm;
(M695M bolt, Magnum): 7mm Rem.
Mag., .300 Win. Mag., .338 Win. Mag.

Tikka Master Trapper

TECHNICAL DETAILS

Calibre	: see below
Cartridge capacity	: 3-rounds cartridge holder (optional 5 rounds)
Magazine catch	: in right of front grip by magazine aperture
Action	: bolt-action
Locking	: 2 locking lugs
Weight	: 3-3.1kg (6lb 10oz-6lb 13oz)
Length	: 102.5-103.5cm (40⅛-40¾in)
Barrel Length	: 52.5cm (20¾in)
Sight	: none, mounting and drilled and tapped for telescopic sight
External safety	: safety catch on right of receiver behind bolt
Internal safety	: locking

CHARACTERISTICS
- material   : steel
- finish   : blued
- stock   : walnut with pistol grip

Available calibres (M595 short bolt): .17
Rem., .222 Rem., .223 Rem., .22-250
Rem., .243 Win., .308 Win.; (M695 long
bolt): .25-06 Rem., 6.5 x 55mm, .270 Win.,
7 x 64mm, .30-06 Spr., 9.3 x 62mm;
(M695M bolt, Magnum): 7mm Rem.
Mag., .300 Win. Mag., .338 Win. Mag.

Uberti

The Italian firm of Aldo Uberti & Company was
set up in 1959 and is situated in Gardone Val
Trompia at the foot of the Italian Alps. The company specialized in producing replicas of
percussion revolvers and rifles and has become
the major manufacturer in this field. The
Uberti company owes its existence to the many
blackpowder shooters there are in the world.
Faithful copies, accurate to the smallest detail,
are made of Colts, Winchesters, Henrys, and
Derringers. All shooting societies and federa-
tions accept these weapons for competition
within their special categories. Uberti insists,
justly, that his products are better than the
originals. This is the result of using modern types
of steel and methods of production, so that firearm parts can be machined to tolerances of
1/1,000mm. Uberti developed a variation of the
hand-process of blueing and tempering firearm
parts in a charcoal fire. The firm
achieves better quality with this revised method
than the original antique weapons. All replica
weapons are tested by the Italian national
verification organization and provided with a
quality proving mark before they are sent to the
customer. Uberti exports to almost every
country in the world. The weapons are often
also provided with a national proving mark
through the importer and given a local trade
mark. In order to give an impression of the
Uberti range of products, some guns are
described here that have also appeared
elsewhere under another name.

Uberti Henry Steel rifle

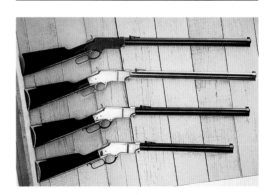

TECHNICAL DETAILS

Calibre	: .44-40
Cartridge capacity	: 13-rounds tubular magazine

Magazine catch	: not applicable, loading port in bottom of casing
Action	: lever-action
Locking	: lever locking
Weight	: 4.2kg (9lb 4oz)
Length	: 111.1cm (43¾in)
Barrel Length	: 61.6cm (24¼in)
Sight	: adjustable rack sight
External safety	: none
Internal safety	: locking, trigger blocked when lever not fully closed

CHARACTERISTICS
• material	: steel
• finish	: blued barrel, tempered casing
• stock	: walnut

Illustrated from top-to-bottom:
1. Uberti Henry Steel rifle
2. Uberti Henry Long rifle
3. Uberti Henry rifle
4. Uberti Henry carbine

Uberti Henry Long rifle

TECHNICAL DETAILS
Calibre	: .44-40, .45 LC (Long Colt)
Cartridge capacity	: 13-rounds tubular magazine
Magazine catch	: not applicable, loading port in bottom of casing
Action	: lever-action
Locking	: lever locking
Weight	: 4.2kg (9lb 4oz)
Length	: 111.1cm (43¾in)
Barrel Length	: 61.6cm (24¼in)
Sight	: adjustable rack sight
External safety	: none
Internal safety	: locking, trigger blocked when lever not fully closed

CHARACTERISTICS
• material	: steel
• finish	: bare steel barrel, brass casing
• stock	: straight walnut stock

Illustrated from top-to-bottom:
1. Uberti Henry Steel rifle
2. Uberti Henry Long rifle
3. Uberti Henry rifle
4. Uberti Henry carbine

Uberti Henry rifle

TECHNICAL DETAILS
Calibre	: .44-40, .45 LC (Long Colt)
Cartridge capacity	: 11-rounds tubular magazine
Magazine catch	: not applicable, loading port in bottom of casing
Action	: lever-action
Locking	: lever locking
Weight	: 4.1kg (9lb)
Length	: 105.4cm (41½in)
Barrel Length	: 56.5cm (22¼in)
Sight	: adjustable rack sight
External safety	: none
Internal safety	: locking, trigger blocked when lever not fully closed

CHARACTERISTICS
• material	: steel
• finish	: blued barrel, brass casing
• stock	: straight walnut stock

Illustrated from top-to-bottom:
1. Uberti Henry Steel rifle
2. Uberti Henry Long rifle
3. Uberti Henry rifle
4. Uberti Henry carbine

Uberti Henry carbine

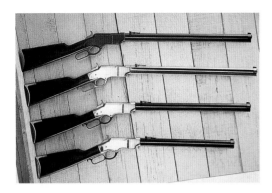

TECHNICAL DETAILS
Calibre : .44-40, .45 LC (Long Colt)
Cartridge capacity : 9-rounds tubular magazine
Magazine catch : not applicable, loading port in bottom of casing
Action : lever-action
Locking : lever locking
Weight : 3.6kg (7lb 15oz)
Length : 96.5cm (38in)
Barrel Length : 47cm (18½in)
Sight : adjustable rack sight
External safety : none
Internal safety : locking, trigger blocked when lever not fully closed

CHARACTERISTICS
• material : steel
• finish : blued barrel, brass casing
• stock : straight walnut stock

Illustrated from top-to-bottom:
1. Uberti Henry Steel rifle
2. Uberti Henry Long rifle
3. Uberti Henry rifle
4. Uberti Henry carbine

Uberti S.A. Cattleman model revolver-carbine

TECHNICAL DETAILS
Calibre : .357 Mag., .44-40, .45 LC, .44 Mag.
Cartridge capacity : cylinder for 6 rounds
Magazine catch : not applicable, loading port
Action : single-action
Locking : cylinder catch
Weight : 2kg (4lb 6oz)
Length : 86.4cm (34in)
Barrel Length : 45.7cm (18in)
Sight : fixed sight
External safety : none
Internal safety : half-cock on hammer

CHARACTERISTICS
• material : steel
• finish : blued barrel, tempered casing
• stock : straight hardwood stock

Uberti 1866 model sporting rifle

TECHNICAL DETAILS
Calibre : .22 LR, .22 WMR, .38 Spec., .44-40, .45 LC
Cartridge capacity : 13-rounds tubular magazine
Magazine catch : not applicable, loading port in right of system housing
Action : lever-action
Locking : lever locking
Weight : 3.7kg (8lb 3oz)
Length : 109.9cm (43¾in)
Barrel Length : 61.6cm (24¼in)
Sight : adjustable rack sight
External safety : none
Internal safety : trigger blocked when lever not fully closed

CHARACTERISTICS
• material : steel barrel, brass casing
• finish : blued barrel, brass casing
• stock : walnut

Illustrated from top-to-bottom:
1. Uberti 1866 model sporting rifle
2. Uberti 1866 model Yellowboy carbine
3. Uberti 1866 model Trapper carbine

Uberti 1866 model Trapper carbine

Uberti 1866 model Yellowboy carbine

TECHNICAL DETAILS

Calibre : .22 LR, .22 WMR, .38 Spec., .44-40, .45 LC
Cartridge capacity : 13-rounds tubular magazine
Magazine catch : not applicable, loading port in right of system housing
Action : lever-action
Locking : lever locking
Weight : 3.3kg (7lb 6oz)
Length : 97.2cm (38¼in)
Barrel Length : 48.3cm (19in)
Sight : adjustable rack sight
External safety : none
Internal safety : trigger blocked when lever not fully closed

CHARACTERISTICS

• material : steel barrel, brass casing
• finish : blued barrel, brass casing
• stock : walnut, with saddle ring

Illustrated from top-to-bottom:
1. Uberti 1866 model sporting rifle
2. Uberti 1866 model Yellowboy carbine
3. Uberti 1866 model Trapper carbine

TECHNICAL DETAILS

Calibre : .22 LR, .22 WMR, .38 Spec., .44-40, .45 LC
Cartridge capacity : 7-10-rounds tubular magazine
Magazine catch : not applicable, loading port in right of system housing
Action : lever-action
Locking : lever locking
Weight : 3.2kg (7lb)
Length : 89.5cm (35¼in)
Barrel Length : 41.4cm (16¼in)
Sight : adjustable rack sight
External safety : none
Internal safety : trigger blocked when lever not fully closed

CHARACTERISTICS

• material : steel barrel, brass casing
• finish : blued barrel, brass casing
• stock : walnut

Illustrated from top-to-bottom:
1. Uberti 1866 model sporting rifle
2. Uberti 1866 model Yellowboy carbine
3. Uberti 1866 model Trapper carbine

Uberti 1871 model Remington Rolling Block rifle

TECHNICAL DETAILS

Calibre : .22 LR, .22 WMR, .22 Hornet, .357 Mag
Cartridge capacity : single shot
Magazine catch : not applicable
Action : separate cocking lever
Locking : rolling block locking
Weight : 2.2kg (4lb 14oz)
Length : 90.2cm (35½in)
Barrel Length : 55.9cm (22in)
Sight : adjustable rack sight

External safety : none
Internal safety : locking, trigger blocked
when lever not fully closed

CHARACTERISTICS
- material : steel
- finish : blued barrel, tempered
casing
- stock : walnut

Illustrated from top-to-bottom:
1. Uberti 1873 model 43in sporting rifle
2. Uberti 1873 model 37in sporting rifle
3. Uberti 1873 model 33in sporting carbine
4. Uberti 1873 model carbine

External safety : none
Internal safety : locking

CHARACTERISTICS
- material : steel
- finish : blued barrel, tempered
casing
- stock : straight walnut stock

Uberti 1873 model 37in sporting rifle

TECHNICAL DETAILS

Calibre : .357 Mag., .44-40, .45 LC
Cartridge capacity : 12-rounds tubular magazine
Magazine catch : not applicable, loading port
in right of system casing
Action : lever-action
Locking : lever locking
Weight : 3.4kg (7lb 8oz)
Length : 110cm (43¼in)
Barrel Length : 61.6cm (24¼in)
Sight : height adjustable sight
External safety : none
Internal safety : locking, trigger blocked
when lever not fully closed

CHARACTERISTICS
- material : steel
- finish : blued barrel, tempered
casing
- stock : walnut

Illustrated from top-to-bottom:
1. Uberti 1873 model 43in sporting rifle
2. Uberti 1873 model 37in sporting rifle

Uberti 1873 model 43in sporting rifle

TECHNICAL DETAILS

Calibre : .357 Mag., .44-40, .45 LC
Cartridge capacity : 13-rounds tubular magazine
Magazine catch : not applicable, loading port
in right of system casing
Action : lever-action
Locking : lever locking
Weight : 3.7kg (8lb 3oz)
Length : 109.9cm (43¼in)
Barrel Length : 76.2cm (30in)
Sight : height adjustable sight

3. Uberti 1873 model 33in sporting carbine
4. Uberti 1873 model carbine

Uberti 1873 model 33 in sporting carbine

TECHNICAL DETAILS

Calibre : .357 Mag., .44-40, .45 LC
Cartridge capacity : 10-rounds tubular magazine
Magazine catch : not applicable, loading port in right of system casing
Action : lever-action
Locking : lever locking
Weight : 3.2kg (7lb 1oz)
Length : 99cm (39in)
Barrel Length : 50.8cm (20in)
Sight : height adjustable sight
External safety : none
Internal safety : locking, trigger blocked when lever not fully closed

CHARACTERISTICS

• material : steel
• finish : blued barrel, tempered casing
• stock : walnut

Illustrated from top-to-bottom:
1. Uberti 1873 model 43in sporting rifle
2. Uberti 1873 model 37in sporting rifle
3. Uberti 1873 model 33in sporting carbine
4. Uberti 1873 model carbine

Uberti 1873 model carbine

TECHNICAL DETAILS

Calibre : .357 Mag., .44-40, .45 LC
Cartridge capacity : 10-rounds tubular magazine
Magazine catch : not applicable, loading port in right of system casing

Action : lever-action
Locking : lever locking
Weight : 3.4kg (7lb 6oz)
Length : 97.2cm (38¼in)
Barrel Length : 48.3cm (19in)
Sight : height adjustable sight
External safety : none
Internal safety : locking, trigger blocked when lever not fully closed

CHARACTERISTICS

• material : steel
• finish : blued
• stock : walnut stock with and without saddle ring

Illustrated from top-to-bottom:
1. Uberti 1873 model 43in sporting rifle
2. Uberti 1873 model 37in sporting rifle
3. Uberti 1873 model 33in sporting carbine
4. Uberti 1873 model carbine

Uberti 1873 model Special Sport

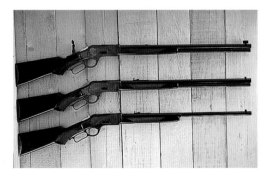

TECHNICAL DETAILS

Calibre : .44-40, .45 LC

Cartridge capacity	: 13-rounds tubular magazine
Magazine catch	: not applicable, loading port in right of system casing
Action	: lever-action
Locking	: lever locking
Weight	: 3.7kg (8lb 3oz)
Length	: 109.9cm (43¼in)
Barrel Length	: 61.6cm (24¼in)
Sight	: adjustable height optical sight and bead tunnel
External safety	: none
Internal safety	: locking, trigger blocked when lever not fully closed

CHARACTERISTICS

- material : steel
- finish : blued barrel, tempered casing
- stock : walnut stock with pistol grip

Illustrated from top-to-bottom:
1. Uberti 1873 model Special Sport
2. Uberti 1873 model Special Sport Standard
3. Uberti 1873 model Special hunting rifle

Uberti 1873 model Special Sport Standard

TECHNICAL DETAILS

Calibre	: .44-40, .45 LC
Cartridge capacity	: 13-rounds tubular magazine
Magazine catch	: not applicable, loading port in right of system casing
Action	: lever-action
Locking	: lever locking
Weight	: 3.7kg (8lb 3oz)
Length	: 109.9cm (43¼in)
Barrel Length	: 61.6cm (24¼in)
Sight	: adjustable height leaf sight
External safety	: none

Internal safety	: locking, trigger blocked when lever not fully closed

CHARACTERISTICS

- material : steel
- finish : blued barrel, tempered casing
- stock : walnut stock with pistol grip

Illustrated from top-to-bottom:
1. Uberti 1873 model Special Sport
2. Uberti 1873 model Special Sport Standard
3. Uberti 1873 model Special hunting rifle

Uberti 1873 model Special hunting rifle

TECHNICAL DETAILS

Calibre	: .44-40, .45 LC
Cartridge capacity	: 6-rounds tubular magazine
Magazine catch	: not applicable, loading port in right of system casing
Action	: lever-action
Locking	: lever locking
Weight	: 3.6kg (8lb)
Length	: 109.9cm (43¼in)
Barrel Length	: 61.6cm (24¼in)
Sight	: adjustable height leaf sight
External safety	: none
Internal safety	: locking, trigger blocked when lever not fully closed

CHARACTERISTICS

- material : steel
- finish : blued barrel, tempered casing
- stock : walnut stock with pistol grip

Illustrated from top-to-bottom:
1. Uberti 1873 model Special Sport

2. Uberti 1873 model Special Sport Standard
3. Uberti 1873 model Special hunting rifle

Unique

Unique is the brand name of the French arms factory MAPF which is short for Manufacture d'Armes des Pyrénées Françaises. The company is located in Hendaye, at the foot of the Pyrenees, on the Bay of Biscay. MAPF makes a range of interesting hunting rifles with interchangeable barrels for using different calibres. The match rifles, such as the T-2000 in small-bore and T-3000 in various larger calibres, are of the highest quality. The company also produces the famous Unique DES-69 sporting pistol and the IS pistol (International Silhouette). The TGC Varmint match rifle is used by French police units as a marksman's rifle.

Unique T-2000 Libre (free rifle)

TECHNICAL DETAILS

Calibre	: .22 LR
Cartridge capacity	: single shot
Magazine catch	: not applicable
Action	: bolt-action
Locking	: bolt locking
Weight	: 6.3kg (13lb 14oz)
Length	: 125cm (49¼in)
Barrel Length	: 71cm (28in)
Sight	: optical sight with bead tunnel
External safety	: safety catch at top of trigger guard
Internal safety	: locking

CHARACTERISTICS

• material	: steel
• finish	: blued
• stock	: special fully-adjustable match stock with thumbhole and shoulder grip

The barrel has special longitudinal grooves for improved cooling.

Unique T-2000 Standard

TECHNICAL DETAILS

Calibre	: .22 LR
Cartridge capacity	: single shot
Magazine catch	: not applicable
Action	: bolt-action
Locking	: bolt locking
Weight	: 5kg (11lb)
Length	: 115cm (45¼in)
Barrel Length	: 71cm (28in)
Sight	: optical sight with bead tunnel
External safety	: safety catch at top of trigger guard
Internal safety	: locking

CHARACTERISTICS

• material	: steel
• finish	: blued
• stock	: match stock with pistol grip

The barrel has special longitudinal grooves for improved cooling.

Unique T-3000 Libre (free rifle) 300-metre

TECHNICAL DETAILS

Calibre	: see below

Cartridge capacity : single shot
Magazine catch : not applicable
Action : bolt-action
Locking : 3 locking lugs
Weight : 6.3kg (13lb 14oz)
Length : 125cm (49¼in)
Barrel Length : 71cm (28in)
Sight : optical sight with bead tunnel
External safety : safety catch at top of trigger guard
Internal safety : locking

CHARACTERISTICS
- material : stainless-steel
- finish : bare metal
- stock : special laminated wood fully-adjustable match stock with thumb hole and shoulder grip

Available calibres: .243 Win., 6.5 x 55S, 7mm-08 Rem., 7.5 x 55 Swiss, .308 Win. The barrel has special longitudinal grooves for improved cooling.

Unique T-3000
Standard 300-metre UIT/CISM

TECHNICAL DETAILS
Calibre : see below
Cartridge capacity : single shot
Magazine catch : not applicable
Action : bolt-action
Locking : 3 locking lugs
Weight : 5.3kg (11lb 11oz)
Length : 115cm (45¼in)
Barrel Length : 71cm (28in)
Sight : optical sight with bead tunnel
External safety : safety catch at top of trigger guard
Internal safety : locking

CHARACTERISTICS
- material : stainless-steel
- finish : bare metal

- stock : walnut match stock with pistol grip

Available calibres: .243 Win., 6.5 x 55S, 7mm-08 Rem., 7.5 x 55 Swiss, .308 Win. The barrel has special longitudinal grooves for improved cooling. The rifle can be used for different calibres by means of interchangeable barrels. There is a 5-rounds CISM version cartridge holder available for this rifle with a 65cm (255/8in) barrel.

Unique TGC hunting carbine

TECHNICAL DETAILS
Calibre : see below
Cartridge capacity : 3-5 rounds cartridge holder
Magazine catch : on right of cartridge holder
Action : bolt-action
Locking : 3 locking lugs
Weight : 3.8kg (8lb 6oz)
Length : 109.5cm (43⅛in)
Barrel Length : 56cm (22in)
Sight : adjustable folding sight with bead tunnel, mounting for telescopic sight
External safety : safety catch on right behind bolt
Internal safety : locking

CHARACTERISTICS
- material : steel
- finish : blued
- stock : walnut with pistol grip and rubber shock absorbing butt plate

Available calibres: .243 Win., 6.5 x 55SE, .270 Win., 7mm-08 Rem., 7 x 64mm, .308 Win., .30-06 Spr., 9.3 x 62mm.

The barrel of this rifle can be changed to use other calibres. It is also available in a left-handed version.

Unique TGC de Chasse hunting rifle

TECHNICAL DETAILS

Calibre	: see below
Cartridge capacity	: 3-5-rounds cartridge holder
Magazine catch	: on right of cartridge holder
Action	: bolt-action
Locking	: 3 locking lugs
Weight	: 3.8kg (8lb 6oz)
Length	: 114.5cm (45⅛in)
Barrel Length	: 61cm (24in)
Sight	: adjustable folding sight with bead tunnel, mounting for telescopic sight
External safety	: safety catch on right behind bolt
Internal safety	: locking

CHARACTERISTICS

- material : steel
- finish : blued
- stock : walnut with pistol grip and rubber shock absorbing butt plate

Available calibres: .243 Win., 6.5 x 55SE, .270 Win., 7mm-08 Rem., 7 x 64mm, 7mm Rem. Mag., .300 Win. Mag., .308 Win., .30-06 Spr., 9.3 x 62mm.

The barrel of this rifle can be changed to use other calibres. It is also available in a left-handed version.

Unique TGC Varmint

TECHNICAL DETAILS

Calibre	: see below
Cartridge capacity	: 3-5-rounds cartridge holder
Magazine catch	: on right of cartridge holder
Action	: bolt-action
Locking	: 3 locking lugs
Weight	: 5.5kg (12lb 1oz)
Length	: 104cm (41in)
Barrel Length	: 51.5cm (20¼in)
Sight	: none, mounting for telescopic sight
External safety	: safety catch on right behind bolt
Internal safety	: locking

CHARACTERISTICS

- material : steel
- finish : blued
- stock : walnut with pistol grip

Available calibres: 6mm BR, .243 Win., 7mm-08 Rem., .300 Savage, .300 Win. Mag., .308 Win., .30-06 Spr.

The barrel of this rifle can be changed to use other calibres. It is also available in a left-handed version.

Unique TGC Varmint - match

TECHNICAL DETAILS

Calibre	: see below
Cartridge capacity	: 3-5-rounds cartridge holder
Magazine catch	: on right of cartridge holder
Action	: bolt-action
Locking	: 3 locking lugs
Weight	: 5.5kg (12lb 1oz)
Length	: 104cm (41in)
Barrel Length	: 51.5cm (20¼in)
Sight	: none, mounting for telescopic sight
External safety	: safety catch on right behind bolt
Internal safety	: locking

CHARACTERISTICS

- material : steel
- finish : blued
- stock : walnut stock with adjustable cheek, pistol grip, and bipod

Available calibres: 6mm BR, .243 Win., 7mm-08 Rem., .300 Savage, .300 Win. Mag., .308 Win., .30-06 Spr.
The barrel of this rifle can be changed to use other calibres. It is also available in a left-handed version.

Verney-Carron

This French company is located in that part of France surrounding Saint-Etienne at the foot of the Pyreneës that is host to a cluster of weapon-manufacturers. It has been the Verney-Carron family business since 1820. Their name is not so well known in northern Europe and North America but their firearms are very popular in France and are exported to countries in southern Europe and South America. The company has a wide range of hunting shotguns and rifles. There are six models of Super-9 shotgun alone, subdivided into classic, luxury, and extra luxury versions. The extra luxe d'or versions are decorated with golden animal figures. The company also has its Sagittaire shotguns, Express rifles, ARC semi-automatic shotguns, PAX pump-action shotguns, and a range of side-by-side barrelled rifles known as Jubile and Jet.

The rifles are branded "Impact." A close study of these weapons shows how much thought has gone into their design and production. The cartridge holder, for instance, is cleverly recessed in the stock. Great care has also been taken with regard to safety. The safety catch is located on the neck of the stock at the transition from receiver to stock. This sliding catch blocks the trigger, the firing pin, the firing pin spring, and the bolt itself. A protruding pin indicates whether there is a round in the chamber or not. In addition, there is an indicator which shows whether the weapon is cocked.

The bolt of the rifle has three heavy-duty lugs and is strengthened by a layer of

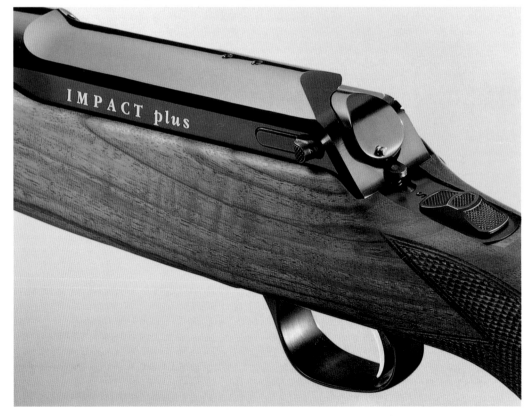

titanium. The rifles in the Impact Affût model range are equipped with Williams sights. The barrels of Verney-Carron rifles are cold-forged under a pressure of 400 tons. The mechanisms are fitted to the wooden stocks by hand to make sure everything fits perfectly and then they are hand-finished.

Verney-Carron Impact Plus Affût (hunting rifle)

TECHNICAL DETAILS
Calibre	: 7 x 64mm, .300 Win. Mag.
Cartridge capacity	: 3-rounds cartridge holder
Magazine catch	: on right of stock
Action	: bolt-action
Locking	: 3 locking lugs
Weight	: 3.15kg (6lb 15oz)
Length	: 113cm (44½in)
Barrel Length	: 60cm (23⅝in)
Sight	: adjustable leaf sight and bead tunnel, drilled and tapped for telescopic sight
External safety	: safety catch on neck of stock
Internal safety	: locking, load and cocking indicators

CHARACTERISTICS
• material	: steel
• finish	: blued
• stock	: walnut stock with pistol grip

Verney-Carron Impact Plus Battue (driven game rifle)

TECHNICAL DETAILS
Calibre	: 7 x 64mm, .300 Win. Mag.

Cartridge capacity	: 3-rounds cartridge holder
Magazine catch	: on right of stock
Action	: bolt-action
Locking	: 3 locking lugs
Weight	: 3kg (6lb 10oz)
Length	: 105cm (413/8in)
Barrel Length	: 52cm (20½in)
Sight	: special sight for driven game with adjustable leaf and bead tunnel, drilled and tapped for telescopic sight
External safety	: safety catch on neck of stock
Internal safety	: locking, load and cocking indicators

CHARACTERISTICS
• material	: steel
• finish	: blued
• stock	: walnut stock with pistol grip

Verney-Carron Sagittaire Double Express Battue (driven game rifle)

TECHNICAL DETAILS
Calibre	: 7 x 65R, 8 x 57 JRS, 9.3 x 74R
Cartridge capacity	: 1 round per each of two barrels
Magazine catch	: not applicable
Action	: breech-action
Locking	: breech-locking
Weight	: 3.3kg (7lb 5oz)
Length	: 100cm (393/8in)
Barrel Length	: 56cm (22in)
Sight	: special sight for driven game with adjustable leaf and bead tunnel, drilled and tapped for telescopic sight
External safety	: safety catch on trigger guard
Internal safety	: locking, load and cocking indicators

CHARACTERISTICS
• material	: steel
• finish	: blued, engraved bare metal breech-action
• stock	: walnut stock and front grip

Voere

The Austrian firm of Voere has been making firearms since 1951. Its history goes back further than this.

A business was established in 1940 in Kufstein by the South German concern of Krieghoff from Suhl, to make equipment for the German army. After World War II, the business was switched to the production of office and school furniture and small machines. This new business was called Tiroler Maschinenbau und Holzindustriegesellschaft mbH. Soon afterwards the factory also began to make drilling and grinding machines. In 1951, a part of the work-force were switched to making weapons. The first of these was the Tyrol LG-51 air rifle. At the same time as these developments, the company name was changed to Tiroler Sportwaffenfabrik und Apparatebau GmbH. The company ran into major financial difficulties in 1964 and in 1965, and the works were taken over by the South German metal-working business of Voere from Vîhrenbach. The business changed name again to Tiroler Jagd- und Sport- Waffenfabrik Voere and then again in 1988 to Voere-Kufsteiner Gerätebau und Handelsgesellschaft mbH. The first model from the late 1980s was a semi-automatic small-bore rifle model 0014, followed by model 1014 with a more "military look". Several years later, these were followed by models 2114 and 2115. These were also semi-automatic small-bore rifles that could be switched to single-shot firing. A number of hunting rifles were developed based on the well-known Mauser 98 rifle. These are the Voere 2150, 2155, and 2165 rifles. In 1992, a large calibre semi-automatic rifle was brought out. This model 2185 was developed by the renowned arms designer Sirkis. The most outstanding triumph by Voere was the introduction in 1991 of the VEC-91 rifle. VEC stands for Voere Electronic Caseless. Externally, the rifle is a classic bolt-action rifle but the insides are revolutionary. The weapon fires caseless cartridges of 5.7 x 26mm calibre that is officially 5.7 x 26 UCC. UCC is an abbreviation for Usel Caseless Cartridge after the Austrian inventor Hubert Usel. The cartridge consists of a body of pressed powder with a detonator and a bullet that is pressed into the powder. The cartridge is fired electronically. The current is supplied by two 15 volt batteries that are carried in the pistol grip. The current from these batteries is converted by a condenser to 18 volt-500mA. This electrical charge is delivered to the detonator by a ceramic pin. Once the cartridge has been fired, there is nothing left in the chamber. Everything is burned and converted to gas-pressure to impel the bullet from the barrel. The concept of caseless cartridges dates back to 1973 when the German company Heckler & Koch began the G-11 project. This was intended to lead to an automatic army rifle for a 4.7mm caseless cartridge. The first prototype was not built until 1980 by H & K but the project was shelved due to a lack of interest for the concept in military circles.

Voere model 2115

TECHNICAL DETAILS

Calibre	: .22 LR
Cartridge capacity	: 10 or 15 rounds
Magazine catch	: at front of magazine aperture
Action	: semi-automatic
Locking	: inertia
Weight	: 2.6kg (5lb 11oz)
Length	: 95cm (37½in)
Barrel Length	: 46cm (18⅛in)
Sight	: adjustable leaf sight and bead tunnel, mounting for telescopic sight
External safety	: safety catch on right of receiver
Internal safety	: locking

CHARACTERISTICS

• material	: steel
• finish	: blued
• stock	: beech with pistol grip

Voere model 2155

TECHNICAL DETAILS

Calibre	: see below
Cartridge capacity	: 3-5 rounds

Magazine catch	: not applicable, internal magazine
Action	: bolt-action
Locking	: 2 locking lugs
Weight	: 3.26kg (7lb 1oz)
Length	: 113.5-118.5cm (44¾-46¾in)
Barrel Length	: 60-65cm (23⅝-25⅝in)
Sight	: fixed leaf sight or driven game sight, drilled and tapped for telescopic sight
External safety	: winged safety catch
Internal safety	: locking

CHARACTERISTICS

• material	: steel
• finish	: blued
• stock	: special walnut stock model 2155/1, walnut stock (model 2155/3, or beech stock (model 2155/5) with pistol grip

Available calibres: 5.6 x 57mm, .22-250 Rem., 6 x 62 Fräres, .243 Win., .25-06, 6.5 x 55mm, 6.5 x 57mm, 6.5 x 65mm, .270 Win., 7 x 57mm, 7 x 64mm, 7mm Rem. Mag., 7.5 Swiss, .30-06 Spr., .300 Win. Mag., .308 Win., 8 x 57mm, 9.3 x 62mm.

The model illustrated is the 2155 driven game model or Battue.

Voere model 2185 Hunter

TECHNICAL DETAILS

Calibre	: see below
Cartridge capacity	: 2-5 rounds
Magazine catch	: at front of magazine aperture
Action	: semi-automatic (gas-pressure)
Locking	: 3 locking lugs on rotating slide
Weight	: 3.5kg (7lb 11oz)
Length	: 110cm (433/8in)
Barrel Length	: 51cm (20⅛in)
Sight	: fixed leaf sight, drilled and tapped for telescopic sight

External safety	: safety catch in front of trigger guard
Internal safety	: locking

CHARACTERISTICS

• material	: steel
• finish	: blued
• stock	: walnut with pistol grip

Available calibres: .243 Win., 6.5 x 57mm, .270 Win., 7 x 57mm, 7 x 64mm, 7mm Rem. Mag., .30-06 Spr., .300 Win. Mag., .308 Win., 8 x 57mm, 9.3 x 62mm.

Voere model 2185/2 Stutzen (hunter's carbine)

TECHNICAL DETAILS

Calibre	: see below
Cartridge capacity	: 2-5 rounds
Magazine catch	: at front of magazine aperture
Action	: semi-automatic (gas-pressure)
Locking	: 3 locking lugs on rotating slide
Weight	: 3.5kg (7lb 11oz)
Length	: 110cm (433/8in)
Barrel Length	: 51cm (20⅛in)
Sight	: fixed leaf sight, drilled and tapped for telescopic sight
External safety	: safety catch in front of trigger guard
Internal safety	: locking

CHARACTERISTICS

• material	: steel
• finish	: blued
• stock	: walnut stock with pistol grip runs under barrel to muzzle

Available calibres: .243 Win., 6.5 x 57mm, .270 Win., 7 x 57mm, 7 x 64mm, 7mm Rem. Mag., .30-06 Spr., .300 Win. Mag., .308 Win., 8 x 57mm, 9.3 x 62mm.

Voere model 2185 Match

TECHNICAL DETAILS

Calibre : .30-06 Spr., .308 Win.
Cartridge capacity : 2-5 rounds
Magazine catch : at front of magazine aperture
Action : semi-automatic (gas-pressure)
Locking : 3 locking lugs on rotating slide
Weight : 5kg (11lb)
Length : 115cm (453/8in)
Barrel Length : 51cm (20⅛in)
Sight : adjustable sight and bead tunnel, drilled and tapped for telescopic sight
External safety : safety catch in front of trigger guard
Internal safety : locking

CHARACTERISTICS

• material : steel
• finish : blued
• stock : laminated wood with pistol grip

Voere model 2185 Sporter

TECHNICAL DETAILS

Calibre : .30-06 Spr., .308 Win.
Cartridge capacity : 2-5 rounds
Magazine catch : at front of magazine aperture
Action : semi-automatic (gas-pressure)
Locking : 3 locking lugs on rotating slide
Weight : 5kg (11lb)
Length : 110cm (433/8in)
Barrel Length : 51cm (20⅛in)
Sight : adjustable sight and bead tunnel, drilled and tapped for telescopic sight
External safety : safety catch in front of trigger guard
Internal safety : locking

CHARACTERISTICS

• material : steel
• finish : blued
• stock : coloured laminated wood with pistol grip

Voere model Vec-91

TECHNICAL DETAILS

Calibre : 5.7 UCC
Cartridge capacity : 5 rounds

Magazine catch : at front of magazine aperture
Action : bolt-action
Locking : 2 locking lugs
Weight : 2.7kg (6lb)
Length : 99cm (39in)
Barrel Length : 51cm (20⅛in)
Sight : adjustable sight, drilled and tapped for telescopic sight
External safety : safety catch on neck of stock
Internal safety : locking

CHARACTERISTICS

• material : steel
• finish : blued
• stock : walnut

This rifle is not equipped with a traditional firing pin. The caseless cartridges are "fired" by a ceramic pin that is electronically charged. The batteries are housed in the pistol grip.

Walther

Carl Walther was born in 1858. He studied the gunsmith's craft and started his own business in Zella-Mehlis, in Germany. At first Walther built target shooting match rifles. At the beginning of the twentieth century, the business was strengthened by three sons, Erich, Fritz, and Georg Walther. Fritz Walther developed the first semi-automatic Walther pistol in 1907 in 6.35mm (.25 ACP) calibre. The famous Walther PP pistol was developed in 1929, followed in 1931 by the PPK of James Bond fame as the pistol that protects Sean Connery as secret agent 007. The PP stands for Polizei Pistole or police pistol. This weapon has been widely used by police forces throughout the world. At the end of the 1930s, a large double-action 9mm parabellum pistol was developed for the armed forces. Because this weapon entered service with the German Wehrmacht in 1938, it was designated P38. The Walther factories were totally destroyed in World War II. Walther started production again at the beginning of the 1950s in an old stable in Ulm on the Danube. Because of the allied ban on production of weapons, Walther initially developed air rifles for precision shooting. The present range includes a wide range of air pistols and rifles. Walther also had a wide choice of small-bore rifles but the company has drastically reduced its range since 1990 and now concentrates on smaller series production of very high quality weapons. The most recent development from Walther is the KK-200 Power Match which achieves a pinnacle of technical excellence. The current range of small-bore rifles have bolts that are coated with titanium-nitrate, which significantly improves the working of the action.

Walther KK-200 Match

TECHNICAL DETAILS
Calibre   : .22 LR
Cartridge capacity : single shot
Magazine catch   : not applicable
Action   : bolt-action
Locking   : bolt-locking
Weight   : 5.3kg (11lb 11oz)
Length   : 109.5cm (43⅛in)
Barrel Length   : 50cm (19¾in)
Sight   : optical sight
External safety   : safety catch on right in front of bolt
Internal safety   : locking
CHARACTERISTICS
• material   : steel
• finish   : bare metal barrel, blued breech
• stock   : laminated beech, open match stock with adjustable cheek and pistol grip

Walther KK-200 Power Match

TECHNICAL DETAILS
Calibre   : .22 LR
Cartridge capacity : single shot
Magazine catch   : not applicable
Action   : bolt-action
Locking   : bolt-locking
Weight   : 5.9kg (13lb)
Length   : 122cm (48in)
Barrel Length   : 64.8cm (25½in)
Sight   : optical sight
External safety   : safety catch on right in front of bolt
Internal safety   : locking
CHARACTERISTICS
• material   : stainless-steel barrel, steel breech, aluminium frame and stock
• finish   : bare metal barrel and frame
• stock   : aluminium and wood stock, fully adjustable with shoulder grip

Walther KK-200-S

TECHNICAL DETAILS
Calibre   : .22 LR
Cartridge capacity : single shot
Magazine catch   : not applicable
Action   : bolt-action
Locking   : bolt-locking
Weight   : 5.3kg (11lb 11oz)
Length   : 109.5cm (43⅛in)
Barrel Length   : 50-55cm (19¾-21¾in)
Sight   : optical sight
External safety   : safety catch on right in front of bolt
Internal safety   : locking

CHARACTERISTICS
• material   : steel

- finish : blued or bare metal barrel, blued breech
- stock : open stock of laminated beech with adjustable cheek and pistol grip

This rifle has no standard barrel length. Every barrel is carefully measured after production and is then sawn to length. The rifle is also equipped with adjustable barrel weights.

Weatherby

Many different types of cartridge have been developed over the years in North America. This is due to the many enthusiasts who have a knowledge of ballistics. These people who develop their own cartridges are known as "wildcatters." Their buzz is to develop cartridges based on standard ones, that outperform the original cartridge on which they were based. Roy Weatherby is a wildcatter. In about 1947, he experimented with a range of cartridges. At that time the tendency was to develop large-calibre hunting cartridges which consequently had a lower velocity. Roy Weatherby looked at the matter from the opposite direction. He considered small calibres with a high velocity would be more effective. The first cartridge he developed was the .220 Rocket, based on the .220 Swift. The first Weatherby Magnums were based on the .300 Holland & Holland Magnum cartridge. These were the .257, the .270, and the .300 Weatherby Magnum cartridges. He started a small gun shop in South Gate, California, and built his own rifles, based on Mauser and Mauser/FN systems. His very powerful super Magnum rifles attracted the attention of weapons experts such as Elmer Keith and Jack O'Connor. In about 1955, Weatherby developed further Magnum calibres, such as the .378 Weatherby Magnum, and the .460 Weatherby Magnum that were more powerful than any other cartridge at that time. In 1957, he brought out his own weapon system, the Weatherby 58 rifle that was to become the Mark V. The Mark V is still the foundation of the Weatherby company. He developed a special nine-lug locking mechanism for this rifle to withstand the extremely high gas-pressures of his new calibres.

Because of the nine lugs, the bolt only needs to rotate through 54 degrees; this was exceptional at that time. In the area of marketing, a concept barely heard of then, Weatherby was gifted. He was able to interest influential people in his rifles such as John Wayne, Gary Cooper, and Roy Rogers, and even the former US president George Bush, and General Norman Schwarzkopf. The Weatherby company has grown considerably since its beginnings and it is currently based at Atascadero in California. The Weatherby family still manage the firm. Weatherby rifles are not just available in the high-velocity Weatherby calibres, they are also available for a range of standard calibres. The Weatherby Magnums cover the following range: .224 Weatherby Magnum, .240 Weatherby Magnum, .257 Weatherby Magnum, .270 Weatherby Magnum, 7mm Weatherby Magnum, .300 Weatherby Magnum, .340 Weatherby Magnum, .378 Weatherby Magnum, .417 Weatherby Magnum, and .460 Weatherby Magnum. There is more information about ammunition in chapter 7.

Weatherby Mark V Accumark

TECHNICAL DETAILS

Calibre	: see below
Cartridge capacity	: 3 rounds
Magazine catch	: button for magazine bottom plate in front of trigger guard
Action	: bolt-action
Locking	: 9 locking lugs
Weight	: 8lb (3.6kg)
Length	: 46¾in (118.8cm)
Barrel Length	: 26in (66cm) with longitudinal grooves for improved cooling
Sight	: none, suitable for telescopic sight
External safety	: safety catch next to bolt blocks firing pin, bolt, and disconnects trigger
Internal safety	: locking, load indicator in rear of receiver

CHARACTERISTICS

- material : steel
- finish : blued
- stock : black plastic Monte Carlo
  stock with pistol grip

Available calibres: .257 Wby. Mag., .270 Wby. Mag., 7mm Rem. Mag., 7mm Wby. Mag., .300 Win. Mag., .300 Wby. Mag., .340 Wby. Mag.

Weatherby Mark V Crown Custom

TECHNICAL DETAILS

Calibre : see below
Cartridge capacity : 3 rounds
Magazine catch : button for magazine bottom plate in front of trigger guard
Action : bolt-action
Locking : 9 locking lugs
Weight : 8lb 8oz (3.9kg)
Length : 46¾in (118.8cm)
Barrel Length : 26in (66cm) with longitudinal grooves for improved cooling
Sight : none, suitable for telescopic sight
External safety : safety catch next to bolt blocks firing pin, bolt, and disconnects trigger
Internal safety : locking, load indicator in rear of receiver

CHARACTERISTICS

- material : steel
- finish : blued
- stock : classic inlaid and engraved walnut Monte Carlo stock with pistol grip with engraved receiver and engraved and gold inlay magazine bottom plate

Available calibres: .257 Wby. Mag., .270 Wby. Mag., 7mm Wby. Mag.,.300 Wby. Mag., .340 Wby. Mag.

Weatherby Mark V Custom Varmint Master

TECHNICAL DETAILS

Calibre : .22-250 Rem.
Cartridge capacity : 3 rounds
Magazine catch : button for magazine bottom plate in front of trigger guard
Action : bolt-action
Locking : 6 locking lugs
Weight : 6lb 8oz (3kg)
Length : 45½in (115.3cm)
Barrel Length : 26in (66cm)
Sight : none, suitable for telescopic sight
External safety : safety catch next to bolt blocks firing pin, bolt, and disconnects trigger
Internal safety : locking, load indicator in rear of receiver

CHARACTERISTICS

- material : steel
- finish : blued
- stock : classic walnut Monte Carlo stock with pistol grip

Weatherby Mark V Euromark

TECHNICAL DETAILS

Calibre : see below
Cartridge capacity : 2-4 rounds depending upon calibre
Magazine catch : button for magazine bottom plate in front of trigger guard
Action : bolt-action
Locking : 9 locking lugs
Weight : 8-9lb 8oz (3.6-4.3kg)
Length : 44¾-46¾in (113.4-118.8cm)

Barrel Length : 24-26in (61-66cm)
Sight : none, suitable for telescopic sight or adjustable sight and bead tunnel
External safety : safety catch next to bolt blocks firing pin, bolt, and disconnects trigger
Internal safety : locking, load indicator in rear of receiver

CHARACTERISTICS
• material : steel
• finish : blued
• stock : classic walnut Monte Carlo stock with pistol grip

Available calibres: .240 Wby. Mag., .257 Wby. Mag., .270 Win., .270 Wby. Mag., 7mm Rem. Mag., 7mm Wby. Mag., .30-06 Spr., .300 Win. Mag., .300 Wby. Mag., .338 Win. Mag., .340 Wby. Mag., .375 H & H Mag., .378 Wby. Mag., .416 Wby. Mag.

CHARACTERISTICS
• material : steel
• finish : blued
• stock : classic walnut Monte Carlo stock with pistol grip

Available calibres: .240 Wby. Mag., .257 Wby. Mag., .270 Win., .270 Wby. Mag., 7mm Rem. Mag., 7mm Wby. Mag., .30-06 Spr., .300 Win. Mag., .300 Wby. Mag., .338 Win. Mag., .340 Wby. Mag., .375 H & H Mag.

Weatherby Mark V Lazermark

TECHNICAL DETAILS
Calibre : see below
Cartridge capacity : 2-4 rounds depending upon calibre
Magazine catch : button for magazine bottom plate in front of trigger guard
Action : bolt-action
Locking : 9 locking lugs
Weight : 8lb 8oz-9lb 8oz (3.9-4.3kg)
Length : 46⅝-46¾in (118.4-118.8cm)
Barrel Length : 26in (66cm)
Sight : none, suitable for telescopic sight
External safety : safety catch next to bolt blocks firing pin, bolt, and disconnects trigger
Internal safety : locking, load indicator in rear of receiver

CHARACTERISTICS
• material : steel
• finish : blued
• stock : classic walnut Monte Carlo stock with pistol grip; oak leaves engraved with laser on stock

Available calibres: .240 Wby. Mag., .257 Wby. Mag., .270 Wby. Mag., 7mm Wby. Mag., .300 Wby. Mag., .340 Wby. Mag.,

Weatherby Mark V Eurosport

TECHNICAL DETAILS
Calibre : see below
Cartridge capacity : 2-4 rounds depending upon calibre
Magazine catch : button for magazine bottom plate in front of trigger guard
Action : bolt-action
Locking : 9 locking lugs
Weight : 8-8lb 8oz (3.6-3.9kg)
Length : 44¾-46¾in (113.4-118.8cm)
Barrel Length : 24-26in (61-66cm)
Sight : none, suitable for telescopic sight or adjustable sight and bead tunnel
External safety : safety catch next to bolt blocks firing pin, bolt, and disconnects trigger
Internal safety : locking, load indicator in rear of receiver

.378 Wby. Mag., .416 Wby. Mag., .460 Wby. Mag.

Weatherby Mark V Sporter

TECHNICAL DETAILS

Calibre : see below
Cartridge capacity : 3-4 rounds depending upon calibre
Magazine catch : button for magazine bottom plate in front of trigger guard
Action : bolt-action
Locking : 9 locking lugs
Weight : 8-8lb 8oz (3.6-3.9kg)
Length : 44¾-46¾in (113.4-118.8cm)
Barrel Length : 24-26in (61-66cm)
Sight : none, suitable for telescopic sight
External safety : safety catch next to bolt blocks firing pin, bolt, and disconnects trigger
Internal safety : locking, load indicator in rear of receiver

CHARACTERISTICS

• material : steel
• finish : blued
• stock : classic walnut Monte Carlo stock with pistol grip

Available calibres: .240 Wby. Mag., .257 Wby. Mag., .270 Win., .270 Wby. Mag., 7mm Rem. Mag., 7mm Wby. Mag., .30-06 Spr., .300 Win. Mag., .300 Wby. Mag., .338 Win. Mag., .340 Wby. Mag., .375 H & H Mag.

Weatherby Mark V Stainless

TECHNICAL DETAILS

Calibre : see below
Cartridge capacity : 2-4 rounds depending upon calibre
Magazine catch : button for magazine bottom plate in front of trigger guard
Action : bolt-action
Locking : 9 locking lugs
Weight : 8lb (3.6kg)
Length : 44¾-46¾in (113.4-118.8cm)
Barrel Length : 24-26in (61-66cm)
Sight : none, suitable for telescopic sight or adjustable sight and bead tunnel
External safety : safety catch next to bolt blocks firing pin, bolt, and disconnects trigger
Internal safety : locking, load indicator in rear of receiver

CHARACTERISTICS

• material : stainless-steel
• finish : bare metal
• stock : synthetic Monte Carlo stock with pistol grip

Available calibres: .240 Wby. Mag., .257 Wby. Mag., .270 Win., .270 Wby. Mag., 7mm Rem. Mag., 7mm Wby. Mag., .30-06 Spr., .300 Win. Mag., .300 Wby. Mag., .338 Win. Mag., .340 Wby. Mag., .375 H & H Mag.

Weatherby Mark V Synthetic

TECHNICAL DETAILS

Calibre : see below
Cartridge capacity : 2-4 rounds depending upon calibre
Magazine catch : button for magazine bottom plate in front of trigger guard
Action : bolt-action
Locking : 9 locking lugs
Weight : 8lb (3.6kg)
Length : 44¾-46¾in (113.4-118.8cm)
Barrel Length : 24-26in (61-66cm)

Sight	: none, suitable for telescopic sight or adjustable sight and bead tunnel
External safety	: safety catch next to bolt blocks firing pin, bolt, and disconnects trigger
Internal safety	: locking, load indicator in rear of receiver

CHARACTERISTICS

• material	: steel
• finish	: blued
• stock	: synthetic Monte Carlo stock with pistol grip

Available calibres: .240 Wby. Mag., .257 Wby. Mag., .270 Win., .270 Wby. Mag., 7mm Rem. Mag., 7mm Wby. Mag., .30-06 Spr., .300 Win. Mag., .300 Wby. Mag., .338 Win. Mag., .340 Wby. Mag., .375 H & H Mag.

Weihrauch

The German company Weihrauch was established in 1899 by master gunsmith Hermann Weihrauch. Until 1899, he worked for another gunsmith, Bartels, in Zella St. Blasi. In 1899, he took the business over and set up under his own name with his three sons.

In their small weapons workshop, they mainly produced hunting rifles. During World War I, the business was set to work making items for the war effort. It made parts and mounts for telescopic sights and for the Mauser-98 rifle. After the war, the firm returned to making sporting weapons. The company also made cycles and door-closers at that time. Once more the company was set to work for the military during World War II, making military cycles and weapon parts. The business was closed down by the allies in 1945. It was not until 1948 that Hermann Weihrauch started up again with his sons in Mellrichstadt in Bavaria, to make cycle and moped parts. This was expanded in 1950 with the manufacture of air weapons and then in 1960 with the Arminius range of revolvers. This make was originally produced by Friedrich Pickert, a gunsmith in Zella-Mehlis who made revolvers.

Today's range from Weihrauch consists of air weapons and small-bore rifles under the Weihrauch name, together with Arminius revolvers. The company also make

a .222 Remington-calibre hunting rifle. Weihrauch has retained its all-round craft skills and the firm still makes cycle parts. It is still in the hands of the Weihrauch family.

Weihrauch HW 60J

TECHNICAL DETAILS

Calibre	: .22 LR, .22 WMR, .22 Hornet
Cartridge capacity	: 5 rounds (LR) or 4 rounds
Magazine catch	: in front of trigger guard
Action	: bolt-action
Locking	: 2 locking lugs
Weight	: 2.95kg (6lb 8oz)
Length	: 106cm (41¾in)
Barrel Length	: 58cm (22¾in)
Sight	: folding sight, mounting for telescopic sight
External safety	: sliding safety catch on right of receiver
Internal safety	: locking, load indicator at rear of bolt

CHARACTERISTICS

• material	: steel
• finish	: blued
• stock	: walnut with pistol grip

This rifle is available with a single pressure-point trigger or with a double pressure-point trigger (Stecher) as illustrated.

Weihrauch HW 60 Match

TECHNICAL DETAILS

Calibre	: .22 LR
Cartridge capacity	: single shot
Magazine catch	: not applicable
Action	: bolt-action

Locking	: 2 locking lugs
Weight	: 4.85kg (10lb 11oz)
Length	: 115cm (45¼in)
Barrel Length	: 66cm (26in)
Sight	: optical sight
External safety	: sliding safety catch on right of receiver
Internal safety	: locking, load indicator at rear of bolt

CHARACTERISTICS
- material : steel
- finish : blued
- stock : special walnut match stock

Locking	: 2 locking lugs
Weight	: 4.85kg (10lb 11oz)
Length	: 115cm (45¼in)
Barrel Length	: 66cm (26in)
Sight	: optical sight and bead tunnel
External safety	: sliding safety catch on right of receiver
Internal safety	: locking, load indicator at rear of bolt

CHARACTERISTICS
- material : steel
- finish : blued
- stock : special walnut match stock

Weihrauch HW 66

TECHNICAL DETAILS

Calibre	: .22 LR, .22 Hornet, .222 Rem.
Cartridge capacity	: 5,4, or 3 rounds respectively
Magazine catch	: internal magazine
Action	: bolt-action
Locking	: 2 locking lugs
Weight	: 3.85kg (8lb 8oz)
Length	: 104.5cm (41½in)
Barrel Length	: 56cm (22⅛in)
Sight	: none, suitable for telescopic sight
External safety	: sliding safety catch on right of receiver
Internal safety	: locking, load indicator at rear of bolt

CHARACTERISTICS
- material : steel with stainless steel barrel
- finish : blued, bare metal barrel
- stock : special walnut match stock

Weihrauch HW 660 Match

TECHNICAL DETAILS

Calibre	: .22 LR
Cartridge capacity	: single shot
Magazine catch	: not applicable
Action	: bolt-action

Weihrauch HW 660 Match Laminate

TECHNICAL DETAILS

Calibre	: .22 LR
Cartridge capacity	: single shot
Magazine catch	: not applicable
Action	: bolt-action
Locking	: 2 locking lugs
Weight	: 4.85kg (10lb 11oz)
Length	: 115cm (45¼in)
Barrel Length	: 66cm (26in)
Sight	: optical sight and bead tunnel
External safety	: sliding safety catch on right of receiver
Internal safety	: locking, load indicator at rear of bolt

CHARACTERISTICS
- material : steel
- finish : blued
- stock : special laminated hardwood match stock

Winchester

The history of Winchester is closely related to that of Smith & Wesson. In 1855, Horace Smith, Daniel B. Wesson, and C.C. Palmer set up the Volcanic Repeating Arms Company. One of the shareholders of the company was Oliver F. Winchester, a clothing manufacturer from New Haven, Connecticut. The company produced the Volcanic lever-action repeating rifle. In 1857, Winchester became the largest shareholder and the company name was changed to New Haven Arms Company. B. Tyler Henry, the company designer, applied in 1860 for a patent for a rifle that subsequently became known as the Henry rifle. In 1866, the company name was changed once more to The Winchester Repeating Arms Company. The first rifle from this new company was the Winchester 1866 model. This weapon was so popular that even though it was succeeded by newer models, it was made until 1899. A total of 171,000 rifles were made of this model. Winchester introduced an improved lever-action repeater in 1873. The production of the 1873 model continued until 1920, amounting to 19,500 in total. The next rifle was the 1876 model of which 64,000 were made. Subsequent models are the 1886 and the famous 1894 model of which more than 3,000,000 were produced. The successor to this type, the 1895 model is still made by Winchester. In addition to lever-action rifles, Winchester also made shotguns and bolt-action hunting rifles. The first bolt-action Winchester was the 1883 model that was based on a patent of Benjamin B. Hotchkiss and was made until 1889. A subsequent bolt-action rifle was the Lee Straight Pull model of 1895 that was made for the US Navy. This rifle was also produced in a sporting version known as the Lee Sporting model. Winchester was the first company to bring out a pump-action repeating rifle, in 1890. The 1890 model used .22 rimfire ammunition and it was produced until 1932, totalling 849,000 in all. The first small-calibre bolt-action rifle from Winchester was the simple, single-shot 1900 model for .22 rimfire. This was based on a patent of John Moses Browning. Winchester was also active in the area of semi-automatic weapons. The first Self-Loading rifle was introduced as model 1903 in that year for .22 rimfire. This was followed by a heavier calibre 1905 model for .35 Winchester SL, and .32 Winchester SL (SL standing for self loading). This rifle had

the first removable cartridge holder. An improved model was introduced in 1907 for .351 Win.-SL and this rifle was made until 1957. This was followed in 1910 by the M1910-SL for .401 Win.-SL. During World War I, Winchester mainly produced the Enfield Pattern 14 army rifle in .303 British, for the British Government. The company supplied 246,000 of these rifles. In 1917 and 1918, Winchester converted part of its machine shops to produce the US model 1917 rifle in .30-06 Springfield. At the start of World War II, Winchester developed the famous .30-M1 carbine of which the company itself made 818,000. This weapon was made under licence until the end of the war by many other companies, including Inland, Underwood, Quality Hardware & Machinery Corp., Rock-Ola, Saginaw, Irwin-Pedersen, National Poster Meter, Standard Products, and IBM. More than 6,000,000 were made during the war. An exceptionally detailed account of the development and production of this weapon can be found in War Baby by the American writer Larry L. Ruth. Winchester was also closely involved with the production of the M1-Garand army rifle. The current name of the company is the US Repeating Arms Company Inc. It is part of the Olin group.

Winchester 1895 model Limited Edition Grade I

TECHNICAL DETAILS

Calibre	: .30-06 Spr.
Cartridge capacity	: box magazine for 4 rounds
Magazine catch	: at rear of magazine
Action	: lever-action
Locking	: lever locking
Weight	: 8lb (3.6kg)
Length	: 42in (106.7cm)
Barrel Length	: 24in (61cm)
Sight	: adjustable height leaf sight
External safety	: safety catch on back of stock
Internal safety	: locking, blocking bar

CHARACTERISTICS

- material : steel
- finish : blued, engraved action casing
- stock : straight walnut stock

Only 4,000 examples were produced in 1995 of this special model.

Winchester 1895 model Limited Edition High Grade

TECHNICAL DETAILS

Calibre : .30-06 Spr.
Cartridge capacity : box magazine for 4 rounds
Magazine catch : at rear of magazine
Action : lever-action
Locking : lever locking
Weight : 8lb (3.6kg)
Length : 42in (106.7cm)
Barrel Length : 24in (61cm)
Sight : adjustable height leaf sight
External safety : safety catch on back of stock
Internal safety : locking, blocking bar

CHARACTERISTICS

- material : steel
- finish : blued, with gold inlay on action housing and gilded trigger
- stock : straight stock of specially selected walnut

Only 4,000 examples were produced in 1995 of this special model.

Winchester .30-M1 carbine

TECHNICAL DETAILS

Calibre : .30-M1 Carbine.
Cartridge capacity : cartridge holder for 5, 15, or 30 rounds
Magazine catch : right-hand front of trigger guard
Action : semi-automatic, gas-pressure
Locking : 2 lugs rotating slide
Weight : 5lb 7oz (2.5kg)
Length : 35⅝in (90.5cm)
Barrel Length : 18in (45.8cm)
Sight : adjustable military optical sight
External safety : safety catch at right front of trigger guard
Internal safety : locking

CHARACTERISTICS

- material : steel
- finish : mat black phosphate coating
- stock : walnut stock with hand guard

Winchester Ram-Line .30-M1 carbine

TECHNICAL DETAILS

Calibre : .30-M1 Carbine.
Cartridge capacity : cartridge holder for 5, 15, or 30 rounds
Magazine catch : right-hand front of trigger guard
Action : semi-automatic, gas-pressure
Locking : 2 lugs rotating slide
Weight : 5lb 7oz (2.5kg)
Length : 37¾in (95.6cm)
Barrel Length : 20in (50.9cm) including muzzle flash reducer
Sight : adjustable military optical sight
External safety : safety catch at right front of trigger guard
Internal safety : locking

CHARACTERISTICS

- material : steel
- finish : mat black phosphate coating
- stock : black plastic Ram-Line stock with pistol grip

The American firm of Ram-Line has designed a plastic stock for this veteran carbine that is illustrated here. Ram-Line also make a folding stock but this type of stock is not permitted for civilian use in many countries.

Winchester Model 70 Classic Featherweight - Boss

TECHNICAL DETAILS
Calibre : see below
Cartridge capacity : cartridge holder for 5 rounds
Magazine catch : at rear of magazine, in front of trigger
Action : bolt-action
Locking : 2 locking lugs
Weight : 7-7lb 4oz (3.2-3.3kg)
Length : 42-42½in (106.7-108cm)
Barrel Length : 22in (55.9cm)
Sight : none, suitable for telescopic sight
External safety : safety catch at right-hand rear of bolt
Internal safety : locking
CHARACTERISTICS
• material : steel
• finish : blued
• stock : hardwood

Available calibres: .22-250 Rem., .243 Win., .308 Win., 7mm-08 Rem., .270 Win., .280 Rem., .30-06 Spr.

The barrel of the rifle illustrated is equipped with the Boss precision system.

Winchester Model 70 Classic Featherweight All-Terrain - Boss

TECHNICAL DETAILS
Calibre : see below
Cartridge capacity : cartridge holder for 5 rounds (Magnum 3)
Magazine catch : at rear of magazine, in front of trigger
Action : bolt-action
Locking : 2 locking lugs
Weight : 7lb 4oz (3.3kg)
Length : 42½-44½in (108-113.7cm)
Barrel Length : 22-24in (55.9-61cm)
Sight : none, suitable for telescopic sight
External safety : safety catch at right-hand rear of bolt
Internal safety : locking
CHARACTERISTICS
• material : stainless-steel
• finish : bare metal
• stock : black plastic

Available calibres: .270 Win., .30-06 Spr., 7mm Rem. Mag., .300 Win. Mag.

The barrel of the rifle illustrated is equipped with the Boss precision system.

Winchester Model 70 Classic Laredo - Boss

TECHNICAL DETAILS
Calibre : 7mm Rem. Mag., .300 Win. Mag.
Cartridge capacity : 3 rounds
Magazine catch : at rear of magazine, in front of trigger
Action : bolt-action
Locking : 2 locking lugs
Weight : 8lb 8oz (3.9kg)
Length : 46½in (118.8cm)
Barrel Length : 26in (66cm)
Sight : none, suitable for telescopic sight
External safety : safety catch at right-hand rear of bolt
Internal safety : locking
CHARACTERISTICS
• material : steel

- finish : blued matt
- stock : grey plastic

This long-range rifle can be equipped with the Boss precision system.

Winchester Model 70 Classic SM

TECHNICAL DETAILS

Calibre : see below
Cartridge capacity : cartridge holder for 3-5 rounds
Magazine catch : at rear of magazine, in front of trigger
Action : bolt-action
Locking : 2 locking lugs
Weight : 7lb 4oz-7lb 8oz (3.3-3.4kg)
Length : 44¾-46¾in (113.7-118.8cm)
Barrel Length : 24-26in (61-66cm)
Sight : none, suitable for telescopic sight
External safety : safety catch at right-hand rear of bolt
Internal safety : locking

CHARACTERISTICS

- material : steel
- finish : blued
- stock : dark grey plastic stock with pistol grip

Available calibres: .270 Win., .30-06 Spr., 7mm Rem. Mag., .300 Win. Mag., .338 Win. Mag., .375 H & H Mag.

Winchester Model 70 Classic SM 375

TECHNICAL DETAILS

Calibre : .375 H & H Mag.

Cartridge capacity : 3 rounds
Magazine catch : at rear of magazine, in front of trigger
Action : bolt-action
Locking : 2 locking lugs
Weight : 7lb 4oz (3.3kg)
Length : 44¾in (113.7cm)
Barrel Length : 24in (61cm)
Sight : none, suitable for telescopic sight
External safety : safety catch at right-hand rear of bolt
Internal safety : locking

CHARACTERISTICS

- material : steel
- finish : blued
- stock : grey plastic with pistol grip

Winchester Model 70 Classic Sporter - Boss

TECHNICAL DETAILS

Calibre : see below
Cartridge capacity : 3-5 rounds
Magazine catch : at rear of magazine, in front of trigger
Action : bolt-action
Locking : 2 locking lugs
Weight : 7lb 12oz-8lb (3.5-3.6kg)
Length : 44¾-46¾in (113.7-118.8cm)
Barrel Length : 24-26in (61-66cm)
Sight : none, suitable for telescopic sight
External safety : safety catch at right-hand rear of bolt
Internal safety : locking

CHARACTERISTICS

- material : steel
- finish : blued
- stock : walnut

Available calibres: .25-06 Rem., .264 Win. Mag., .270 Win., .270 Wby. Mag., .30-06 Spr., 7mm Rem. Mag., .300 Win. Mag., .300 Wby. Mag., .338 Win. Mag.

This rifle can be equipped with the Boss precision system.

Winchester Model 70 Classic Sporter SM

TECHNICAL DETAILS

Calibre	: see below
Cartridge capacity	: 3-5 rounds
Magazine catch	: at rear of magazine, in front of trigger
Action	: bolt-action
Locking	: 2 locking lugs
Weight	: 7lb 4oz-7lb 8oz (3.3-3.4kg)
Length	: 44¾-46¾in (113.7-118.8cm)
Barrel Length	: 24-26in (61-66cm)
Sight	: none, suitable for telescopic sight
External safety	: safety catch at right-hand rear of bolt
Internal safety	: locking

CHARACTERISTICS

• material	: steel
• finish	: blued matt
• stock	: black synthetic stock

Available calibres: .270 Win., .30-06 Spr., 7mm Rem. Mag., .300 Win. Mag., .338 Win. Mag., .375 H & H Mag.

This rifle can be equipped with the Boss precision system.

Winchester Model 70 Classic Stainless Boss

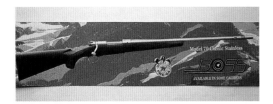

TECHNICAL DETAILS

Calibre	: see below
Cartridge capacity	: 3-5 rounds
Magazine catch	: at rear of magazine, in front of trigger
Action	: bolt-action
Locking	: 2 locking lugs
Weight	: 6lb 12oz-7lb 8oz (3.1-3.4kg)
Length	: 42¼-46¾in (107.3-118.8cm)
Barrel Length	: 22-26in (55.9-66cm)
Sight	: none, suitable for telescopic sight
External safety	: safety catch at right-hand rear of bolt
Internal safety	: locking

CHARACTERISTICS

• material	: stainless-steel
• finish	: matt finish
• stock	: black synthetic stock with pistol grip

Available calibres: .22-250 Rem., .243 Win., .270 Win., .308 Win., .30-06 Spr., 7mm Rem. Mag., .300 Win. Mag., .300 Wby. Mag., .338 Win. Mag.

Winchester Model 70 Custom Classic Express

TECHNICAL DETAILS

Calibre	: see below
Cartridge capacity	: 3 rounds
Magazine catch	: at rear of magazine, in front of trigger
Action	: bolt-action
Locking	: 2 locking lugs
Weight	: 10lb (4.5kg)
Length	: 44¾-45in (113.7-114.3cm)
Barrel Length	: 22-24in (55.9-61cm)
Sight	: Express folding sight and bead tunnel, suitable for telescopic sight
External safety	: safety catch at right-hand rear of bolt
Internal safety	: locking

CHARACTERISTICS

- material : steel
- finish : blued
- stock : walnut with pistol grip

Available calibres: .375 H & H Mag., .375 JRS, .416 Rem. Mag., .458 Win. Mag.

Winchester Model 70 Custom Classic Sharpshooter II Stainless

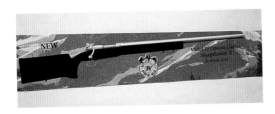

TECHNICAL DETAILS

Calibre	: see below
Cartridge capacity	: 3-5 rounds
Magazine catch	: at rear of magazine, in front of trigger
Action	: bolt-action
Locking	: 2 locking lugs
Weight	: 11lb (5kg)
Length	: 44¾-46¼in (113.7-118.8cm)
Barrel Length	: 24-26in (55.9-61cm)
Sight	: none, suitable for telescopic sight
External safety	: safety catch at right-hand rear of bolt
Internal safety	: locking

CHARACTERISTICS

- material : stainless-steel
- finish : matt finish
- stock : black synthetic stock with pistol grip

Available calibres: .22-250 Rem., .308 Win., .30-06 Spr., .300 Win. Mag.

Winchester Model 70 Custom Classic Sporting Sharpshooter II Stainless

TECHNICAL DETAILS

Calibre	: 7mm STW, .300 Win. Mag.
Cartridge capacity	: 3 rounds
Magazine catch	: at rear of magazine, in front of trigger guard

Action	: bolt-action
Locking	: 2 locking lugs
Weight	: 8lb 8oz (3.9kg)
Length	: 46¼in (118.8cm)
Barrel Length	: 26in (66cm)
Sight	: none, suitable for telescopic sight
External safety	: safety catch at right-hand rear of bolt
Internal safety	: locking

CHARACTERISTICS

- material : steel receiver, stainless-steel barrel
- finish : matt blued receiver, matt finish barrel
- stock : dark grey plastic stock with pistol grip

The abbreviation with 7mm STW calibre stands for Shooting Time Westerner. This special cartridge was introduced through the Shooting Times magazine in 1988 by Layne Simpson, a writer about shooting.

Winchester Model 70 Heavy Varmint

TECHNICAL DETAILS

Calibre	: see below
Cartridge capacity	: 5-6-rounds
Magazine catch	: at rear of magazine, in front of trigger guard
Action	: bolt-action
Locking	: 2 locking lugs
Weight	: 10lb 12oz (4.9kg)
Length	: 46in (116.8cm)
Barrel Length	: 26in (66cm)
Sight	: none, suitable for telescopic sight
External safety	: safety catch at right-hand rear of bolt
Internal safety	: locking

CHARACTERISTICS
- material : stainless-steel
- finish : matt finish
- stock : dark grey plastic or Kevlar stock with pistol grip

Available calibres: .220 Swift, .223 Rem., .22-250 Rem., .243 Win., .308 Win.

Winchester Model 94 Big Bore

TECHNICAL DETAILS
Calibre	: .307 Win., .356 Win.
Cartridge capacity	: tubular magazine for 6 rounds
Magazine catch	: not applicable, loading port at right of mechanism housing
Action	: lever-action
Locking	: lever locking
Weight	: 6lb 8oz (3kg)
Length	: 37¾in (95.9cm)
Barrel Length	: 20in (50.8cm)
Sight	: adjustable height sight with bead tunnel
External safety	: safety catch at right-hand side of casing
Internal safety	: locking, trigger blocked when lever not fully closed

CHARACTERISTICS
- material : steel
- finish : blued
- stock : straight walnut stock

Winchester Model 94 Legacy

TECHNICAL DETAILS
Calibre	: .30-30 Win.

Cartridge capacity	: tubular magazine for 6 rounds
Magazine catch	: not applicable, loading port at right of mechanism housing
Action	: lever-action
Locking	: lever locking
Weight	: 6lb 8oz (3kg)
Length	: 37¾in (95.9cm)
Barrel Length	: 20in (50.8cm)
Sight	: adjustable height sight
External safety	: safety catch at right-hand side of casing
Internal safety	: locking, trigger blocked when lever not fully closed

CHARACTERISTICS
- material : steel
- finish : blued
- stock : straight walnut stock

Winchester Model 94 Ranger

TECHNICAL DETAILS
Calibre	: .30-30 Win.
Cartridge capacity	: tubular magazine for 6 rounds
Magazine catch	: not applicable, loading port at right of mechanism housing
Action	: lever-action
Locking	: lever locking
Weight	: 6lb 8oz (3kg)
Length	: 37¾in (95.9cm)
Barrel Length	: 20in (50.8cm)
Sight	: adjustable height sight
External safety	: safety catch at right-hand side of casing
Internal safety	: locking, trigger blocked when lever not fully closed

CHARACTERISTICS
- material : steel
- finish : blued
- stock : straight hardwood stock

This rifle is also available with a Bushnell 4 x 32 telescopic sight with a mounting that permits the normal sights to be used as well.

Winchester Model 94 Trapper

TECHNICAL DETAILS

Calibre : see below
Cartridge capacity : tubular magazine for 5 rounds (.30-30) or 9 rounds
Magazine catch : not applicable, loading port at right of mechanism housing
Action : lever-action
Locking : lever locking
Weight : 6lb (2.7kg)
Length : 33¾in (85.7cm)
Barrel Length : 16in (40.6cm)
Sight : adjustable height sight
External safety : safety catch at right-hand side of casing
Internal safety : locking, trigger blocked when lever not fully closed

CHARACTERISTICS
- material : steel
- finish : blued
- stock : straight walnut stock

Available calibres: .30-30 Win., .44 Mag./.44 Spec., .357 Mag., .45 LC

Winchester Model 94 Walnut

TECHNICAL DETAILS

Calibre : .30-30 Win.
Cartridge capacity : tubular magazine for 6 rounds
Magazine catch : not applicable, loading port at right of mechanism housing
Action : lever-action
Locking : lever locking
Weight : 6lb 8oz (3kg)
Length : 37¾in (95.9cm)
Barrel Length : 20in (50.8cm)

Sight : adjustable height sight with bead tunnel
External safety : safety catch at right-hand side of casing
Internal safety : locking, trigger blocked when lever not fully closed

CHARACTERISTICS
- material : steel
- finish : blued
- stock : straight walnut stock

Winchester Model 94 Walnut - Checkered (chequered)

TECHNICAL DETAILS

Calibre : .30-30 Win.
Cartridge capacity : tubular magazine for 6 rounds
Magazine catch : not applicable, loading port at right of mechanism housing
Action : lever-action
Locking : lever locking
Weight : 6lb 8oz (3kg)
Length : 37¾in (95.9cm)
Barrel Length : 20in (50.8cm)
Sight : adjustable height sight with bead tunnel
External safety : safety catch at right-hand side of casing
Internal safety : locking, trigger blocked when lever not fully closed

CHARACTERISTICS
- material : steel
- finish : blued
- stock : straight walnut stock with deeply-carved fish-scale pattern on the front grip

Winchester Model 94 WinTuff

TECHNICAL DETAILS

Calibre	: .30-30 Win.
Cartridge capacity	: tubular magazine for 6 rounds
Magazine catch	: not applicable, loading port at right of mechanism housing
Action	: lever-action
Locking	: lever locking
Weight	: 6lb 8oz (3kg)
Length	: 37¾in (95.9cm)
Barrel Length	: 20in (50.8cm)
Sight	: adjustable height sight with bead tunnel
External safety	: safety catch at right-hand side of casing
Internal safety	: locking, trigger blocked when lever not fully closed

CHARACTERISTICS

- material : steel
- finish : blued
- stock : straight laminated wood stock

Winchester Model 94 Wrangler

TECHNICAL DETAILS

Calibre	: .30-30 Win., .44 Mag./.44 Spec.
Cartridge capacity	: tubular magazine for 5 rounds (.30-30 Win.) or 9 rounds
Magazine catch	: not applicable, loading port at right of mechanism housing
Action	: lever-action
Locking	: lever locking
Weight	: 6lb (2.7kg)
Length	: 33¾in (85.7cm)
Barrel Length	: 16in (40.6cm)
Sight	: adjustable height sight
External safety	: safety catch at right-hand side of casing
Internal safety	: locking, trigger blocked when lever not fully closed

CHARACTERISTICS

- material : steel
- finish : blued

- stock : straight walnut stock

This rifle, which is almost identical to the 94 Trapper, has an enlarged trigger-guard/locking and cocking lever for use with gloves.

Winchester Model 9422 High Grade

TECHNICAL DETAILS

Calibre	: .22 LR, .22 Long, .22 Short
Cartridge capacity	: 15, 17, or 21 rounds respectively
Magazine catch	: tubular magazine with closing button at front
Action	: lever-action
Locking	: lever locking
Weight	: 6lb (2.7kg)
Length	: 37 3/8in (94.8cm)
Barrel Length	: 20½in (52.1cm)
Sight	: adjustable folding sight, mounting for telescopic sight
External safety	: the trigger is disengaged from the firing mechanism when the weapon is cocked
Internal safety	: locking, half-cock on hammer and safety system on firing pin

CHARACTERISTICS

- material : steel
- finish : blued with engraved casing
- stock : walnut

Winchester Model 9422 Trapper

TECHNICAL DETAILS

Calibre	: .22 LR, .22 Long, .22 Short

Cartridge capacity : 11, 12, or 15 rounds
respectively
Magazine catch : tubular magazine with
closing button at front
Action : lever-action
Locking : lever locking
Weight : 5lb 8oz (2.5kg)
Length : 333/8in (84.6cm)
Barrel Length : 16½in (41.9cm)
Sight : adjustable folding sight,
mounting for telescopic sight
External safety : the trigger is disengaged
from the firing mechanism
when the weapon is cocked
Internal safety : locking, half-cock on ham-
mer and safety system on
firing pin

CHARACTERISTICS
• material : steel
• finish : blued
• stock : walnut

Winchester Model 9422 Walnut

TECHNICAL DETAILS
Calibre : .22 LR, .22 Long, .22 Short,
or .22 WMR
Cartridge capacity : 15, 17, or 21 rounds res-
pectively (11 for .22 WMR)
Magazine catch : tubular magazine with
closing button at front
Action : lever-action
Locking : lever locking
Weight : 6lb (2.7kg)
Length : 373/8in (94.8cm)
Barrel Length : 20½in (52.1cm)
Sight : adjustable folding sight,
mounting for telescopic sight
External safety : the trigger is disengaged
from the firing mechanism
when the weapon is cocked
Internal safety : locking, half-cock on ham-
mer and safety system on
firing pin

CHARACTERISTICS
• material : steel
• finish : blued with engraved casing
• stock : walnut

Winchester Model 9422 WinCam

TECHNICAL DETAILS
Calibre : .22 WMR
Cartridge capacity : 11-rounds
Magazine catch : tubular magazine with
closing button at front
Action : lever-action
Locking : lever locking
Weight : 6lb 4oz (2.8kg)
Length : 373/8in (94.8cm)
Barrel Length : 20½in (52.1cm)
Sight : adjustable folding sight,
mounting for telescopic
sight
External safety : the trigger is disengaged
from the firing mechanism
when the weapon is cocked
Internal safety : locking, half-cock on
hammer and safety system
on firing pin

CHARACTERISTICS
• material : steel
• finish : blued
• stock : stock laminated with layers
of different coloured hard-
woods

Winchester Model 9422 WinTuff

TECHNICAL DETAILS
Calibre : .22 LR, .22 Long, .22 Short,
or .22 WMR
Cartridge capacity : 15, 17, or 21 rounds respec-
tively (11 for .22 WMR)
Magazine catch : tubular magazine with
closing button at front
Action : lever-action
Locking : lever locking

Weight	: 6lb 4oz (2.8kg)
Length	: 37 3/8in (94.8cm)
Barrel Length	: 20½in (52.1cm)
Sight	: adjustable folding sight, mounting for telescopic sight
External safety	: the trigger is disengaged from the firing mechanism when the weapon is cocked
Internal safety	: locking, half-cock on hammer and safety system on firing pin

CHARACTERISTICS

• material	: steel
• finish	: blued
• stock	: laminated hardwood

Zoli

The history of the Italian arms maker Zoli stretches back to the Middle Ages. It is known that the Zoli family were making blunderbuss-type weapons early in the fifteenth century. Members of the family remained associated with the making of weapons in the ensuing centuries in the area surrounding Gardone Val Trompia. Until the Industrial Revolution, many families throughout this region made weapons by hand on a small scale. It is known that Giovanni Zoli was making locking mechanisms for firearms in 1867. A fine example of his handicraft is the marvellous front-loading pistol that is displayed in the present-day Zoli factory. Antonio Zoli, who founded Antonio Zoli S.p.a., was born in 1905. His father, Giuseppe Zoli, had a small workshop for weapons in Magno di Valtrompia where he made rifle locking systems.

Prior to World War II, Antonio Zoli worked as a gunsmith for various weapon manufacturers in the region. In October 1945, he decided to set up his own business with his sons. At first they made double-barrelled shotguns but their range was later increased to include Express rifles and bolt-action rifles. Zoli was the first firm, in 1956, to recognize the demand for replicas of blackpowder firearms. The third generation of the family since the company was formed is now engaged in the business. The family is justly proud that they carry on the traditions established by the old craftsmen but with the latest technology. The superbly finished Zoli rifles are exported to many different countries.

Zoli model AZ-1900 Lux

TECHNICAL DETAILS

Calibre	: see below
Cartridge capacity	: 4-5 rounds
Magazine catch	: catch at front of trigger guard
Action	: bolt-action
Locking	: 2 locking lugs
Weight	: 3.4-3.5kg (7lb 8oz-7lb 11oz)
Length	: 117.4-122.4cm (46¼-48¼in)
Barrel Length	: 60-65cm (23⅝-25⅝in)
Sight	: adjustable folding sight and bead tunnel, drilled and tapped for telescopic sight
External safety	: safety catch on right behind bolt
Internal safety	: locking, load indicator at rear of bolt

CHARACTERISTICS

• material	: steel
• finish	: blued barrel with bare steel receiver
• stock	: walnut with pistol grip

Available calibres: .243 Win., 6.5 x 55mm, 6.5 x 57mm, .270 Win., .270 Wby. Mag., 7 x 64, 7mm Rem. Mag., .308 Win., .30-06 Spr., .300 Win. Mag., .338 Win. Mag., 9.3 x 62mm.

Zoli model AZ-1900 Lux Battue (rifle for driven game)

TECHNICAL DETAILS

Calibre	: see below
Cartridge capacity	: 4-5 rounds
Magazine catch	: catch at front of trigger guard
Action	: bolt-action
Locking	: 2 locking lugs
Weight	: 3.3kg (7lb 5oz)
Length	: 110.4cm (43½in)
Barrel Length	: 53cm (207/8in)
Sight	: sight for driven game and bead tunnel, drilled and tapped for telescopic sight
External safety	: safety catch on right behind bolt
Internal safety	: locking, load indicator at rear of bolt

CHARACTERISTICS
- material : steel
- finish : blued barrel with bare steel receiver
- stock : walnut with pistol grip

Available calibres: .243 Win., 6.5 x 55mm, 6.5 x 57mm, .270 Win., 7 x 64, 7mm Rem. Mag., .308 Win., .30-06 Spr., .300 Win. Mag., .338 Win. Mag., 9.3 x 62mm.

Zoli model AZ-1900 Standard

TECHNICAL DETAILS

Calibre	: see below
Cartridge capacity	: 4-5 rounds
Magazine catch	: catch at front of trigger guard
Action	: bolt-action
Locking	: 2 locking lugs
Weight	: 3.4-3.5kg (7lb 8oz-7lb 11oz)
Length	: 117.4-122.4cm (46¼-48¼in)
Barrel Length	: 60-65cm (23⅝-25⅝in)
Sight	: adjustable folding sight and bead tunnel, drilled and tapped for telescopic sight

External safety	: safety catch on right behind bolt
Internal safety	: locking, load indicator at rear of bolt

CHARACTERISTICS
- material : steel
- finish : blued
- stock : walnut with pistol grip

Available calibres: .243 Win., 6.5 x 55mm, 6.5 x 57mm, .270 Win., .270 Wby. Mag., 7 x 64, 7mm Rem. Mag., .308 Win., .30-06 Spr., .300 Win. Mag., .338 Win. Mag., 9.3 x 62mm.

A left-hand version of this rifle is also available (AZ-1900 Standard-Left).

Zoli model AZ-1900 Standard Battue (rifle for driven game)

TECHNICAL DETAILS

Calibre	: see below
Cartridge capacity	: 4-5 rounds
Magazine catch	: catch at front of trigger guard
Action	: bolt-action
Locking	: 2 locking lugs
Weight	: 3.3kg (7lb 5oz)
Length	: 110.4cm (43½in)
Barrel Length	: 53cm (207/8in)
Sight	: sight for driven game and bead tunnel, drilled and tapped for telescopic sight
External safety	: safety catch on right behind bolt
Internal safety	: locking, load indicator at rear of bolt

CHARACTERISTICS
- material : steel
- finish : blued
- stock : walnut with pistol grip

Available calibres: .243 Win., 6.5 x 55mm, 6.5 x 57mm, .270 Win., 7 x 64, 7mm Rem.

Mag., .308 Win., .30-06 Spr., .300 Win. Mag., .338 Win. Mag., 9.3 x 62mm.

Zoli model AZ-1900 Stutzen (hunting carbine)

TECHNICAL DETAILS

Calibre	: see below
Cartridge capacity	: 4-5 rounds
Magazine catch	: catch at front of trigger guard
Action	: bolt-action
Locking	: 2 locking lugs
Weight	: 3.3kg (7lb 5oz)
Length	: 110.4cm (43½in)
Barrel Length	: 53cm (207/8in)
Sight	: adjustable sight with bead tunnel, drilled and tapped for telescopic sight
External safety	: safety catch on right behind bolt
Internal safety	: locking, load indicator at rear of bolt

CHARACTERISTICS

• material	: steel
• finish	: blued barrel, bare steel receiver
• stock	: walnut stock, with pistol grip, runs through under barrel to muzzle

Available calibres: .243 Win., 6.5 x 55mm, 6.5 x 57mm, .270 Win., 7 x 64, 7mm Rem. Mag., .308 Win., .30-06 Spr., .300 Win. Mag., .338 Win. Mag., 9.3 x 62mm.

Zoli model AZ-1900 Stutzen-Battue (hunting carbine for driven game)

TECHNICAL DETAILS

Calibre	: see below
Cartridge capacity	: 4-5 rounds
Magazine catch	: catch at front of trigger guard
Action	: bolt-action

Locking	: 2 locking lugs
Weight	: 3.3kg (7lb 5oz)
Length	: 110.4cm (43½in)
Barrel Length	: 53cm (207/8in)
Sight	: adjustable sight for driven game, with bead tunnel; drilled and tapped for telescopic sight
External safety	: safety catch on right behind bolt
Internal safety	: locking, load indicator at rear of bolt

CHARACTERISTICS

• material	: steel
• finish	: blued barrel, bare steel receiver
• stock	: walnut stock with pistol grip, runs through under barrel to muzzle

Available calibres: .243 Win., 6.5 x 55mm, 6.5 x 57mm, .270 Win., 7 x 64, 7mm Rem. Mag., .308 Win., .30-06 Spr., .300 Win. Mag., .338 Win. Mag., 9.3 x 62mm.

Zoli model AZ-1900 Super-Lux

TECHNICAL DETAILS

Calibre	: see below
Cartridge capacity	: 4-5 rounds
Magazine catch	: catch at front of trigger guard
Action	: bolt-action
Locking	: 2 locking lugs
Weight	: 3.4-3.5kg (7lb 8oz-7lb 11oz)
Length	: 117.4-122.4cm (46¼-48¼in)

Barrel Length	: 60-65cm (23⅝-25⅝in)
Sight	: none, drilled and tapped for telescopic sight
External safety	: safety catch on right behind bolt
Internal safety	: locking, load indicator at rear of bolt

CHARACTERISTICS
- material : steel
- finish : blued barrel, bare steel receiver
- stock : walnut with pistol grip

Available calibres: .243 Win., 6.5 x 55mm, 6.5 x 57mm, .270 Win., .270 Wby. Mag., 7 x 64, 7mm Rem. Mag., .308 Win., .30-06 Spr., .300 Win. Mag., .338 Win. Mag., 9.3 x 62mm.

Zoli model Savana Lux

TECHNICAL DETAILS
Calibre	: 7 x 65R, 8 x 57 JRS, 9.3 x 74R
Cartridge capacity	: not applicable, double-barrelled
Magazine catch	: not applicable
Action	: breech-action
Locking	: breech locking
Weight	: 4.5kg (9lb 14oz)
Length	: 115cm (45¼in)
Barrel Length	: 60cm (23⅝in)
Sight	: fixed leaf sight, drilled and tapped for telescopic sight
External safety	: safety catch on neck of stock
Internal safety	: locking, cocking indicator

CHARACTERISTICS
- material : steel
- finish : blued barrel, bare steel pivot-breech
- stock : walnut with pistol grip

Bibliography

Title	Author/ Publisher
Alles over geweren	Achard/Rebo
Alles over handvuurwapens	Mouret/Rebo
Alles over jachtgeweren	Berton/Rebo
ArmasHobby	Press SA
Armas y Municiones	Gun Press SA
Combat Digest	Boger
Deutches Waffen Journal	Schwend Verlag
Exploded Long Gun Drawings	H. A. Murtz
Feuerwaffen für Sammler	Steinwedel
Firearms	Myatt
Firearms Assembly/Disassembly	Gun Digest
Firearms History	Hogg
Frankonia Jagd Katalog	Frankonia Jagd
Gewehre, Pistolen und Revolver	Müller
Gun Annual	Modern Day Period
Gun Digest	DBI Books Inc
Gun Journal	Charlton Publishing Inc.
Gun Parts No. 19	Gun Parts Corp.
Gun World	Gallant Charger Publishers
Guns	Publishers Development Guns & Ammo Petersen Publishing Corp.
Guns & Gunsmiths	North & Hogg
Guns & Shooting	Aceville Publishing Ltd
Guns Illustrated	DBI Books Inc.
Guns of the World	Tanner and others
Handboek voor de herlader	Hartink and others/ASI
Hornady Handbook of Cartridge Reloading	Hornady
Internationale Wapen Spiegel	Vervloet/Hartink and others
Internationaler Waffen Spiegel	Civil Arms Verlag
Internationales Waffen Magazin	Orell Füssli Verlag
Kaliber	Magnum Uitgeverij
Man/Magnum	SA Man 1982 (Pty) Ltd
Metallic Cartridge Reloading	Matunas
Miltary Small Arms	Hogg & Weeks
Modern Law Enforcement Weapons & Tactics	Clapp
Pistols & Revolvers	Hartink/Rebo
Pleasure of Guns	Rosa & May
Sam	NVTU De Schakel
Sam	S.I. Pulicaties
Schusswaffen tunen und testen	Heymann
Schweizer Waffen Magazin	Orell Füssli Verlag
Shooter's Bible	Stoeger Publishing Co.
Shooting Times	PJS Publishing Inc.
Small Arms	Myatt
Small Arms of the World	Ezell/Smith/Stackpole Books
Small Arms of the World	Smith & Smith
Technik von Faustfeuerwaffen	König
Visier	Pietsch + Scholten
Vuurwapens van 1840 tot heden	Lenselink
Waffen Digest	Motorbuch Verlag
Waffen Lexikon	Lampel & Mahrholdt
Waffen Revue	Schwend Verlag
Waffen Sammeln	König & Hugo
War Baby	L. L. Ruth
WM Waffenmarkt Jahrbuch	GFI Verlag GmbH

Index

Acknowledgements

The author and publisher would like to thank the following persons and companies, in alphabetical order, for their co-operation. It would perhaps not have been possible to complete this book without their help or the information contained would have been less comprehensive.

—AKAH: Albrecht Kind GmbH & Co
  Postfach 310283
  D-51617 Gummersbach
  Germany

—AMT/IAI
  6226 Santos Diaz Street
  Irwindale
  CA 91702 USA

—Anschütz GmbH
  Jagd- und Sportwaffenfabrik
  Daimlerstrasse 12
  D-7900 Ulm/Donau
  Germany

—Armscor/KBI Inc
  PO Box 5440
  Harrisburg
  PA 17110-0440 USA

—A.S.I. Uitgeverij
  Postbus 2279
  8203 AG Lelystad
  The Netherlands

– Benelli Armi SA
  Via della Stazione 50
  I-61029 Urbino
  Italy

—Pietro Beretta
  25063 Gardone V.T.
  (Brescia)
  Italy

—Bernardelli
  PO Box 74
  I-25063 Gardone V.T.
  (Brescia) Italy

—Blaser Jagdwaffen GmbH
  Ziegelstadel 1
  D-88316 Isny im Allgäu
  Germany

—Brown Precision Inc
  7786 Molinos Avenue
  Los Molinos
  CA 96055 USA

—Browning Inc
  One Browning Place
  Morgan
  UT 84050 USA

—Browning SA
  Parc Industriel des Hauts Sarts
  B-4040 Herstal
  Belgium

—BSA Guns (UK) Ltd
  Armoury Road
  Birmingham B11 2PX
  Great Britain

—Bushmaster/Quality Parts Co
  PO Box 1479
  Windham
  ME 04062 USA

—Calico
  405 East 19th Street
  Bakersfield
  CA 93305 USA

—Chapuis
  Z.I. La Gravoux BP 15
  F-42380 Saint Bonnet le Chéteau
  France

—Colt's Manufacturing Company Inc.
  (Freebairn & Co)
  Hartford
  CT 06144-1868 USA

—CZ-Ceska Zbrojovka A.s.
  688 27 Uhersky Brod
  Czech Republic

—Daewoo/Kimber of America Inc
  9039 SE Jannsen Road
  Clackamas
  OR 97015 USA

—Dakota Arms Inc
  HC55
  Box 326
  Sturgis
  SD 57785 USA

—Erma Werke GmbH
Postfach 1269
D-85202 Dachau
Germany

—Feinwerkbau
Westinger & Altenburger GmbH
Neckarstrasse 43
D-7238 Oberndorf am Neckar
Germany

—FN-Browning SA
Parc Industriel des Hauts Sarts
B-4040 Herstal Belgium

—Frankonia Jagd
D-97064 Würzburg
Germany

—Gaucher Armes SA
46 rue Desjoyaux
F-42000 St.-Etienne
France

—Gibbs Rifle Company
Route 2
Box 214
Hoffman Road
Cannon Hill Industrial Park
Martinsburg
WV 25401 USA

—GOL-Waffen G. Prechtl
Mierensdorffstrasse 29
D-69469 Weinheim
Germany

—Griffin & Howe
33 Claremont Road
Bernardsville
NJ 07924 USA

—Grünig + Elmiger AG
Sportwaffenfabrik
CH-6102 Malters
Switzerland

—Harrington & Richardson 1871 Inc
60 Industrial Row
Garner
MA 01440-2832 USA

—Harris Gunworks Inc
3840 N 28th Avenue
Phoenix
AZ 85017-4733 USA

—Heckler & Koch GmbH
Postfach 1329
D-78722
Oberndorf/Neckar
Germany

—Hege/Zeughaus GmbH
Zeughausgasse 2
D-88662 Oberlingen
Germany

—Heym GmbH
Postfach 1163
D-97697 Münnerstadt
Germany

—Helmut Hofmann GmbH
Postfach 60
D-97634 Mellrichstadt
Germany

—Howa/Interarms (North American
Group)
PO Box 208
Alexandria
VA 22313 USA

—I.M.I./TAAS-ISRAEL Industries Ltd
(Israel Military Industries)
PO Box 1044
Ramat Hasharon 47100
Israel

—Jarret Rifles Inc
383 Brown Road
Jackson
SC 29831 USA

—KBI Inc/Armscor
PO Box 5440
Harrisburg
PA 17110-0440 USA

—Keppeler & Fritz GmbH
Aspachweg 4
D-74427 Fictenberg
Germany

—Krico-A. Kriegeskorte GmbH Jagd und
Sportwaffen fabrik
Kronacher Strasse 63
D-90765 Fürth-Stadeln
Germany

—Lakefield/Savage Arms (Canada) Inc
PO Box 129
Lakefield
Ontario
K0L 2H0 Canada

—H. de Lange, sporting shooter of
Streefkerk, The Netherlands

—L.A.R. Manufacturing Inc
4133 West Farm Road -
8540 South West Jordan
Utah 84084 USA

—Magnum Research Inc
7110 University Avenue
NE Minneapolis
MN 55432 USA

—Magnum shooting association Het Magnum Broederschap of Nieuwpoort, The
Netherlands

—MagTech/CBC
Av. Humberto de Campos 3220
Ribeirao Pires
Sao Paolo Brazil

—Manufacture d'Armes des Pyrénées
Franáaises
BP 420
F-64700 Hendaye France

—Marlin Firearms Company
100 Kenna Drive
PO Box 248
North Haven
CT 06473-0905 USA

—Mauser Werke Oberndorf
Postfach 1349
D-78722 Oberndorf am Neckar
Germany

—Merkel/Suhler Jagd- und Sportwaffen
GmbH
Auenstrasse 5
Postfach 130
D-98501 Suhl
Germany

—Mitchell Arms Inc
3400 W MacArthur Blvd 1
Santa Ana
CA 92704 USA

—Musgrave/Denel (Pty) Ltd
PO Box 183
Jagersfontein Road
Bloemfontein-3000
Republic of South Africa

—Navy Arms Company
689 Bergen Blvd
Ridgefield
NJ 07657 USA

—New England Firearms
60 Industrial Row
Gardner
MA 01440-2832 USA

—Norinco/Norconia GmbH
Ostring 19
D-97228 Rottendorf
Germany

—Regional Police Zuid-Holland-Zuid
based at Dordrecht The Netherlands

—Remington Arms Company Inc
Delle Donne Corporate Centre
1011 Center Road
Wilmington
DE 19805-1270 USA

—Rhöner Sportwaffen GmbH
Untere Torstrasse 9
D-97656 Oberelsbach/Weisbach
Germany

—Robar Companies Inc
21438 North Seventh Ave
Suite B
Phoenix AZ 85027 USA

—J. Roukema, weapons expert and sports
shooter of Papendrecht, The Netherlands

—A. Rozendaal, sports shooter, photo-
grapher, Nieuwpoort, The Netherlands

—Ruger/Sturm
Ruger & Company Inc
Lacey Place
Southport CT 06490 USA

—Sako Limited
PO Box 149
FIN-11101 RiihimÑki
Finland

—Savage Arms Inc
100 Springdale Road
Westfield MA 01085 USA

—marksman's association Scherpschutters-
ver. Zuid Holland of Nieuwpoort, The
Netherlands